National Insurance Contributions 2021/22

National Insurance Contributions 2021/22

Sarah Bradford BA (Hons) FCA CTA (Fellow)

Bloomsbury Professional

LONDON • DUBLIN • EDINBURGH • NEW YORK • NEW DELHI • SYDNEY

BLOOMSBURY PROFESSIONAL

Bloomsbury Publishing Plc

50 Bedford Square, London, WC1B 3DP, UK

1385 Broadway, New York, NY 10018, USA

29 Earlsfort Terrace, Dublin 2, Ireland

British Library Cataloguing-in-Publication Data

A catalogue record for this book is available from the British Library.

ISBN: 978 1 52651 867 5

Typeset by Compuscript Ltd, Shannon
Printed and bound by CPI Group (UK) Ltd, Croydon, CR0 4YY

MIX
Paper from responsible sources
FSC® C013604

Preface

Since the last edition of this book, the country has endured another year of Covid-19 restrictions, and the Brexit transitional period has come to an end. Going forward, there will be a period of adjustment as the country seeks to return to a new normal after the pandemic, while getting to grips with the post-Brexit landscape.

During the first half of 2021/22, support continues to be available to employees and the self-employed who have been unable to work, or who have suffered a downturn in profits, as a result of the pandemic and the associated restrictions.

The Coronavirus Job Retention Scheme (CJRS) which provides grants to pay employees who are furloughed or flexibly furloughed continues to run until 30 September 2021. Payments made to furloughed employees count as earnings for Class 1 National Insurance purposes, and are liable to employee's and employer's Class 1 National Insurance contributions, as for normal wages and salary payments.

Grants received by the self-employed under the Self-Employment Income Support Scheme (SEISS) are taxable in the tax year in which they are received (rather than by reference to the basis period). They are also liable to Class 4 National Insurance.

A number of specific exemptions were introduced to deal with particular aspects of the pandemic response. These include an exemption from tax and National Insurance for employer provided and employer-reimbursed Coronavirus antigen tests, and for employer-reimbursed homeworking equipment initially purchased by the employee to enable them to work from home due to the pandemic, and also an exemption from Class 1 and Class 4 for self-isolation payments made to those on low incomes who were required to self-isolate to stop the spread of the virus.

As far as Brexit is concerned, withdrawing from the EU meant that the UK also ceased to participate in the European Economic Area (EEA) as the UK falls outside its geographic scope. The rules applying prior to the UK's withdrawal from the EU continued to apply until the end of the transitional period on 31 December 2020. The UK reached an agreement with the EU on the social security rules that apply from 1 January 2021 onwards. These rules ensure that workers who move between the UK and the EU, Norway or Switzerland only have to pay into one country's social security scheme at a time. Separate rules apply to workers who are working only temporarily in the EU, Norway, Iceland or Switzerland, who may be able to obtain a certificate to enable them to continue to pay UK National Insurance contributions while working abroad.

Looking ahead, the National Insurance Contributions Bill 2021, which was introduced into Parliament on 12 May 2021, introduces a zero rate of secondary contributions for employers of armed forced veterans on their earnings up to a new upper secondary threshold, which is to be aligned with the upper secondary thresholds for employees under the age of 21 and apprentices under the age of 25. The zero rate is available retrospectively for 2021/22, and also for 2022/23 and 2023/24.

The Bill also provides that employers located in a Freeport tax site will also be able to benefit from a zero rate of secondary contributions on the earnings of new Freeport employees up to £25,000. The zero rate will be available from 6 April 2022 for a limited period and will apply for the first 36 months of the Freeport employee's employment.

As always, HMRC remain vigilant as regards countering attempts to avoid National Insurance contributions. In this vein, the Bill also includes measures to strengthen the Disclosure of Tax Avoidance Scheme rules as they apply to the promotion of schemes that seek to avoid National Insurance contributions.

As always, I would extend my thanks to all at Bloomsbury Professional for bringing the 2021/22 edition to publication, and to Paul Crick for his excellent editing of the title. I hope very much that it continues to be a useful addition to your bookshelves.

Sarah Bradford
June 2021

Contents

Table of Examples

Table of Statutes

[*All references are to paragraph number*]

M

N

T

V

W

Table of Statutory Instruments

[All references are to paragraph number]

Table of HMRC Guidance, etc

[*All references are to paragraph number and appendices*]

Table of EC Material

[*All references are to paragraph number*]

Table of Cases

[*All references are to paragraph number*]

F

H

I

L

M

N

List of Abbreviations

APP	Appropriate personal pension
APPSHP	Appropriate personal pension stakeholder pension
ASPP	Additional statutory paternity pay
CAA 2001	Capital Allowances Act 2001
CNR	Centre for Non-residents
COMP	Contracted-out money purchase
COMPSHP	Contracted-out money purchase stakeholder pension
COSR	Contracted-out salary related
DCC	Defined contribution convention
DCNI	Direct Contribution National Insurance schemes
DPNI	Direct Payment National Insurance schemes
DWP	Department for Works and Pensions
EAS	Employer alignment submission
EEA	European Economic Area
EC	European Community
EFTA	European Free Trade Association
EEOYP	Electronic End of Year Processing
EPS	Employer payment summary
ESC	Extra statutory concession
ESI	Employment status indicator
ET	Earnings threshold
EU	European Union
FA	Finance Act
FPS	Full payment submission
HMRC	HM Revenue and Customs
HRP	Home responsibilities protection
ITA 2007	Income Tax Act 2007
ITEPA 2003	Income Tax (Earnings and Pensions) Act 2003
ITTOIA 2005	Income Tax (trading and Other Income) Act 2005
LEL	Lower earnings limit
MSC	Managed service company
NIA 1965	National Insurance Act 1965
NICA 2008	National Insurance Contributions Act 2008
NICA 2011	National Insurance Contributions Act 2011
NICA 2014	National Insurance Contributions Act 2014
NICO	National Insurance Contributions Office
NICs	National Insurance contributions
NISPI	National Insurance Services to Pension Industry
NISR 2	National Insurance Recording System 2
OSPP	Ordinary statutory paternity pay
OTS	Office of Tax Simplification
PAYE	Pay as you earn

PEOYP	Paper End of Year Processing
PSA	PAYE settlement agreement
PSEC	Pension Scheme of the European communities
PT	Primary earnings threshold
RA	Reciprocal agreement
RTI	Real time information
ROW	Rest of the world
S2P	Second state pension
SAP	Statutory adoption pay
SCON	Scheme contracted-out number
SEE	Small earnings exception
SERPS	State earnings-related pensions
SMP	Statutory maternity pay
SPP	Statutory paternity pay
SSA 1975	Social Security Act 1975
SSAA 1992	Social Security Administration Act 1992
SSCBA 1992	Social Security Contributions and Benefits Act 1992
SSP	Statutory sick pay
ST	Secondary earnings threshold
TMA 1970	Taxes Management Act 1970
UAP	Upper accrual point
UEL	Upper earnings limit
UK	United Kingdom

Chapter 1

Overview of the National Insurance system

SIGNPOSTS

- Purpose – the National Insurance scheme was created after the Second World War to provide a universal insurance system (see **1.1**).
- Contributory principle of National Insurance (see **1.2**).
- Call for closer alignment of tax and National Insurance (see **1.3**).
- Each individual has a unique National Insurance number which is used to record contributions paid and credited (see **1.4**).
- HMRC are responsible for administering and collecting National Insurance contributions (see **1.8**).
- There are different classes of National Insurance contribution and different contributors are liable or eligible to pay different classes (see **1.18**).
- Entitlement to contributory benefits is conditional on having paid enough of the right type of contribution; non-contributory benefits do not depend on contributions (see **1.26**).
- To target avoidance, certain types of schemes and arrangements must be notified to HMRC under the National Insurance Disclosure Scheme (see **1.38**).

INTRODUCTION

The National Insurance Fund

1.1 The National Insurance scheme was created after the Second World War with the aim of providing a universal insurance system. National Insurance contributions are paid into the National Insurance Fund, which is kept separate from other revenue raised by national taxes. It is used pay the social security benefits, such as the state pension and contributory benefits. The existence of a separate fund to 'house' National Insurance contributions is a central feature of the National Insurance system. The fund is established by statute and separate accounts are prepared by HMRC.

The fund was established in 1948 to pay social security benefits to individuals. The self-employed were included in the Welfare State for the first time in 1952. Some benefits are contingent on the payment of sufficient contributions, whereas others are not and are payable regardless of the individual's contribution record.

National Insurance contributions are paid by the employed and self-employed once their earnings reach a minimum level. Voluntary contributions can also be paid by individuals to top up their contribution record. National Insurance contributions are paid into the National Insurance Fund after deducting the National Health Service allocation, which is determined in accordance with *SSAA 1992, s 162(5)*. National Insurance contributions allocated to the National Health Service in this way fund about 20% of the overall costs of the National Health Service. In 2018/19, the NHS allocation was £25.4 billion, up from £24.3 billion in 2017/18. Interest and penalties charged in relation to National Insurance contributions are also paid into the National Insurance Fund.

The UK state benefit structure is complex as is its link with National Insurance. Some benefits are dependent on the individual having paid sufficient National Insurance contributions or received sufficient National Insurance credits (contributory benefits). Others are means tested and not linked to National Insurance contributions. The link between National Insurance contributions and contributory benefits is explored further at **1.26**.

Contributory benefits are funded by the National Insurance Fund and are paid from current contributions rather than from accumulated funds. This system means that this year's contributions fund this year's benefits. To ensure that the National Insurance Fund is able to meet about two months' worth of benefit commitments, it is topped up by grants from the Consolidated Fund (which is funded by general taxation). Retirement pensions account for about 90% of benefit expenditure from the National Insurance Fund. Surpluses on the Fund are invested in the Government's Call Notice Deposit Account.

The existence of a separate National Insurance Fund also plays a role in relation to the UK's international and social security obligations and agreements.

The National Insurance Fund accounts are prepared annually in accordance with the requirement imposed by *SSAA 1992, s 161(2)*. The National Insurance Fund Accounts are available on the gov.uk website (see www.gov.uk/government/publications/national-insurance-fund-accounts).

A separate National Insurance Scheme applies to Northern Ireland, although it operates on virtually identical rules to the UK scheme.

Contributory principle of National Insurance

1.2 A key element of the National Insurance system is the contributory principle. This is the idea that entitlement to social security benefits and the state pension is 'earned' by paying National Insurance contributions. The contributory principle is based on an insurance concept – individuals pay contributions as an insurance against times of sickness and unemployment. However, there is very little direct correlation between what an individual pays by way of contributions and what they receive in terms of benefits; individual contributions are not ring-fenced to pay benefits to that individual. Rather, contributions are set at such a level as is necessary to meet the cost of funding current year benefits. The National Insurance Fund operates on a pay-as-you go basis. Contributions paid by those of working age provide protection for those who are no longer able to work. In this way, the National Insurance system is a system of social insurance.

At an individual level, an individual's contribution record is expressed in terms of the number of qualifying years for which sufficient contributions have been paid or credits given for that year to be a qualifying year. Entitlement to the state pension, for example, is contingent on having sufficient qualifying years (35 years for the full single-tier state pension and a minimum of ten for a reduced pension) rather than having paid a certain monetary amount by way of contributions. Other contributory benefits use a contribution test which requires contributions to have been paid in the two years preceding the year of the benefit claim.

Over time the link between contributions paid and benefits received has been weakened and there is much confusion surrounding the link between National Insurance contributions and benefit entitlement. In their report on the Closer Alignment of Tax and National Insurance, the Office of Tax Simplification noted that individuals were generally unclear on the relationship between National Insurance contributions and benefit entitlement and called for a more transparent system so that people can better understand the contributory principle such that any future debate on whether it should be retained can be based on a full understanding of the facts.

Views of the retention of the contributory principle are diverse. Some people regard National Insurance as simply another tax and would be in favour of its abolition and the merger of tax and National Insurance, whereas others regard it as a cornerstone of the welfare system. The government has frequently stated their commitment to the retention of the contributory principle and presented it as an argument against the possibility of a full merger between tax and National Insurance.

Focus

The contributory principle is a key feature of the National Insurance system, under which entitlement to the state pension and certain benefits is 'earned' by paying National Insurance contributions.

Call for closer alignment of tax and National Insurance

1.3 Differences in the income tax and National Insurance rules cause difficulties in practice and impose a burden on those operating the two systems. To reduce this burden, calls are made regularly for the merger of income tax and National Insurance. However, despite apparent support for such a merger, this looks unlikely to happen in the foreseeable future.

The issue of merging tax and National Insurance was considered by the Treasury in the 2007 paper Income Tax and National Insurance Alignment: an Evidence Based Assessment. Subsequently, the Mirrlees Review by the Institute of Fiscal Studies found in favour of integrating the tax and National Insurance system.

The issue was raised again by the Office of Tax Simplification (OTS) in their review of small business taxation. In their interim report of March 2011 they highlighted the major simplification that could result in a merger of tax and National Insurance contributions. Following the publication of the report, the government announced that they would consult on options to integrate tax and National Insurance, issued a call for evidence in July 2011 and announced next steps for consultation in November 2011. This consultation has not taken place. The issue came to prominence again in July 2015. Following the Summer 2015 Budget, the Financial Secretary to the Treasury, David Gauke, wrote to the Office of Tax Simplification (OTS) to ask them to undertake a study into the closer alignment of tax and National Insurance contributions. The OTS published their terms of reference in July 2015. The main aim of the project is to explore more fully the steps that need to be taken to achieve a closer alignment of income tax and National Insurance contributions and the costs, benefits and impacts of each of those steps. The OTS were charged with considering the evidence already available, including their own previous work, and undertook further research with stakeholder and taxpayers. In particular, the OTS considered:

- the case for change, including the distortions, burdens and costs associated with the current system;
- the changes that could be introduced to bring the two systems closer together in relation to the taxation of earned income (for employers and employees) and the self-employed;
- the costs, benefits and impacts of each step;
- all forms of NIC charge including employers' NICs; and
- how any changes would fit with wider government objectives, including the system for determining entitlement to contributory benefits, Exchequer costs and burdens for business.

The review also considered the base of the systems, but it did not consider the extension of NICs to non-employment income such as property income, dividends and pensions.

In undertaking its work and framing its recommendations, the OTS had regard to:

- the effect on the taxpayer and business understanding of the system;
- the likely effect on compliance burdens;
- the impact on any distortions to current taxpayer behaviour caused by the current system;
- avoidance risks,
- the principles and design of HMRC Making Tax Easier reforms, including digital tax accounts, integrated reporting and payment;
- HMRC operational impacts;
- likely revenue implications, both in terms of Exchequer impact and the impact on different types of taxpayers;
- administrative costs for government (including the administration of the contributory benefit system); and
- fairness of consistency of treatment of taxpayers.

The OTS published a final report in March 2016 ahead of the 2016 Budget. In their report, the OTS set out a seven-stage programme for bringing tax and National Insurance closer together. The proposed steps are as follows:

- moving to an annual cumulative and aggregate basis for National Insurance contributions;
- basing employers' National Insurance on whole payroll costs and renaming the charge;
- aligning National Insurance contributions for the self-employed more closely with employees' contributions and benefits;
- improving transparency for National Insurance and the contributory principle;
- aligning the definition of both earnings and expenses for income tax and National Insurance;
- bringing taxable benefits in kind within Class 1; and
- having a joined-up approach for income tax and National Insurance laws and practice.

The report envisages bringing National Insurance more into line with income tax and the goal at this stage is one of closer alignment rather than a merger between the two.

The report, 'The closer alignment of tax and National Insurance contributions' is available to download from the gov.uk website (see www.gov.uk/government/publications/closer-alignment-of-income-tax-and-national-insurance-contributions).

The OTS noted that further work needs to be undertaken and, following the March 2016 Budget, the Financial Secretary to the Treasury wrote to the Office of Tax Simplification welcoming proposals to undertake two further reviews – one of the impact of moving employee National Insurance contributions to an annual, cumulative and aggregated basis and the other on the reform of employer National Insurance. A further review was published in November 2016 setting out proposals to move the calculation of Class 1 National Insurance contributions to an annual aggregated basis. Under the proposals, Class 1 National Insurance would be calculated in a similar way to PAYE tax, earnings from all jobs would be aggregated and earners would receive one annual allowance, which would be split between jobs. Although such a move would bring tax and National Insurance more closely into line, at this stage the Government intend to keep the two systems separate, reflecting the different roles which each performs. The OTS also outlined proposals for the reform of employer's National Insurance contributions, including replacing the existing system with a payroll levy. The OTS recommended that the Government act to start the process of reforming Class 1 National Insurance contributions and envisages a five-year timetable for delivery of the full package of reforms.

A Commons Briefing Paper on National Insurance was published in July 2017 (Number 4517, 17 July 2017: see http://researchbriefings.files.parliament.uk/documents/SN04517/SN04517.pdf). The first part of the paper provides an introduction to the National Insurance system, while the second part looks at the major reforms that have been made since the 1990s and, in particular, the consideration by successive governments of the case for merging National Insurance with income tax. The introduction notes that:

> 'The issue has been considered, off and on, for almost twenty years, and even though there have been a number of changes to bring NICs and income tax into closer alignment, there remain considerable difficulties for a full merger.'

However, the possibility of revisiting the structure of National Insurance contributions and aligning more closely the contributions payable by employed and self-employed has been raised again, and this may pave the way for re-examining the question of alignment of tax and National Insurance. The *Coronavirus Act 2020, ss 72 – 74* contains provisions to lift temporarily the caps on increases in National Insurance, and this may allow for structural changes and greater alignment between the employed and the self-employed, as well as for an increase in contributions to meet some of the costs arising from the Covid-19 pandemic.

National Insurance numbers

1.4 A National Insurance number is a unique personal number which is used to record the contributions paid and credited to that person. National Insurance numbers are fundamental to the operation of the National Insurance system.

National Insurance numbers comprise three letters and six numbers in the form LLNNNNNNL. The final letter is A, B, C or D (for example AB123456C).

A National Insurance number is allocated automatically to those who live in the UK, are under 16 years of age and in respect of whom child benefit is payable. The person is sent a letter which has the number on it shortly before his or her 16th birthday.

Employees need to give their employer their National Insurance number when they start work. The self-employed need to supply their National Insurance number when applying to pay self-employed National Insurance contributions. A person also needs his or her National Insurance number when claiming benefits.

There is no legal right to a National Insurance number. However, there are various circumstances in which one is required. A person will need a National Insurance number when:

- he or she starts work;
- he or she is looking for work;
- he or she starts self-employment; or
- he or she wants to pay voluntary National Insurance contributions.

If any of the above circumstances apply and the person does not have a National Insurance number, it will be necessary to apply for one. Guidance on applying for a National Insurance number can be found on the gov.uk website at www.gov.uk/apply-national-insurance-number. The application can be made online. The applicant may need to send documents or attend an interview to prove their identity. Once the application process is complete, it can take up to 16 weeks for a National Insurance number to be issued.

A person does not need a National Insurance number to apply for benefits or a student loan, but will receive one if they do not already have one if their application is successful.

When a person comes from abroad to work in the UK and does not have a National Insurance number, they will also need to apply for one.

Where an employer does not know an employee's National Insurance number or the employee does not have a National Insurance number (as would be the case if the employee is under the age of 16), the National Insurance number field should be left blank when making RTI returns. A dummy or temporary National Insurance number should not be used. Where a National Insurance number forms part of a RTI submission, it is vital that the number used is correct.

If a person has lost or mislaid their National Insurance number, it can be found on their personal tax account. A letters confirming a person's National Insurance number can be saved or printed from their personal tax account. If the person does not have a personal tax account, he or she can contact HMRC to find out what their National Insurance number is. An application form, CA5403, will need to be completed. This is available on the gov.uk website (see further www.gov.uk/lost-national-insurance-number).

> **Focus**
>
> Each individual has a National Insurance number that is unique to them.

National Insurance records

1.5 Details of National Insurance contributions paid or credited to a person are held on that person's National Insurance record. National Insurance contributions records are maintained on computer on the National Insurance Recording System 2 (NISR2). A person's National Insurance number is essentially their National Insurance account number. Contributions which have been paid are credited to the account by reference to the person's National Insurance number. A person may also have National Insurance credits allocated to their account. Broadly, these are Class 1 or Class 3 contributions which are credited but not actually paid in certain circumstances, including when a person is unemployed, incapable of work, in education or training or on jury service.

Entitlement to contributory benefits, including the state pension, is dependent on a person having paid, or been credited with, sufficient National Insurance contributions. Entitlement to the state pension is dependent on having sufficient qualifying years. For contributory benefits, entitlement depends on having met the associated benefit condition. It is therefore essential that each person has his or her own National Insurance record to enable individual benefit entitlement to be determined. However, it should be noted that the contributions actually paid by each individual are not earmarked for paying benefits to that person. Benefits are paid from current year contributions paid into the National Insurance Fund rather than from contributions actually paid by a particular individual.

To enable benefit entitlement to be determined correctly, it is important that a person's National Insurance record is accurate and up to date. An accurate record is also important to enable any shortfalls in contributions to be identified so that a person can, if they so wish, make voluntary contributions to protect pension and benefit entitlement.

Where a person is employed, the accuracy of their National Insurance record depends on the supply of accurate and timely information by his or her employer. Under Real Time Information (RTI) the employer must provide pay and deduction details to HMRC at or before the time at which a payment is made to an employer.

A person can check their National Insurance record online. They will be able to see what they have paid up to the start of the current tax year, any National Insurance credits that they have received, and whether there are any gaps in their record which means that some years aren't 'qualifying years' and do not count towards the state pension. The person will also be able to see how much it would cost to pay voluntary contributions to make up for gaps in their contributions record. Individuals can check their insurance record online on the gov.uk website at www.gov.uk/check-national-insurance-record.

> **Focus**
>
> Each person has a National Insurance record on which details of contributions paid and credited are maintained.

Legislative framework

1.6 The main body of law governing National Insurance contributions is contained in the *Social Security Contributions and Benefits Act 1992* (*SSCBA 1992*), whereas the running of the scheme is governed by the *Social Security Administration Act 1992* (*SSAA 1992*). The primary legislation was last consolidated in 1992.

These Acts are supplemented by regulations, the main regulations being the *Social Security Contributions Regulations 2001* (*SI 2001/1004*) (the *Social Security Regulations*), which contain much of the detail.

The main body of contributions law is supplemented by various other Acts and regulations.

Supplementary Acts include:

- *Pension Schemes Act 1993*;
- *Social Security Act 1998*;
- *Social Security (Transfer of Functions, etc.) Act 1999*;
- *Welfare Reform and Pensions Act 1999*;
- *Child Support, Pensions and Social Security Act 2000*;
- *Social Security Fraud Act 2001*;
- *Social Security Contributions (Share Options) Act 2001*;

- *State Pension Credit Act 2002*;
- *National Insurance Contributions and Statutory Payments Act 2004*;
- *Welfare Reform Act 2007*;
- *Pension Act 2007*;
- *National Insurance Contributions Act 2008*;
- *National Insurance Contributions Act 2011*;
- *National Insurance Contributions Act 2014*;
- *National Insurance Contributions Act 2015*;
- *National Insurance Contributions (Rate Ceilings) Act 2015*; and
- *National Insurance Contributions (Termination Award and Sporting Testimonials) Act 2019.*

The main *Social Security Regulations* and Acts are amended and updated by amending regulations. However, from time to time substantive regulations are made which add to the body of National Insurance contributions law.

Other guidance

1.7 The legislative framework is supplemented by a wealth of non-statutory guidance on National Insurance contributions.

Detailed guidance on all aspects of National Insurance contributions can be found on the National Insurance pages of the gov.uk website (see www.gov.uk/national-insurance).

HMRC's National Insurance Manual (which is available on the gov.uk website at www.hmrc.gov.uk/manuals/nimmanual/index.htm) contains comprehensive guidance on National Insurance contributions.

HMRC also operate various helplines dealing with National Insurance contributions. The helplines are listed in the table below:

Helpline	**Number**
Employer helpline	0300 200 3200
National Insurance enquiries for employees and individuals	0300 200 3500
National Insurance registrations	0300 200 3502
National Insurance deficiency enquiries	0300 200 3503
Newly self-employed helpline	0300 200 3504
National Insurance enquiries for self-employed employees	0300 200 3505
National Insurance enquiries for non-UK residents	0300 200 3506
Contracted-out pensions enquiries	0300 200 3507

ADMINISTRATION

HMRC

1.8 HMRC are responsible for administering and collecting National Insurance contributions. They are also responsible for statutory payments. However, responsibility for state benefits rests with the Department for Work and Pensions (DWP).

Within HMRC, the National Insurance Contributions Office (NICO) is responsible for handling National Insurance contributions.

> **Focus**
>
> HMRC collect and administer National Insurance contributions.

Complaints procedure

1.9 Details of HMRC's complaints procedure is set out generally on the gov.uk website at www.gov.uk/guidance/complain-to-hm-revenue-and-customs. HMRC advise those wishing to make a complaint about National Insurance matters to contact the complaints manager at the office dealing with the issue. The complaint can be made by telephone, in writing or in person. If the complainant does not know which office to contact, the complaint can be made by telephone by calling 0300 200 3500. Where a complaint is made in writing, it is useful to state 'complaint' at the top of the letter.

When making a complaint, the complainant should quote his or her National Insurance number and also provide as much information as possible as regards what went wrong, when, who dealt with it and how the complainant would like it settled.

When dealing with the complaint, HMRC undertake to supply the complainant with the name of the person who is looking into the complaint, investigate the complaint thoroughly, deal with it confidentially and to try and resolve it as quickly as possible. They will also tell the complainant who to contact if they remain unhappy.

If the complainant is unhappy with the response from HMRC, he or she can ask for the complaint to be looked at again. A senior officer who has not been involved in the case will take a look at it and how it has been handled. This officer will give the complainant a final decision. If the complainant remains unhappy, he or she can ask the Adjudicator to investigate the complaint (see **1.10**).

The complainant can also ask his or her MP to take up the case or refer the case to the Parliamentary Ombudsman (see **1.13**). However, the Parliamentary Ombudsman would normally expect HMRC and the Adjudicator to have already considered the complaint.

Where HMRC upheld a complaint they undertake to apologise and explain what went wrong. They will also meet reasonable costs, such as postage, phone calls and professional fees.

Adjudicator's Office

1.10 Where a complaint made to HMRC is not satisfactorily resolved, the complainant can take his or her complaint to the Adjudicator's Office (see www.adjudicatorsoffice.gov.uk). The Adjudicator's Office acts as a fair and unbiased referee and looks into complaints concerning HMRC, the Valuation Office and The Insolvency Service. The office will look into complaints regarding HMRC's handling of National Insurance matters.

A complaint can only be made to the Adjudicator's Office once HMRC's own complaints procedure has been exhausted and a final response received (see **1.13**). The Adjudicator's Office can then consider whether HMRC have handled the complaint appropriately and reached a reasonable decision. If the Adjudicator's Office decides that HMRC have not resolved the complaint satisfactorily, they will recommend what needs to be done to put matters right.

The Adjudicator's Office can look into complaints concerning:

- mistakes;
- unreasonable delays;
- poor or misleading advice;
- inappropriate staff behaviour; and
- the use of discretion.

However, the Office cannot investigate matters of government or departmental policy or matters that can be considered by appeal to an independent tribunal, such as the amount of National Insurance that is payable. Nor can the Adjudicator's Office look into issues that the courts have already considered or could consider, complaints that are being investigated by the Parliamentary Ombudsman or complaints about whether HMRC have complied with the legislation when dealing with requests under the *Freedom of Information Act 2000* and the *Data Protection Act 1998.*

A complaint to the Adjudicator's Office must be made in writing or by fax, although general enquiries can be made by telephone. When making a complaint, the complainant should supply the following details:

- his or her name. address and telephone number;
- details of the office that dealt with the complaint;
- specific details of the complaint, including what the complainant thinks HMRC should have done to put matters right and why the complainant is unhappy with HMRC's response;

- any evidence in support of the claim, such as relevant notices and letters etc; and
- if HMRC have already acknowledged shortcomings and have offered redress, why the complainant does not believe this to be adequate.

The Adjudicator's Office can deal with a representative acting on the complainant's behalf if this is preferred, providing the complainant has provided written authority for the Adjudicator's Office to deal with the representative.

In the event that the complaint concerns a matter that the Adjudicator's Office cannot handle, the Office will advise the complainant of this as soon as is possible.

Complaints process

1.11 The Adjudicator's Office introduced a new approach to dealing with complaints from early 2019 and no longer request a report from HMRC about their handling of the complaint and the reasons for it.

A complaint cannot be investigated by the Adjudicator's Office until it has gone through HMRC's own two-tier complaints procedure. It is expected that a complaint will be brought within six months of that process.

When a complaint is received by the Adjudicator's Office, the first stage is to decide whether they can investigate it. The Adjudicator's Office's remit is based on the Service Level Agreement (SLA) with HMRC.

If the complaint concerns a matter that the Adjudicator's Office can investigate and the complaint has already been through HMRC's complaints procedure, the Adjudicator's Office will investigate the case. The Office will also consider what information they need to investigate the complaint satisfactorily. The Adjudicator's Office may telephone or write to the complainant to confirm the complaint and, if they need further information, to request it.

Due to the volume of complaints received, the Adjudicator's Office may not be able to investigate a complaint immediately on receipt.

Whilst a complaint is being investigated, the Adjudicator's Office has no authority to ask HMRC to suspend any action they may be taking in relation to the matter. The Adjudicator's Office will review the complaint and all the relevant evidence alongside HMRC's guidelines, records or procedures. They will ask HMRC for specific information that they may need to complete their investigation.

Settling the complaint

1.12 There are various ways in which a complaint may be settled.

A complaint may be settled by recommendation letter. This is a letter which sets out what the Adjudicator recommends, if anything, that HMRC should do to put things right.

If the Adjudicator believes that HMRC has already dealt with the complaint in a satisfactory manner, the Adjudicator will write to the complainant stating this.

Complaints may also be settled by a mediation process. This involves finding a resolution that is acceptable to both the complainant and to HMRC.

If the complainant is unhappy with the decision reached by the Adjudicator's Office, he or she can make a further complaint to the Parliamentary Ombudsman.

Parliamentary and Health Service Ombudsman

1.13 The Parliamentary and Health Service Ombudsman (see www.ombudsman.org.uk) carries out independent investigations into complaints, unfair or improper actions or poor service by UK government departments and the NHS.

A complainant can also ask his or her MP to take up the case or refer the case to the Parliamentary and Health Service Ombudsman. However, the Parliamentary and Health Service Ombudsman would normally expect HMRC and the Adjudicator to have already considered the complaint. Thus a complaint to the Parliamentary and Health Service Ombudsman should only be made if the complainant is unhappy with the response received from both HMRC and the Adjudicator's Office.

Details of the service offered by the Parliamentary and Health Service Ombudsman can be found on the Parliamentary Ombudsman's website (www.ombudsman.org.uk).

Appeals process

1.14 A person who disagrees with a decision made by HMRC in relation to National Insurance contributions may be able to challenge that decision by appealing to an independent tribunal. The same appeals process applies for National Insurance purposes as for direct tax purposes. Guidance on decisions and appeals for National Insurance can be found in HMRC's Decisions and Appeals for National Insurance and Statutory Payments Manual.

A dispute in relation to National Insurance may arise for a number of reasons, such as an error being found when examining an employer's records or a worker disputing their employment status.

There are three stages in the process. The first stage is the information stage in which an initial opinion will be offered based on the information available, together with references to the legislation and HMRC guidance. The second stage is that of a formal decision. It may be possible to resolve disputes by discussion and agreement before a formal decision is given. However, if a decision cannot be reached after agreement or a decision is requested, HMRC should issue a formal decision.

The third stage is the appeals stage.

When HMRC issue a decision, the letter will also state if a right of appeal exists, how to appeal, the time limits that apply and where the appeal should be sent. Appeals must normally be made in writing within 30 days of the date of the decision. They can either be made by letter or on the appeals form enclosed with HMRC's decision. Appeals sent after the 30-day deadline may be accepted if there is a reasonable excuse for missing the deadline.

When appealing, the following information must be supplied:

- name or business name;
- reference number as shown on the decision letter;
- the decision against which the appeal is being made;
- an explanation of why HMRC's decision is disagreed; and
- what the appellant believes are the correct figures and, where relevant, how these have been calculated.

Where a decision is appealed, HMRC can offer a review, the appellant can ask for a review or the appeal can be notified to the tribunal

Most agreements are settled by agreement with HMRC. HMRC will consider the reasons for the appeal and may agree with the appellant. Where an agreement is reached HMRC will confirm the agreement in writing. A further 30-day appeal window runs from the date that the confirmation is sent. HMRC will confirm the National Insurance and any penalties due following agreement.

HMRC review

1.15 In the event that agreement cannot be reached, HMRC may offer a review. Further, at any time after sending the appeal, the contributor can ask HMRC to review the decision or for a tribunal to consider the appeal. However, both cannot be done at the same time.

Where HMRC offer a review, the contributor has 30 days to accept this offer. If the offer of review is accepted outside this timeframe, HMRC may still carry out a review if they believe that the contributor has a reasonable excuse for missing the deadline. Otherwise, they may refer the matter to the tribunal.

During the review, HMRC will appoint an officer who has not previously been involved with the decision under review. The person appealing can put his or her case to the review officer. Normally this is done in writing.

The review is usually completed within 45 days. If it cannot be completed within this timeframe HMRC may ask the contributor to agree to a longer period. If an extension is not agreed, HMRC will write to state that the review has upheld the original decision. The contributor then has 30 days to appeal to the tribunal if he or she wishes to do so.

Once the review has been completed, HMRC will advise the contributor of the review decision in writing. If the contributor does not agree with the review conclusions, he or she can ask for the appeal to be heard by an independent tribunal. This request must be made within 30 days of the review conclusion letter. If no appeal is made and no reply is received in relation to the review conclusion letter, agreement with the findings is assumed. HMRC will then amend the decision in line with the outcome of the review.

Appealing to the tribunal

1.16 In the event that a contributor wishes his or her appeal to be heard by the tribunal, he or she must send the appeal to the tribunal. If a review has not been offered by HMRC, this can be done at any time after the appeal has been sent to HMRC.

However, if a review has been offered and declined, the appeal must be sent to the tribunal within 30 days of the letter offering the review. If a review has taken place, the appeal must be sent to the tribunal within 30 days of the review conclusion letter.

A tribunal can only be asked to consider an appeal that has already been made to HMRC.

Appeal forms are available on the Her Majesty's Courts and Tribunals Services website (www.justice.gov.uk). Completed forms should be sent to:

First-tier Tribunal (Tax)

Tribunals Service
2nd Floor
54 Hagley Road
Birmingham
B16 8PE

The appeal is to the First-tier Tribunal (tax).

Where the appeal is settled by tribunal, the tribunal will either tell the contributor (or his or her agent) at the hearing and confirm the decision in writing or write to the contributor with its decision. In the event that the contributor loses the appeal and wishes to take matters further, in some circumstances it may be possible to appeal to the upper tribunal. If HMRC lose, they may also take their appeal to the upper tribunal.

Where an appeal is made to the tribunal it is usually advisable for the contributor to appoint a professional adviser to act on his or her behalf.

Penalties for inaccurate documents

1.17 A single cross-tax penalty regime applies for inaccurate tax documents across the main taxes, including National Insurance contributions.

Under this system penalties are not charged if mistakes are made provided reasonable care was taken. For these purposes, 'taking reasonable care'; means:

- keeping accurate records to ensure that returns are correct;
- checking the correct position if something is not understood; and
- telling HMRC promptly if an error is discovered in a return after it is sent in.

However, if reasonable care is not taken, penalties will be charged for inaccuracies. The penalty charged depends on the type of inaccuracy, with harsher penalties charged for more serious inaccuracies. Where disclosure of the error is made to HMRC without prompting, the penalty is lower than for a 'prompted' disclosure. A disclosure is regarded as unprompted if the person had no reason to suspect that HMRC were aware of the error.

The system recognises three types of inaccuracy:

- careless;
- deliberate but not concealed;
- deliberate and concealed.

The following table summarises the penalties that may be charged.

Type of inaccuracy/disclosure	**Maximum penalty**	**Minimum penalty**
Reasonable care	No penalty	No penalty
Careless unprompted	30%	0%
Careless prompted	30%	15%
Deliberate unprompted	70%	20%
Deliberate prompted	70%	35%
Deliberate concealed unprompted	100%	30%
Deliberate concealed prompted	100%	50%

Penalties may be levied on third parties.

When working out the quality of the disclosure, HMRC take into account how long it has taken the taxpayer to tell HMRC about the inaccuracy. Where a significant period (normally three years) has elapsed before making the disclosure, the reduction given for disclosure will be restricted by 10 percentage points above the minimum. The penalty will still be nil if the taxpayer took reasonable care, but if the error is judged to be careless, the minimum penalty will be 10% where disclosure is made after three years.

The penalty regime recognises that mistakes are made. However, provided reasonable care is taken in filling in returns and any mistakes are drawn promptly to HMRC's attention when they come to light, penalties will not be charged.

It is therefore important that the task of filling in returns is taken seriously and every effort is made to ensure that they are correct.

CLASSES OF NATIONAL INSURANCE CONTRIBUTIONS

Different classes of National Insurance contributions

1.18 There are seven different types of classes of National Insurance contributions. Different contributors are liable or eligible to pay different classes of National Insurance contributions. Contributions payable under each of the classes are computed in different ways. Some are flat rate contributions; others are determined by reference to earnings or profits. The class of NIC paid also affects the benefits to which the contributor is entitled.

The classes of National Insurance contributions are as follows:

- Class 1
- Class 1A
- Class 1B
- Class 2
- Class 3
- Class 3A
- Class 4

> **Focus**
>
> Different classes of contribution are payable by different types of contributor, and give rise to differing pension and benefit entitlements.

Class 1

1.19 Class 1 contributions are payable by employees and employers on the employee's earnings. Employees pay primary Class 1 contributions and employers pay secondary Class 1 contributions.

Employees pay primary Class 1 contributions at a nil rate on earnings between the lower earnings limit and the primary earnings threshold. Contributions are payable on earnings between the primary earnings threshold at the main primary rate, whereas earnings above the upper earnings limit attract contributions at the lower additional primary rate.

Employers pay secondary contributions at the secondary rate on the employee's earnings above the secondary earnings threshold. Higher secondary thresholds apply to earners under the age of 21 and to apprentices under the age of 25.

For further details on Class 1 National Insurance contributions, see Chapter 3.

Class 1A

1.20 Class 1A National Insurance contributions are employer-only contributions paid on most taxable benefits, and also on taxable termination payments and taxable sporting testimonials. The liability on benefits in kind is calculated annually by reference to the total cash equivalent of taxable benefits within the Class 1A net. The liability on termination payments and sporting testimonials is calculated in the earnings period in which the award is made. Contributions are payable at the Class 1A rate, which is the same as the secondary Class 1 rate.

For further details of Class 1A National Insurance contributions, see Chapter 4.

Class 1B

1.21 Class 1B National Insurance contributions are employer-only contributions paid on items included in a PAYE settlement agreement in place of the Class 1 or Class 1A liability that would otherwise arise, and also on the tax due under the PAYE settlement agreement.

Class 1B contributions are payable annually at the Class 1B rate, which is the same as the secondary Class 1 rate.

For further details of Class 1B National Insurance contributions, see Chapter 5.

Class 2

1.22 Class 2 contributions are paid by the self-employed. Class 2 contributions are payable at a flat weekly rate. Different contribution rates apply to share fishermen and volunteer development workers. Class 2 contributions provide the self-employed with the opportunity to build up entitlement to the state pension and to contributory benefits.

Self-employed earners with earnings below the small profits threshold are not liable to pay Class 2 contributions, but can pay voluntarily if they so wish.

For further details on Class 2 National Insurance contributions, see Chapter 6.

Class 3

1.23 Class 3 National Insurance contributions are voluntary contributions. A contributor is never liable to pay Class 3 contributions but can choose to pay them to make up a shortfall in his or her contributions record and protect entitlement to the state pension and other benefits.

Class 3 contributions are payable at a flat weekly rate.

For further details on Class 3 National Insurance contributions, see Chapter 7.

Class 3A

1.24 Class 3A National Insurance contributions were introduced in October 2015 and were available for a limited period only. The window for paying Class 3A contributions closed on 5 April 2017. Class 3A contributions were voluntary contributions which allowed those who reached state pension age before 6 April 2016 (and who receive the basic state pension rather than the single-tier state pension) to pay a voluntary contribution to enhance their state pension.

For further details on Class 3A National Insurance contributions, see Chapter 7.

Class 4

1.25 Class 4 National Insurance contributions are payable by the self-employed on profits from their self-employment. The liability to Class 4 contributions is in addition to the Class 2 liability.

Class 4 contributions are payable at the main Class 4 percentage on profits between the lower profits limit and the upper profits limit. Profits above the upper profits limit attract a liability to Class 4 contributions at the (lower) additional Class 4 percentage.

Class 4 contributions do not provide entitlement to the state pension or to contributory benefits.

For further details on Class 4 National Insurance contributions, see Chapter 8.

NATIONAL INSURANCE CONTRIBUTIONS AND BENEFIT ENTITLEMENT

Link between National Insurance contributions and benefit entitlement

1.26 The cost of paying social security benefits is met by the National Insurance fund. The fund derives its money from National Insurance contributions paid over to HMRC. Thus National Insurance contributions fund social security benefits. Benefits are funded on a current year basis such that current contributions into the fund meet the benefit liability for the current year. This means that contributions paid by an individual are not ring-fenced to meet the cost of pension and benefits paid to them. Contributions paid in any year go towards funding pensions and benefits paid out that year.

Entitlement to some benefits is dependent on the claimant having paid sufficient National Insurance contributions or received sufficient National

Insurance credits over a sufficient period of time. These benefits are known as contributory benefits. Payment of a contributory benefit is contingent on the associated contribution condition being met. Each person has a contributions record. Contributions paid build up qualifying years and it is the years rather than the monetary value of contributions paid which determine entitlement.

Benefits which are paid to qualifying claimants regardless of their National Insurance record are known as non-contributory benefits.

The different classes of National Insurance contributions do not all carry the same entitlement to contributory benefits. The extent to which payment of National Insurance confers benefit entitlement is examined further at **1.27**.

> **Focus**
>
> Entitlement to some benefits (contributory benefits) is contingent on having paid enough of the right type of contribution; some benefits (non-contributory benefits) do not have a contribution condition and others are means tested.

Administration of benefits

1.27 The payment of social security benefits is administered by the Department for Work and Pensions (see www.dwp.gov.uk). By contrast, HMRC have responsibility for the collection and administration of National Insurance contributions (see **1.8**).

As entitlement to many benefits depends on the claimant having paid sufficient National Insurance contributions, the two departments work closely together.

Classes of NIC and benefit entitlement

1.28 Payment of contributory benefits is dependent on the claimant having paid sufficient National Insurance contributions of the right type over a sufficient period of time. When it comes to earning the right to contributory benefits, not all classes of NICs are equal. Some National Insurance contributions count towards meeting the contribution condition for the full range of contributory benefit, whereas others only count for a limited range of benefits. Some National Insurance contributions have no associated benefit entitlement.

The position is summarised in the following table.

Contribution class	Benefit rights
Class 1	Basic state pension, additional state pension, single-tier state pension, contribution-based jobseeker's allowance, contribution-based employment and support allowance, maternity allowance and bereavement payment, bereavement allowance, widowed parents allowance, bereavement support payment
Class 1A	Employer-only contributions – no benefit entitlement
Class 1B	Employer-only contributions – no benefit entitlement
Class 2	Basic state pension, single-tier state pension, contribution-based employment and support allowance, maternity allowance and bereavement allowance. Share fishermen and volunteer development workers who pay a higher rate of Class 2 contribution are also entitled to contribution-based jobseeker's allowance
Class 3	Basic state pension. Single-tier state pension and bereavement payment, bereavement allowance, widowed parent's allowance
Class 3A	Buys additional state pension for those who reach state pension age before 6 April 2016.
Class 4	No benefit entitlement (although the self-employed derive the right to contributory benefits from the payment of Class 2 contributions).

Different benefits have different contributions conditions (see **1.32**).

Some benefits are not linked to the claimant's National Insurance record. These are known as 'non-contributory benefits' (see **1.35** and **1.36**).

National Insurance credits

1.29 National Insurance credits are available in certain circumstances to people who are unable to work, for example because they are ill or because they are caring for someone else. National Insurance credits help maintain entitlement to the basic state pension and to certain other state benefits.

There are two types of National Insurance credit:

- Class 1 credits, which count towards entitlement to the state pension and to certain other state benefits; and
- Class 3 credits, which count towards entitlement to the state pension only.

Where National Insurance credits are awarded, they are added to any National Insurance contributions paid for the tax year in question and are considered together on determining whether the year is a qualifying year. In deciding whether to pay voluntary contributions for a particular year a person should not overlook any National Insurance credits to which he or she may be entitled.

National Insurance credits are given in various circumstances, including the following:

- where a person is unemployed or unable to work because of illness and is claiming certain benefits;
- for the year in which a person has their 16th, 17th or 18th birthday (starting credits). However, new awards of starting credits are not made to a person whose 16th birthday falls on or after 6 April 2010;
- where a person is on an approved training course;
- where a person is doing jury service;
- where a person is receiving statutory maternity pay, statutory paternity pay, statutory adoption pay, statutory sick pay, maternity allowance or working tax credit;
- where a person has wrongly been put in prison;
- where the person is a man approaching age 65 (although these credits are being phased out from 6 April 2010 in line with the increase in pension age for women);
- where a person is caring for a child or for a person who is sick or disabled; or
- where a person's spouse or civil partner is a member of Her Majesty's Forces and the person is accompanying them on a tour of duty outside the UK.

National Insurance credits are also available for weeks in which carer's allowance, incapacity benefit or employment and support allowance or jobseeker's allowance is claimed.

Spouses and civil partners of armed forces personnel may be able to get National Insurance credits if they accompany their spouse or civil partner on an overseas posting. Class 1 credits may be available where the posting took place on or after 6 April 2010. Class 3 credits are available for a posting on or after 6 April 1975. Credits are not given for a posting prior to 6 April 1975.

The following table summarises the National Insurance credits available in different circumstances.

Circumstances	Type of credit	Conditions
Looking for work	Class 1 credits	Class 1 credits given automatically where in receipt of jobseeker's allowance but must be claimed where person is unemployed and looking for work but not on jobseeker's allowance.
On an approved training course	Class 1 credits	Aged 18 or over on an approved full-time (20 hours or more per week) course expected to last less than one year. Excludes courses that are part of a job, GCSE, A level or equivalent courses. Special rules apply to disabled persons.
On jury service	Class 1 credits	Must have attended court and either not working or have earnings too low to pay NICs. Credits are not available to the self-employed while on jury service.
Wrongly imprisoned	Class 1 credits	Conviction quashed in the Court of Appeal.
On maternity, paternity, adoption or shared parental pay	Class 1 credits	Must have received SMP, ASPP, SAP or ShPP and earnings are insufficient to make the year a qualifying year. Class 1 credits must be claimed.
On maternity allowance	Class 1 credits	Class 1 credits are given automatically.
Receiving working tax credit	Class 3 credits or Class 1 credits	In receipt of working tax credit. Class 1 credits are given automatically where in receipt of working tax credit with a disability premium. Where working tax credit is paid without a disability premium Class 3 credits are given. If self-employed, earnings must be below the small profits threshold.
Ill, disabled or on sick pay	Class 1 credits	Payable automatically where on employment support allowance or employability supplement or allowance. Credits can be claimed where not on employment support allowance but meet conditions for it or on statutory sick pay but don't earn enough for the year to be a qualifying year.

Circumstances	**Type of credit**	**Conditions**
On universal credit	Class 3 credits	Credits given automatically where on universal credit.
Man approaching age 65	Class 1 credits	These credits were only available to those born before 6 October 1953. They were payable where the person was either not working or did not have insufficient earnings to make tax year a qualifying year and lived in UK for at least 183 days in the tax year. The self-employed needed earnings below the small profits threshold.
Caring for a child	Class 3 credits	Class 3 credits are given automatically to a parent registered for child benefit for a child under the age of 12 (even if the parent does not receive the child benefit). An application can be made to transfer credits between parents and to family members. An approved foster carer or kinship carer in Scotland can apply for Class 3 credits.
Caring for a sick or disabled person	Class 1 or Class 3 credits	Class 1 credits are paid automatically to someone receiving carer's allowance. Class 3 credits are paid automatically to someone on income support who provides regular and substantial care. A person caring for one or more disabled person for at least 20 hours per week and person cared for receives the care component of disability living allowance at the middle or highest rate, attendance allowance or constant attendance allowance or qualify for a care certificate can apply for the Class 3 carer's credits.
Accompanying a spouse or civil partner who is in HM Forces on an overseas assignment	Class 1 credits	On an accompanied assignment outside the UK with a spouse or civil partner who is a member of HM Forces.

National Insurance credits are not normally available to a married woman with a reduced rate election in force (see **3.112**) or to a person who reached state pension age before 6 April 2010.

Child benefit and the state pension

1.30 A person who has a child under the age of 12 and who either does not work or does not earn enough to pay National Insurance contributions qualifies for a carer's credit (see **1.32**) which helps protect entitlement to the state pension. The carer's credit is paid for each week that a person qualifies for child benefit in respect of a child under the age of 12.

A high income child benefit charge applies where the recipient of child benefit or his or her partner has income of £50,000 or more for the tax year. Where both partners have income in excess of £50,000, the charge is levied on the partner with the higher income. Where income is between £50,000 and £60,000 the charge is equal to one per cent of child benefit received for each £100 by which income exceeds £50,000. Where income is £60,000 or above, the charge is equal to the child benefit received in the tax year.

Those who are affected by the high income child benefit charge can choose either to continue to receive the child benefit and to pay it back. In many cases, the benefit will be received by one parent (typically the mother), but may be paid back by the recipient's partner if he or she is the higher earner. Alternatively, those affected by the charge can elect to stop receiving child benefit as for many people this will be easier than receiving it and paying it back later in the form of the high income child benefit charge.

As previously noted, a person who is in receipt of child benefit for a child under the age of 12 will receive the carer's credit if they do not work or do not earn enough to pay National Insurance contributions. In the situation where child benefit is paid to a non-earning parent but clawed back by means of the high income child benefit charge levied on the recipient's partner, it is important that the recipient still fills in the child benefit claim form, even if they elect for it not to be paid, in order to protect entitlement to the carer's credit and the state pension. Failing to register for the benefit may result in the loss of at least 12 qualifying years where the parent does not work or earns below the lower earnings limit or small profits threshold.

Specified adult childcare credits

1.31 Specified adult childcare credits transfer the National Insurance benefit attached to child benefit from the child benefit recipient to a family member who is providing care for a related child under the age of 12. For these purposes, the following count as a 'family member':

- mother or father who does not live with the child;
- grandparent, great-grandparent or great-great grandparent;
- brother or sister (including half- and step-siblings);
- aunt or uncle;

- husband or wife of former husband or wife of civil partner or former civil partner of any of the above or their partner or former partner or their son or daughter; and
- husband or wife of former husband or wife of civil partner or former civil partner of any of the above or their partner or former partner of the son or daughter of an aunt or uncle.

The credit must be claimed. However, as the credits are attached to child benefit, if no one has claimed child benefit for the child, there is no National Insurance credit to transfer and specified adult childcare credit cannot be awarded.

HMRC have confirmed that where, since March 2020, normal caring arrangements have been affected by the Covid-19 pandemic and lockdown, if care has been provided in other ways, for example, over the telephone or by video, National Insurance credits can still be claimed for 2019/20 and 2020/21.

Carer's credit

1.32 Carer's credit was introduced from 6 April 2010 and replaced the Home Responsibilities Protection scheme. It enables those who are not working or who do not earn enough because they are looking after someone else to build up entitlement to the additional state pension (also known as the second state pension). It is a Class 3 credit and as such counts towards entitlement to the basic state pension and bereavement benefits only. The carer's credit is available to:

- people who are getting child benefit for children up to the age of 12;
- approved foster carers;
- those caring for at least 20 hours a week for people who are getting attendance allowance, disability allowance at the middle or highest rate care component, constant attendance allowance, personal independence allowance daily living component at the standard or enhanced rate or armed forces independence payment or the need for care has been certified by a health or social care professional.

A person in receipt of carer's allowance automatically receives the carer's credit. However, they would not have received home responsibilities protection prior to 6 April 2010. National Insurance credits are also paid for any week in which a person would receive carer's allowance but for the fact that for that week they are also receiving widow's benefit at the same or a higher weekly rate or bereavement benefits at the same or higher weekly rate.

People who work for part of a tax year and qualify for the new National Insurance credits for the remainder of the tax year are able to combine them to form a qualifying year for basic state pension and second state pension purposes.

Home Responsibilities Protection

1.33 Home responsibilities protection (HRP) was a scheme that operated from 6 April 1978 to 5 April 2010 to protect state pension entitlement for those who do not work because they are caring for someone. Foster carers qualified for HRP from April 2003.

Home responsibilities protection was replaced from 6 April 2010 by a system of weekly credits for carers (see **1.32**).

HRP was given automatically to those who are awarded child benefit in respect of a child under 16 and who have given the Child Benefit office their National Insurance number. HRP was only given to the person who has claimed and been awarded child benefit. It was not given to the other parent. HRP was also given automatically to those on income support who do not need to register for work because they are caring for someone who is sick or disabled.

The HRP scheme worked by reducing the number of years needed to qualify for the basic state pension. It was only given for full tax years.

Where a person reaches state pension age on or after 6 April 2010, complete tax years of home responsibilities protection built up before 6 April 2010 are converted into qualifying years (to a maximum of 22 years). These qualifying years also count towards bereavement benefits.

Contributory benefits

1.34 Contributory benefits are only payable to those who have paid, or have had credited, sufficient National Insurance contributions of the right type over a sufficient period and who meet the contribution condition for the benefit in question. Contributory benefits are not means tested.

The following benefits are contributory benefits:

- basic state pension (payable to those reaching state pension age before 6 April 2016);
- additional state pension (payable to those reaching state pension age before 6 April 2016);
- single-tier state pension (payable to those who reach state pension age on or after 6 April 2016)
- contribution-based jobseeker's allowance;
- contribution-based employment and support allowance;
- maternity allowance;
- bereavement benefits.

The contribution conditions that determine whether a claimant is eligible for a particular benefit are complicated and vary from benefit to benefit.

For example, contribution-based jobseeker's allowance depends on the National Insurance contributions paid over the last two tax years whereas entitlement for contributory employment and support allowance requires the claimant to have actually paid sufficient Class 1 or Class 2 National Insurance contributions in one of the last two complete tax years before the year of the claim or that the claimant has paid or been credited with sufficient National Insurance contributions for the last two tax years of the claim.

Detailed consideration of the contribution conditions for contributory benefits is outside the scope of this work. Advice is available from the DWP.

Non-contributory benefits

1.35 Entitlement to non-contributory benefits is not dependent on the claimant's National Insurance record. These benefits are not means tested.

Non-contributory benefits include:

- child benefit;*
- personal independence allowance;
- guardian's allowance;
- attendance allowance;
- disability living allowance (care component and mobility component);
- carer's allowance;
- severe disablement allowance;
- industrial injuries disablement benefit;
- war widow or widower's pension.

* From January 2013 a tax applies to claw back child benefit where recipient or his or her partner earns more than £50,000.

Means tested benefits

1.36 Some benefits are means tested and eligibility is dependent on the claimant's financial situation rather than the claimant's National Insurance record. Benefits falling into this category include:

- income support;
- income-based jobseeker's allowance;
- income-related employment and support allowance;
- working tax credit;
- pension credit;

- housing benefit;
- council tax benefit;
- payments from the social fund; and
- universal credit.

Statutory payments

1.37 Statutory payments – statutory sick pay (SSP), statutory maternity pay (SMP), statutory paternity pay (SPP), shared parental pay (ShPP), statutory adoption pay (SAP) and statutory parental bereavement pay (SPBP) – are paid by the employer to the employee as a replacement for earnings when the employee is absent from work due to sickness or on becoming a parent, either as a result of birth or adoption.

Although the payment of statutory payments is not dependent on the employee's contributions record, the employee must meet several conditions in order to qualify for a statutory payment. Each statutory payment requires the employee to meet an earnings requirement, which depends on the employee having average weekly earnings which are at least equal to the lower earnings limit for National Insurance purposes.

Statutory payments are administered by HMRC.

NATIONAL INSURANCE DISCLOSURE SCHEME

Introduction to the scheme

1.38 The National Insurance disclosure scheme targets avoidance of National Insurance contributions by requiring certain types of arrangements to be disclosed to HMRC. The aim of the scheme is to provide HMRC with early information as regards NIC arrangements, how they work and who has used them. The scheme largely mirrors that applying for tax purposes and contained within *Part 2* of the *Finance Act 2004*. The scheme was introduced for National Insurance purposes with effect from 1 May 2007.

Penalties are charged for a failure to comply with the scheme.

> **Focus**
>
> The National Insurance disclosure scheme requires that certain types of benefit be notified to HMRC in order to target avoidance of National Insurance contributions.

Legislative framework governing the disclosure scheme

1.39 The primary legislation governing the National Insurance disclosure scheme is found in *SSAA 1992, s 132A* which enables the Treasury to make regulations requiring, or relating to, the disclosure of information in relation to any notifiable contributions arrangement or notifiable contributions proposal. The regulation power is widened by provisions introduced by the National Insurance Contributions Bill 2021, cl. 11, to include any arrangements or proposals which HMRC reasonably suspect to be notifiable arrangements or a notifiable contribution proposal (as the case may be).

For these purposes, a 'notifiable contributions arrangement' is any arrangement that:

- enables, or might be expected to enable, a person to obtain an advantage in relation to a contribution; and
- is such that the main benefit, or one of the main benefits, that might be expected to arise from the arrangement is the obtaining of that advantage.

A 'notifiable contributions proposal' is a proposal for arrangements, which if entered into, would be notifiable contributions arrangements. It does not matter whether the proposal relates to a particular person or to any person who may seek to take advantage of it.

For these purposes, an 'advantage' in relation to a contribution is the avoidance or reduction of a liability for that contribution or the deferral of the payment of that contribution. The term 'arrangements' extends to any scheme, transaction or series of transactions.

The details of the National Insurance disclosure scheme were initially set out in the *National Insurance Contributions (Application of Part 7 of the Finance Act 2004) Regulations 2007 (SI 2007/785)* (as amended). These were consolidated in 2012 and the *National Insurance Contributions (Application of Part 7 of the Finance Act 2004) Regulations 2012 (SI 2012/1868)* replaced the 2007 Regulations with effect from 1 September 2012. The rules were strengthened by changes made to the *Finance Act 2004* provisions by *FA 2015, Sch 17* with effect from 26 March 2015.

Further guidance on the disclosure of tax avoidance schemes (DOTAS) regime as it applies to National Insurance contributions can be found in HMRC's National Insurance Manual at NIM58000ff.

Features of the scheme

1.40 Under the terms of the scheme, a National Insurance arrangement must be disclosed where:

- it will, or might be, expected to enable any person to obtain a National Insurance advantage;

- that advantage is, or might be, expected to be, the main benefit or one of the main benefits of the arrangement; and
- the arrangement falls within any of the 'hallmarks' set out in the regulations.

The hallmarks are descriptions of arrangements that are of a type which are likely to warrant disclosure. They are not mutually exclusive and an arrangement may have more than one hallmark.

The fact that a scheme exhibits one or more of the hallmarks does not necessarily mean that it is unacceptable.

The hallmarks applying for National Insurance purposes are as follows:

- wishing to keep the arrangement confidential from a competitor;
- wishing to keep the arrangements confidential from HMRC;
- arrangements for which a premium fee could reasonably be obtained; and
- arrangements that are standardised ('shrink wrapped') NIC products;
- pension benefit schemes; and
- employment income arrangements.

In most cases, the duty to disclose falls on the promoter. In relation to a notifiable contribution proposal, a person is a promoter if, in the course of a relevant business, he is to any extent responsible for the design of the proposed arrangements or he makes a notifiable contribution proposal available for implementation by others. In the case of notifiable contribution arrangements, a person is a promoter if he is to any extent responsible for the design or organisation or management of those arrangements (the *National Insurance Contributions (Application of Part 7 of the Finance Act 2004) Regulations 2012 (SI 2012/1868), reg 8*).

For these purposes, a relevant business is any trade, profession or business that involves the provision of services relating to National Insurance contributions or is carried on by a bank or securities house.

The promoter must make the disclosure within five days of the earlier of the dates on which the scheme is made available for implementation by another person or the promoter becomes aware that the scheme has been implemented by a transaction taking place that forms part of it (*SI 2012/1868, reg 5(4)*).

However, if the promoter is based outside the UK, is a lawyer to whom legal privilege applies if there is no promoter, the obligation to disclose falls on the scheme user. The scheme user must make the disclosure within 30 days of entering into the first transaction that forms part of the scheme.

Where a scheme provides both a tax and a National Insurance advantage, as is the case for many employment schemes, only one disclosure needs to be made but each advantage must be separately disclosed.

Promoters must also notify HMRC of a change to a notified scheme.

Making a disclosure

1.41 HMRC produce forms that are to be used for making a disclosure.

Disclosures can be made online or by post. Where an online disclosure is made, the following forms are used (which are accessed by clicking on the link on the gov.uk website at www.hmrc.gov.uk/aiu/forms-tax-schemes.htm):

- AAG1: completion by promoter of notifiable arrangements;
- AAG2: completion by users of notifiable arrangements when an offshore promoter does not notify;
- AAG3: completion by users of notifiable arrangements where there is no promoter of the arrangements, or the arrangements are promoted by a lawyer who is unable to make full disclosure.

For disclosure by post, the relevant form from the following should be used,

- AAG1: notification of scheme by promoter;
- AAG2: notification by scheme user where offshore promoter does not notify;
- AAG3: notification by scheme user where no promoter or scheme promoted by a lawyer who is unable to make a full disclosure; and
- AAG5: continuation sheet.

The forms are available on the gov.uk website (see www.gov.uk/forms-to-disclose-tax-avoidance-schemes. Paper copies can be ordered by calling 0300 200 3610. A disclosure can be made online or by post. Where the disclosure is made by post, the forms should be sent to

HM Revenue and Customs – Counter Avoidance (Intelligence)
CTIAA Intelligence S0528
PO Box 194
Bootle
L69 9AA

Alternatively, they can be emailed to aag@hmrc.gov.uk.

Scheme reference numbers

1.42 A scheme that has been disclosed to HMRC is issued with a unique scheme reference number. This is an eight-digit number. The reference number is issued within 90 days of the disclosure. Scheme promoters have a duty to provide scheme users with the reference number and may be charged a penalty for failing to do so.

The reference number enables HMRC to identify users of each disclosed scheme.

Impact on scheme users

1.43 Scheme users must notify HMRC that they have used or are using an NIC scheme and supply the scheme reference number.

In the case of most NIC schemes, the scheme user is generally an employer.

Employers using a National Insurance scheme must notify HMRC that they are using the scheme on form AAG4. Where the arrangements relate to Class 1 National Insurance contributions, the disclosure should be made by 19 May after the end of the tax year in which the advantage is expected to arise. Where the arrangements concern Class 1A National Insurance contributions, disclosure should be made by 6 July following the end of the tax year in which the advantage is expected to arise. Where the arrangements cover both Class 1 and Class 1A National Insurance contributions, disclosure should be made by 19 May.

The scheme reference number should be disclosed on form AAG4. A penalty may be charged for a failure to do this.

Penalties

1.44 Penalties may be charged where a scheme promoter fails to disclose an avoidance scheme which falls within the scope of the DOTAS rules to HMRC. Penalties comprise an initial penalty of up to £5,000 per day and a further daily penalty of up to £600 per day where the failure to disclose continues. However, where the initial penalty appears 'inappropriately low' it may be increased to such amount as appears 'appropriate' up to £1 million. This is to deter promoters for whom the level of the penalty is such that it can be regarded as simply a cost of doing business rather than an actual deterrent.

A penalty of up to £5,000 may also be charged for a failure to give the scheme reference number to scheme users. Scheme users who fail to show the scheme reference number on their returns may be charged an initial penalty of £5,000, rising to £7,500 for a second failure and to £10,000 for a third failure.

GENERAL ANTI-ABUSE RULE (GAAR)

What is the GAAR?

1.45 The general anti-abuse rule (GAAR) was introduced by the *Finance Act 2013* and came into effect for tax purposes on 7 July 2013. The GAAR legislation defines arrangements which for tax purposes are abusive.

HMRC have published guidance on the GAAR, which is available on the Gov.uk website (see www.gov.uk/government/publications/tax-avoidance-general-anti-abuse-rules). The guidance is updated regularly.

The GAAR effectively rejects the assertion that taxpayers are free to reduce their tax bills by lawful means, regardless of how contrived those means may be irrespective of any divergence between the tax and true economic consequences. The GAAR imposes a statutory limit on how far a taxpayer can go in lawfully reducing his or her tax bill. This limit is reached where the arrangements that are put in place by the taxpayer go beyond anything that can reasonably be regarded as a reasonable course of action.

The aim of the GAAR is to deter taxpayers from entering into tax-abusive arrangements and to deter promoters from promoting such arrangements. Where a taxpayer enters into an abusive arrangement, the GAAR will counter any advantage gained from that arrangement.

However, the legislation recognises under the UK tax code there are different and valid courses of action that a taxpayer can choose, which may have different tax consequences. Choosing one course that generates a lower tax bill than an alternative course is not necessarily an abusive arrangement. The GAAR contains safeguards which aim to ensure that a reasonable course of action remains outside its scope.

Application to National Insurance contributions

1.46 The *National Insurance Contributions Act 2014, s 10* extends the application of the GAAR to National Insurance contributions. The Act came into effect on 13 March 2014 and applies to arrangements made on or after that date. Provision is made in *s 11* to make regulations to modify the application of the GAAR in its application to National Insurance contributions.

PLANNING POINTS

1.47

- Ensure that you know your National Insurance number.
- Check whether you are entitled to National Insurance credits.
- If you are entitled to child benefit, but your partner falls within the HICBC, make sure that you register for the benefit, even if you elect for it not to be paid, so that you benefit from the associated National Insurance credit.
- Check your contributions record regularly to ensure that you are on target to receive a full state pension.

Chapter 2

Categorisation of earners

SIGNPOSTS

- Different categories of earners pay different classes of National Insurance contribution. Consequently, it is important that workers are categorised correctly (see **2.1**).
- To ensure that the correct class of National Insurance is paid, it is necessary to determine the status of the worker (see **2.5**).
- Regulations set the status of certain workers, overriding the decision that may be reached by applying the normal tests (see **2.37**).
- Anti-avoidance rules apply where services are provided through an intermediary, such as a personal service company, or via a managed service company (see **2.49**).
- The off-payroll working sector rules apply where the end client is in the public sector (see **2.50**) and where the end client is a large and medium-sized private sector organisation from 6 April 2021 (see **2.51**).

IMPORTANCE OF CATEGORISATION

Link between category of earner and Class of National Insurance contribution payable

2.1 Different categories of persons pay different classes of National Insurance contributions. Employed earners and their employers pay Class 1 National Insurance contributions, whereas self-employed earners pay Class 2 and Class 4 National Insurance contributions. Class 3 National Insurance contributions are voluntary contributions which may be paid by earners and others to make up shortfalls in contribution and protect benefit entitlement. The 'cost' of the contribution varies from class to class and the different classes confer very different state pension and benefit entitlements.

As a result, it is very important that an earner is correctly categorised for National Insurance purposes. If an earner is wrongly categorised, for example as being a self-employed earner when in reality he or she is an employed earner, the earner will pay the wrong class of National Insurance contribution. This may affect his or her state pension and benefit entitlement as well as the amount that the earner pays by way of contributions.

> **Focus**
>
> Different classes of National Insurance contributions are payable by different categories of persons. It is therefore important that a worker is categorised correctly so that the correct class of contribution is paid.

The categorisation problem

2.2 Categorising workers correctly is not always straightforward. The tax and National Insurance systems recognise two categories of worker – employed and self-employed. A further category, that of 'worker' (broadly an individual with a contract who is not an employee but has some rights) exists for employment law purposes.

Many workers do not fit neatly into the 'employed earner' and 'self-employed earner' boxes required by the National Insurance system and are essentially a hybrid of the two, exhibiting characteristics of both employed and self-employed earners. The growth in freelancing and the expansion of the 'gig' economy mean that this is increasingly the case, such that categorising a worker for National Insurance purposes is often the case of finding the best fit.

The issue of employment status and the problems caused by the polarised definitions that apply for tax and National Insurance purposes was considered by the Office for Tax Simplification (OTS) in 2015. The OTS studied employment status because it was identified in earlier projects undertaken by the OTS as an area of difficulty and one which caused complexity in practice. In their work, the OTS examined the dividing line between employment and self-employment and whether it was drawn in the right place. False self-employment (driven by a desire to save National Insurance contributions) was a concern for the government and has led to the development of various pieces of anti-avoidance legislation to date, including the IR35, off-payroll working and managed service company rules.

The OTS considered a number of direct and indirect routes to improve the current situation, including setting a de minimus limit below which an employee would not be regarded as an employee, requiring the engager to deduct tax and National Insurance from the self-employed and the introduction of a statutory employment test. The OTS also considered ways in which HMRC's employment status indicator (ESI) tool could be improved. They also looked into ways in which the incentive for false self-employment could be reduced by reducing the tax and National Insurance differentials between the employed and the self-employed. Employer's National Insurance was seen as a major driver in false self-employment, although due to the revenue that it raises its abolition was not seen as a realistic option. The idea of introducing a third category of worker for tax and National Insurance purposes was rejected.

The OTS published their report in March 2015, followed by the publication of a summary of responses in July 2015. The reports are available on the gov.uk website (www.gov.uk/government/organisations/office-of-tax-simplification).

In October 2016, the Prime Minister commissioned Matthew Taylor, the Chief Executive of the Royal Society of Arts to look into how modern employment practices need to change in order to keep pace with modern business models, including the gig economy and digital platforms. The review, 'Good work: the Taylor review of modern working practices', was published in July 2017 (see www.gov.uk/government/publications/good-work-the-taylor-review-of-modern-working-practices). The government responded to the Review in February 2018 (see www.gov.uk/government/publications/government-response-to-the-taylor-review-of-modern-working-practices) and launched four consultations on key areas covered by the Review, including a consultation on employment status.

The employment status consultation, which is available on the gov.uk website at www.gov.uk/government/consultations/employment-status, sets out proposals to make the employment status rules clearer for individuals and for businesses. The consultation considers both tax and employment law issues. From a tax perspective, consideration is given to where the boundary between employment and self-employment should lie. Consideration is given to the case for incorporating the existing employment status tests (see **2.5**) into legislation; and also at replacing the existing approach with clearer tests, with the key principles enshrined in primary legislation with secondary legislation providing more detail and guidance. Comments are sought how this might work in practice. An alternative approach set out in the document is to develop a less complex test based on fewer factors, and attention is drawn to the 'supervision, direction and control' test used in the agency legislation. Comments on the proposals set out in the consultation document were sought by 1 June 2018. As at May 2021, the government had yet to publish a response.

Categories of earner

2.3 The National Insurance legislation (*SSCBA 1992, s 2(1)*) recognises two categories of earner – employed earners and self-employed earners.

An employed earner is defined as 'a person who is gainfully employed in Great Britain under a contract of service, or in an office (including elective office) with earnings'.

Earnings includes any remuneration or profit derived from an employment (*SSCBA 1992, s 3(2)*). Earner is construed accordingly (*SSCBA 1992, s 3(1)*).

The definition of an employed earner was amended from 13 May 2014 (by *NICA 2014, s 15(1)*). Prior to that date the definition referred to general earnings rather than to the wider term of earnings.

A self-employed earner is defined as 'a person who is gainfully employed in Great Britain otherwise than in an employed earner's employment (whether he is also employed in such employment)'.

A person can simultaneously be an employed earner and a self-employed earner if he or she has earnings from more than one source.

The primary legislation (*SSCBA 1992, s 2(2)(b)*) also makes provision for regulations to be made deeming certain earners to be treated in a particular way. The *Categorisation of Earners Regulations 1978, SI 1978/1689* fulfil this purpose and prescribe how certain earners are to be treated for National Insurance purposes. These are examined in more detail at **2.36**.

The legislation (*SSCBA 1992, s 2(2)(a)*) also permits the making of regulations to take certain prescribed employments outside the liability to National Insurance contributions.

Others who may pay National Insurance contributions

2.4 National Insurance contributions may be paid by persons who are not earners.

Secondary contributors pay secondary Class 1 National Insurance contributions. These are also known as employers' National Insurance contributions. The definition of 'secondary contributor is found in *SSCBA 1992, s 7(1)*.

> 'A secondary contributor, in relation to a payment of earnings to or for the benefit of an employed earner is
>
> (a) in the case of an earner employed under a contract of service, his employer;
>
> (b) in the case of an earner employed in an office with general earnings, either
>   (i) such person as may be prescribed in relation to that office; or
>   (ii) if no such person is prescribed, the government department, public authority or body of persons responsible for paying the general earnings of the office.'

It may not always be easy to identify the secondary contributor, particularly where the earner is paid by more than one person in a particular week or if the person works under the control or management of a person other than the immediate employer.

The legislation provides the power (in *SSCBA 1992, s 7(2A))* to make regulations making provision to treat a person as the secondary contributory in respect of earnings paid to or for the benefit of the earner if arrangements have been entered into, the main purpose or one of the main purposes of which is to ensure that the person is not treated as the secondary contributor. For this purpose, arrangements includes any scheme, transaction or series of transactions, agreement or understanding, whether legally enforceable or not, and any associated operations.

Where an earner is deemed to be an employed earner by regulations, the associated secondary contributor is also prescribed by the regulations (see **2.38ff**). The regulations also set the secondary contributor in other cases (see **2.46**).

Class 3 contributions may be paid by 'others' as well as by earners. 'Others' are persons who are not earners. Class 3 contributions are voluntary contributions which may be paid to make up shortfalls in a person's contribution record. Class 3A contributions (voluntary contributions, which were payable for a limited period by those who reach state pension age before 6 April 2016) could have been paid by persons who are not earners.

DETERMINING STATUS

Overview of employment status

2.5 As noted above, different categories of earner pay different classes of National Insurance contributions. The legislation categorises earners into employed earners and self-employed earners.

To ensure that an earner is correctly categorised it is necessary to determine the status of a worker. The status of the worker will also determine whether there is a secondary contributor. Where the worker is an employed earner, there will be a secondary contributor. Where the worker is a self-employed earner, there will be no secondary contributor. Although in many instances it will be clear as to whether a worker is employed or self-employed, this will not always be the case. It is therefore necessary to understand the difference between an employed earner and a self-employed earner and how to distinguish between the two.

Whether an earner is an employed earner or a self-employed earner is a question of fact rather than choice. The nature of the engagement will determine the worker's status. The worker and the engager cannot simply agree that the worker will be treated as self-employed if the nature of the engagement is one of employment. The exception to this rule is where the status of the worker is set by regulation or statute, deeming a worker to be an employed earner or a self-employed earner irrespective of whether the facts of the engagement would suggest otherwise.

Where a worker has more than one job, status must be determined separately for each job, having regard to the factors relevant to that engagement. The fact that a worker is an employed earner in one job does not automatically make him or her an employed earner in any other jobs that he or she carries out. Each case must be considered separately on its facts.

The same considerations apply to determine the status of the worker, regardless of whether the worker is working on a part-time or casual basis.

It should be noted that different rules apply to determine a worker's status for employment law purposes. Consequently, a worker may be employed for tax and National Insurance purposes but self-employed for employment law purposes.

> **Focus**
>
> Employment status must be considered separately for each job, and it is the nature of the engagement that determines the status; the worker and the engager cannot simply decide whether a worker is employed or self-employed.

Employed or self-employed

2.6 The statutory definitions of employed earner and self-employed earner applying for National Insurance purposes are set out at **2.3**.

Broadly, an employee is someone who works under a contract of service whereas the self-employed work under a contract for services. If it is not immediately apparent which camp a worker falls into, applying certain tests and asking certain questions should enable a decision to be made. The tests of employment and self-employment are considered at **2.8**.

Office holders

2.7 The definition of an employed earner also includes office holders. An office has an existence that is independent from the person holding that office. Examples include Members of Parliament, company directors, government ministers, mayors, etc. However, for the office holder to be an employed earner, he or she must have remuneration or profit from employment. If the officer holder has no earnings, there will be no liability to Class 1 National Insurance contributions as the liability is earnings-related.

Tests to determine whether worker is employed or self-employed

2.8 Determining employment status frequently causes difficulties in practice, not least because there is no single definition applying for both tax and National Insurance and for employment law purposes. Rather, it is a case of looking at the characteristics of the engagement and deciding whether on balance the characteristics are of an employment or self-employment relationship.

Guidance on determining employment status for tax and National Insurance purposes can be found on the gov.uk website at www.gov.uk/employment-status/overview. More detailed guidance can be found in HMRC's Employment Status Manual at ESM0500ff. The guidance stresses the importance of fact finding, underlining the need to look beyond the job title.

> **Focus**
>
> Employment status is often not clear cut and there is no definitive test. Instead it is a case of looking at the characteristics of the engagement and whether the picture that emerges is one of employment or self-employment.

Employed

2.9 In their guidance on the gov.uk website, HMRC set out a list of characteristics as following which apply where a person is an employee.

A person who works for a business is probably an employee if most of the following are true:

- they are required to work regularly unless they are on leave (eg holiday, on sick leave or maternity, paternity, adoption or parental leave);
- they are required to work for a minimum number of hours and expect to be paid for the time worked;
- a manager or supervisor is responsible for their workload, saying when a piece of work should be finished and how it should be done;
- they can't send someone else to do their work;
- the business deducts tax and National Insurance from their wages;
- they get paid holiday;
- they are entitled to statutory sick pay and statutory maternity pay;
- they can join the business's pension scheme;
- they are subject to the business's disciplinary and grievance procedures;
- they work at the business's or at an address specified by their business;
- their contract sets out redundancy procedures;
- the business provides the materials, tools and equipment for their work;
- they only work for the business, or if they do have another job, it is completely different from their work for the business; and
- their employment contract, statement of terms or offer letter uses terms like 'employer' and 'employee'.

Example 2.1—Determining employment status

Susie works as a marketing administrator for a large company. Her working hours are 9am to 5pm with an hour for lunch. She is provided with a computer and with the other equipment necessary for her to do her job.

She is paid a salary of £20,000 a year, which is paid monthly in arrears. Occasionally, she is required to work overtime, for which she is paid.

Her duties are set out in her job description. She is given work by her boss, who oversees what she does.

Susie exhibits the characteristics of employment. She is an employed earner for National Insurance purposes and is liable to pay primary Class 1 National Insurance contributions. Her employer is liable for secondary Class 1 National Insurance contributions in respect of her earnings.

Self-employed

2.10 A person is self-employed if they run their own business for themselves and take responsibility for its success or failure. HMRC regards a person as self-employed for tax and National Insurance purposes if most of the following are true:

- they are in business for themselves and are responsible for the success or failure of the business and can make a profit or a loss;
- they can decide what work they do and when, where or how they do it;
- they can hire someone else to do their work;
- they are responsible for fixing unsatisfactory work in their own time;
- the engager agrees on a fixed price for their work – it doesn't depend on how long it takes the worker to do the job;
- they use their own money to buy business assets, cover running costs and provide tools and equipment for their work; and
- they can work for more than one client.

Where these characteristics apply the worker would be a self-employed earner for National Insurance purposes.

Example 2.2—Determining employment status

Mark is a painter and decorator. He agrees to decorate a living room for a client and charges a fee of £600 for the job.

He provides the necessary equipment and purchases trade paint for the job.

He budgeted on the job taking three days. However things do not go as planned and it takes four. He absorbs the cost of this overrun.

The following week, he paints the exterior of a house for a different client. He charges £800 for the job.

Mark exhibits the characteristics of a self-employed worker. He would be regarded as a self-employed earner for National Insurance purposes and would need to pay Class 2 and Class 4 contributions.

Determining employment status in marginal cases

2.11 The nature of a person's work may be such that it exhibits some characteristics of employment and some of self-employment, rather than predominantly the characteristics of either employment or self-employment.

There is no single satisfactory test that can be applied to determine whether a person is employed or self-employed. Where the position is not clear-cut, it is necessary to consider all the factors that are present or absent in the case in point and then to stand back at look at the bigger picture to see if the worker tends towards employment or towards self-employment. It is important to establish all the facts.

In reaching a decision, there are various factors that need to be considered. These include:

- the nature of the contract and other written terms;
- the nature of the engager's business;
- the nature of the job;
- personal service and right of substitution;
- mutuality of obligation;
- right of control;
- provision of own equipment;
- financial risk;
- opportunity to profit;
- length of engagement;
- extent to which the worker is part and parcel of the organisation;
- entitlement to employee-type benefits;
- right to terminate the contract;
- personal factors; and
- intention.

Each factor is examined further below.

> **Focus**
>
> In marginal cases, it is necessary to look at all the factors of the engagement and see whether the overall picture tends towards employment or self-employment.

Contract of service versus contract for services

2.12 The contract should be the starting point when seeking to determine the status of a worker. An employee has a contract of service. A self-employed worker has a contract for services.

A contract of service essentially denotes a master-servant relationship. This indicates employment. A person is employed to work for another person.

A contract for services denotes self-employment. There is no master-servant relationship. The contract provides for the agreed services to be provided under the terms set out in the contract.

A contract does not need to be in writing. A contract may also be oral or implied. However, a valid contract must have certain elements:

- the intention to enter into legal relations;
- an agreement, formed by the offer of work and its acceptance; and
- consideration (usually in the form of payment for the work done).

Once it has been established that a contract exists, it is necessary to consider the terms of the contract to determine the status of the worker.

Where there is a comprehensive written contract that contains all the terms agreed between the parties, the courts will normally look to that to determine employment status, often without considering other evidence. However, if the written contract does not reflect the true underlying situation and agreement between the parties, the courts will disregard the contract and look to the reality of the arrangement to reach a status decision. Where it is suspected that the contract is a sham, the onus is on HMRC to prove that this is the case and HMRC will reserve the right to check that the working arrangements are in line with the contract.

Guidance on the role of contracts in determining employment status can be found in HMRC's Employment Status Manual at ESM0506ff.

> **Focus**
>
> A contract of service suggests employment and a contract for services suggests self-employment. The contract should reflect the true nature of the engagement.

Nature of the engager's business

2.13 In determining employment status, it is also important to gain an insight into the nature of the engager's business and the way that the business operates. In their Employment Status Manual at ESM0503, HMRC identify the following as information that is needed in order to build up a picture of the business:

- the organisational and management structure of the business;
- whether the business is a retailer, wholesaler, manufacturer or a firm within the service industry sector;
- the number of employees;
- whether any of the work is subcontracted out;
- whether there are any employees who undertake work that is similar to work that is subcontracted out;
- whether the business is office-based or factory-based or whether it is carried out at a number of sites or at a client's premises; and
- whether there are any homeworkers.

Understanding the engager's business and what is normal for that business will help determine the status of the worker.

Nature of the job

2.14 In determining whether a worker is employed or self-employed, HMRC will consider the nature of the worker's job. In particular, they will look at whether there are any other workers who are employees who are doing a similar job to the worker under similar terms and conditions. They will also look into whether the worker replaced another worker who was an employee or whether the worker was previously an employee of the business who became self-employed (HMRC Employment Status Manual at ESM0504).

Right of substitution

2.15 In deciding whether a worker is employed or self-employed it is necessary to consider whether the worker must provide his or her services personally or whether he or she can provide a replacement or substitute in his or her absence. Under a contract of services, denoting employment, the worker is required to provide his or her services personally.

The right to send a replacement, known as the right of substitution, is indicative of self-employment. If the worker has to pay the helper or substitute sent in his or her place, this would further indicate self-employment.

However, the lack of a right of substitution does not preclude a worker being self-employed. The worker may be engaged because of his or her specialist skills and it may not be possible for replacement to be sent instead.

In looking at any rights of substitution, the extent to which the engager has a right to reject any proposed substitute should also be considered. If the engager has the final say or if the worker only has the right to propose a substitute, the pointer to self-employment is weaker than if the worker has an unequivocal right to send a substitute.

HMRC guidance on the right on substitution in determining employment status can be found in their Employment Status Manual at ESM0533ff.

Focus

The ability to send a substitute rather than undertake the work personally is a strong indicator of self-employment.

Mutuality of obligations

2.16 For there to be a contract of services there must be minimum mutual obligations – without minimum obligations there is no contract in existence. It is necessary to first determine whether a contract exists before ascertaining whether the contract is one of service or for services. Having determined that a contract exists, it is then necessary to determine whether there is the irreducible minimum for a contract of employment.

These minimum obligations form the badges of a contract between master and servant.

As a minimum, the alleged employer must be obliged under the contract to offer continuing employment to the alleged employee.

In return, the alleged employee must be obliged to:

- accept work from the alleged employer to a reasonable extent;
- make himself or herself available to the alleged employer to provide his or her services; and
- to refrain from looking for or taking work from another employer while tied to the alleged employer.

It should be remembered that these are the minimum mutual obligations necessary for a contract of service and usually the contract will impose further obligations on each party. Without the obligation on the part of the employer to offer work and the obligation on the part of the employee to accept work there can be no contract of service. Without a contract of service, the worker cannot be an employed earner and liable for Class 1 National Insurance contributions.

However, when looking at mutuality of obligations it is necessary to appreciate these may change over time. It may be that there is no mutuality of obligation at the start of the arrangement, but that the regular offer of work and the repeated acceptance of that work over a period of time give rise to a contract. The actions of the parties over the period are such that mutual obligations are formed.

The existence of minimum mutuality of obligations is indicative of employment.

HMRC guidance on mutuality of obligations can be found in their Employment Status Manual at ESM0543.

Focus

For a contract of service to exist, there must be minimum mutual obligations.

Right of control

2.17 The right of control that the engager has over the worker is relevant is determining the status of that worker. Within an employment situation, a master-servant relationship exists. For this to be the case, one party must be the master and the other the servant. This implies that where there is a contract of service (and thus the worker is employed) the engager will have more control over the worker than where the worker is engaged under a contract for services (and thus self-employed). What is important here, is the right of the engager to exert control, rather than whether that contract is actually exerted.

For example, it would be quite normal for an employee to be told when and where to work. A contract of employment would usually set out the employee's working hours. Any flexibility would generally require the employer's agreement. However, a self-employed worker would have more flexibility as to when and how he or she worked.

The fact that a worker is told how to perform the duties would point towards employment. However, the absence of such control in itself is not necessarily indicative of self-employment. Where an employee is an expert in his or her field or has a senior role it would be normal for his or her work to be unsupervised or self-managed.

However, as a general rule, the higher the degree of control that the engager has over the worker, the more likely it is that the worker is employed. Although a high level of control is a strong pointer towards employment, it may not be conclusive on its own and should be considered in light of all relevant factors and the overall picture.

HMRC guidance on the role of the right of control in determining employment status can be found in their Employment Status Manual at ESM0518ff.

> **Focus**
>
> The higher the level of control over where and how the worker performs the duties, the stronger the indicator of employment.

Provision of own equipment

2.18 A person who is self-employed will normally provide the tools and equipment needed to perform the work which he or she has been engaged to do. By contrast, an employer will generally provide the tools and equipment needed for an employee to perform the duties of the employment.

When looking at the degree to which provision of equipment is indicative of self-employment, greater weight is given to the provision of substantial items of capital equipment. The provision of capital equipment also signifies investment in the business – another characteristic suggesting self-employment. Provision of equipment is of most significance where it is fundamental to the service provided and of sufficient importance to affect the substance of the contract.

Many employees provide small items of equipment, such as small tools. The provision of such items does not in itself make the worker self-employed. As always, it is necessary to consider the bigger picture.

HMRC guidance on the role of the provision of equipment in determining employment status can be found in their Employment Status Manual at ESM0540ff.

> **Focus**
>
> The provision of equipment, particularly substantial capital items, is an indicator of self-employment.

Financial risk

2.19 A person who is self-employed bears a higher degree of financial risk than one who is employed. A self-employed person will bear any financial risk associated with the business. He or she will correct any mistakes at his or own expense and bear the cost of jobs that overrun or exceed budget. A self-employed person will also have to meet the cost of hiring help or the cost of a replacement if he or she is personally unable to undertake the work. A self-employed person will also suffer the financial risk associated with bad debts and increasing costs.

An employee will not be exposed to financial risks of this nature.

Financial risk is a very important factor in determining the status of a worker. The risk of making a loss is taken as a very strong indicator of self-employment.

HMRC guidance on the role of financial risk in determining employment status can be found in their Employment Status Manual at ESM0541.

> **Focus**
>
> Bearing financial risk is a strong indicator of self-employment.

Opportunity to profit

2.20 The other side of the coin to bearing financial risk is the opportunity to profit. A self-employed person enjoys the opportunity to profit when the business does well or if jobs come in ahead of budget. The self-employed person is in a position to enjoy the profits associated with good business decisions in a way that is not generally available to an employee and as such is able to enjoy the profits of his or her business.

An employee does not have the opportunity to profit in such a direct way. However, an employee on commission will earn more if he or she sells more. Likewise, an employee who performs well may receive a bonus or greater pay rise than one who performs less well and may be offered promotion opportunities. However, an employee does not suffer the losses and take the profits to the same degree as someone who is self-employed.

HMRC guidance on the role of the opportunity to profit in determining employment status can be found in their Employment Status Manual at ESM0547.

> **Focus**
>
> Bearing financial risk is a strong indicator of self-employment.

Length of engagement

2.21 The length of engagement itself is not a strong indicator of employment or self-employment and must be considered as part of the overall picture.

However, the existence of an open-ended contract is likely to signify employment, although the absence of such a contract does not necessarily indicate self-employment as many employees are engaged on fixed-term contracts.

Although numerous short-term engagements may suggest self-employment, it may also be the case that the worker is a casual employee.

It is therefore necessary to consider the length of the engagement in the light of other relevant factors when determining the status of a worker. However, there may be a correlation between the length of the engagement and other factors, which means that the longer the engagement, the more likely it is to be one of employment. For example, the longer the engagement, the more likely the engager will wish to exert control over the worker, and the higher the level of control, the more likely the relationship is to be one of employment.

HMRC guidance on the impact of the length of the engagement in determining employment status can be found in their Employment Status Manual at ESM0548.

Focus

The length of the engagement itself is not a strong indicator of status; it should be considered in light of other characteristics of the engagement.

Extent to which the worker is part and parcel of the organisation

2.22 The extent to which the worker is an integral part of the client's organisation can be a strong indicator of status.

If a worker is taken on to manage staff and is involved in making key decisions, it is highly likely that the worker will be an employee. Other indicators that the worker is 'part and parcel' of the organisation would include being invited on staff outings, being allowed to join the pension scheme and being subject to disciplinary grievance procedures.

By contrast, if the worker is not part of the fabric of the organisation and is not regarded by the client's staff as 'one of us', it is more likely that the worker is self-employed.

Although this is an important test, it is not enough on its own to determine the status of a worker and should be considered in line with other relevant factors.

HMRC guidance on the significance of whether an employee is 'part and parcel' of the organisation in determining employment status can be found in their Employment Status Manual at ESM0545.

> **Focus**
>
> A worker who is 'part and parcel' of the organisation is more likely to be an employee.

Entitlement to employee-type benefits

2.23 An employee will receive non-cash remuneration in addition to his or her cash salary or wages. Non-cash benefits include the right to paid holiday, pension provision and possibly items such as private health care, a company car etc.

By contrast, a self-employed worker will be paid the agreed fee for the job and will not receive any additional perks which may be given to employees. The absence of such benefits usually indicates an intention for the worker to be self-employed.

HMRC guidance on the role of the right to holiday pay, maternity pay sick pay and pension rights in determining employment status can be found in their Employment Status Manual at ESM0544.

> **Focus**
>
> Receiving employee-type benefits suggests the worker is an employee.

Right to terminate the contract

2.24 Under the terms of an employment contract, the employee can terminate the contract by giving the required notice. The employer can also terminate the contract on the giving of notice.

A contract for services does not usually include such a clause. The contract will come to an end on the completion of the task or if the contract terms are breached.

HMRC guidance on the impact of the right to terminate the contract on employment status can be found in their Employment Status Manual at ESM0546.

Personal factors

2.25 Factors personal to the worker may also need to be considered in reaching a decision as to the status of a worker. The importance of these factors may depend on the worker's level of skill or expertise.

Personal factors may be less important if the worker is unskilled and highly supervised by the engager. A high level of supervision and control over the person's work will suggest employment, regardless of the personal factors involved.

HMRC's guidance on the role of personal factors in determining employment status can be found in their Employment Status Manual at ESM0549ff.

Intention of the parties

2.26 The intention of the parties can be a useful decider when the factors pointing to employment and self-employment are evenly matched. However, intention alone cannot determine status. A worker who exhibits the characteristics of an employed earner will not be regarded as self-employed, even if this is the intention of both parties. If the true nature of the relationship is one of employment, the worker will be an employed earner.

It must be remembered that the status of the worker is a question of fact and something that can only be determined after considering all relevant factors. Employment status is not something that the worker and engager can merely agree between themselves.

Regularly working for one engager

2.27 The fact that a worker regularly works for one engager does not in itself mean that the engagement is one of employment – each engagement must be considered separately in light of the factors relevant to that engagement. The position may also change over time. For example, a worker may begin to work for an engager in a self-employed capacity and take on a number of short-term contracts. However, this may in time be replaced with a contract of employment.

Similarly, a person working in a self-employed capacity may work or may intend to work for more than one engager, but due to problems securing work, may find themselves working part-time for one engager. However, this may be on a self-employed basis.

It is the nature of the arrangement rather than the number of engagers for whom the worker works that is important in determining the employment status.

HMRC guidance on the impact of working for one engager only on the determination of employment status can be found in HMRC's Employment Status Manual at ESM0553.

Case law

2.28 The case law on employment status is extensive and the courts consider the factors set about above in reaching a decision.

Where a decision on status is made for tax purposes, the decision that is reached normally holds for National Insurance purposes and vice versa.

Ready Mixed Concrete (South East) Ltd v Minister of Pensions and National Insurance

2.29 The leading case of *Ready Mixed Concrete (South East) Ltd v Minister of Pensions and National Insurance* [1968] 2 QB 497 established conditions that are needed for a contract of service to exist. The case considered whether an owner-driver of a vehicle used exclusively for the delivery of a company's ready mixed concrete was engaged under a contract of services or a contract for services.

The company made and sold ready mixed concrete. They had engaged an independent contractor to deliver the concrete to the customers, but that contract was terminated. The company then introduced a scheme whereby the concrete was delivered by owner-drivers working under written contracts. The drivers entered into a hire purchase agreements with Readymix Finance Ltd to purchase a lorry. However, the mixing equipment on the lorry was the company's property. The Minister for Social Security was asked for a determination of the employment status of one of the drivers, Mr Latimer.

Mt Latimer had a written contract. The contract allowed him, with the company's consent, to appoint a suitably qualified driver to operate the truck in his place, but this was subject to the requirement that he drove the truck himself unless he had a valid reason for not doing so. If a substitute driver was used, Mr Latimer was responsible for paying him. The contract also required Mr Latimer to wear a company uniform, to carry out all reasonable orders from a competent servant of the company, and maintain the lorry at his own expense and meet the running costs. There was a mutual intention that Mr Latimer was an independent contractor.

Other relevant facts were that he did not work set hours and had no fixed meal break, the company did not tell him how to drive the truck or which routes to take. There were nine owner-drivers in the depot and they arranged their holiday to ensure that only one of them was away at any one time. A relief driver was engaged to cover the driver on holiday and all the drivers contributed equally to his wage. Additional drivers were engaged in the busy period under contracts of service.

The Minister for Pensions and Social Security found that Mr Latimer was employed under a contract of service. However, this decision was reversed on appeal to the High Court, where MacKenna J found that Mr Latimer was a 'small business man', not a servant. His contract was one of carriage not service. He found that a contract of service only existed where the following three conditions were met:

- the servant agrees that, in consideration of a wage or other remuneration, he will provide his own work and skill in the performance of some service of his master;

- he agrees, expressly or implicitly, that in the performance of that service he will be subject to the other's control in a sufficient degree to make that other master; and
- the other provisions of the contract are consistent with it being a contract of service.

The case established that for there to be a contract of service:

- the worker must be subject to a right of control;
- personal service must be given; and
- other factors are consistent with a contract of service.

Hall v Lorimer

2.30 The case of *Hall v Lorimer* [1993] STC 23 is a leading employment status case from which some important principles emerged.

Mr Lorimer was a freelance vision mixer in the television industry. He undertook work for a number of different production companies.

He did not provide his own equipment or tools and was one of many people involved in each production. He usually worked on premises owned or hired by the production company. He sometimes provided advice on the equipment that was to be used and also advised on areas relevant to his areas of expertise.

On becoming freelance, Mr Lorimer circulated his curriculum vitae to potential clients in a bid to obtain work. Most of his engagements were for a single day. The longest engagement was for a week. In the period from February 1985 to August 1989 he undertook 580 engagements.

He was free to accept or reject offers of work. He had no formal contract. He took bookings by telephone and confirmed them in writing, stating date, rate of pay, time and place.

He contributed no money to the production and did not share in profits or losses. However, he paid the expenses of running his office and his agent's fees out of his income. He also had a separate business bank account.

Mr Lorimer contended that he was self-employed. What is now HMRC contended that he was employed. Mr Lorimer won in the High Court and HMRC appealed. The appeal was dismissed by the Court of Appeal, upholding the decision of the High Court and the Tribunal.

The court considered the questions set out at **2.8ff**. These failed to give a decisive answer as to Mr Lorimer's employment status. The court also took the view that the sum total of the answers to the individual questions would not necessarily give the right answer as some factors would carry more weight than others. Applying this approach, the courts found Mr Lorimer to be self-employed.

The decision had implications for labour-only subcontractors, who are not excluded from being self-employed regardless of the fact that they do not provide their own equipment. However, when seeking to demonstrate self-employment, an individual should be able to demonstrate that he or she runs a business. Factors that would suggest this include invoicing for work done, running an office at home, registering for VAT, keeping personal and business finances separate, running the risk of bad debts, promoting the business and employing staff.

Dragonfly Consulting Ltd v R & C Commrs

2.31 The case of *Dragonfly Consulting Ltd v R & C Commrs* [2008] BTC 639 illustrated that a limited right to substitution in not in itself sufficient to ensure that a worker is regarded as self-employed.

The case concerned an IT contractor who provided his services to a client through an intermediary company. The issue was whether, had the contractor provided his services direct to the client, the contractor would have been an employee of the client. If this were the case the IR35 provisions (see **2.49**) would bite.

The special commissioners found that, but for the intermediary company, the contractor would have been an employee of the client. The taxpayer appealed, arguing that the right of substitution within the notional contract was not compatible with employment. The appeal also considered the degree of control that the client had over the work of the contractor and the intention of the parties.

The appeal was dismissed. The court found that the taxpayer did not have an unqualified right to substitution and could only provide a substitute with the client's consent. Further, on the evidence provided, it was reasonable to conclude that the contractor's work was subject to a degree of substitution.

Whether a worker is employed or self-employed is a question of fact. The true nature of the relationship prevails over any statement of intention between the parties.

The taxpayer also sought to establish a further category, namely that of 'worker', arguing that he was a worker rather than employed or self-employed. This failed as the courts do not recognise intermediate categories of worker. A worker is either employed or self-employed. There is no halfway house.

This case was important because it destroyed the myth that including a substitution clause in a contract was sufficient to ensure that a worker was treated as self-employed (and where services were provided through a personal service company that the IR35 provisions would not bite). It illustrates the necessity to look at the overall picture and see whether the relationship that emerges is one of employment or self-employment.

Christa Ackroyd Media Limited v HMRC and similar cases

2.32 The *Christa Ackroyd* case (*Christa Ackroyd Media Limited v HMRC* [2018] TC 06334) attracted considerable press attention. The case focussed on typical freelance contracts that are used in the broadcasting company, whereby presenters and broadcasters provided their services through a personal service company.

Christa Ackroyd was a presenter on the BBC's *Look North* programme for more than ten years. She supplied her services through a personal service company, Christa Ackroyd Media Limited (CAM), working under two fixed-term contracts between her personal service company and the BBC. HMRC contended that IR35 applied and CAM should have accounted for PAYE and NIC on the deemed payment under the IR35 rules.

Under the terms of the engagement, the BBC had the ultimate right to specify the services that Christa Ackroyd must provide and she was subject to the BBC's guidelines and the BBC controlled the editorial format of the *Look North* programme. Further Christa Ackroyd was not able to provide services to any other organisation without the BBC's consent. She was required to work for the BBC for at least 225 days a year, for which she would be paid the relevant monthly contracted fee. She may also be called upon by the BBC to provide other broadcasting services and attend public events. Christa Ackroyd had to provide the contracted services personally – she could not send a substitute.

In reaching a decision, reliance was placed on the case of *Ready Mix Concrete (South East) Ltd v Minister of Pensions and National Insurance* (1968) 2 QB 497 and the Tribunal found the key characteristics of employment of mutuality of obligation and control to a sufficient degree to be present in this case.

Having made an overall qualitative assessment of the circumstances, the Tribunal found the relationship between Christa Ackroyd and the BBC to be one of employment. As a result, the engagement fell within IR35 and her personal service company, CAM, would be liable for PAYE and NIC on the deemed payment.

However, by contrast, in *Albatel Limited v HMRC* [2019] TC 070405, the First-tier Tribunal found that Lorraine Kelly was not an employee of ITV, but rather a 'theatrical artist' who presents a brand that ITV specifically sought when hiring her services. The judge ruled that her contract was a contract for services, not that of employer and employee.

HMRC have brought various cases under the IT35 legislation against those in the media working through personal services companies, with mixed success. In February 2021, the Upper Tribunal held that contracts held by presenter Kaye Adams with the BBC fell outside the scope of IR35 (*HMRC v Atholl House Productions Ltd* [2021] UKUT 0037 (TCC)). At the time of writing, HMRC were pursuing a case against Gary Lineker, claiming that he was employed in his role as a presenter for the BBC and BT Sport rather than self-employed. In each case, the decision hinges on the facts of each particular engagement.

Other case law

2.33 There are numerous cases of relevance to employment status decisions and it is not possible to cover them all in this work. However, HMRC's Employment Status Manual includes a summary of the following cases:

- *Davies v Braithwaite* 18 TC 198 – existence of contract of service (see ESM7920);
- *Morren v Swinton and Pendlebury Borough Council* [1965] 1 WLR 576 – contract of service or contract for services (see ESM7025);
- *Ready Mixed Concrete (South East) Ltd v Minister of Pensions and National Insurance* [1968] 2 QB 497 – contract of service (see ESM7030);
- *Market Investigations v Ministers of Social Security* [1969] 2 QB 173 – contract of service or series of contracts for services (see ESM7040);
- *Fall v Hitchen* 49 TC 433 – contract of service or contract for services (see ESM7955);
- *Airfix Footwear Ltd v Cope* [1978] ICR 1210 – whether engaged under a contract of employment and entitled to claim unfair dismissal (see ESM7060);
- *Massey v Crown Life Insurance Company* [1978] I WLR 676 – contract of service/claim for unfair dismissal (see ESM7070);
- *Edwards v Clinch* 56 TC 367 – whether fees were chargeable under former Schedule E as emoluments of employment or under former Schedule D (see ESM7080);
- *O'Kelly and Others v Trusthouse Forte plc* [1984] 1 QB 90 – contract of service or contract for services (see ESM7100);
- *Nethermere (St Neots) Ltd v Gardiner and Taverna* [1984] IRLR 240 – contract of service or contract for services (see ESM7110);
- *Sidet v Phillips* 59 TC 458 – contract of service or contract for services (see ESM7120);
- *Wallis v Sinnett* 60 TC 150 – contract of service or contract for services (see ESM7130);
- *Lee Ting Sang v Chung Chi-Keung* [1990] IRLR 236 – contract of service (see ESM7140);
- *Andrews v King* 64 TC 332 – whether gangmaster self-employed or an employee (see ESM7150);
- *Lane v The Shire Roofing Company (Oxford) Ltd* [1995] TLR 104 – contract of service or contract for services (see ESM7165);
- *Barnett v Brabyn* 69 TC 133 – nature of employment status (see ESM7170);

- *Secretary of State for Employment v McMeechan* [1997] IRLR 353 – whether an employee of agency and entitled to redundancy pay (see ESM7180);
- *Clark v Oxfordshire Health Authority* [1998] IRLR 125 – whether there was a contract of service/claim to unfair dismissal and race discrimination (see ESM7190);
- *Carmichael & Another v National Power plc* [1999] 1 WLR 2042 – whether contract of employment and entitlement to written statement of particulars (see ESM7200);
- *Express and Echo Publications Ltd v Tanton* [1999] IRLR 367 – contract of service or contract for services (see ESM7210);
- *(1) MacFarlane & (2) Skivington v Glasgow City Council* EAT/1277/99 – contract of service or contract for services (see ESM7229);
- *St John's College School, Cambridge v Secretary of State for Social Security* (unreported) – whether visiting instrumental teachers engaged under contract of service or contract for services (see ESM7230);
- *Mongomery v Johnson Underwood Ltd* (unreported) – contract of service or contract for services (see ESM7240);
- *Todd & Others v Adamns and Another* (unreported) – contract of service/ claim for damages (see ESM7250);
- *Synaptek Ltd v Young* 75 TC 51 – application of Social Security Contributions (Intermediaries) Regulations 2000, *SI 2000/727* to IT consultant working through his own service company (see ESM7260);
- *Usetech Ltd v Young* [2004] STC (SCD) 213 – application of *Social Security Contributions (Intermediaries) Regulations 2000, SI 2000/727* to IT consultant working through his own service company (see ESM7270);
- *Future Online Ltd v Foulds* 76 TC 590 – application of *Social Security Contributions (Intermediaries) Regulations 2000, SI 2000/727* to IT consultant working through his own service company (see ESM7280);
- *HMRC Commissioners v Larkstar Data Ltd* [2008] EWHC 3284 (Ch) – appeal against determination of liability under the *Social Security Contributions (Intermediaries) Regulations 2000, SI 2000/727* (see ESM7300);
- *Autoclenz Ltd v Belcher & Ors* [2009] EWCA Civ 1046 – whether car valeters were self-employed or limb employees within *Employment Rights Act 1996, s 230(3)* (see ESM7310); and
- *Talentcore Limited (t/a Team Spirits) v Revenue and Customs Commissioners* [2011] UKUT 423 (TCC) – appeal against determinations to tax and NIC in relation to application of agency legislation (see ESM7315).

HMRC guidance

2.34 Guidance on determining employment status for tax and National Insurance purposes can be found on the gov.uk website at www.gov.uk/employment-status/overview. More detailed guidance can be found in HMRC's Employment Status Manual at ESM0500ff. The Employment Status Manual is available on the gov.uk website at www.gov.uk/manuals/esmanual/index.htm.

Check Employment Status for Tax (CEST) tool

2.35 HMRC have produced an online tool – the Check Employment Status for Tax (CEST) tool – which can be used for a specific engagement to determine whether the worker would be classified as employed or self-employed for tax and National Insurance purposes and also to determine whether the off-payroll working rules apply.

The tool was updated in late 2019 in preparation for the extension of the off-payroll working rules, which came into effect from 6 April 2021. Detailed guidance on using the CEST tool can be found in HMRC's Employment Income Manual at ESM1100ff. A handy glossary of terms in located at ESM11020.

The service can be used to determine the view of HMRC on whether:

- the intermediaries (IR35) legislation (see **2.49**) applies to an engagement;
- for a public sector engagement, whether the off-payroll working in the public sector (see **2.50**) apply; and
- whether a worker should pay tax through PAYE.

The service can be used for both current and future engagements in both the public and the private sector. It can be used by an organisation hiring a worker, a worker providing their services, an agency placing a worker through an intermediary and by other parties in the contractual chain.

HMRC state that they will stand by the result given by the CEST tool, unless the information provided is not accurate. However, HMRC warn that they will not be bound by the result if it is achieved through contrived arrangements designed to achieve a particular outcome from the service. They regard this as deliberate non-compliance.

The check should be re-performed if there are changes in the nature of the engagement or the way in which the work is done. HMRC warn that where there are subsequent material changes to the contractual or working arrangements, they will not stand by the original outcome. It is recommended that the CEST tool is run again in light of the new arrangements in order to secure a result by which HMRC will stand.

The service is anonymous and does not store information or the result given. Users can print out the result as evidence of their employment status. This is recommended.

Under the off-payroll working rules as they apply where the end client is a public sector body and as extended to the private sector from April 2021, the engager is required to determine the status of any workers who provide their services through an intermediary and provide a copy of that determination to the worker and to other parties in the chain. The CEST tool can be used to meet the obligation to undertake a determination. The result should be printed out and given to the worker and to other parties in the chain.

It is important to note that CEST should only be used to determine the status of worker for tax and National Insurance purposes; it should not be used to make a determination for employment law purposes as different considerations apply.

The following information is required to use the service:

- the worker's responsibilities;
- who decides what work is done;
- who decides when, where and how the work is done;
- how the worker will be paid;
- whether the engagement provides any benefits or reimbursement of expenses.

Users are instructed to choose the answers that best match the usual working practices of the engagement. The Employment Status Manual (at ESM 11035ff.) provides detailed guidance on answering particular questions within the CEST tool.

The CEST tool is available on the gov.uk website at www.gov.uk/guidance/check-employment-status-for-tax.

HMRC rulings

2.36 Where a decision on the employment status of a worker cannot be determined, a ruling can be sought from an HMRC status officer. The decision given is binding for both tax and National Insurance purposes.

However, an appeal can be made if the earner does not agree with the decision reached.

SPECIAL CASES

Categorisation of Earners Regulations

2.37 The primary legislation (*SSCBA 1992, s 2(2)*) provides the power for regulations to be made which categorise an earner for National Insurance purposes. The *Social Security (Categorisation of Earners) Regulations 1978*,

SI 1978/1689 makes various provisions with regard to categorisation of certain earners. The regulations override any decisions on status that may be reached by applying the tests set out above.

In particular, *reg 2* deems the earners specified in *Sch 1, Pt I* to be employed earners for National Insurance purposes. This treatment applies regardless of whether such earners exhibit the characteristics normally associated with self-employment. The effect of deemed employed earner status is that the earners in question are brought by the regulations within the Class 1 National Insurance net. They will therefore be liable to Class 1 contributions rather than to Class 2 and Class 4 contributions.

The categories of earners deemed to be employed earners by the regulations are discussed at **2.38** to **2.43**.

The regulations also deem certain earners to be self-employed earners. These are listed in *Sch 1, Pt II*. These are discussed at **2.44**.

Employments listed in *Sch 1, Pt III* of the regulations are disregarded for National Insurance purposes. These are discussed at **2.45**.

Where earners are deemed employed earners by virtue of the regulations, the associated deemed secondary contributor is specified by *reg 5* and *Sch 3*. *Schedule 3* also sets the deemed secondary contributor in other cases (see **2.46**).

The regulations also provide (in *reg 3* and *Sch 2*) that where an earner is, or is deemed to be, a self-employed earner, the earner continues to be treated as a self-employed earner until such time as the self-employment ceases. The effect of this is that the self-employed earner remains liable for Class 2 contributions for weeks when he or she is on holiday or otherwise not working as long as the self-employment has not come to an end.

Finally, the regulations make provision (in *reg 4*) for the procedures to be followed if a decision as to status is made by the High Court which is inconsistent with a previous direction of the Secretary of State. Broadly, the regulation gives the Secretary of State the power to treat the earner as having the status corresponding to the Class of contributions paid prior to the High Court decision for the period for which such contributions were paid if this is considered to be in the interests of the earner (see **2.55**).

Office cleaners and cleaners of telephone apparatus

2.38 Office cleaners and operatives working in any similar capacity in any premises other than one used as a private dwelling house are deemed to be employed earners by virtue of the *Social Security (Categorisation of Earners) Regulations 1978, SI 1978/1689, reg* 2 and *Sch 1 para 1*. Likewise a cleaner of telephone apparatus and associated fixtures other than in a private dwelling house is deemed to be an employed earner.

The deemed secondary contributor (by virtue of *Sch 3, para 1*) depends whether or not the person is supplied through an agency. Where the cleaner is supplied by or through an agency or other third party and receives his or her remuneration from or through that agency or third party, the agency or third party is deemed to be the secondary contributor. In any other case, the secondary contributor is deemed to be the person with whom the deemed employee contracted to do the work.

Provision of personal services via agencies and intermediaries

2.39 The rules regarding the treatment of workers supplied through agencies and other intermediaries were changed with effect from 6 April 2014.

As they apply from 6 April 2014, the regulations deem persons supplied by agencies to be employed earners where certain conditions are met. The deeming provisions bite where:

- the worker personally provides workers to the end client;
- there is a contract between the end client and an agency under, or in consequence of which, the services are provided or the end client pays, or otherwise provides consideration for the services, and
- remuneration is receivable by the worker (from any person) in consequence of providing the services.

This deeming provision does not apply where the services are provided in the home of the person supplying them or on other premises not under the control or management of the end client (except where the other premises are premises at which the employed person is required to work as a result of working for the client). Also excluded from this rule are persons who work for the end client as an actor, singer, musician or other entertainer, or as a fashion, photographic or artist's model.

The person providing the services is not deemed to be an employed earner where it can be shown that the manner in which the worker provides the services is not subject to (or to the right of) supervision, direction or control by any person. If the worker is subject to supervision, direction and control and the conditions listed above are met, the worker is deemed to be an employed earner and within the scope of Class 1 National Insurance contributions.

Where a deemed employment arises as a result of these provisions, the secondary contributor is normally the UK agency who is party to the contract with the end client. However, if the client provides the UK agency with fraudulent documents in connection with the control, direction or supervision which is to be exercised over the worker, it is the end client rather than the agency who is the secondary contributor.

In the event that a person, other than the end client, who is resident in Great Britain and who has a contractual relationship with the UK agency provides fraudulent documents to the UK agency in connection with the purported deduction or payment of contributions in connection with the employed person, the secondary contributor is the person who provides the fraudulent documents (*Sch 3, para 2*).

Employment by a spouse or civil partner

2.40 A person is deemed to be an employed earner where that person is employed by his or her spouse or civil partner for the purposes of the spouse or civil partner's employment (or self-employment) (*Sch 2, para 3*).

In this situation, the spouse or civil partner is deemed to be the associated secondary contributor (*Sch 3, para 3*).

Lecturers, teachers and instructors

2.41 The National Insurance treatment of lecturers, teachers and instructors who are self-employed for tax purposes was changed with effect from 6 April 2012. The previous deeming provision that applied prior to that date was revoked, so that where a lecturer or teacher would otherwise be treated as self-employed by applying the usual tests, from 6 April 2012 they are also treated as self-employed for National Insurance purposes.

Ministers of religion

2.42 A person employed as a minister of religion, but not in employment under a contract of services with general earnings, is deemed to be an employed earner, unless the remuneration (excluding payments in kind) does not consist wholly or mainly of stipend or salary (*Sch 1, para 5*). This prevents a Roman Catholic priest from being deemed an employed earner under this provision.

The associated secondary contributor is the Church Commission for England (*Sch 3, para 7*).

However, where the minister of religion is not employed as a minister of the Church of England or under a contract of service or where the remuneration is not wholly or mainly a stipend or salary, the relevant secondary contributor depends on the source from which the remuneration is paid.

If the remuneration is paid only from one fund, the secondary contributor is the person responsible for that fund.

If the remuneration is paid from more than one fund and remuneration from one of those funds is also paid to other ministers of religion, the secondary contributor is the person responsible for the administration of that fund. If, however, remuneration is paid from two or more funds to other ministers of religion, the secondary contributor is the person responsible for the administration of the fund from which remuneration is paid to the greatest number of ministers of religion who carry out their duties in Great Britain.

In any other case where payment is made from more than one fund, the secondary contributor is the person who carries out the administration of the fund from which the minister of religion first receives a payment of remuneration in the tax year (*Sch 3, para 8*).

Entertainers

2.43 The treatment of entertainers was changed from 6 April 2014. From that date, entertainers are no longer deemed to be employed earners where, applying the normal tests, the entertainer would be self-employed (*Sch 1 para 5A* as omitted by *SI 2014/635 reg 3(c)*).

The case of *ITV Services Ltd v Revenue and Customs Commissioners* [2012] UKUT 47 (TCC) concerned the employment status for National Insurance purposes of actors engaged by ITV under a variety of contracts. The First-tier Tribunal found that except for the ITV 'All Rights Agreement', all other contracts, including contracts for walk-ons, fell within the scope of the regulations (as they applied prior to 6 April 2014) as the contracts provided for the actor's remuneration to include 'payment by way of salary'. Consequently a liability to Class 1 National Insurance arises under the contracts. The decision was upheld by the Upper Tribunal.

The tribunal decision triggered a change in HMRC's view as to the ambit of the regulations, with HMRC accepting that the regulations applied to a minority of actors who had previously entered into Equity contracts on the common understanding that, as the production was dependent on them for box office success, they would remain outside the ambit of the regulations. The tribunal decided that there was an element of salary in these contracts and confirmed that the essential quality of salary was 'to purchase the individual's time for some definite or indefinite period, short or long, rather than to pay for specific services'. HMRC's view is that the wider implication of the decision is that this test should be applied to all actors, regardless of their status in the profession and that, prior to 6 April 2014, Class 1 National Insurance contributions will be due wherever the nature of the contract is such that it includes payment by way of salary. HMRC took the decision to apply the regulations to all Equity contracts that were newly entered into, revised, renewed or extended on or after 2 March 2011 and from 6 April 2011 to existing Equity contracts in place before that date which continue beyond the end of 2010/11 which HMRC had previously accepted as being outside the scope of the regulations. HMRC subsequently confirmed that highly-paid celebrity entertainers referred to in the industry as 'key talent' or 'marquee talent' who are engaged contractually are within the ambit of the regulations. From 6 April 2014 the status of entertainers is determined by reference to the usual tests and the deeming rules do not apply.

Further guidance on the employment status of entertainers can be found in HMRC's Employment Status Manual at ESM4145 to ESM4147.

Examiners, moderators and invigilators

2.44 The *Social Security (Categorisation of Earners) Regulations 1978, SI 1978/1689* also deem certain earners to be self-employed earners for National Insurance purposes. Deemed self-employed earners are within the Class 2 and Class 4 National Insurance contributions net rather than within the charge to Class 1. Deemed self-employed earners are specified in *Sch 1, Pt II*.

The regulations (in *Sch 1, para 6*) deem a person responsible for the conduct or administration of any examination or professional qualification as an examiner, moderator or invigilator or in any similar capacity or in which the person concerned is engaged to set questions or tests for any such examination under a contract where the whole of the work is to be performed in less than 12 months to be a self-employed earner for National Insurance purposes.

Disregarded employments

2.45 Certain employments are disregarded for National Insurance purposes by virtue of the *Social Security (Categorisation of Earners) Regulations 1978, SI 1978/1689, reg 2* and *Sch 3, Pt III*. These include:

- employment by a relative in a private dwelling house in which both reside other than for the purposes of any business or trade carried on there by the employer (*Sch 1, para 7*). For these purposes, a relative is a father, mother, grandfather, grandmother, son, daughter, grandson, granddaughter, brother, sister, half-brother or half-sister;
- employment by spouse or civil partner other than for the purposes of the employment of the spouse or civil partner (*Sch 1, para 8*);
- any self-employment or deemed self-employment where the earner is not ordinarily so employed (*Sch 1, para 9*). This would cover the situation of, say, someone who is an employed earner and undertakes a one-off job for which he or she is paid a small fee. Such a person would not be regarded as 'ordinarily self-employed'. HMRC generally disregard self-employed income by an employed person of less than £1,300 a year;
- employment for the purposes of any election or referendum authorised by Act of Parliament as a returning officer or acting returning officer, a Chief Counting Officer or counting officer or employment by any of these officers (*Sch 1, para 10*);

- employment as a member of the naval, military or air forces of a country to which a provision of the *Visiting Forces Act 1952, s 1* applies or as a civilian by any such force unless such a civilian is ordinarily resident in the UK (*Sch 1, para 11*);
- employment as a member of any international headquarters or defence organisation designated under the *International Headquarters and Defence Organisations Act 1964, s 1*, other than employment by a person who is a serving member of the regular naval, military or air forces of the Crown raised in the UK or having its depot or headquarters in the UK or of a civilian ordinarily resident in the UK who is not a member of a scheme providing a pension, lump sum, gratuity or like benefit on cessation of the employment which is established under arrangements made by the international headquarters or, as the case may be, defence organisation of which he is a member (*Sch 1, para 12*);
- employment by the International Finance Corporation (IFC) of a person who is exempt from tax by virtue of *art 3* of, and *s 9* of *art 6* of the *Agreement establishing the IFC* as set out in the Sch to the *International Finance Corporation Order 1955*, and a member of a scheme established by or on behalf of the IFC which provides for pension or other benefit on cessation of the employment (*Sch 1, para 14*); and
- employment by the Asian Infrastructure Investment Bank (AIIB) of a person who is exempt from tax by virtue of *reg 18(2)* of the *Asian Infrastructure Investment Bank (Immunities and Privileges) Order 2015*, and a member of a scheme established by or on behalf of the AIIB which provides for a pension or other benefit on cessation of the employment (*Sch 1, para 15*).

Prior to 5 July 2007, employment as a Queen's Gurkha officer or as any other member of the Brigade of Gurkhas of a person who was recruited for that brigade in Nepal was also disregarded for National Insurance purposes.

Other deemed secondary contributors

2.46 As well as specifying the associated secondary contributor in the case of earners deemed to be employed earners by virtue of *Sch 1, Pt 1* of the *Social Security (Categorisation of Earners) Regulations 1978, SI 1978/1689, Sch 3* of the regulations also specify the secondary contributor in other situations.

Where a person is employed by a company that is in voluntary liquidation and which carries on business under a liquidator, the person holding the office of liquidator is deemed to be the secondary contributor (*Sch 3, para 4*).

The secondary contributor in respect of a person employed in chambers as a barrister's clerk is deemed to be the head of chambers (*Sch 3, para* 5).

Where the person is employed by a foreign employer or by a foreign agency, the secondary contributor is as shown in the table below (*Sch 3, para 9)*.

Employment	Secondary contributor
by a foreign employer (other than as listed below) where the employed person, under an arrangement involving the foreign employer and the host employer provides, or is personally involved in the provision of services, to a host employer	the host employer
under or in consequence of a contract between a foreign agency and an end client where the worker provides services to that end client	the end client
by a foreign employer where the worker provides services to an end client under or in consequence of a contract between that end client and a UK agency	the UK agency who has the contractual relationship with the end client (but see notes 1 and 2 below)
by a foreign agency where the worker provides services to an end client under or in consequence of that end client and a UK agency	the UK agency who has the contractual relationship with the end client (but see notes 1 and 2 below
by a UK employer where the worker provides services to a person outside the UK under or in consequence of a contract between that person and a UK agency and the worker is liable to pay contributions in the UK in relation to that employment	the UK employer or the UK agency who has the contractual relationship with the person outside the UK
by a foreign employer where the worker provides services to a person outside the UK under or in consequence of a contract between that person and a UK agency and that worker is eligible to pay contributions in the UK in relation to that employment	the UK agency who has the contractual relationship with the person outside the UK

Notes

1. If the end client provides, at any time, to the UK agency fraudulent documents in connection with the control, direction or supervision which is to be exercised over the employed person, the secondary contributor is the end client.

2. If a person who is resident in Great Britain (and who is not the end client) who has a contractual relationship with the UK agency provides, at any time, to the UK agency fraudulent documents in connection with the purported deduction or payment of contributions in connection with the employed person, the secondary contributor is the person who provides the fraudulent documents.

However, where the employment is as a mariner, this rule applies only if the duties of the employment are performed wholly or mainly in category A, B, C or D waters.

Anti-avoidance

2.47 The regulations also contain anti-avoidance provisions (in *reg 5A*), which apply to treat the earner as employed where:

- the earner has an employment in which the earner personally provides services to a person who is resident or present or has a place of business in the UK;
- a third person enters into relevant arrangements; and
- but for this deeming provision, the earner would not be treated as an employed earner.

For these purposes, relevant anti-avoidance provisions are arrangements the main purpose, or one of the main purposes, of which are to secure that:

- the earner is not treated under Sch 1, para 2 of the regulations as being an employed earner in relation to the employment; and
- that person is not treated under Sch 1, para 2 or 9(b) as the secondary contributor in respect of payments of earnings to or for the benefit of the earner in respect of the employment.

The term 'arrangements' includes any scheme, transaction, series of transactions, agreement or understanding, whether or not legally enforceable, and any associated transactions.

In relation to payments of earnings made on or after 2 February 2015 or arrangements made on or after 6 April 2014, under *reg 5A(5)*, a person who is resident or present or who has a place of business in Great Britain is treated as a secondary contributory where that person enters into arrangements in respect of which the main purpose, or one of the main purposes, is to secure that that person is not treated as the secondary contributor in respect of payments of earnings to or for the benefit of an employed earner in respect of an employment and otherwise no person who is resident or present or has a place of business in Great Britain would be the secondary contributor in respect of such payments or be treated under the regulation (by virtue of *Sch 1, para* 2 or *9(b)*) as the secondary contributor.

The provisions were introduced by *NICA 2015, s 6(1)* and apply in the main with effect from 6 April 2014.

Salaried partners in limited liability partnerships

2.48 Legislation was introduced in the *Finance Act 2014* which provides for certain salaried partners in limited liability partnerships (LLP) to be treated as employees rather than as self-employed for tax purposes.

From 2014/15 a partner in a LLP who meets each of the following conditions will be treated as an employee for tax purposes.

Condition A is that at least 80% of the total amount paid by the LLP to the member for his or her services is 'disguised salary'. This will be the case where the amount paid is a fixed amount or, if it is a variable amount, it is variable without reference to the profits and losses of the LLP.

Condition B is that the member does not have significant influence over the affairs of the LLP.

Condition C is that the member's contribution to the LLP is less than 25% of the disguised salary for the tax year.

The *Social Security Contributions (limited Liability) Partnership Regulations 2014, SI 2014/3159* reclassify certain members of LLPs as employed earners (and as employees for statutory payments purposes). The conditions mirror those for tax purposes as set out above and, where they apply, with effect from 2014/15, the LLP member is treated as an employed earner for National Insurance purposes and is liable to primary Class 1 National Insurance contributions, rather than to Class 2 and Class 4. The LLP will be the secondary contributor and as such liable to pay secondary Class 1 National Insurance contributions. The regulations modify *SSCBA 1992, Pt 1* and *Pt 6* insomuch as they apply to contributions to provide that 'employment' includes membership of an LLP which carries on a trade, profession or business with a view to profit (*reg 2A*). For the purposes of the *SSCBA 1992*, a person who is in employment in Great Britain as a member of an LLP which carries on a trade, profession or vocation with a view to profit is treated as a self-employed earner unless such a person is treated as an employed earner by virtue of the regulations (*reg 2C*).

Provision of services through an intermediary and IR35

2.49 Anti-avoidance provisions were introduced with effect from 6 April 2000 to counter perceived avoidance of tax and National Insurance contributions where a worker provides services to an end client, via an intermediary, such as a personal service company. The provisions are generally known as 'IR35' after the Budget press release in which they were first publicised. They have attracted much criticism since their introduction and generated a wealth of case law.

The rules have now largely been superseded by the off-payroll working rules. From 6 April 2021 onwards, the IR35 rules are only relevant where services are provided by a worker through an intermediary, such as a personal service company, to an end client which is a small private sector organisation. Where, from 6 April 2021, the end client is a medium-sized or large private sector organisation, or, from 6 April 2017, a public sector body, the off-payroll working rules apply, and it is the responsibility of the end client to consider whether they apply, and operate them if they do. The IR35 rules do not apply in these circumstances and do not need to be considered by the worker's intermediary.

The National Insurance provisions governing IR35 are contained in the *Social Security Contributions (Intermediaries) Regulations 2000, SI 2000/727*.

The regulations provide that:

- where an individual (the worker) personally performs, or has an obligation personally to perform, services for another person (the client);
- the performance of those services by the worker is referable to arrangements involving a third party (such as, but not limited to, a personal service company); and
- the circumstances are such that were the services to be performed by the worker under a contract between the worker and the client, the worker would be an employee of the client;

the relevant payments and benefits paid to the worker are treated as earnings from the employment that are liable to Class 1 National Insurance contributions.

Essentially, the regulations consider whether, but for the presence of the intermediary, the worker would be an employed earner of the client. If this is the case, the regulations try to ensure that broadly the same amount of National Insurance contributions are payable as would be payable were the worker employed directly by the client. In determining whether, ignoring the intermediary, the worker would be an employee of a client, the tests outlined at **2.7ff** should be applied.

The rules were replaced by the off-payroll working rules where the end client is a public sector body from 6 April 2017 (see **2.50**) and where the end client is a medium-sized or large private sector organisation, from 6 April 2021 (see **2.51**). To the extent that they continue to apply, they apply as follows.

Under the rules as they continue to apply beyond 6 April 2021, where a worker supplies his or her services through an intermediary, such as a public sector body, to an end client which is a small private sector organisation, it is the intermediary, rather than the client, who is responsible for operating the regulations.

In an IR35 scenario, the intermediary is typically a one-man company, but this does not have to be the case. However, the worker has responsibility for the control and management of intermediary. This can be contrasted with the managed service company scenario described at **2.52** where control of the intermediary lies with the scheme provider.

Under the regulations as they continue to apply, the worker is charged to Class 1 National Insurance contributions on any attributable earnings. These are broadly the earnings that would have been earnings from the employment had the worker been directly employed by the client and on which Class 1 National Insurance contributions have not been paid. The intermediary is liable for secondary Class 1 National Insurance contributions on the attributable earnings. The calculation of attributable earnings and associated Class 1 National Insurance liability is explained at **3.22**.

The rules effectively render ineffective the policy of the intermediary paying the worker dividends (which do not attract National Insurance contributions) rather than earnings in an attempt to reduce the overall National Insurance bill.

Under the IR35 rules, the worker's attributable earnings are deemed to be paid to the worker in a single payment on 5 April at the end of the tax year to which they relate. Thus attributable earnings for 2021/22 are deemed to be paid to the worker on 5 April 2022.

The worker's attributable earnings are aggregated with other earnings paid to the worker in the earnings period and the earnings-related contributions due on the aggregate amount are calculated in the normal way.

The rules were replaced by off-payroll working rules with effect from 6 April 2017 where the end client is a public sector body (see **2.50**) and from 6 April 2021 where the end client is a medium-sized or large private sector organisation.

> **Focus**
>
> The off-payroll working rules apply where the end client is a large or medium-sized business in the private sector from April 2021 (delayed by one year as a result of the Covid-19 pandemic). The existing IR35 rules only apply from 6 April 2021 onwards where the engager is a small private business.

Off-payroll working in the public sector

2.50 The IR35 rules were reformed from 6 April 2017 where the end client is a public sector body, with new off-payroll working rules applying in place of the IR35 regime.

In respect of payments made on or after 6 April 2017 (including those where the contract was made before that date), where a worker provides services through an intermediary, such as a personal service company, to a public sector body, the onus of deciding whether the off-payroll working rules apply falls on the public sector body. Under the rules as they apply from that date, it is the fee payer (which may be the public sector body or may be an agency) who is responsible for calculating the deemed payments and applying PAYE and NIC. The change in the rules shifts the responsibility for deciding whether the rules apply from the worker's intermediary to the public sector end client.

The *Social Security Contributions (Intermediaries) Regulations 2000, SI 2000/727* were amended by the *Social Security (Miscellaneous Amendments No 2) Regulations 2017, SI 2017/373* with effect from 6 April 2017 to give statutory effect to the National Insurance changes and bring the IR35 rules for public sector end clients for National Insurance purposes into line with the tax changes.

Where the rules apply, the fee payer, which may be the public sector authority, agency or other third party paying the intermediary is responsible for calculating the tax and primary Class 1 National Insurance contributions and paying them over to HMRC. These amounts are deducted from the fee that is paid to the intermediary for the work carried out by the worker for the public sector body. The worker's intermediary is able to set against its own income tax for the year an amount which is equal to the payment received from the fee-payer from which income tax and National Insurance has already been deducted. The calculation of the tax and National Insurance is explained at **3.29**.

Under the rules, the worker providing his or her services through a personal service company or other intermediary is responsible for providing the fee payer with the information that they need to determine whether the off-payroll working in the public sector rules apply. The worker must also provide information necessary to enable tax and National Insurance to be deducted from the payment.

The fee payer (whether this is the public authority, agency or other third party) is responsible for operating employment taxes in accordance with the contract, reporting details of the tax and National Insurance deducted to HMRC through real time information (RTI) and paying the relevant employer's National Insurance contributions.

The public authority end client is responsible for determining whether the rules apply and, where labour is provided by an agency or third party, advising them as to whether the rules apply. For the purposes of the rules, a public authority is one as defined for the purposes of the *Freedom of Information Act 2000* and the *Freedom of Information (Scotland) Act 2000*.

HMRC's Employment Status Indicator tool can be used to check the status of workers for the purpose of determining whether the rules apply.

Focus

Where the end client is a public sector body, under the reformed rules applying from 6 April 2017, it is the public sector body which is responsible for determining if the off-payroll rules apply rather than the intermediary.

Off-payroll working in the private sector

2.51 Following the introduction of the new off-payroll working rules that apply where the end client is a public sector body (see **2.50**), the government consulted in 2018 on extending the rules to the private sector. At the time of the 2018 Budget, it was announced that the private sector reforms would only apply to medium-sized and large private sector businesses and that the government would consult further on the detail of the rules. The reforms were due to be introduced from April 2020 – one year later than originally planned. Just three weeks before they were due to come into effect, the government announced that the start date would be delayed by a further year – to 6 April 2021 – to help businesses already struggling to cope with the impact of the Covid-19 pandemic. Legislation giving statutory effect to the changes is included in the *Finance Act 2020.*

The rules, as amended and extended, apply from 6 April 2021 where the end client is a large or medium-sized business in the private sector or a public sector body. The end client must decide whether the worker would be an employee if they provided their services directly rather than through an intermediary, and where they do, operate the rules.

Where the end client is a small business in the private sector, the IR35 rules continue to apply (see **2.49**) with the personal service company deciding whether IR35 is in point and where it is, calculating the deemed payment and applying tax and National Insurance.

The off-payroll rules apply to the private sector where the end client is a company or an unincorporated business that falls outside the definition of 'small'.

The definition in *CA 2006, s 232*, which applies for the purposes of the *Companies Act 2006* to determine whether a company is regarded as 'small' will apply to determine whether a private sector business which engages workers that provide their services through an intermediary, such as a personal service company, falls within the scope of the rules as extended from April 2021. The rules apply unless the private sector engager meets the definition of 'small'. Under this definition a company is small if it satisfies at least two of the following conditions:

- the annual turnover is not more than £10.2m;
- the balance sheet total is not more than £5.1m;
- the company has no more than 50 employees.

The test is modified in its application to unincorporated bodies. Where the private sector business either becomes small or ceases to be small, it will move in or out of the new rules, as appropriate, from the start of the tax year following the end of the accounting period in which the change occurred.

Where the engager is within the scope of the rules, they must determine whether, if the intermediary is ignored and the worker supplied their services direct to the client, the worker would be an employee of the client. HMRC's Check Employment Status for Tax (CEST) tool can be used for this purpose (see **2.35**). As long as the information entered into the tool is accurate and reflects the true working relationship between the parties, HMRC will stand by the result. The engager must notify the worker of the determination reached and the reasons for reaching that determination. If the worker does not agree with the determination, they should notify the engager, who has 45 days to respond. The worker is advised to undertake their own determination using the CEST tool.

Where the outcome is that the worker would be an employee of the end client if they provided their services directly rather than through an intermediary, the fee payer, which may be the end client or which may be a third party, such as an agency, must deduct tax and National Insurance from payments made to the worker's intermediary.

The deemed payment is the amount which is treated as earnings for tax and National Insurance purposes. It is calculated as follows:

(1) Work out the value of payments to the worker's intermediary having first deducted any VAT charged.

(2) Deduct the direct cost of materials that have or will be used by the worker in providing his or her services.

(3) Deduct any expenses that would be deductible for tax purposes if the worker was employed.

(4) The resulting amount is the deemed payment.

If the result of the above calculation is nil or negative, there is no deemed payment.

The fee payer must report the pay and deductions to HMRC on a full payment submission under real time information. The submission should indicate that the worker is an off-payroll worker. The fee payer can either use their existing PAYE scheme or open a new one for this purpose.

Where the client is a 'small' private sector organisation, the extended off-payroll worker rules do not apply. Instead, the existing IR35 rules continue in place and the intermediary remains responsible for working out whether the engagement falls within IR35 and where it does, calculating the deemed payment and paying over the associated tax and National Insurance to HMRC.

Managed service companies

2.52 Provisions were introduced for tax purposes from 6 April 2007 by the *Finance Act 2007* which aimed to prevent workers from avoiding income tax by providing their services through a managed service company. Corresponding provisions have applied for National Insurance purposes since 6 August 2007. The National Insurance provisions are contained in the *Social Security (Managed Service Companies) Regulations 2007, SI 2007/2070*.The regulations target the perceived use of managed service companies to avoid National Insurance contributions.

A managed service company is an intermediary company through which the services of a worker are provided to an end client. The workers are not in business on their own account (as in an IR35 case). Instead the managed service company is controlled by a scheme provider. The scheme provider is a business and generally a company which provides a generic structure and administers the managed service company.

Managed service companies are not personal service companies and are not within the IR35 rules described at **2.49** or the off-payroll working rules described at **2.50** and **2.51**. Under a managed service company arrangement, the worker obtains work via an agency. Unlike the IR35/off-payroll working scenario, the worker has no involvement in running the managed service company and no part in its management or control. The scheme provider organises the work between the agency and the managed service company and also arranges payment of the workers. A fee is charged for this service.

Under a managed service company scenario, the exact arrangements may vary. However a typical set up would be a composite company with between 10 and 20 unrelated worker shareholders. Each worker holds a different class of share to enable differing dividend payments to be made. The scheme provider is usually the director of the managed service company.

Alternatively, the managed service company may be a personal service company with only one worker shareholder. However, this arrangement is distinguished from a personal service company within the scope of IR35 or the off-payroll working rules in that control and management of the company rests with the scheme provider rather than with the worker.

The worker is usually paid a mix of dividends, salary and reimbursed expenses by the managed service company. In the absence of the anti-avoidance provisions, no National Insurance liability would arise in respect of payments made in the form of dividends.

The managed service company rules apply where:

- the services of an individual are provided either directly or indirectly by a managed service company;
- the worker, or an associate of the worker, receives a payment or benefit that can be reasonably taken to be in respect of the services; and
- the payment or benefit is not earnings derived from the employed earner's employment with the managed service company.

Under the regulations (*reg 3*) the managed service company is treated as making a payment of earnings to the worker. Likewise the worker is treated as receiving earnings. The earnings are known as the workers attributable earnings. The earnings for National Insurance purposes are calculated as for tax purposes. The calculation is discussed at **3.26**. The worker's attributable earnings are aggregated with other earnings paid in the earnings period and the Class 1 National Insurance liability is calculated in the usual way.

By virtue of *reg 4* of the regulations, the worker is treated as an employed earner and the managed service company is treated as the secondary contributor in respect of the worker's attributable earnings. This is the case regardless of whether the managed service company fulfils the conditions prescribed for secondary contributors in *SSCBA 1992, s 1(6)*.

Essentially the rules operate so as to treat all payments by the managed service company to the worker as payments of earnings liable to Class 1 National Insurance contributions, regardless of how the payment is described. This means that even if the payment by the managed service company to the worker is described as a dividend, it will attract a Class 1 National Insurance liability.

Employee shareholder status

2.53 The concept of an 'employee shareholder' was introduced by the *Growth and Infrastructure Act 2013*. Employee shareholder status is a form of employment status under which those adopting the status are issued or allotted with at least £2,000 of shares in the company in which they work. The shares form the consideration under an employee shareholder agreement. In return for the shares, various employment rights are forfeited. The first £2,000 of shares acquired in consideration of an employee shareholder agreement are free of tax and National Insurance contributions. However, amounts allotted in excess of £2,000 attract tax and National Insurance. Employee shareholders also enjoy other tax and National Insurance advantages as long as certain conditions are met.

The tax and National Insurance advantages are obtained in exchange for forfeiting certain employment rights, such as the right to claim unfair dismissal, the right to a redundancy payment, the right to request flexible working and the right to request training.

Workers were able to adopt employee shareholder status from 1 September 2013. However, the initiative was short-lived, as the tax advantages attached to ESS shares were abolished for arrangements entered into on or after 1 December 2016.

RECATEGORISATION

Recategorising earners

2.54 The issue of whether a worker has been categorised incorrectly for National Insurance purposes often only comes to light as a result of a status enquiry.

Where it is discovered that a worker has been categorised incorrectly and, as a result, has been paying the wrong Class of National Insurance contributions, the worker is brought within the correct Class of contribution.

If a categorisation decision was not sought at the outset of the working arrangement, the recategorisation will generally be retrospective so as to apply from the date on which the working relationship began. Where a person who has paid Class 2 contributions is found to be an employed earner, arrears of Class 1 contributions will be assessed. Arrears of contributions can be sought for the previous six years.

However, if the person has paid Class 1 contributions and is subsequently found to be self-employed, the usual policy is to treat the recategorisation as applying only from the date of the categorisation decision. This prevents a repayment of Class 1 contributions from being made. Although the worker is denied a refund of Class 1 contributions, this policy is regarded as being in the worker's best interest as it preserves the benefit entitlement earned in respect of the

Class 1 contributions paid as a result of the incorrect categorisation. However, the worker can challenge any decision not to apply the recategorisation retrospectively.

Incorrect recategorisation

2.55 A categorisation decision may be overturned by the courts. This can make the contribution position quite complicated.

Where a decision is made as to the categorisation of an earner, the earner is immediately treated as being liable for the class of contribution relevant to the categorisation decision. Thus if it is determined that an earner is employed he will be brought within the Class 1 net immediately. As noted at **2.54** the decision may be applied retrospectively.

An earner can appeal against a categorisation decision. If the decision is found by the court to be incorrect the status decision will be overturned. This will return the worker to the status that he or she had prior to the status decision. However, HMRC have the discretion to prevent this revision from being applied retrospectively if this is in the earner's interests (*Social Security (Categorisation of Earners) Regulations 1978, SI 1978/1689, reg 4*).

Example 2.3—Incorrect recategorisation

A worker pays Class 2 and Class 4 contributions on the basis that he is self-employed. His status is queried and he is found to be an employed earner. He is assessed to Class 1 contributions. The earner appeals against the decision and the High Court find him to be self-employed.

During the period when the earner was treated as being employed he (and his employer) paid Class 1 contributions. This is felt to be beneficial to the worker as it offers greater benefit entitlement. Therefore the return to self-employed status is only applied from the date of the High Court decision. The Class 1 National Insurance contributions paid are not refunded.

PLANNING POINTS

2.56

- Ensure that the status of workers is considered at the outset. Problems arise where a worker is incorrectly categorised and pays the wrong Class of contribution.
- Ensure that the contract and other documentation support the reality of the situation. If the contract is a contract for services, but the reality of the situation is that the worker is an employed earner, the contract will be disregarded.

- Where services are provided through a personal service company, to prevent falling within the IR35 or off-payroll working rules, ensure that, in the absence of the intermediary, the worker would be self-employed. Consider the pointers of self-employment, such as bearing financial risk, ability to reject work, provision of own equipment etc, and ensure that these are present.
- Where workers are provided to a public sector end client or a medium-sized or large private sector organisation through an intermediary, consider the application of the off-payroll working rules and ensure that, where the rules bite, tax and National Insurance is correctly deducted by the fee-payer from payments made to the intermediary.
- Ensure that any status decision reached can be supported by evidence where possible and, where HMRC's CEST tool is used, keep a copy of the decision. This is important to back up a status determination under the off-payroll working rules.
- Seek a decision from HMRC where the employment status of a worker is in doubt.
- Be aware of the *Categorisation of Earners Regulations* and the status of workers covered by those regulations.
- Be aware that the rules governing how a worker's status is determined is an area under review and keep abreast of developments, reassessing the position in the light of any changes to the rules.

Chapter 3

Class 1 National Insurance contributions

SIGNPOSTS

- Class 1 National Insurance contributions are earnings-related contributions, payable by both the employed earner and the secondary contributor (see **3.1**).
- Liability to primary Class 1 contributions arises on earnings of employed earners aged 16 and over and under pensionable age on earnings above the earnings threshold; secondary contributions are payable on earnings of employed earnings over the age of 16 on earnings above the relevant secondary threshold (see **3.4**).
- Class 1 contributions are calculated in accordance with the rates and thresholds for the tax year in question (see **3.5**).
- A higher secondary threshold applies to the earnings of employees under the age of 21 and to apprentices under the age of 25 (see, respectively, **3.9** and **3.10**).
- A higher secondary threshold is introduced from 6 April 2021 on the earnings of veterans during their first 12 months in a civilian employment after leaving the armed forces (see **3.11**).
- A zero rate of secondary contributions applies to the first £25,000 of employees working in freeport tax sites for a period of up to 36 months (see **3.12**).
- An employment allowance of £4,000 is available to qualifying employers to offset against their secondary Class 1 liability for the year (see **3.13**).
- Employers claiming a grant for furloughed employees under the Coronavirus Job Retention Scheme must meet the cost of the associated employer's National Insurance for periods of furlough from 1 August 2020 onwards (see **3.20**).
- Class 1 contributions are payable on earnings from the employed earner's employment. The definition of 'earnings' is set by legislation and supplemented by regulations (see **3.22**).

- The liability is computed separately for each earnings period, rather than cumulatively, although directors have an annual earnings period (see **3.88**).
- In certain cases, earnings from related employments must be aggregated. The provisions prevent avoidance of contributions by artificially splitting employments to benefit from multiple thresholds (see **3.102**).
- Class 1 contributions are normally calculated using the exact percentage method (see **3.108**).
- Class 1 National Insurance are collected under PAYE and paid over to HMRC. Contributions are reported to HMRC under Real Time Information (RTI) each time a payment is made to an employee (see **3.121**).

OVERVIEW OF CLASS 1 NATIONAL INSURANCE CONTRIBUTIONS

Nature of Class 1 National Insurance contributions

3.1 Class 1 National insurance contributions are earnings-related contributions payable on earnings from the employed earner's employment.

Class 1 National Insurance contributions comprise two parts – primary contributions (see **3.2**) payable by the employed earner and secondary contributions (see **3.3**) payable by the employed earner's employer or other such person paying (or treated as paying) the earnings.

Focus

Class 1 National Insurance contributions are earnings-related contributions payable by the employed earner and the person paying the contributions, normally the employer.

Primary Class 1 National Insurance contributions

3.2 Primary Class 1 National Insurance contributions are payable by an employed earner on his or her earnings.

An employed earner is a person who is gainfully employed in Great Britain either under a contract of service, or in an office (including elective office) with earnings (*SSCBA 1992, s 2(1)(a)*: see also **2.3**).

The definition of 'employed earner' was widened with effect from 13 May 2014 to make it clear that a person with 'earnings' is within the definition (rather than requiring such as person to have 'general earnings' as previously).

The primary legislation makes provision for regulations to be made to prescribe the category of earner into which a worker is treated as falling (*SSCBA 1992, s 2(2)*). Certain persons are deemed to be employed earners by virtue of the *Social Security (Categorisation of Earners) Regulations 1978* (*SI 1978/1689*) (see **2.32ff**). Such persons are liable for primary Class 1 National Insurance contributions on their earnings.

Regulations may also be made which make provision for treating a person as falling in one or other of the categories of earner in relation to an employment where arrangements have been entered into the main purpose, or one of the main purposes of which, is to secure that the person is not treated as the earner or the secondary contributor in relation to the employment. (*SSCBA 1992, s 2(2ZA), (2ZB)).* For these purposes, arrangements include any scheme, transaction or series of transactions, agreement or understanding, regardless of whether they are legally enforceable, and any associated regulations. This allows the Treasury the power to make regulations to counter perceived false self-employment.

For details of what constitutes earnings, see **3.22ff**.

Focus

Primary contributions are payable by an employed earner on his or her earnings.

Secondary Class 1 National Insurance contributions

3.3 Secondary Class 1 National Insurance contributions are payable by the secondary contributor. This will normally be the employer. The legislation prescribes who is regarded as the secondary contributor in relation to a payment of earnings.

The secondary contributor in relation to a payment of earnings to or for the benefit of an employed earner is:

- in the case of an earner employed under a contract of service, his employer;
- in the case of an earner employed in an office with earnings, either such person as may be prescribed in relation to that office, or, if no person is prescribed, the government department, public authority or body of persons responsible for paying the earnings of the office (*SSCBA 1992, s 7(1)*: see also **2.4**).

However, where an employed earner is paid earnings in a tax week by more than one person in respect of different employments or the employed earner works under the general management of a person other than the immediate employer, the secondary contributor may be prescribed by regulations where the Treasury feels this to be necessary (*SSCBA 1992, s 7(2)*).

In certain cases, the person who is to be treated as the secondary contributor is prescribed by legislation. The *Social Security (Categorisation of Earners) Regulations 1978* (*SI 1978/1689*), *Sch 3* set out persons to be treated as secondary contributors in certain cases (see **2.32ff** and **2.41**). The secondary contributor in respect of oil and gas workers on the UK continental shelf is prescribed by the Social Security Regulations 2001 (*SI 2001/2004*), *reg 114*.

Regulations may also be made which make provision for treating a person as the secondary contributor in respect of earnings paid to or for the benefit of an earner where arrangements have been entered into the main purpose, or one of the main purposes of which, is to secure that the person is not treated as the secondary contributor in relation to the employment. (*SSCBA 1992, s 7(2A), (2B)).* For these purposes, arrangements include any scheme, transaction or series of transactions, agreement or understanding, regardless of whether they are legally enforceable, and any associated regulations

> **Focus**
>
> Secondary contributions are payable by the employer on the employed earner's earnings to the extent to which they exceed the relevant secondary threshold.

Liability for Class 1 National Insurance contributions

3.4 Liability to Class 1 National Insurance contributions arises where an employed earner age 16 or over has earnings in excess of the earnings threshold. The liability for primary contributions (but not secondary contributions) ceases when the employed earner reaches state pension age.

Primary contributions are payable by employees aged 16 and over and under state pension age on earnings over the primary threshold. For 2021/22 the primary threshold is set at £184 per week (£797 per month; £9,568 per year). The government plans to increase the primary threshold over time to bring the point at which individuals start paying tax in line with the personal allowance. For 2021/22, the primary threshold is £9,568 and the personal allowance is £12,570.

Where an employee earns between the lower earnings limit and the primary threshold, he or she is treated as having paid notional primary contributions at a nil rate. For 2021/22, the lower earnings limit is £120 per week and the primary threshold is £184 per week. The effect of the notional contributions is to preserve the contributions record of those earning between these limits. No liability to primary Class 1 National Insurance contributions arises where the earner is at or over state pension age. However, the liability to secondary contributions remains. This means that once an employee reaches state pension age, the employee pays no further Class 1 contributions on his or her earnings, whereas the employer must continue to pay secondary Class 1 National Insurance contributions.

Secondary contributions in respect of employees aged 21 and over are payable by the secondary contributor once the secondary threshold is reached. For 2021/22, the secondary threshold is set at £170 per week (£737 per month; £8,840 per year).

There is no liability for secondary contributions in respect of earners under the age of 21 on earnings below the upper secondary threshold for under-21s for the year in question, although the primary liability remains (*SSCBA 1992, s 9A*, as inserted from 6 April 2015*)*. The exemption from secondary contributions was extended to earnings paid to apprentices under 25 up to the apprentice upper secondary threshold (AUST) from 6 April 2016 (*SSCBA 1992, s 9B)*. The upper secondary threshold for under-21s and the apprentice upper secondary threshold are aligned with the upper earnings limit. The upper earnings limit, upper secondary threshold for under-21s and the apprentice upper secondary threshold for under-25s are set at £967 per week (£4,189 per month, £50,270 per year) for 2021/22.

From 6 April 2022, employers do not pay any secondary contributions on the earnings of a veteran for the first year of their civilian employment until earnings exceed the relevant secondary threshold, which is to be aligned with the upper earning limit for employee contributions, set at £967 per week (£4,189 per month, £50,270 per year) for 2021/22. Secondary contributions are payable at the usual rate of 13.8% on earnings above this threshold. The veteran pays employee contributions as normal on their earnings to the extent that they exceed the primary threshold.

From 6 April 2022, relief from secondary contributions up to a new upper secondary threshold, expected to be set at £25,000, is to be introduced on the earnings of employees who spend at least 60% of their time working at a freeport Tax site. The relief will apply for a period of up to 36 months. Secondary contributions are payable as normal on earnings in excess of the new upper secondary threshold; and the employee continues to pay primary contributions. The zero rate applies for 2021/22 (applied retrospectively), 2022/23 and 2023/24, although the Treasury have the power to extend the application of the zero rate to later tax years.

An employment allowance was introduced from 2014/15 onwards, which is available to qualifying employers to offset it against their secondary Class 1 National Insurance bill. The allowance must be claimed; this can be done through the employer's payroll software (see further **3.127**). The allowance is set at £4,000 for 2021/22. However, it is not available to companies where the sole employee is also a director. From 6 April 2020 onwards, the availability of the employment allowance is restricted to companies whose NIC bill in the previous year was £100,000 or less.

Where, during the Covid-19 pandemic, employees are furloughed and a grant is claimed under the Coronavirus Job Retention Scheme, the grant paid to the employee is liable for primary and secondary Class 1 National Insurance contributions. For periods of furlough from 1 August 2021 onwards, employers have been responsible for meeting the cost of the associated secondary Class 1 National Insurance contributions. For periods of furlough prior to 1 August 2021, employers were able to reclaim the associated employer's National Insurance from the government.

> **Focus**
>
> Liability for National Insurance starts at age 16 and for primary contributions stops when the employed earner reaches state pension age; however, liability for secondary contributions continues beyond state pension age.

Class 1 rates and threshold

Thresholds

3.5 There are various thresholds that apply for Class 1 National Insurance purposes.

The lower earnings limit is linked to the weekly rate of the basic pension in a Category A retirement pension (*SSCBA 1992, s 5(2)*). Once earnings reach the lower earnings limit, set at £120 per week (£520 per month; £6,240 per year) for 2021/22, a person is within the scope of Class 1 National Insurance contributions and able to accrue the benefit and pension entitlement associated with Class 1 contributions. However, a person does not actually pay any primary Class 1 contributions until earnings exceed the primary threshold, set at £184 per week (£797 per month and £50,270 per year). The lower earnings limit is also important in relation to statutory payments as to qualify the employee must have average earnings at least equal to the lower earnings limit.

The primary earnings threshold is the trigger point at which primary Class 1 contributions become payable by an employee. Likewise, the secondary threshold is the trigger point at which secondary Class 1 contributions become payable by the employer where the employee is over the age of 21. For 2021/22, the primary and secondary thresholds are not aligned. For 2021/22, the secondary threshold is set at £170 per week (£737 per month; £8,840 per year) and the primary threshold is set at the higher level of £184 per week (£797 per month; £9,568 per year). A higher secondary threshold applies where the employee is under the age of 21, an apprentice under the age of 25 or, from 6 April 2021 onwards, a veteran in the first year of civilian employment since leaving the armed forces. A further secondary threshold is to be introduced from 6 April 2022 to provide an element of relief from secondary contributions on the earnings of employees spending at least 60% of their time in a Freeport tax site in Great Britain. A corresponding relief is to be introduced for Freeport Tax Sites in Northern Ireland.

Where the employee is under the age of 21, from 2015/16 onwards no secondary contributions are payable by the employer until the employee's earnings reach the upper secondary threshold for under 21s. Likewise, from 6 April 2016 onwards, no secondary contributions are payable by the employer on earnings paid to an apprentice under the age of 25 until the apprentice's earnings reach the apprentice upper secondary threshold. For 2021/22, the upper secondary threshold for under 21s and the apprentice upper secondary threshold are set at £967 per week (£4,189 per month, £50,270 per year). The upper earnings limit for under 21s and the apprentice upper secondary threshold are aligned with the upper earnings limit applying for primary Class 1 National Insurance purposes.

From 6 April 2022, no liability to secondary contributions arises on the earnings of a veteran in his or her first year of their first civilian employment since leaving the armed forces until earnings exceed a new higher secondary threshold, which is to be aligned with those applying to the earnings of employees under the age of 21 and apprentices under the age of 25. The threshold is set at £967 per week (£4,189 per month, £50,270 per year) for 2021/22. However, for 2021/22, the employer must account for secondary contributions as normal. Provisions are to be introduced to enable the employer to claim the relief retrospectively from 6 April 2022. From 2022/23, the employer should be able to claim the relief through the payroll.

The upper earnings limit places a ceiling on payment of primary contributions at the main rate. Primary contributions are payable at the main Class 1 rate on earnings between the primary threshold and the upper earnings limit. Earnings in excess of the upper earnings limit attract primary Class 1 National Insurance contributions at the additional rate. For 2021/22 the upper earnings limit is set at £967 per week (£4,189 per month, £50,270 per year). This is aligned with the level at which higher rate tax becomes payable by UK taxpayers, excluding Scottish taxpayers.

The upper earnings limit does not apply to secondary contributions (although the upper secondary threshold for under 21s, the apprentice upper secondary threshold and the new upper secondary threshold for veterans in the first year of their first civilian employment since leaving the armed forces are aligned with the upper earnings limit). All contributions in excess of the secondary threshold, including any earnings above the upper earnings limit, attract secondary contributions at the secondary Class 1 rate. For 2021/22, the secondary threshold (applying where the earner is aged 21 and above) is set at £170 per week (£737 per month; £8,840 per year). Where the employee is under the age of 21, there is no liability to secondary contributions until the employee's earnings reach the upper secondary threshold for under 21s and where the employee is an apprentice under the age of 25, until the apprentice's earnings reach the upper secondary threshold for apprentices under 25.

From 6 April 2021, a new relief removes the secondary liability on the earnings of veterans on earning up to a new secondary threshold during the first year of their civilian employment since leaving the armed forces. For 2021/22, these thresholds are set at £967 per week (£4,189 per month, £50,270 per year).

Rates

3.6 Primary Class 1 contributions are payable by employed earners. There are two rates of primary Class 1 contributions. The main rate (set at 12% for 2021/22) is payable on earnings between the primary threshold and the upper earnings limit. The additional rate (set at 2% for 2021/22) is payable on earnings in excess of the upper earnings limit. A notional rate of 0% is payable on earnings between the lower earnings limit and the primary threshold.

For 2021/22, the lower earnings limit is £120 per week (£520 per month; £6,240 per year), the primary threshold is £184 per week (£797 per month; £9,568 per year) and the upper earnings limit is £967 per week (£4,189 per month; £50,270 per year). The main rate, payable on earnings between the primary threshold and upper earnings is set at 12% and the additional rate, payable on earnings above the upper earnings limit, is set at 2%. The reduced rate for married women with a reduced rate election is set at 5.85%.

Secondary contributions are payable by the secondary contributor on all earnings above the secondary threshold, except where the employee is under the age of 21 or an apprentice under the age of 25. The secondary threshold is set £170 per week (£737 per month, £8,840 per year) for 2021/22. Secondary contributions are payable at a rate of 13.8% for 2021/22. Unlike primary contributions, the rate of secondary contributions does not fall once earnings exceed the upper earnings limit. However, no secondary contributions are payable in respect of earners under the age of 21 on earnings below the upper secondary threshold for under-21s (*SSCBA 1992, s 9A*) or on the earnings of apprentices under the age of 25 on earnings below the apprentice upper secondary threshold (*SSCBA 1992, s 9B*). For 2021/22, the upper secondary threshold for under-21s and the apprentice upper secondary threshold are set at £967 per week (£4,189 per month, £50,270 per year). From 6 April 2021, for 2021/22, 2022/23 and 2023/24, no secondary contributions are payable on the earnings of veterans in the first 12 months of their first civilian job after leaving the armed forces below the relevant secondary threshold, set at £967 per week (£4,189 per month, £50,270 per year) for 2021/22. However, for 2021/22, employers must account for secondary contributions as normal on veteran's earnings. Relief will be given retrospectively from 6 April 2022. For 2022/23 and 2023/24, relief will be given in real time through the payroll. Secondary contributions are payable as normal at 13.8% on earnings of employees under 21, apprentices under 25 and veterans in the first 12 months of civilian employment to the extent that they exceed the associated upper secondary threshold.

From 6 April 2022, no secondary contributions will be payable on the earnings of employees spending at least 60% of their working time at a Freeport tax site in Great Britain up to £25,000 a year. The relief will apply for 36 months per employee. Secondary contributions will be payable as normal on earnings in excess of £25,000 a year.

Legislation contained in the *Social Security (Administration) Act 1992, ss 143* and *145* caps increases in rates at 0.25%. However, the *Coronavirus Act 2020, ss 72* and *73* lifts this cap during the period 19 March 2020 to 25 March 2022, paving the way for higher increases, potentially to recover some of the costs associated with the Covid-19 pandemic.

Weekly rates and thresholds

3.7 The rates and weekly thresholds applying for Class 1 National Insurance contributions purposes for 2020/21 are as follows. See Appendix 1 for the rates for earlier years.

	2020/21	**2021/22**
Lower earnings limit	£120 per week	£120 per week
Secondary threshold	£169 per week	£170 per week
Primary threshold	£183 per week	£184 per week
Upper earnings limit	£962 per week	£967 per week
Upper secondary threshold for U21s	£962 per week	£967 per week
Apprentice upper secondary threshold for U25s	£962 per week	£967 per week
Main primary rate (on earnings at or above the primary threshold and below upper earnings limit)	12%	12%
Additional primary rate (on earnings above the upper earnings limit)	2%	2%
Secondary rate (on earnings at or above the secondary threshold)	13.8%	13.8%
Married women's reduced rate on earnings at or above the primary threshold and below the upper earnings limit	5.85%	5.85%
Married women's additional rate (on earnings above the upper earnings limit)	2%	2%
Employment allowance (per employer, per year)	£4,000	£4,000

Weekly, monthly and annual thresholds

3.8 The table at **3.7** shows the weekly thresholds for 2021/22. Where the employee has a monthly or annual earnings period, it will be necessary to apply these thresholds on a monthly or annual basis, as appropriate.

The following table shows the weekly, monthly and annual thresholds as they apply for 2021/22:

	Weekly	Monthly	Annual
Lower earnings limit	£120	£520	£6,420
Primary threshold	£184	£797	£9,568
Secondary threshold	£170	£737	£8,840
Upper earnings limit	£967	£4,189	£50,270
Upper secondary threshold (under 21s)	£967	£4,189	£50,270
Apprentice upper secondary threshold (under 25s)	£967	£4,189	£50,270

Employees under 21

Age-related secondary percentage

3.9 Legislation contained in *SSCBA 1992, s 9A* (as inserted by *NICA 2014, s 9(3))* makes provision for an age-related secondary percentage to apply in relation to earnings of employed earners under 21 up to an upper secondary threshold. For 2021/22 the age-related percentage is set at 0% *(SSCBA 1992, s 9A(3))*. The upper secondary threshold for the under-21 age group is prescribed by the *Social Security (Contributions) Regulations 2001, SI 2001/1004, reg 10(e)* and is set at £967 per week (£4,189 per month, £50,270 per year) for 2021/22.

The effect of this section is that employers do not pay any secondary contributions (or, more correctly, pay them at a zero rate) on the earnings of employed earners under the age of 21 to the extent that those earners are above the secondary threshold (£170 per week for 2021/22) but do not exceed the upper secondary threshold for under 21s (set at £967 per week for 2021/22). Secondary contributions on earnings above this threshold attract secondary contributions at the normal rate (13.8% for 2021/22).

The measure makes it cheaper for employers to take on employees under the age of 21.

To ensure that effect is given to the zero rate in payroll software packages, it is important that the correct category letter is used. This is M where the employee is under 21 or Z where the employee is under 21 but can defer National Insurance because they have more than one job and are paying it in another job.

Where the employee is under 21 but also an apprentice, the provisions for apprentices under 25 outlined at **3.10** take precedence.

It should be noted, however, that employees under the age of 21 are required to pay employee contributions once their earnings reach the primary threshold (set at £184 per week for 2021/22). Systems should be in place to identify when an employee reaches age 21.

> **Focus**
>
> Where the employee is under 21, secondary contributions are only payable once earnings exceed £967 per week for 2021/22. Make sure that category letter M is used to denote that the employee is under 21.

Apprentices under 25

Zero-rate of secondary contributions

3.10 With effect from 6 April 2016 onwards, secondary contributions are payable at a zero rate in respect of the earnings paid to a 'relevant apprentice' to the extent that their earnings do not exceed the apprentice upper secondary threshold (AUST) (*SSCBA 1992, s 9B*, as inserted by *NICA 2015, s 1(4)*).

A 'relevant apprentice' is someone who is aged under 25 and who is employed in the employment as an apprentice. An 'apprentice' is defined (in *SI 2001/1004, reg 154A)* as a person employed under:

- an approved English apprenticeship agreement within the meaning of the *Apprenticeships, Skills, Children and Learning Act 2009, s A1*;
- an English apprenticeship agreement within the meaning of *s 32* of the 2009 Act as saved by the *Deregulation Act 2015 (Commencement No 1 and Transitional and Saving Provisions) Order 2015, Sch 1, Pt 2, para 2*;
- a Welsh apprenticeship agreement within *s 32* of the 2009 Act;
- arrangements made by the Secretary of State or the Scottish Ministers under the *Employment and Training Act* 1973, *s.2*;
- arrangements made by the Secretary of State or the Scottish Ministers under the *Enterprise and New Towns (Scotland) Act 1990*; or
- arrangements made by the Secretary of State of Northern Ireland or Northern Irish Ministers under the *Employment and Training Act (Northern Ireland) Act 1950.*

Further, to qualify as an apprentice, the person must be being trained in pursuant to arrangements:

- in relation to which the Secretary of State has secured the provision of financial resources under *s 100* of the 2009 Act; or
- which are set out in a written agreement made between that person, the employer and the training provided which contains information as

to the type of apprenticeship framework or standard being followed, the start date of the apprenticeship and the expected date of completion of the apprenticeship.

For 2021/22 the AUST is set at £967 per week (£4,189 per month, £50,270 per year) (*SI 2001/1004, reg. 10(f))*. Secondary contributions are payable at the normal secondary rate of 13.8% on earnings in excess of the AUST.

It should be noted that these provisions do not impact on the liability of the apprentice to primary contributions, which are payable as normal to the extent that earnings exceed the primary threshold (set at £184 per week for 2021/22).

Care should be taken to use the correct category letter, category letter H, for apprentices under the age of 25 that meet the definition of a 'relevant apprentice'.

The provisions in relation to apprentices under 25 take precedence over those applying to employees under the age of 21, where an employed earner is both under 21 and a relevant apprentice (*SSCBA 1992, s 9A(1A))*.

Focus

Employers do not need to pay secondary contributions in respect of apprentices under the age of 25 as long as their earnings are below £962 per week for 2020/21 or £967 per week for 2021/22. Category letter H should be used to denote an apprentice under the age of 25.

Veterans in their first year of civilian employment

Limited relief from secondary contributions

3.11 Legislation contained in the *National Insurance Contributions Bill 2021, cll 6* and *7* introduces new relief from secondary contributions for employers who employ an armed forces veteran in their first civilian employment after leaving the armed forces. The relief is available from 6 April 2021 for the first 12 months of the veteran's first civilian employment after leaving the armed forces. Where the employment commenced between 6 April 2020 and 5 April 2021, the relief applies from 6 April 2021 until the first anniversary of the start date of the first civilian employment. Subsequent and concurrent employers are also able to benefit from the relief during the relief period.

The zero rate is available for 2021/22 (applied retrospectively), 2022/23 and 2023/24. However, the Treasury have the power to make regulations to extend the application of the zero rate to later tax years.

To qualify for the relief, the earner must meet the veteran conditions (*National Insurance Contributions Bill 2021, cl 7*). These are that:

- the earner has served at least one day as a member of any of the regular forces;
- the employment is in a civilian capacity; and
- the earnings are paid during the period of one year beginning with the earner's first day of employment in a civilian capacity since the earner last ceased to be a member of any of the regular armed forces.

The relief operates in a similar way to that for employers of employees under 21 (see **3.9**) and apprentices under the age of 25 (see **3.10**) in that secondary contributions are payable at a zero rate on the veterans earnings up to the upper secondary threshold and at the normal secondary percentage of 13.8% on earnings in excess of the upper secondary threshold. The upper secondary threshold is to be aligned with that for employees under 21 and apprentices under 25, which for 2021/22 is set at £967 per week (£4,189 per month, £50,270 per year).

The employer must elect for the relief to apply.

For 2021/22, the employer must account for secondary contributions as normal on the earnings of the veteran to the extent that they exceed the secondary threshold of £170 per week (£737 per month, £8,840 per year). The relief will be given retrospectively from 6 April 2022. For 2022/23 and 2023/24 provisions are to be introduced to enable the relief to be given through the payroll via Real Time Information. It is likely that this will be achieved by the introduction of a new category letter for veterans in the first year of their first civilian job after leaving the armed forces.

The legislation provides for the relief to be available for a limited time period only – from 6 April 2021 to 5 April 2024. However, the government are to review the relief in 2023 and have the ability to extend its availability beyond 6 April 2024.

> **Focus**
>
> The new relief for employers of armed forces veterans provides a financial incentive to encourage employers to take on employees who have recently left the armed forces.

Freeports

Relief from secondary contributions for freeport employers

3.12 The *National Insurance Contributions Bill 2021, cll 1–3* provides for freeport employers to benefit from a zero rate of secondary contributions on certain earnings of employees employed in Freeports in Great Britain.

The relief provides for the zero secondary rate to apply to the earnings of freeport employees for 36 months starting from the first day of their employment (or the date that the employment terminates, if earlier), up to an upper secondary threshold. The upper secondary threshold is to be set by regulations and is expected to be set at £25,000.

For the purposes of the relief, a freeport employer is a business which is operating with a physical premises in a freeport tax site. A freeport employee is an employed earner of a freeport employer who spends 60% or more of their employed time in a single freeport site in which their employer has a business premises. Freeport sites in Great Britain are specified in the *Finance Act 2021*.

The relief applies to freeport employers in respect of new employments from 6 April 2022. An employment counts as a new employment if the earner was not employed by the employer or a person connected with the employer in the two years prior to the date on which the employment commenced.

For the relief to be available, the freeport employment must begin on or after 6 April 2022 and before 6 April 2026. In the event that the government decide not to continue this relief beyond 5 April 2026, new claims will not be permitted on or after 6 April 2026. However, relief will be available for the full 36 months where the freeport employment commences prior to 6 April 2026 (or the date that the employment terminates, if earlier).

Effect will be given to the relief through Real Time Information.

Anti-avoidance provisions apply to deny the relief where it would only be available as a result of avoidance arrangements, which are contrived arrangements designed primarily to secure the relief.

The *National Insurance Contributions Bill 2021, cl 5* makes provision for regulations to be introduced to provide corresponding relief for employments in freeport sites in Northern Ireland.

> **Focus**
>
> The introduction of Freeports is part of the government's levelling up strategy and the introduction of the temporary relief from secondary contributions provides an incentive for employers to operate from a freeport site.

EMPLOYMENT ALLOWANCE

Nature of the allowance

3.13 The employment allowance was introduced from 6 April 2014 and provides eligible employers with a reduction of up to the amount of the allowance in their secondary Class 1 National Insurance bill for the tax year.

The allowance can only be offset against the employer's secondary Class 1 liability. It cannot be used to reduce or extinguish any Class 1A or Class 1B liability.

The allowance is set at £4,000 for 2021/22.

The legislation giving statutory effect to the allowance can be found in *NICA 2014, ss 1–7*. HMRC guidance on the employment allowance is available on the gov.uk website at www.gov.uk/government/publications/employment-allowance-more-detailed-guidance.

The allowance is set at the lower of the amount of the allowance and the employer's secondary Class 1 liabilities for the year (which are not excluded liabilities) (*NICA 2014, s 1(2)*).

From 6 April 2020, availability of the employment allowance is restricted to companies whose secondary Class 1 National Insurance liability in the previous tax year was less than £100,000. Where an employer has multiple PAYE schemes, the employment allowance is only available if the secondary Class 1 liability across all PAYE schemes was less than £100,000 in the previous tax year.

From 2016/17 onwards the allowance is not available to companies with a single employee where that employee is also a director. For 2015/16 and earlier tax years, the allowance was available to most employers, however, there are some exceptions (see **3.12**).

The allowance can only be used against one PAYE scheme, even if the employer runs multiple PAYE schemes. The allowance is given per employer rather than per PAYE scheme. Anti-avoidance provisions apply.

From April 2020, the employment allowance counts towards the de minimis state aid allowed over a three-year period. The employment allowance is not available where the de minimis state aid threshold for the relevant sector has been exceeded.

Where during the Covid-19 pandemic a grant was claimed under the Coronavirus Job Retention Scheme (see **3.20–3.21**), a claim for periods prior to 1 August 2020 could only be made for the associated employer's (secondary) Class 1 National Insurance to the extent that it was not offset by the employment allowance.

> **Focus**
>
> The employment allowance is available to offset against secondary contributions unless there is only one employee who is also a director. However, remember to claim it; this can be done through the payroll software.

Excluded employers and excluded liabilities

3.14 Certain categories of employers are not eligible for the employment allowance (*NICA 2014, s 2*). These include:

- employers employing someone for personal, household or domestic work (such as someone who employs a nanny, an au pair, a chauffeur, a gardener or a care support worker), unless (with effect from 6 April 2015) the duties are performed for an individual and the individual needs those duties to be performed because of his or her old age, mental incapacity, past or present dependence on alcohol or drugs, past or present illness or mental disorder);
- employers who already claim the allowance through a connected company or charity;
- public authorities (including local, district and town councils); and
- employers who carry out functions either wholly or mainly of a public nature (eg NHS services, general practitioner services, managing housing stock owned by a local council, provision of a meals on wheels service for a local council, prison services or refuse collection).

However, the provision of security and cleaning services for a public building, such as government or local council offices or the supply of IT services for a government department or local council are not regarded as the carrying out of a function of a public nature. Consequently, employers providing these services are not excluded from claiming the employment allowance.

The allowance cannot be claimed in respect of a liability to pay secondary contributions which is incurred in respect of earnings of workers supplied by service companies. Nor is the allowance available where the secondary contributions are payable in respect of an earner who is employed for purposes connected with a transferred business or part (*NICA 2014, s 2(4)–(8)*). These are excluded liabilities for the purposes of the employment allowance.

From 2016/17 onwards, companies with a single employee who is also a director are precluded from claiming the allowance (see further **3.15**).

From 6 April 2020, availability of the employment allowance is restricted to employers whose secondary Class 1 liability in the previous tax year was less than £100,000. Where the employer has multiple PAYE schemes, the £100,000 cap applies across all PAYE schemes.

Companies with a single employee who is also a director

3.15 From 2016/17 onwards the list of companies excluded from claiming the employment allowance is extended to include a body corporate where all the payments of earnings in relation to which that body corporate is the secondary contributor in that year are paid to, or for the benefit of, the same employed earner and when each of those payments is made, that employed earner is a director of that body corporate (*NICA 2014, s 2(4A)*).

Consequently, as provided by the legislation, the exclusion applies when:

- there is only one employed earner in respect of whom earnings are paid; and
- at the time that those earnings are paid, that employed earner is also a director of the company.

On the strict application of the legislation, it would appear that the employment allowance continues to be available if a company has more than one employed earner or has only one employed earner and that employed earner is not a director.

HMRC have published guidance on this exclusion. The guidance, *Single-director companies and Employment Allowance: further guidance* is available on the gov.uk website at www.gov.uk/government/publications/employment-allowance-more-detailed-guidance/single-director-companies-and-employment-allowance-further-employer-guidance.

It is when comparing this guidance to the actual wording of the legislation that things start to get interesting. The first thing to note is that the guidance is called 'single-director companies' where under the terms of the legislation the trigger for the loss of the employment allowance is that the company is a single *employee* company where that employee is also a director. A company that has only one director will, under the terms of the legislation, continue to qualify for the employment allowance if there is more than one employee or if that director is not also an employee. Consequently, referring to 'single-director companies' is somewhat misleading.

The guidance states, at para 1:

> 'From 6 April 2016, limited companies where the director is the only employee paid earnings above the secondary threshold for Class 1 National Insurance contributions will no longer be able to claim the Employment Allowance'.

Again, the guidance is misleading as the legislation imposes no condition on the earnings level of the employees. Under the terms of the legislation, the allowance is lost if there is a single employee who is also a director. Consequently, if there is more than one employee, the allowance is, under the terms of the legislation, preserved, regardless of whether any of the employees earn above the secondary threshold. Granted that the employment allowance only has value where at least one employee (including the director) has earnings above the secondary threshold as to utilise the allowance, secondary contributions must be payable, and for secondary contributions to be payable at least one employee must have earnings equal or greater than the secondary threshold (set at £170 per week for 2021/22).

The definition of an employed earner (in *SSCBA 1992, s 2*) is 'a person who is gainfully employed in Great Britain either under a contract of service, or in an office (including an elective office, with earnings'. An earner is an employed earner if he or she has earnings – there is no stipulation that the earnings be of a minimum level. Further, by virtue of *NICA 2014, s 2(4A)*, for the restriction to bite all the earnings must be paid to or for the benefit of the same employed earner (who is also a director at the time that the payments are made). The restriction is dependent simply on there being only one employed earner, rather than one employed earner with earnings above the secondary threshold.

Consequently, by applying the HMRC guidance, companies who would qualify for the employment allowance under the strict wording of the legislation (ie companies with more than one employed earner but only one employed earner who is paid at or above the level of the secondary threshold), may find that by applying HMRC's interpretation of the legislation they would be denied the allowance. It should be noted that HMRC's guidance is only that – guidance. It is the legislation which determines whether the employment allowance is available. Companies that are denied the allowance on the basis of HMRC's guidance may wish to consider an appeal.

That said, where the employment allowance is beneficial, it is worthwhile taking steps to ensure that there are at least two employees or where there is a single employee that employee is not also a director. For example, someone running a personal company could employ a family member or resign as director and appoint a spouse as director to ensure that the structure of the company was such that it remained within the ambit of the employment allowance.

The HMRC guidance makes it clear that if a company which did not qualify for the allowance qualifies for the allowance later in the tax year, that company will be eligible for the allowance in full if it takes on an additional employee. This may result from employing a spouse, taking on seasonal workers, etc. However, the guidance is misleading in that one again imposes an earnings requirement on the additional employee in that they must have earnings at least equal to the secondary threshold on any additional employee. The guidance states quite clearly that:

> 'The decisive factor is that the additional employee(s) must be paid above the secondary threshold'.

This is not required by the legislation. Any additional employee, regardless of the earnings level of that employee will, under the wording of the legislation, mean that the company qualifies for the employment allowance for the whole year (unless excluded on other grounds),

It should be noted that this restriction only applies to companies.

> **Focus**
>
> The legislation denies availability of the employment allowance to companies where there is only one employee who is in receipt of earnings and that employee is also a director. However, HMRC guidance misleadingly refers to 'single director companies' and adds a further condition that any additional employee must be paid above the secondary threshold. This is not a requirement of the legislation and thus employing a second employee, regardless of how much that employee is paid, will preserve the employment allowance.

Companies employing illegal workers

3.16 Under measures set out in a consultation paper published in November 2016 employers who have employed workers subject to immigration control and who have been penalised by the Home Office and who have exhausted their appeal rights in relation to that penalty will be denied the right to claim the employment allowance for the tax year following that in which their appeal rights were exhausted. At the time of the consultation, the intention was to introduce the measure with effect from 6 April 2018, but at the time of writing it had not been brought into effect, nor had a date been set for its introduction. The consultation provides that employers who lose their right to the employment allowance as a result of this measure will be responsible for amending their payroll software to ensure that the employment allowance is not claimed.

Claiming the allowance

3.17 The employment allowance is not given automatically. It must be claimed. The claim is made via the employer's RTI payroll software package or via HMRC's Basic PAYE Tools, where used. It can be claimed at any point in the tax year – there is no requirement that it must be claimed at the start of the tax year.

Claims can be made for the previous four tax years if the claim was not made at the time.

Employers will be able to use HMRC's PAYE Online Service to view how much of the allowance has been used by selecting 'view PAYE Liabilities and Payments'.

Where the employer's secondary Class 1 liability is less than the amount of the allowance (£4,000 for 2020/21), the unused allowance is carried forward to the next tax month until the allowance is fully utilised. To the extent that the allowance has not been fully utilised by the end of the tax year, it is lost. However, the clock starts again at the beginning of each new tax year.

Example 3.1—Utilising the employment allowance

Basil Ltd has a monthly employer's Class 1 NIC liability of £1,265. The company claims the employment allowance for 2021/22 via their RTI payroll software package.

In Month 1, the allowance fully covers the employer's Class 1 NIC liability of £1,265. The company must, however, pay PAYE and employees' Class 1 NIC over to HMRC as usual by the due date.

The employment allowance for the year is £4,000. In Month 1, £1,265 of the allowance is used, leaving the balance of £2,735 to be carried forward for use in subsequent months.

In Month 2, a further £1,265 of the available allowance is used, leaving a balance of £1,470 (£1,765 – £1,265) to be carried forward to subsequent months. In Month 3, a further £1,265 of the available allowance is used, leaving a balance of £205 (£1,470 – £1,265) to be carried forward to subsequent months.

In Month 4, the remaining allowance (£205) is less than the liability for the month. In Month 4, the company can set the remainder of the allowance against the employer's Class 1 NIC liability for the month, reducing the amount that needs to be paid over to HMRC (together with PAYE and employees' Class 1 NIC) to £1,060 (£1265 – £205).

The employment allowance has now been fully utilised.

In Month 5 and subsequent months in 2021/22 the company must pay the full amount of their employer's Class 1 NIC liability over to HMRC.

The clock starts again at the start of the 2022/23 tax year, assuming that the company still qualifies for the allowance.

Focus

The employment allowance must be claimed through the payroll software – it is not given automatically. It does not have to be claimed from the start of the tax year: it can be claimed at any point. Claims can be made for past years for the four previous tax years.

Stopping the allowance

3.18 A company which has claimed the employment allowance in the past but is not eligible for 2020/21 (for example, because their secondary Class 1 liability in 2019/20 is more than £100,000) should stop their claim for the allowance. This can be done by selecting 'no' in the Employment Allowance Indicator' field within the payroll software and submitting an employer payment summary (EPS) to HMRC. A company that is not entitled to the employment allowance must pay the full amount of their secondary contributions over to HMRC without deducting the allowance.

Employment allowance anti-avoidance measures

3.19 The employment allowance legislation contains anti-avoidance measures. In addition, HMRC published a Spotlight in June 2015 (Spotlight 24: see https://www.gov.uk/government/publications/spotlight-24-employment-allowance-avoidance-scheme-contrived-arrangements-caught-by-existing-rules), which highlights a scheme of which they are aware and which in their view does not work.

The allowance is given per employer rather than per PAYE scheme. This means that it is not possible to claim multiple allowances by splitting the PAYE scheme into numerous smaller schemes.

Spotlight 24 highlights an avoidance scheme that is designed to exploit the employment allowance. The basis of the marketed scheme is that a payroll company takes on the employer's staff and sets up underlying companies, each of which employs small numbers of staff. Each company claims the full employment allowance to wipe out the secondary National Insurance liability. The payroll company invoices the former employer for the services provided by their former staff, who are now employed by the companies created by the payroll company.

HMRC is of the view that this scheme is caught by the existing legislation and does not work. The scheme, if used, should be notified under the DOTAS rules. Promoters of such schemes who fail to notify under these rules may be liable for a fine of up to £1 million.

The employment allowance legislation contains a targeted anti-avoidance rule, which aims to ensure that schemes which use artificial and contrived arrangements to secure an unintended advantage do not work.

Focus

The employment allowance is given 'per employer' rather than 'per PAYE scheme'. This means that if an employer has more than one PAYE scheme they will only receive one employment allowance. Anti-avoidance legislation exists to prevent employers trying to claim multiple employment allowances by splitting the payroll by creating a number of smaller companies.

CORONAVIRUS JOB RETENTION SCHEME

Nature of the scheme

3.20 The Coronavirus Job Retention Scheme is a temporary scheme designed to help employers to maintain their workforce during the Covid-19 pandemic by allowing them to furlough workers and claim a grant from the government. The scheme runs from 1 March 2020 to 30 September 2021.

Under the scheme as originally introduced in March 2020, employers could furlough workers who were on the payroll as at 19 March 2020 and in respect of whom a RTI submission had been made to HMRC by that date (so that HMRC were aware that they were on the payroll). Where an employee was on the payroll at 28 February 2020 but made redundant or left after that date but before 19 March 2020, they can be put back on the payroll and furloughed.

The first phase of the scheme applies to periods of furlough from 1 March 2020 to 30 June 2020. During this period, the employer could claim a grant of 80% of the furloughed employee's wages, capped at £2,500, plus the associated employer's National Insurance and minimum employer pension contributions (3%) where these are required under auto-enrolment. To be eligible for the grant, the employee had to be furloughed for at least three weeks and was not allowed to do any work for the employer during this period. Grants claimed under the scheme had be paid to the employee in full and were liable to tax and primary Class 1 National Insurance, as for normal payments of wages and salary. The employer could, if they wished, top up the grant (for example, so that the employee continued to receive their full salary while on furlough), but this is optional. Claims for grants under the first period of the scheme had to be made by 30 July 2020.

The second phase of the scheme ran from 1 July 2020 to 31 October 2020. From 1 July 2020, employers were still able to claim 80% of the employee's wages while furloughed, but employers were be able to bring employees back to work part-time (with the employer paying the wages for the period that the employee works, and claiming the grant for the hours for which the employee is furloughed).

From 1 August 2020, the grant remained at 80% of wages (subject to the cap of £2,500 per month), but employers were be required to meet the associated employer's National Insurance contributions.

For claim periods falling in September 2020, employees on furlough continued to receive a grant of 80% of their wages, subject to the cap, but the employer was only able to claim 70% from the government and was required meet the cost of the remaining 10%.

For claim periods falling in October 2020, the government grant covered 60% of the furloughed employee's wages (subject to the cap), with the employer making it up to 80%.

Availability of grants under the second phase of the scheme was only available in respect of employees who had to be put on furlough by 10 June 2020; this was in order to meet the minimum three-week furlough period required for a claim to be made by the cut-off date of 30 June 2021.

The scheme was due to come to an end on 30 October 2020, but was further extended, initially to run until 30 April 2020, before being extended further as announced in the March 2021 Budget, to 30 September 2021. From 1 November 2020, the scheme is available to employees on the payroll as at 30 October 2020 and where a RTI submission had been made in respect of them by that date. Claims for November 2020 to April 2021 must be made by the 14th of the following month, or the next working day where this falls on a weekend or a bank holiday. Employers can claim a grant of 80% of the employee's usual pay for their furloughed hours, capped at £2,500 (or equivalent where the employee is not fully furloughed for the full month). The full amount of the grant must be paid over to the employee.

The final phase of the scheme runs from 1 May 2021 to 30 September 2021. Claims can be made in respect of employees who were on the payroll at midnight on 2 March 2021 and in respect of whom an RTI submission had been made at that date. Throughout the final phase, employees who are furloughed or flexibly furloughed continue to receive 80% of their usual pay for their unworked hours (capped at £2,500 per month). However, while an employer can claim the full 80% for May and June 2021, the amount that they can claim drops to 70% (capped at £2,187.50) for July 2021 and to 60% (capped at £1,875.00) for August and September 2021. For July 2021, the employer must meet the cost of 10% of the employee's usual wages for their furloughed hours (capped at £312.50 for the month); this rises to 20% (capped at £625 a month) for August and September 2021.

Grant payments are liable to employee and employer Class 1 National Insurance contributions, which must be paid over to HMRC.

National Insurance contributions and the Coronavirus Job Retention Scheme

3.21 Grant payments must be paid to employees in full and are liable to tax and to primary and secondary Class 1 National Insurance contributions.

In respect of claims relating to periods of furlough from 1 March 2020 to 31 July 2020, the employer could claim back the secondary Class 1 National Insurance payable on the grant, to the extent that these are not covered by the employment allowance. Employer's National Insurance on the grant is worked out in the usual way.

From 1 August 2020, the employer must meet the cost of the associated employer's National Insurance.

Example 3.2—National Insurance contributions on grants paid to employees under the Coronavirus Job Retention Scheme

An employee is furloughed for July 2020. The employee has been on the payroll for five years and is paid a regular salary, which in February 2020 was £2,000.

The employer claims a grant of £1,400 (70% of £2,000) under the Coronavirus Job Retention Scheme (CJRS). The employer does not top up the employee's pay. The employee is aged 35.

The employer must, however, top up the amount claimed so that the employee receives 80% of his salary, equal to £1,600 (80% of £2,000). Of this, £1,400 is covered by the CJRS grant and £200 by the employer.

The amount paid to the employee is subject to employee's and employer's Class 1 National Insurance contributions.

For 2021/22, the monthly secondary threshold is £737, the monthly primary threshold is £797 and the upper earnings limit is £797.

Employee's National Insurance on a payment of £1,600 is £96.36 ((£1,600 – £797) × 12%).

Employer's National Insurance on a payment of £1,600 is £119.09 ((£1,600 – £737) × 13.8%).

EARNINGS

Importance of earnings

3.22 The liability to Class 1 National Insurance contributions arises by reference to the employed earner's earnings.

The *Social Security (Contributions) Regulations 2001, SI 2001/1004, reg 24* provide that for the purpose of determining the amount of earnings-related contributions, the amount of a person's earnings from the employed earner's employment are calculated on the basis of his or her gross earnings from the employment or employments in question.

Therefore, before the extent of any liability to Class 1 contributions can be determined it is first necessary to establish the earner's earnings for the earnings period in question.

It should be noted that due to some differences in the rules, earnings for National Insurance purposes will not necessarily be the same as those for tax purposes. Separate provisions apply to determine earnings for National

Insurance purposes and emoluments from the employment for income tax purposes. Due to increasing alignment, the two figures will often be the same, but this will not always be the case.

> **Focus**
>
> Class 1 National Insurance contributions are payable on all employed earnings from the employment. Determining the amount of the earnings is not always straightforward, and what constitutes earnings for National Insurance purposes is not always the same as for tax. Certain items are disregarded from earnings by regulations.

Meaning of earnings

3.23 Determining a person's earnings is not always straightforward. The starting point is *SSCBA 1992, s 3(1)(a)*, which prescribes that earnings includes any remuneration or profit derived from the employment.

To be treated as earnings, the remuneration or profit must be derived from the employment. Although the National Insurance legislation does not define 'remuneration' or 'profit' for these purposes, it does (in *SSCBA 1992, s 122*) make it clear that 'employment includes any trade, business, profession, office or vocation'.

The primary legislation also makes provision for regulations to be made specifying how earnings for a period are to be calculated. Regulations may also be made for the purposes of providing for certain payments to be disregarded from calculation of earnings (*SSCBA 1992, s 3(2)–(5)*). To this end, the *Social Security (Contributions) Regulations 2001* (*SI 2001/1004*), *Schs 2* and *3* make specific provision as regards items included in the calculation of earnings (see **3.27**) and for items to be disregarded in the calculation of earnings (see **3.47**).

Statutory payments and sickness payments

3.24 Statutory payments – statutory sick pay, statutory maternity pay, statutory adoption pay, statutory paternity pay, statutory shared parental pay and statutory parental bereavement pay – are treated as remuneration derived from the employed earner's employments (*SSCBA 1992, s 4(1)(a)*). This means that payments of this nature are liable to Class 1 National Insurance contributions.

In addition, sickness payments made to or for the benefit of the employed earner and in accordance with arrangements under which the person who is the secondary contributor in relation to the employment concerned has made, or remains liable to make, payments towards the provision of sickness payments are included within earnings (*SSCBA 1992, s 4(1)(b)*). However, if the payments are made from funds contributed by the earner, the sickness payment is disregarded to the extent that it relates to funds so provided (*SSCBA 1992, s 4(2)*). For these purposes, a sickness payment is regarded as any payment made in respect of absence from work due to incapacity.

Where a sickness payment is treated as remuneration derived from an employed earner's employment, that payment is made through the person who is the secondary contributor, except where the payment is payable by another person, that person has agreed with the secondary contributor to make the payment and arrangements have been made between them for the person who agreed to make the payment to furnish the secondary contributor with such information as is necessary for the secondary contributor to comply with his obligations (the *Social Security (Contributions) Regulations 2001* (*SI 2001/1004*), *reg 23*).

Focus

Statutory payments are within the definition of earnings and consequently liable to Class 1 National Insurance contributions.

Gains on chargeable events in relation to securities options

3.25 A gain on a chargeable event in relation to a securities option which is calculated under *ITEPA 2003, s 479* and which is charged as employment income by virtue of *ITEPA 2003, s 476* is treated as earnings for Class 1 National Insurance purposes by virtue of *SSCBA 1992, s 4(4)(a)*).

Restrictive undertakings

3.26 A payment that is paid (or treated as paid) to or for the benefit of the earner in consideration for certain restrictive undertakings and which is taxed as employment income by virtue of *ITEPA 2003, s 225, s 226* is treated as earnings for Class 1 National Insurance purposes by virtue of *SSCBA 1992, s 4(4)(b)*.

Earnings of workers supplied by service companies

3.27 Regulations provide for the National Insurance rules where workers provide their services through an intermediary, such as a personal service company, and either the IR35 rules apply or the engagement falls within the scope of the off-payroll working rules.

By virtue of *SSCBA 1992, s 4A*, regulations may be made so as to provide that where:

- an individual (the worker) personally performs, or is under an obligation personally to perform, services for the purposes of a business carried on by another person (the client);
- the performance of those services by the worker is (within the meaning of the regulations) referable to an arrangement involving a third person (and not referable to any contract between the client and the worker); and
- the circumstances are such that were the services to be performed by the worker under a contract between him and the client, he would be regarded as employed in the employed earner's employment (see **2.43**),

relevant payments or benefits are, to the specified extent, treated as earnings paid to the worker in respect of his or her employed earner's employment. The regulations are the *Social Security Contributions (Intermediaries) Regulations 2000* (*SI 2000/727*), Pt. 1 of which applies the IR35 rules for National Insurance purposes and bring the worker's attributable earnings within the liability to Class 1 National Insurance contributions, while Pt. 2 provides for the National Insurance rules where an engagement falls within the off-payroll working rules. The rules also apply to workers who provide services through an intermediary in a domestic capacity (such as nannies operating through a personal service company) by virtue of the *Social Security (Contributions and Benefits Act 1992) (Modification of Section 4A) Order 2003* (*SI 2003/2079*), *reg 5*.

The regulations were amended from 6 April 2017 (by *SI 2017/373*) to provide new rules that apply where a worker's services are provided to a public authority and the off-payroll working rules apply, and from 6 April 2021 (by *SI 2020/1220*) to extend those rules where the end client is a medium-sized or large private sector body (see **2.51**) and the engagement is within the off-payroll working. The rules governing public sector engagements and those where the end client is a medium-sized and large private sector organisation and the off-payroll working rules apply are found in *Pt 2* of the regulations.

From 6 April 2021 onwards, the rules in Pt 1 of the regulations apply only where the services are supplied through an intermediary to a small private sector organisation in circumstances such that the IR35 rules apply. The rules in Pt 2 apply to engagements that fall within the off-payroll working rules.

Engagements within IR35: Calculating attributable earnings

3.28 The calculation of attributable earnings set out below only applies from 6 April 2021 onwards where the worker's services are provided through an end client to a small private sector organisation in circumstances in which the IR35 rules apply. The rules set out below do not apply to payments made on or after 6 April 2017 where the worker's services are provided to a public authority and the engagement is one to which the *Social Security Contributions (Intermediaries) Regulations 2000* (*SI 2000/727*), *Pt 2* applies by virtue of *reg 13*, or from 6 April 2021 where services are provided through an intermediary to an end client that is a medium or large public sector body.

Where the engagement is within IR35, attributable earnings are calculated in accordance with the *Social Security Contributions (Intermediaries) Regulations 2000* (*SI 2000/727*), *reg 7* as follows:

Step one

Find the total amount of all payments and benefits received by the intermediary in that year under the arrangements, and reduce that amount by 5%.

If the payments are made under the deduction of tax under the Construction Industry Scheme, the intermediary is treated as receiving the amount that would have been received had no payment been made.

Step two

Add the amount of any payments and benefits received by the worker in that year under the arrangements, otherwise than from the intermediary, that:

- are not chargeable to income tax as employment income under *ITEPA 2003*, and
- would be so chargeable if the worker were employed by the client.

Step three

Deduct the amount of any expenses met in that year by the intermediary that under *ITEPA 2003* would have been deductible from the taxable earnings of the employment, within the meaning of *ITEPA 2003, s 10* in accordance with *ITEPA 2003, s 327(3)–(5)*, if the worker had been employed by the client and the expenses had been met by the worker out of those earnings.

It is assumed when calculating the deductible expenses that all engagements of the worker under the arrangements involving the intermediary are undertaken in the course of the same employment.

Expenses met by the intermediary include expenses met initially by the worker and reimbursed by the intermediary.

Where the intermediary provides a vehicle for the worker, any mileage allowance relief that the worker would have been entitled to under *ITEPA 2003, s 231*, if the worker had been employed by the client and the vehicle were not a company vehicle, is treated as a deductible expense. If the intermediary is a partnership, the worker is a member of the partnership and the worker provides a vehicle for the purposes of the partnership, the vehicle is regarded as being provided by the intermediary for the worker.

Step four

Deduct the amount of any capital allowances in respect of expenditure incurred by the intermediary in that year that could have been claimed by the worker under the *Capital Allowances Act 2001, Pt 2* (plant and machinery allowances) by virtue of *CAA 2001, s 15(1)(i)* (which provides that employment is a qualifying activity for the purposes of that Part) if the worker had been employed by the client and had incurred the expenditure.

Step five

Deduct any contributions made in that year for the benefit of the worker by the intermediary to a registered pension scheme (within the meaning of *FA 2004, Pt 4*) that if made by an employer for the benefit of an employee would not be chargeable to income tax as income of the employee, and any payments made in that year in respect of the worker by the intermediary in respect of any of the Pensions Acts levies.

This does not apply to excess contributions made and later repaid.

The Pensions Acts levies are:

- the administration levy referred to in the *Pensions Act 2004, s 117(1)*;
- the initial levy referred to in the *Pensions Act 2004, s 174(1)*;
- the risk-based pension protection levy referred to in the *Pensions Act 2004, s 175(1)(a)* of that Act;
- the scheme-based pension protection levy referred to in the *Pensions Act 2004, s 175(1)(b)*;
- the fraud compensation levy referred to in the *Pensions Act 2004, s 189(1)*;
- a levy in respect of eligible schemes imposed by regulations made under the *Pensions Act 2004, s 209(7)* (the Ombudsman for the Board of the Pension Protection Fund).

Step six

Deduct the amount of secondary Class 1 contributions and Class 1A contributions paid by the intermediary for that year in respect of earnings of the worker.

Step seven

Deduct:

- the amount of any payments made by the intermediary to the worker in that year that constitutes remuneration derived from the worker's employment by that intermediary including, where the intermediary is a body corporate and the worker is a director of that body corporate, payments treated as remuneration derived from that employment by virtue of *SI 2001/1004, reg 22(2)* (payments to directors to be treated as earnings), but excluding payments which represent items in respect of which a deduction was made under Step three, and
- the amount of any benefits provided by the intermediary to the worker in that year, being benefits that constitute amounts of general earnings

in respect of which Class 1A contributions are payable, but excluding any benefits which represent items in respect of which a deduction was made under Step three.

If the result at this point is nil or a negative amount, the worker has no attributable earnings for that year.

If the intermediary makes exempt mileage allowance or passenger payments in accordance with *ITEPA 2003, ss 229* or *233* to the worker, the payments are treated as if they have been made by the intermediary to the worker and constituted remuneration derived from the worker's employment with the intermediary.

Step eight

Find the amount that, together with the amount of secondary Class 1 contributions payable in respect of it, is equal to the amount resulting from Step seven (if that amount is a positive amount).

Step nine

The result is the amount of the worker's attributable earnings for that year.

The attributable earnings are deemed to be paid to the worker on 5 April at the end of the tax year.

Example 3.3—Calculating attributable earnings under IR35

James supplies consultancy services through his personal service company, Bond Consulting, to a private sector client M Ltd. The arrangements fall with IR35.

For the tax year 2021/22, M Ltd pays Bond Consulting £60,000 in respect of the services received by James.

James does no other work during the year.

James pays himself a salary of £20,000 on which PAYE and National Insurance contributions are paid.

He has a company car provided by Bond Consulting with a cash equivalent value of £4,000. He also receives private medical insurance with a cash equivalent value of £500. Bond Consulting Ltd also makes pension contributions to a registered pension scheme of £2,000 on James' behalf.

Bond Consulting Ltd pays a subscription to an approved professional body on James' behalf of £200.

Bond Consulting Ltd owns the equipment necessary for James' work. Had James purchased that equipment himself, been employed by M Ltd and used the equipment in that employment, he would have been entitled to claim capital allowances of £400.

Bond Consulting Ltd paid secondary Class 1 National Insurance contributions of £1,540.08 ((£20,000 – £8,840) @ 13.8%) and also Class 1A National

Insurance contributions of £621 ((£4,000 + £500) @13.8%) in respect of the benefits provided to James.

The attributable earnings are calculated as follows:

		£
Step one	Payments and benefits received by Bond Consulting Ltd and to which IR35 applies	60,000
	Less 5% (£50,000 × 5%)	(2,500)
Step two	Payments and benefits received by James directly from M Ltd	0
Step three	Expenses met by Bond Consulting Ltd that would have been deductible were James an employee of M Ltd	(200)
Step four	Capital allowances in respect of equipment provided by Bond Consulting Ltd that James could have claimed personally had he provided the equipment and been an employee of M Ltd.	(400)
Step five	Contributions made by Bond Consulting Ltd to a registered pension scheme on James' behalf	(2,000)
Step six	Salary received by James from Bond Consulting Ltd which was subject to tax and National Insurance contributions	(20,000)
Step seven	Benefits in kind from Bond Consulting Ltd subject to tax and Class 1A NICs	(4,500)
	SUB TOTAL	**30,400**
Step eight	Amount together with employer's National Insurance that equals £30,400 $\frac{£30{,}400 \times 100}{100 + 13.8}$	26,714
Step nine	**ATTRIBUTABLE EARNINGS**	**26,714**
	Employer's NIC on attributable earnings £26,714 × 13.8%	3,686

James is treated as having **received** attributable earnings of £26,714. These are liable to Class 1 National Insurance contributions.

The attributable earnings are deemed to be paid on 5 April 2022. These are aggregated with any other earnings paid in the same earnings period and the Class 1 National Insurance liability is computed in the usual way.

Focus

Where IR35 applies, Class 1 National Insurance contributions are due on the deemed attributable earnings, which are treated as paid on 5 April at the end of the relevant tax year.

Calculating deemed direct earnings: engagements to which the off-payroll working rules apply

3.29 Part 2 of the regulations applies to engagements that fall within the off-payroll working rules. These are engagements where the end client is a public sector body (6 April 2017 onwards) or a medium-sized or large private sector organisation (6 April 2021 onwards) and the worker provides his or her services to the end client via an intermediary such as a personal service company and the nature of the engagement is such that if the worker provided his or her services to the end client directly, the worker would be an employee of the end client.

The IR35 rules were superseded by new off-payroll working rules from 6 April 2017 in relation to payments received on or after that date where the end client is a public sector worker. From a National Insurance perspective, new rules (contained in Pt 2 of the regulations) were introduced from 6 April 2017 to deal with engagements that fell within the off-payroll working rules as they applied where the end client was a public sector body from that date. An engagement falls within the *Social Security Contributions (Intermediaries) Regulations 2000, SI 2000/727, Pt 2*, from 6 April 2017 onwards by virtue of *reg 13* where:

- the individual ('the worker') personally performs, or is under an obligation to perform services for another person ('the client');
- the client is a public authority;
- the services are provided not under a contract directly between the client and the worker but under arrangements involving a third party ('the intermediary'); and
- the circumstances are such that if the services were provided under a contract directly between the client and the worker, the worker would be regarded for the purposes of *SSCBA 1992, Pts I to V* as employed in the employed earner's employment by the client, or the worker is an office holder who holds that office under the client and the services relate to that office.

For these purposes, a public authority is as defined in the *Social Security Contributions (Intermediaries) Regulations 2000 (SI 2000/727), reg 3A*.

These rules (the off-payroll working rules) were extended from 6 April 2021 to engagements where the end client is a medium-sized or large private sector organisation (see **2.51**) and the worker provides his or services through an intermediary, such as a personal service company, and the nature of the engagement is such that if the worker provided his or her services directly to the end client, the worker would be an employee of the end client.

Where the engagement falls within Pt. 2 of the regulations, the fee-payer (which may be a relevant end client or may be an agency or other intermediary or third party responsible for paying the worker) must calculate the deemed direct earnings in accordance with the *Social Security Contributions (Intermediaries) Regulations 2000 (SI 2000/727) reg 17* as follows:

Step one

Identify the amount or value of the chain payment made by the person who is treated as making the deemed direct earnings, and deduct from that amount so much of it (if any) as is in respect of value added tax.

Step two

Deduct, from the amount resulting from Step 1, so much of that amount as represents the direct costs to the intermediary of materials used, or to be used, in the performance of the services.

Step three

Deduct, at the option of the person treated as making the deemed direct earnings, from the amount at step 2, so much of the amount as represents expenses met by the intermediary which would have been deductible in accordance with *ITEPA 2003, s 10* in accordance with *ITEPA 2003, s 327(3)–(5)* (deductions from earnings) if:

- the worker had been employed by the client; and
- the expenses had been met out of those earnings

Step four

If the amount resulting from the preceding steps is nil or negative, there are no deemed earnings. Otherwise the resulting amount is the amount of the deemed direct earnings.

The deemed direct payment is subject to PAYE and National Insurance contributions as for a direct employee and the real time information reporting requirements apply.

Example 3.4—Calculating the deemed direct earnings

Richard provides his services through a personal service company, R Ltd. R Ltd wins a six-month contract with a local authority. Under the terms of the contract, R Ltd invoices the local authority an amount of £8,000 plus VAT each month (a total of £9,600). R Ltd incurs expenses of £400 per month, which would have been deductible as employment expenses had Richard been employed directly by the local authority, R Ltd also spends £1,000 on materials necessary to enable him to fulfil the contract.

The local authority ascertains that the contract falls within the rules for off-payroll working in the public sector and consequently the local authority must deduct tax and National Insurance from the amount paid in settlement of R Ltd's invoices each month.

The deemed direct payment is calculated as follows:

		£
Step one	The amount of the chain payment net of VAT	8,000
Step two	Less: cost of direct materials	(1,000)
Step three	Less: eligible expenses	(400)
Step four	Deemed direct payments	6,600

The local authority will need to account for PAYE tax and National Insurance (employer's and employee's) on the deemed period and deduct this from the amount paid in settlement of the invoice.

When working out the tax and National Insurance on payments made by R Ltd to Richard, the amount paid by the personal service company can be reduced by an amount up to the deemed direct payment. However, the deduction is capped at the end-of-line remuneration paid by the intermediary.

Focus

Where the off-payroll working rules apply, the end client (or fee payer where this is a third party) must account for Class 1 National Insurance contributions on the deemed payment.

Salaried partners in limited liability partnerships

3.30 Anti-avoidance measures were introduced for tax purposes by the *Finance Act 2014* to target disguised employment using limited liability partnerships (LLPs). Under the provisions, salaried partners who meet certain conditions (see **2.42**) are treated as employees for tax purposes, rather than as self-employed. As a result, their earnings are subject to PAYE and Class 1 National Insurance contributions.

For National Insurance purposes, the Treasury is given the power (by *SSCBA 1992, s 4AA*) to make regulations to reclassify certain LLP members as employed earners when certain conditions are met. The regulations are the *Social Security Contributions (Limited Liability Partnership) Regulations 2014 (SI 2014/3159)*. The regulations set out the conditions in which a partner of a limited liability partnership is treated as an employed earner for National Insurance purposes. The conditions, which mirror those applying for tax purposes, are discussed further at **2.43**.

For the purposes of the regulations, any amount treated as employment income from the deemed employment under *ITTOIA 2005, ss 863A* or *863G(4)*, other than employment income in the form of benefits in kind which would be taxed under the benefits code, is treated as earnings for National Insurance purposes and as such is liable to Class 1 contributions.

> **Focus**
>
> The earnings of salaried partners in LLPs are generally treated as earnings from an employment rather than from self-employment, with the result that the National Insurance liability is to Class 1 rather than to Classes 2 and 4.

Managed service companies

3.31 Provision is made (in *SSCBA 1992, s 4A*, as modified by the *Social Security Contributions and Benefits Act 1992 (Modification of Section 4A) Order 2007* (*SI 2007/2071*) for regulations to be made for securing that where the services of an individual are provided directly or indirectly by a managed service company, relevant payments and benefits (to the extent as specified in the regulations) are treated as earnings paid to the worker in respect of an employed earner's employment. The regulations are the *Social Security Contributions (Managed Service Companies Regulations 2007* (*SI 2007/2070*).

The attributable earnings provisions (in *SI 2007/2070, reg 3*) apply where:

- the services of an individual (the worker) are provided (directly or indirectly) by a managed service company (MSC);
- the worker, or an associate of the worker, receives (from any person) a payment or benefit which can be reasonably expected to be taken to be in respect of services; and
- the payment or benefit is not earnings derived from an employed earner's employment of the worker with the MSC.

The attributable earnings for National Insurance purposes are computed as for tax purposes in accordance with *ITEPA 2003, s 61E* as follows:

Step one

Find the amount of the payment or benefit received by the worker (or an associate of the worker) that can reasonably be expected to be taken in respect of the services provided to the MSC.

A payment or benefit is anything that is received by the employee for performing the duties of the employment that would be general earnings from the employment (*ITEPA 2003, s 61F*). If the payment is in cash, the amount of that payment is the amount received. If the payment is in the form of a non-cash payment, the amount of that payment is the cash equivalent of the benefit.

Step two

Deduct the amount of any expenses met by the worker that would have been deductible from the taxable earnings of the employment had the worker been employed by the client to provide those relevant services and the expenses had been met by the worker out of those earnings.

If the result at this point is nil or a negative amount there are no attributable earnings.

Step three

Assume the result of step two represents the amount together with employer's National Insurance contributions on it, and deduct (on that assumption) what would be the amount of those contributions.

The result is the attributable earnings.

The attributable earnings are aggregated with other earnings in the earnings period and Class 1 National Insurance contributions are computed in the usual way.

Example 3.5—Managed service company: calculation of attributable earnings

Richard provides his services through a managed service company. In 2021/22 he receives a dividend of £20,000 from the managed service company. The payment is in respect of services provided to the managed service company.

Richard incurs expenses of £2,000 that would be deductible had he been employed by the client.

The attributable earnings are as follows:

		£
Step one	Payment in respect of services provided to MSC	20,000
Step two	Deductible expenses	(2,000)
Step three	Attributable earnings plus employer's National Insurance contributions	18,000
	Employer's National Insurance contributions $\frac{£18{,}000 \times 13.8}{100 + 13.8}$	(2,183)
	ATTRIBUTABLE EARNINGS	**15,817**

> **Focus**
>
> Where services are provided by a managed service company, the attributable earnings are liable to Class 1 National Insurance contributions.

Other amounts treated as earnings

3.32 Certain payments are deemed to be earnings by the regulations and are treated as remuneration derived from the employed earner's employment (the *Social Security (Contributions) Regulations 2001* (*SI 2001/1004*), *reg 22*). The payments in question are:

- any payment by a company to or for the benefit of any of its directors if, apart from the deeming provision, the payments would not otherwise be earnings for National Insurance purposes and the payment is made on or account of or by way of an advance of a sum which would be earnings for those purposes;
- the amount treated as earnings from the employment by virtue of *ITEPA 2003, s 222(2*) in respect of tax due on notional payments not made good by the employee within 90 days. This provision brings such payments within the Class 1 NIC net rather than the Class 1A NIC net despite the fact that they are returned on form P11D;
- the amount treated as employment income in respect of conditional shares or interests in conditional shares acquired before 16 April 2003, computed in accordance with *ITEPA 2003, s 428* (as originally enacted);
- the amount treated as employment income by virtue of *ITEPA 2003, Pt 7, Ch 4* (as originally enacted) in respect of post-acquisition charges on shares or interests in shares acquired before 16 April 2003;
- amounts treated as employment income in relation to employment-related securities (within the meaning of *ITEPA 2003, s 421B(8)*) and to which PAYE applies by virtue of *ITEPA 2003, s 698*;
- amounts which count as employment income in relation to share incentive plans and in respect of which PAYE is recoverable by virtue of the PAYE regulations;
- amounts which count as employment income by virtue of the operation of the employee security anti-avoidance provisions in *F(No. 2)A 2005, Sch 2* under *ITEPA 2005, Pt 7, Chs 2–4* where the relevant date for that income (determined in accordance with *ITEPA 2003, s 698(6)*) is on or after 2 December 2004 and before 20 July 2005;

- amounts which count as employment income by virtue of anti-avoidance provisions in *FA 2006, s 92* (amending *ITEPA 2003, s 420*) in relation to options where the relevant date is on or after 2 December 2004 and before 19 July 2006;
- with effect from 1 September 2013, amounts treated as earnings from employment by virtue of *ITEPA 2003, s 226A* in respect of shares given to an employee shareholder with a market value of more than £2,000 (the excess over £2,000 being treated as earnings);
- with effect from 6 April 2016, any amount paid or reimbursed to an employee in respect of expenses, provided pursuant to a salary sacrifice arrangement (within the meaning of *ITEPA 2003, s 289A(5))* and which is not a payment or reimbursement of relevant motoring expenditure (within *SI 2001/1004, reg 22A)*;
- with effect from 6 April 2016, any amount paid or reimbursed to an employed earner in respect of expenses which is calculated by reference to a set rate rather than by reference to the actual amount incurred in respect of the expenses where such a rate is not contained in regulations made under *ITEPA 2003, s 289A(6)(a)* or approved under *ITEPA 2003, s 289B;*
- with effect from 6 April 2018, the amount of a termination award which is treated as earnings from the employment of the employed earner by virtue of *ITEPA 2003, s 402B*.

The items listed above are within the charge to Class 1 National Insurance contributions rather than to Class 1A.

The regulation (*reg 22(3)*) also specifies that the cash equivalent of the benefit arising in respect of car fuel provided for private motoring in a company car (calculated in accordance with *ITEPA 2003, s 149*) is deemed to be earnings. However, this has little practical application as employer-provided company car fuel is within the Class 1A charge rather than the Class 1 charge. The Class 1A charge is discussed in detail in Chapter 4.

Mileage allowance payments

3.33 Mileage allowance payments in excess of the approved amount are deemed to be earnings for Class 1 National Insurance purposes by virtue of the *Social Security (Contributions) Regulations 2001* (*SI 2001/1004*), *reg 22A*.

However, the rules for determining whether the payments are in excess of the approved amount apply differently for National Insurance purposes and for tax purposes. This is because, unlike tax, National Insurance contributions are calculated independently for each earnings period on a non-cumulative basis (see **3.83** for commentary on earnings periods).

The amount that is treated as earnings for the earnings period in respect of mileage allowance payments paid in connection with the use of qualifying vehicles other than cycles is found by applying the formula:

$$RME - QA$$

Where:

- RME is the aggregate of the relevant motoring expenditure in the earnings period; and
- QA is the qualifying amount.

However, from 6 April 2018, the amount that is treated as qualifying earnings is RME without the deduction of the qualifying amount (QA), where the aggregate relevant motoring expenditure is paid pursuant to optional remuneration arrangements.

A payment is relevant motoring expenditure if it is a mileage allowance payment within the meaning of *ITEPA 2003, s 229(2)* or would be such a payment but for the fact that it is paid for the benefit of another employee or it is any form of payment, except a payment in kind, made by or on behalf of the employer and made to, or for the benefit of, the employee in respect of the use by the employee of a qualifying vehicle. The amount does not have to be paid in the form of a rate per mile.

A payment can still be a relevant motoring expenditure if it is paid in the form of a lump sum allowance or a lump sum allowance and a lower rate per mile. In *Cheshire Employer and Skills Development Ltd (formerly Total People Ltd) v Revenue and Customs Commissioners* [2013] BTC 1, the Court of Appeal held that lump sum payments made to reimburse employees for business mileage were not emoluments for NIC purposes.

The qualifying amount (which is the amount that can be paid before triggering a Class 1 National Insurance liability) is found by the formula:

$$M \times R$$

Where:

- M is the sum of the number of miles of business travel undertaken, at or before the time when the payment is made, in respect of which the payment is made and in respect of which no other payment has been made, and the number of business miles undertaken since the last payment of relevant motoring expenditure was made, or if no previous payments have been made, since the employment began and for which no payment has been made.
- R is the rate applicable to the vehicle in question at the time when the payment is made in accordance with *ITEPA 2003, s 230(1)* and, if more than one rate is applicable to the class of vehicle in question, the highest of those rates.

The rates applying for National Insurance purposes for 2011/12 and later tax years are as follows:

Type of vehicle	Rate per mile
Car or van	45p
Motorcycle	24p

The determination of National Insurance contributions separately for each earnings period means that no account is taken of payments made in earlier periods and likewise no account of business miles previously reimbursed. For tax purposes, the rate used to work out the qualifying amount for cars and vans falls to 25p once 10,000 business miles have been reimbursed in the tax year. However, for National Insurance purposes, all business miles can be reimbursed at the higher rate of 45p per mile without triggering a Class 1 National Insurance liability, regardless of the number of business miles reimbursed in the tax year.

Example 3.6—Mileage allowance payments

An employee is paid each calendar month. He is required to use his own car for business. His employer pays him a mileage rate of 50p per mile.

In September he drives 4,000 business miles in his company car. He is paid a mileage allowance of £2,000 (4,000 miles @ 50p per mile).

The earnings period is the month of September.

The qualifying amount for the earnings period is £1,800 (4,000 miles @ 45p per mile).

The employee is paid £200 more than the qualifying amount. This is treated as a payment of earnings of £200 for the earnings period (September 2020). This amount is aggregated with other payments of earnings in the earnings period and Class 1 National Insurance contributions are worked out on the total in the usual way.

The qualifying amount of a mileage allowance payment paid in respect of cars, vans and motor cycles is excluded from earnings for Class 1 National Insurance purposes by virtue of the *Social Security (Contributions) Regulations* 2001 *(SI 2001/1004), Sch 3, Pt VIII, para 7A* (see **3.62**).

The tax legislation also provides for exemption from tax for the qualifying amount of a mileage payment made in respect business travel using a cycle. The qualifying amount is found applying the formula M × R, where R is 20p per mile. This amount is excluded from earnings for Class 1 National Insurance purposes by virtue of the *Social Security (Contributions) Regulations* 2001 *(SI 2001/1004), Sch 3, Pt VIII, para 7B* (see **3.62**).

Also exempt from tax is the qualifying amount of a passenger payment. This is found by applying the formula M × R, where R is 5p per mile and business mileage is the business mileage for which the employee receives passenger payments. Unlike approved mileage payments, approved passenger payments can be made to company car drivers as well as to those who use their own cars for business travel. To qualify for the payment, the passenger must also be an employee or a volunteer for whom the journey is also business travel. Qualifying passenger payments are excluded from earnings for Class 1 National Insurance purposes by virtue of the *Social Security (Contributions) Regulations 2001 (SI 2001/1004) Sch 3, Pt VIII, para 7C* (see **3.69**).

> **Focus**
>
> The calculation of mileage allowance payments for National Insurance purposes differs from that for tax in that the 45p per mile rate for cars and vans is used for all mileage, rather than only for the first 10,000 business miles in the tax year, as for tax. Payments in excess of the qualifying amount are treated as earnings and are liable for Class 1 National Insurance contributions.

Disguised remuneration

3.34 Since a National Insurance liability arises in respect of amounts charged to income tax as employment income under the disguised remuneration provisions in *ITEPA 2003, Pt 7A*. Broadly, these provisions treat amounts that are provided by third parties as employment income where the amounts provided are effectively remuneration. The amount treated as employment income for tax purposes is treated as earnings for Class 1 National Insurance purposes (the *Social Security (Contributions) Regulations 2001 SI 2001/1004), reg 22B)*.

However, this does not apply where the amount in question is a disguised remuneration loan which is subject to the 2019 loan charge and where secondary contributions have been paid on the crystalised loan.

To prevent a liability arising twice on the same amount, the amount treated as employment income is not regarded as earnings under this provision if it is treated as earnings by virtue of another provision.

Calculation of earnings in special cases

3.35 Although Class 1A National Insurance contributions (see Chapter 4) apply to most taxable benefits in kind, the legislation brings a number of non-cash payments within the Class 1 National Insurance net by treating them as earnings for Class 1 National Insurance purposes. This is to prevent the avoidance of National Insurance by making payments in non-cash forms. Unlike items within the Class 1A (employer-only) charge, non-cash payments that are treated as earnings for Class 1 purposes suffer both an employer and an employee liability. The legislation contains special rules for determining the amount that is taken into account as earnings where this is not straightforward (the *Social Security (Contributions) Regulations 2001* (*SI 2001/1004*), *Sch* 2).

Beneficial interests in assets

3.36 In calculating a person's earnings, the amount comprised in a payment by way of conferment of any beneficial interest listed below is taken into consideration (the *Social Security (Contributions) Regulations 2001* (*SI 2001/1004*), *reg 24* and *Sch 2, para 2*):

- options to acquire or dispose of currency of the UK or any other country or territory, gold, silver, palladium or platinum, any of the assets listed below;
- alcoholic liquor on which duty has not been paid;
- gemstones;
- certificates and other instruments conferring rights in assets; and
- vouchers capable of being exchanged for any of the items listed above.

The amount included within the calculation of earnings is the amount that the beneficial interest might reasonably be expected to fetch if sold in the open market on the day on which it is conferred.

This general rule is subject to the exceptions listed in **3.37** to **3.45** below.

Beneficial interest comprised in units in a unit trust scheme

3.37 In the event that the amount of earnings is comprised in a payment by way of the conferment of a beneficial interest in a unit trust scheme (within the meaning of the *Financial Services and Markets Act 2000, s 227*) which has a published selling price, the amount that is taken into account in the calculation of earnings is determined by reference to the published selling price on the day in question (the *Social Security (Contributions) Earnings Regulations 2001* (*SI 2001/1004*), *reg 24* and *Sch 2, para 3*).

The published selling price is the lowest selling price published on the date on which the payment in question is made. If no price is published on that date, the lowest selling price on the last previous date on which such a price was published is used instead.

Beneficial interest in an option to acquire certain assets

3.38 The amount of earnings comprised in a beneficial interest comprising an option to acquire any of the assets listed in **3.25** above is determined by reference to the value of the asset acquired by the exercise of the option on the day on which the option was acquired (the *Social Security (Contributions) Regulations 2001* (*SI 2001/1004*), *reg 24* and *Sch 2, para 4*).

The amount taken into account as earnings is reduced by any consideration for the acquisition of the asset. If the consideration is variable, the earnings are reduced by the least amount of consideration for which the asset may be acquired.

If the asset can be exchanged for another asset of higher value, the amount of earnings is determined by reference to the asset with the higher value.

Readily convertible assets

3.39 The amount taken into account in the calculation of earnings in respect of a payment by way of the conferment of a beneficial interest in a readily convertible asset is the best estimate of the amount that can be made of the amount that is likely to be chargeable to tax in respect of that asset as general earnings (the *Social Security (Contributions) Regulations 2001* (*SI 2001/1004*), *reg 24* and *Sch 2, para* 5).

If the earnings comprise a voucher or similar document that is capable of being converted into a readily convertible asset, the amount taken into account in the calculation of earnings is the best estimate that can reasonably be made of the amount of general earnings in respect of the asset for which the voucher is capable of being exchanged.

Assets that are not readily convertible

3.40 Where the earnings comprise:

- a payment by way of alcoholic liquor on which duty has not been paid or by way of gemstones, not disregarded as a payment in kind which is not a readily convertible asset;
- a voucher, stamp or similar document that is not capable of being converted into a readily convertible asset; or
- a non-cash voucher not capable of being turned into a readily convertible asset,

the amount of those earnings is determined by reference to the cost of the asset in question (the *Social Security (Contributions) Regulations 2001* (*SI 2001/1004*), *reg 24* and *Sch 2, para 6*).

Where the asset is a voucher, the cost of that voucher also includes the cost of any asset for which the voucher or similar is capable of being exchanged.

Convertible and restricted interests in securities and restricted securities

3.41 The amount of earnings comprised in a payment by way of the conferment of a convertible interest in securities, a restricted interest in securities or an interest in convertible or restricted securities is the amount taken into account as employment income for tax purposes in accordance with *ITEPA 2003, Pt 7, Chs 1–5*. However, in computing the earnings for National Insurance purposes, no relief is given for any secondary Class 1 contributions paid by the employee (the *Social Security (Contributions) Regulations 2001* (*SI 2001/1004*), *reg 24* and *Sch 2, para 7*).

For details of the limited circumstances in which the secondary liable may be met by, or transferred to, the employee, see **3.123**.

Exercise of a replacement right to acquire shares obtained as an earner before April 1999

3.42 If, before 6 April 1999, an earner obtained a right to acquire shares in a body corporate, the earner subsequently obtained a replacement right, the replacement right was exercised, the market value of the option or resulting shares was not increased by things done other than for a genuine commercial reason (see **3.43**) and the gain is not disregarded, the amount taken into account as earnings is calculated or estimated in accordance with the rules set out below (the *Social Security (Contributions) Regulations 2001* (*SI 2001/1004*), *reg 24* and *Sch 2, para 11*).

Step one

Find the amount (if any) by which the sum of the market value of the shares acquired by the exercise of the replacement right and the market value of any other benefit in money or money's worth obtained by the exercise of the replacement right exceeds the amount required to be paid for the exercise of that right.

Step two

Find the amount (if any) by which the market value of the shares, which were the subject of the right assigned or released on the first occasion in respect of which the condition in *Sch 3, Pt 9, para 16(4)* (see **3.66**) is not satisfied exceeds the amount required to be paid for the exercise of that right immediately before that time.

Step three

Subtract the amount found by step two from the amount found by step one.

Step four

Subtract from the result of step three any amount taken into account in computing the earner's earnings for the purposes of the Class 1 contribution at the time of the grant of the first right and any amount given by or on behalf of the earner as consideration for the acquisition of the first right or any subsequent right. However, for these purposes, 'consideration' does not include the value of any right assigned or released in exchange for the acquisition of a replacement right.

The result of step four is the amount taken into account as earnings. However, if the result is negative, the amount of earnings is taken to be nil.

For the purposes of this computation, the market value is the price which the shares that are the subject of the right in question might reasonably be expected to fetch on sale in the open market.

Exercise, assignment or release of share option: market value of option or resulting shares increased by things done other than for genuine commercial reasons

3.43 Where a payment arises from exercise, assignment or release of an option which is not disregarded from earnings (see **3.71** – *Sch 3, Pt 9, para 17*)**,** the amount that is taken into account is the amount of the gain as computed for income tax purposes (*Social Security (Contributions) Regulations 2001* (*SI 2001/1004*), *reg 24* and *Sch 2, para 11A*).

However, if:

- the right to acquire shares in a body corporate is not capable of being exercised more than ten years after the date on which it was obtained;
- an amount of earnings was taken into account for the purposes of earnings-related contributions in respect of the earners obtaining that right, at the time that he obtained it (known as 'the deductible amount'); and
- no exercise, assignment or release of the whole or any part of that right, any right replacing it ('the replacement right') or any subsequent right has occurred on or after 10 April 2003,

the deductible amount is deducted from the amount otherwise taken into account as earnings.

Valuation of non-cash vouchers

3.44 The amount of earnings comprised in a non-cash voucher not disregarded from earnings (see **3.50**) is an amount equal to the expense incurred. This is referred to in the legislation as the 'chargeable expense' (the *Social Security (Contributions) Regulations 2001* (*SI 2001/1004*), *reg 24* and

Sch 2, para 14).However, the chargeable expense is reduced by any amount that the employed earner makes good to the person providing the non-cash voucher.

However, different valuation rules apply from 6 April 2018 where the non-cash voucher is made available under an optional remuneration arrangement, such as a salary sacrifice scheme (the *Social Security (Contributions) Regulations 2001* (*SI 2001/1004*), *reg 24* and *Sch 2, para 14A*). Where the non-cash voucher is made available under an optional remuneration arrangement, the amount of earnings in respect of that voucher is the relevant amount.

The first step in determining the relevant amount is to determine the greater of the chargeable expense (ignoring any amount made good by the employed earner) and the amount foregone under the optional remuneration arrangement in exchange for the non-cash voucher. If the chargeable expense is the greater, the relevant amount is the chargeable expense, less any amount made good. If the amount foregone is the greater, the relevant amount is the amount foregone, less any amount made good. Where an amount would be exempt from income tax but for the alternative valuation, rules apply where provision is made via an optional remuneration scheme, the chargeable expense is assumed to be zero for the purposes of working out the relevant amount.

Separate rules apply to determine the value of qualifying childcare vouchers (see **3.51**).

Vouchers provided for the benefit of two or more employed earners

3.45 Where a voucher or non-cash voucher is provided for the benefit of two or more employed earners, the amount which is taken into account as earnings depends on the circumstances (the *Social Security (Contributions) Regulations 2001* (*SI 2001/1004*), *reg 24* and *Sch 2, para 15*).

In the event that the respective proportion of the benefit of the vouchers to which each of the earners is entitled is known at the time of the payments, the amount taken into account as earnings in respect of each earner is on the basis that each receives a payment equal to that proportion. If the respective proportions are not known at the time of the payments, the earnings comprised in the payments are apportioned equally between the earners.

The amount apportioned is reduced by any amount made good by the earner.

Payments disregarded in the calculation of earnings for earnings-related contributions

3.46 The *Social Security (Contributions) Regulations 2001* (*SI 2001/1004*), *reg 25* and *Sch 3* specify certain payments that are disregarded in the calculation of earnings for the purposes of earnings-related contributions.

The payments specified are taken outside the Class 1 National Insurance net. However, this does not necessarily mean that they escape liability to National Insurance contributions entirely as, in the case of most taxable benefits in kind, they may be liable for Class 1A contributions instead.

The Class 1A charge is examined in Chapter 4.

The items disregarded by virtue of *SI 2001/1004, reg 25* and *Sch 3* are examined at **3.47ff**.

The legislation also provides for certain items to be excluded from the general earnings disregard for payments in kind. These payments remain within the definition of earnings and thus within the Class 1 charge.

The regulations also make provisions for certain payments by trustees (*SI 2001/1004, reg 26*) and payments to directors (*SI 2001/1004, reg 27*) to be disregarded. These are discussed, respectively, at **3.74** and **3.75**.

Focus

The *Social Security (Contributions) Regulations, Sch 3* take certain payments out of the Class 1 net. However, while there is no Class 1 liability, there may be a liability to Class 1A, as is the case for most taxable payments in kind. Although the general rule is that payments in kind are within Class 1A rather than Class 1, the general disregard for payments in kind does not apply to certain payments specified in the regulations (and discussed below), which therefore remain liable to Class 1.

Payments in kind

3.47 The *Social Security (Contributions) Regulations 2001* (*SI 2001/1004*) contain a general exclusion from earnings for payments in kind or by way of provision of board and lodgings or other facilities. This is found in *Sch 3, Pt II, para 1*.

However, payments in kind (unless specifically excluded) are generally liable to Class 1A National Insurance rather than Class 1 National Insurance contributions. Thus the earnings disregard does not take payments in kind completely out of the National Insurance contributions net, merely outside the Class 1 charge. As the Class 1A charge is an employer-only charge (see **4.1**), this is beneficial to the employee as it means that no primary contributions are due. However, where a Class 1a liability arises, the employer remains liable to pay National Insurance contributions.

The general disregard is subject to a number of exceptions. The items disregarded from the general exclusion from earnings for payments in kind remain liable to Class 1 National Insurance contributions. These are examined below.

Payments by way of assets not disregarded

3.48 The general disregard from earnings for payments in kind (see **3.47**) does not apply (by virtue of *SI 2001/1004, Sch 3, Pt II)* to:

- the conferment of a beneficial interest in a readily convertible asset not disregarded as a payment in kind (see **3.49**);
- the conferment of a beneficial interest in a specific asset not disregarded as a payment in kind (see **3.50**);
- the conferment of any beneficial interest in any contract of long-term insurance which falls within *Sch 1, Pt II, para 1* of the *Financial Services and Markets Act 2000 (Regulated Order) 2001*;
- a non-cash voucher not of a description mentioned in **3.51** or which is in respect of incidental overnight expenses.

However, an asset as described in **3.49** or **3.50** below is disregarded from earnings if that asset is given to the employee as a long service award and is exempt from tax by virtue of *ITEPA 2003, s 323.*

Items outside the disregard are liable to Class 1 National Insurance contributions.

Payments by way of readily convertible assets not disregarded as payments in kind

3.49 Certain payments by way of readily convertible assets are excluded from the payments in kind disregard by virtue of *SI 2001/1004, Sch 3, Pt III* and consequently remain within the charge to Class 1 National Insurance contributions.

The payments in kind disregard does not apply to readily convertible assets within *ITEPA 2003, s 702* (*SI 2001/1004, Sch 3, Pt III, para 1*). This covers:

- assets capable of being sold or otherwise realised in a recognised investment exchange (within the meaning of the *Financial Services and Markets Act 2000*), the London Bullion Market, the New York Stock Exchange or any other market specified in the *Income Tax (Pay As You Earn) Regulations 2003* (*SI 2003/2682*);
- assets consisting in the rights of an assigner, or any other rights, in respect of a money debt that is or may become due to the employer or to any other person; property that is subject to a warehousing regime, or any right in respect of property so subject, or anything that is likely (without anything being done by the employee) to give rise to or become, a right enabling a person to obtain an amount or total amount of money which is likely to be similar to the expense incurred in the provision of an asset; and

- assets for which trading arrangements are in existence or are likely to come into existence in accordance with any arrangements of another description existing when the asset is provided or any understanding existing at that time.

Also excluded from the disregard are assets that would be regarded as a readily convertible asset for PAYE purposes by virtue of the provisions on income provided in the form of an enhancement to the value of an asset in *ITEPA 2003, s 697* (*SI 2001/1004, Sch 3, Pt III, para 2).*

Any voucher, stamp or similar document (whether used singularly or together with other such vouchers, stamps or documents) which is capable of being exchanged for a readily convertible asset of the type described above and excluded from the payments in kind disregard is also excluded from the disregard. Such vouchers remain within the Class 1 National Insurance net (*SI 2001/1004, Sch 3, Pt III, para 3*).

Payments by way of specific assets not disregarded as payments in kind

3.50 The following assets are excluded from the payments in kind disregard and remain liable to Class 1 National Insurance contributions by virtue of *SI 2001/1004, Sch 3, Pt IV*:

- securities (*SI 2001/1004, Sch 3, Pt IV, para 1)*;
- options to acquire or dispose of currency in the UK or in any other country or territory; gold, silver, palladium or platinum, an asset falling within any of the bullets within this list or an option to acquire or dispose of such an option (*SI 2001/1004, Sch 3, Pt IV, para 6)*;
- any alcoholic liquor (within the meaning of the *Alcoholic Liquor Duties Act 1979*) in respect of which no duty has been paid (*SI 2001/1004, Sch 3, Pt IV, para 9)*;
- any gemstone, including stones such as diamond, emerald, ruby, sapphire, amethyst, jade, opal or topaz and organic gemstones such as amber or pearl, whether cut or uncut and whether or not having industrial use (*SI 2001/1004, Sch 3, Pt IV, para 10)*;
- certificates or other instruments which confer property rights in respect of assets in the form of securities, alcoholic liquor or gemstones, any right to acquire, dispose or underwrite an asset, being a right to which the holder would be entitled if he held any such assets to which the certificate or instrument relates or a contractual right other than an option to acquire any such asset otherwise than by way of subscription (*SI 2001/1004, Sch 3, Pt IV, para 11)*;
- any voucher, stamp or document (whether used singularly or together with other such stamps or vouchers or documents) which is capable of

being exchanged for an asset falling within the preceding bullets in this list (*SI 2001/1004, Sch 3, Pt IV, para 12).*

Certain non-cash vouchers disregarded as payments in kind

3.51 A non-cash voucher is a voucher that can be exchanged only for goods or services. It has no associated monetary value on surrender.

A non-cash voucher is disregarded in the calculation of earnings (and thus taken outside the Class 1 National Insurance net) only if it falls within one of the categories listed below (*SI 2001/1004, Sch 3, Pt V*):

- non-cash vouchers for the provision of car fuel charged to tax under *ITEPA 2003, s 149* by virtue of *SI 2001/1004, Sch 3, Pt. VIII, para 7D (SI 2001/1004, Sch 3, Pt V, para 1(2)(a))*;
- non-cash vouchers for the provision of van fuel charged to tax by virtue of *ITEPA 2003, s 160* by virtue of *SI 2001/1004, Sch 3, Pt VIII, para 7E (SI 2001/1004, Sch 3, Pt V, para 1(2)(aa))*;
- non-cash vouchers for incidental overnight expenses in circumstances specified in *SI 2001/1004, Sch 3, Pt X, para 4 (SI 2001/1004, Sch 3, Pt V, para 1(2)(b))*;
- for 2015/16 and earlier years only, transport vouchers under pre-26 March 1982 arrangements provided to employees under the rules as they applied for 2015/16 and earlier tax years who were in lower paid employments and excluded from general earnings for tax purposes by virtue of *ITEPA 2003, s 86 (SI 2001/1004, Sch 3, Pt V, para 2)*;
- non-cash vouchers exempted from liability to income tax by virtue of *ITEPA 2003, ss 266(1)(A)* or *269 (SI 2001/1004, Sch 3, Pt V, para 3);*
- non-cash vouchers in respect of the provision of transport between home and work for disabled employees where such provision would be exempt from income tax by virtue of *ITEPA 2003, s 246 (SI 2001/1004, Sch 3, Pt V, para 5(a))*;
- a non-cash voucher in respect of the provision of cars for disabled employees where such provision would be exempt from income tax by virtue of *ITEPA 2003, s 247 (SI 2001/1004, Sch 3, Pt V, para 5(b))*;
- a non-cash voucher in respect of the provision of transport home when the employee works late or car sharing arrangements fail and where such provision would be exempt from income tax by virtue of *ITEPA 2003, s 248 (SI 2001/1004, Sch 3, Pt V, para 5(c))*;
- with effect from 1 January 2015, a non-cash voucher in respect of the provision of recommended medical treatment which would be exempt from tax by virtue of *ITEPA 2003, s 320C (SI 2001/1004, Sch 3, Pt V, para 5(d))*;

- a non-cash voucher in respect of the provision of works transport services where such provision would be exempt from tax by virtue of *ITEPA 2003, s 242 (SI 2001/1004, Sch 3, Pt V, para 5A(a))*;
- a non-cash voucher in respect of the provision of support for public bus services where such provision would be exempt from income tax by virtue of *ITEPA 2003, s 243 (SI 2001/1004, Sch 3, Pt V, para 5A(b))*;
- a non-cash voucher in respect of the provision of cycles and cyclists' safety equipment where such provision would be exempt from income tax in accordance with *ITEPA 2003, s 244 (SI 2001/1004, Sch 3, Pt V, para 5A(c))*;
- a non-cash voucher for the provision of a mobile phone where such provision would be exempt from income tax by virtue of *ITEPA 2003, s 319 (SI 2001/1004, Sch 3, Pt V, para 5A(d))*;
- a non-cash voucher for the provision of travelling and subsistence during public transport strikes where the direct provision of such travel would be exempt in accordance with *ITEPA 2003, s 245 (SI 2001/1004, Sch 3, Pt V, para 5B(a))*;
- a non-cash voucher in respect of the provision of recreational benefits where the direct provision of such benefits would be exempt from income tax by virtue of *ITEPA 2003, s 261 (SI 2001/1004, Sch 3, Pt V, para 5B(b))*;
- a non-cash voucher in respect of the provision of annual parties and functions the direct provision of which would be exempt from income tax by virtue of *ITEPA 2003, s 264 (SI 2001/1004, Sch 3, Pt V, para 5B(c))*;
- a non-cash voucher in respect of the provision of leave travel facilities for members of the armed forces where the direct provision of such travel would be exempt from income tax by virtue of *ITEPA 2003, s 296 (SI 2001/1004, Sch 3, Pt V, para 5B(d))*;
- a non-cash voucher in respect of the provision of subsidised meals where the direct provision of such meals would be exempt from income tax by virtue of *ITEPA 2003, s 317* (note that from 6 April 2011 the exemption no longer applies where the meals are provided as part of a salary sacrifice arrangement) *(SI 2001/1004, Sch 3, Pt V, para 5B(e))*;
- a non-cash voucher for the provision of eye tests and special corrective appliances, the direct provision of which would be exempt from income tax by virtue of *ITEPA 2003, s 320A (SI 2001/1004, Sch 3, Pt V, para 5B(f))*;
- a non-cash voucher in respect of the provision of mainland transfers for offshore oil and gas workers where such provision would be exempt from income tax under *ITEPA 2003, s 305 (SI 2001/1004, Sch 3, Pt V, para 6(b))*;

- a non-cash voucher in respect of a suggestion scheme award where such an award would be exempt from income tax by virtue of *ITEPA 2003, s 321 (SI 2001/1004, Sch 3, Pt V, para 6(c))*;
- a non-cash voucher in respect of a long service award where such an award would be exempt from income tax under *ITEPA 2003, s 323 (SI 2001/1004, Sch 3, Pt V, para 6(d))*;
- trivial benefits provided by employers exempt from tax under *ITEPA 2003, s 323A (SI 2001/1004, Sch 3, Pt V, para 6(da))*;
- a non-cash voucher representing a small gift from a third party which would be exempt from income tax by virtue of *ITEPA 2003, s 324 (SI 2001/1004, Sch 3, Pt V, para 6(e))*;
- a non-cash voucher provided to or for the benefit of the employed earner by a person who is not the secondary contributor (*SI 2001/1004, Sch 3, Pt V, para 8)*; and
- a non-cash voucher providing health screening or medical check-ups to the extent that no liability to income tax arises in respect of such provision (*SI 2001/1004, Sch 3, Pt V, para 9)*.

Also disregarded from earnings are qualifying childcare vouchers up to the exempt amount (*Sch 3, Pt V, paras 6B, 7, 7A*).

The rules relating to tax relief for childcare vouchers and employer supported childcare were changed with effect from 6 April 2011. Where an employee joins an employer supported childcare or childcare scheme on or after 6 April 2011, tax relief is restricted to the basic rate of tax. Those who joined the scheme prior to that date continue to benefit from relief at their marginal rate of tax.

As a result of the changes, the calculation of the exempt amount from 6 April 2011 depends on whether the employee joined the scheme before 6 April 2011 or on or after that date.

Where an eligible employee (as defined in *ITEPA 2007, s 207AA* with effect from 6 April 2018) joined a childcare voucher scheme before 6 April 2011, provided that the employee has not ceased to be an employee and there has not been a continuous period of at least 52 weeks during which vouchers were not being provided to an employee under the scheme, the exempt amount is found by applying the formula:

$$E \times QW$$

Where:

- E is the sum of £55 plus the administration costs for the childcare voucher; and
- QW is the number of qualifying weeks for which the earner has been employed by the secondary contributor during the tax year in which

the qualifying childcare voucher is provided and for which no other qualifying childcare has been provided by the secondary contributor.

Where an eligible employee joins a childcare voucher scheme on or after 6 April 2011, the exempt amount is found by the formula:

$$E \times QW$$

Where:

- E is the sum of £25 per week plus the administration costs for the childcare voucher if the employee's estimated relevant earnings exceed the higher rate limit for the tax year (£150,000 for 2017/18);
- E is £28 per week plus the administration costs for the childcare voucher if the employee's estimated relevant earnings exceed the basic rate limit for the tax year (£33,500 for 2017/18) but do not exceed the higher rate limit; and
- E is £55 per week plus the administration costs for the childcare voucher in all other cases; and
- QW is the number of qualifying weeks for which the earner has been employed by the secondary contributor during the tax year in which the qualifying childcare voucher is provided and for which no other qualifying childcare has been provided by the secondary contributor.

An earner is only entitled to one exempt amount even if childcare vouchers are provided in respect of more than one child. However, vouchers may be provided to each parent in respect of the same child so that the child effectively benefits from childcare to the value of twice the exempt amount.

A qualifying childcare voucher is one which meets the following conditions:

- it is provided to an employee to enable the employee to obtain childcare for a child who is a child or step-child of the employee and who is maintained wholly or partly at the employee's expense, or is resident with the employee and in respect of whom the employee has parental responsibility;
- it can only be used to obtain qualifying childcare;
- it is provided under a scheme that is open to the employer's employees generally or to those at a particular location (although it is permissible to preclude relevant lower paid employees from joining the scheme where the vouchers are made available under a salary sacrifice arrangement); and
- for those joining the scheme on or after 6 April 2011, the employee has made an estimate of the employee's relevant earnings.

The tax exemption for childcare vouchers is only available where the employee joined the employer's scheme and received a voucher by 4 October 2018. Employees can continue to benefit from the exemption while the employer continues to offer the scheme but must choose whether to benefit from the tax exemption or the tax-free government top where sums are deposited in a designated online account.

Pension and pension contributions

3.52 Certain pension payments and pension contributions are disregarded when computing earnings for the purposes of Class 1 National Insurance contributions. These are set out in the *Social Security (Contributions) Regulations 2001* (*SI 2001/1004*), *Sch 3, Pt VI.*

Contributions to and benefits from registered pension schemes

3.53 A payment:

- by way of an employer's contribution to a registered pension scheme which is exempt from income tax by virtue of *ITEPA 2003, s 308(1)*; or
- by way of a benefit pursuant to a registered pension scheme to which *FA 2004, s 204(1)* and *Sch 31* or to which *FA 2004, s 208, 209* applies,

is disregarded in the calculation of earnings (*SI 2001/1004, Sch 3, Pt VI, para* 2).

Migrant member relief and corresponding reliefs

3.54 A payment by way of:

- an employer's contribution which attracts relief under *FA 2004, Sch 33, para 2* and any benefit referable to that contribution;
- an employer's contribution with pre-commencement entitlement to relief under the *Taxation of Pension Schemes (Transitional Provisions Order) 2006* (*SI 2006/2004*) and any benefit referable to that contribution;
- an employer's contribution to a pension scheme established outside the UK for the benefit of its employees or primarily for their benefit and any benefit referable to such a contribution whenever made;
- benefits from a pension scheme which are referable to contributions made before 6 April 2006 provided that a tax charge did not arise under former *ITEPA 2003, s 386* by virtue of former *ITEPA 2003, s 390*; or
- benefits subject to an unauthorised payment charge imposed by *FA 2004, s 208* as applied to a relevant non-UK scheme by virtue of *FA 2004, Sch 34, para, 1*,

is disregarded in the computation of earnings for Class 1 National Insurance purposes (*SI 2001/1004, Sch 3, Pt VI, para 3*).

Funded unapproved retirement benefit schemes

3.55 A payment by way of relevant benefits (within the meaning of *ICTA 1988, s 612*) pursuant to a retirement benefits scheme that has not been approved and is attributable to payments made prior to 6 April 1998 is disregarded in the computation of earnings for Class 1 National Insurance purposes (*SI 2001/1004, Sch 3, Pt VI, para 4*).

Payments to pension previously taken into account in calculating earnings

3.56 A payment by way of any benefit pursuant to a retirements benefit scheme that had not been approved and is attributable to payments after 6 April 1998 and before 6 April 2006 which have previously been included in a person's earnings for the purposes of assessment of his or her liability for earnings-related contributions is disregarded in the computation of earnings for Class 1 National Insurance purposes (*SI 2001/1004, Sch 3, Pt VI, para 5*).

Payments to pension schemes exempt from UK taxation under double taxation agreements

3.57 A payment to a pension scheme which is afforded tax relief by virtue of:

- *art 25(8)* of the Convention set out in the Schedule to the *Double Taxation Relief (Taxes on Income) (France) Order 1968*;
- *art 17A* of the Convention set out in the Schedule to the *Double Taxation Relief (Taxes on Income) (Republic of Ireland) Order 1976;*
- *art 27(2)* of the Convention set out in the Schedule to the *Double Taxation Relief (Taxes on Income) (Canada) Order 1980*;
- *art 28(3)* of the Convention set out in the Schedule to the *Double Taxation Relief (Taxes on Income) (The United States of America) Order 2002*;
- *art 17(3)* of the Convention set out in the Schedule to the *Double Taxation Relief (Taxes on Income) (South Africa) Order 2002*;
- *art 17(3)* of the Convention set out in the Schedule to the *Double Taxation Relief (Taxes on Income) (Chile) Order 2003*,

is disregarded from the computation of earnings for Class 1 National Insurance purposes (*SI 2001/1004, Sch 3, Pt VI, para 7*).

Contributions to and benefits from employer-financed retirement benefit schemes

3.58 A payment by way of an employer's contribution towards an employer-financed retirement benefits scheme (within the meaning given in *ITEPA 2003, s 393A*) and benefits pursuant to a retirement benefits scheme to which **3.60** applies is disregarded from the computation of earnings for Class 1 National Insurance purposes (*SI 2001/1004, Sch 3, Pt VI, para 8*).

Contributions to, and pension payments from, employer-financed pension only schemes

3.59 A payment by way of an employer contribution towards an employer-financed pension only scheme and a pension pursuant to an employer-financed pension only scheme which is income charged to tax pursuant to *ITEPA 2003, Pt 9* and to which **3.60** applies is disregarded from the computation of earnings for Class 1 National Insurance purposes (*SI 2001/1004, Sch 3, Pt VI, para 9(1)*).

For these purposes, an employer-financed pension only scheme is a scheme that is financed by payments made by or on behalf of the secondary contributor and providing only a pension. Such a scheme is not an employer-financed retirement benefits scheme because it does not provide relevant benefits (within the meaning of *ITEPA 2003, s 393B*).

Payments from employer-finance retirement benefits schemes and employer-financed pension only schemes

3.60 This paragraph applies to payments mentioned in **3.58** and **3.59** above which, if the scheme had been a registered pension scheme would have been authorised member payments (within the meaning of *FA 2004, s 164*) and would satisfy the conditions listed below and which are made after the employment of the employed earner by the secondary contributor, a subsidiary of the secondary contributor or a person connected with the secondary contributor or a subsidiary of the secondary contributor (*SI 2001/1004*), *Sch 3, Pt VI, para 10*).

The conditions are:

- any pension payable under the rules would have satisfied pension rules 1 and 3, pension rule 4 and pension rule 6 and *FA 2004, Sch 29, para 1(1)(e)*;
- in relation to any pension commencement lump sum payable under its rules, *FA 2004, s 166(1)(a)* and *Sch 29, paras 1* to *3* (as modified for these purposes) would have been satisfied;

- in relation to any ill-health lump sum payable under its rules, *FA 2004, s 166(1)(b)* and *Sch 29, paras 1* to *3* (as modified for these purposes) would have been satisfied; and
- any pension is payable until the member's death in instalments at least annually.

The amount that is disregarded is as computed in accordance with *FA 2004, Sch 29 Pt 1* as modified in accordance with *SI 2001/1004*), *Sch 3, Pt VI, para 10(6)*.

Armed forces early departure scheme payments

3.61 A payment under a scheme established by the *Armed Forces Early Departure Payments Scheme Order 2005* (*SI 2005/437*) or the *Armed Forces Early Departure Scheme Regulations 2014 (SI 2014/2328)* is disregarded in the computation of earnings for Class 1 National Insurance purposes (*SI 2001/1004, Sch 3, Pt VI, para 10A*). The disregard was originally introduced for 2013/14 onwards but was extended retrospectively to apply also to the years 2005/06 to 2012/13 (*NICA 2014, s 16*).

Superannuation funds to which ICTA 1988, s 615(3) applies

3.62 A payment by way of an employer contribution to a superannuation fund to which *ICTA 1988, s 615(3)* applies and any payment by way of a pension or annuity paid by such a fund is disregarded in the computation of earnings for Class 1 National Insurance purposes (*SI 2001/1004, Sch 3, Pt VI, para 11*).

Independent advice in respect of conversions and transfers of pension scheme benefits

3.63 A payment or reimbursement comprising independent advice in respect of conversions and transfers of pension scheme benefits to which no liability to income tax arises by virtue of *ITEPA 2003, s 308B* is disregarded in the computation of earnings for Class 1 National Insurance purposes with effect from 6 April 2015 (*SI 2001/1004, Sch 3, Pt VI, para 12*).

Payments and reimbursements of the cost of pensions advice

3.64 With effect from 6 April 2017, a payment or reimbursement of costs is incurred, by or in respect of an employee or former employee or prospective employee, in obtaining pension advice if condition A or B below is met (*SI 2001/1004, Sch 3, Pt VI, para 13)*. The disregard is capped at £500 per tax year per employment. For the purposes of the disregard, 'relevant pensions advice' is advice in relation to a person's pension arrangements or the use of a person's pension funds.

Condition A is that the payment or reimbursement is provided under a scheme that is open to the employer's employees generally or generally to the employer's employees at a particular location.

Condition B is that the payment or reimbursement is provided under a scheme that is open generally to the employer's employees, or generally to those of the employer's employees at a particular location who have reached the minimum qualifying age or meet the ill-health condition. The minimum qualifying age is the employee's relevant pension age less five years. The 'relevant pension age' where an employee is a member of a registered pension scheme is the employee's protected pension age, and in any other case is the minimum pension age as defined by *FA 2004, s 279(1)*.

The ill-health condition is met by an employee if the employer is satisfied on the basis of evidence provided by a registered medical practitioner that the employee is (and will continue to be) incapable of carrying on his or her occupation because of physical or mental impairment.

Payments in respect of training and similar courses

3.65 The payments and vouchers listed below in respect of training and similar courses are disregarded in the computation of earnings for Class 1 National Insurance purposes by virtue of the *Social Security (Contributions) Regulations 2001* (*SI 2001/1004*), *Sch 3, Pt VII, paras 2–11*:

- a payment of or contribution towards expenditure incurred in providing work-related training that is exempt from income tax by virtue of *ITEPA 2003, ss 250–254 (Sch 3, Pt VII, para 2)*;
- a payment in respect of expenditure for individual learning account training which is exempt from income tax by virtue of *ITEPA 2003, s 25 (Sch 3, Pt VII, para 3)*;
- a payment to a person as a participant in the New Deal 50 Plus scheme (*Sch 3, Pt VII, para 4)*;
- a payment made to a participant in a special scheme for claimants of jobseeker's allowances in accordance with the *Welfare Reform and Pensions Act 1999, s 60(2) (Sch 3, Pt VII, para 5)*;
- a payment made to a participant in a Jobmatch Scheme, including a pilot, arranged under the *Employment and Training Act 1973, s 2(1) (Sch 3, Pt VII, para 6)*;
- a payment by way of a discharge of any liability by the use of a voucher given to a participant in a Jobmatch Scheme (including a pilot), arranged under the *Employment and Training Act 1973, s 2(1) (Sch 3, Pt VII, para 7)*;

- a payment made to a participant in an Employment Retention and Advancement Scheme arranged under the *Employment and Training Act 1973, s 2(1) (Sch 3, Pt VII, para 8);*
- a payment made to a participant in a Return to Work Credit Scheme, arranged under the *Employment and Training Act 1973, s 2(1) (Sch 3, Pt VII, para 9)*;
- a payment made to a participant in a Working Neighbourhoods Pilot, arranged under the *Employment and Training Act 1973, s 2(1) (Sch 3, Pt VII, para 10)*;
- a payment made to a participant in an In-Work Credit scheme arranged under the *Employment and Training Act 1973, s 2(1) (Sch 3, Pt VII, para 11)*; and
- from 29 September 2020, a care leaver's apprenticeship bursary payment which is exempted from income tax under *ITEPA 2003, s 254A (Sch 3, Pt VII, para 13)*

Also disregarded in the computation of earnings for Class 1 National Insurance contributions purposes is a payment made to an employed earner receiving full-time education at a university, technical college or similar educational establishment (within the meaning of *ICTA 1988, s 331*), provided that the following conditions are met (*SI 2001/1004, Sch 3, Pt VII, para 12*):

- the employed earner must have enrolled at the educational establishment for a course lasting at least one academic year when the payment is made;
- the secondary contributor must require the employed earner to attend the course for an average of at least 20 weeks in an academic year;
- the educational establishment must be open to members of the public generally and must offer more than one course of practical or academic instruction;
- the educational establishment must not be run by the secondary contributor or a person connected with him (within the meaning of *ICTA 1988, s 839*) or a trade organisation of which the secondary contributor is a member; and
- the total amount of earnings payable to the earner in respect of his or her attendance, including lodgings, travelling and subsistence allowances but excluding any tuition fees must not exceed the statutory amount (£15,480 in respect of the academic year beginning on 1 September 2007 and subsequent academic years).

This disregard does not extend to payments by the secondary contributor to the employed earner for, or in respect of, work done for the secondary contributor, whether during vacations or otherwise.

From 29 September 2020 onwards, a care leaver's apprenticeship bursary payments which is exempt from tax under *ITEPA 2003, s 254A* is disregarded in the computation of earnings for Class 1 National Insurance purposes (*SI 2001/1004, Sch 3, Pt VII, para 13*).

Travelling, relocation and other expenses and allowances of the employment

3.66 Certain travelling, relocation and other expenses and allowances of employment are disregarded in the computation of earnings for Class 1 National Insurance purposes by virtue of the *Social Security (Contributions) Regulations 2001* (*SI 2001/1004*), *Sch 3, Pt VIII).*

However, it should be noted that none of the following are disregarded in the calculation of an employed earner's earnings (*SI 2001/1004, Sch 3, Pt VIII, para 1A)*:

- any amount paid or reimbursed pursuant to a relevant salary sacrifice arrangement as provided for in *ITEPA 2003, s 289A(5)*;
- any amount paid or reimbursed to an employed earnings which falls within *SI 2001/1004, reg 22* (see **3.32**);
- any amount paid to an employed earner in respect of anticipated expenses that have yet to be incurred (whether or not such expenses are actually incurred after the payment is made).

Relocation expenses

3.67 A payment of or contribution towards expenses reasonably incurred by a person in relation to a change of residence in connection with the commencement of, or an alteration in, the duties of the employment or the place where those duties are normally carried out are disregarded in the computation of earnings where the following conditions are met (*SI 2001/1004, Sch 3, Pt VIII, para* 2).

The first condition is that the payment or contribution is exempt from income tax by virtue of *ITEPA 2003, s 271* (or would be so were it not disregarded by another provision of *ITEPA 2003*).

The second condition is that the change of residence results from the employee becoming employed by the employer, an alteration of the duties of the employee's employment (where the employer remains the same) or an alteration of the place where the employee is normally to perform the duties of the employment (where both the employer and the duties of the employment remain the same).

The third condition is that the change of residence must be made wholly and mainly to allow the employee to have his or her residence within a reasonable daily travelling distance of the place or new place where the employee is to perform the duties of the employment, new employment or altered employment as the case may be.

The fourth condition is that the employee's former residence is not within a reasonable daily travelling distance of the place where the employee performs or is to perform the duties of the employment.

Travelling and subsistence expenses

3.68 Certain travel and subsistence expenses are disregarded from the computation of earnings for Class 1 National Insurance purposes. These include:

- a payment of, or a contribution towards, travel expenses that the holder of an office or employment is obliged to incur and pay as holder of that office or employment (*SI 2001/1004, Sch 3, Pt VIII, paras 3, 3A, 3ZA, 3ZB*);
- with effect from 6 April 2016, anti-avoidance rules apply where a worker personally provides services to a client and the services are provided under arrangements involving an employment intermediary, unless the arrangements fall within *ITEPA 2003, Pt 2 Ch 8*, the conditions in *ITEPA 2003, ss 51, 52* or *53* are met and the employment intermediary is not a managed service company (*SI 2001/1004, Sch 3, Pt VIII, para 3ZA, 3ZB*);
- with effect in relation to expenses incurred on or after 6 April 2014, a payment of, or a contribution towards, the expenses of the earner's employments if or to the extent that payment or contribution is wholly and exclusively for the purposes of paying or reimbursing travel expenses that meet the following conditions. The first condition (Condition A) is that the earner is obliged to incur the expenses as the holder of the employment and the expenses are attributable to the earner's necessary attendance at any place for the performance of the duties of the employment, the second condition (Condition B) is that the employment is a director of a not-for-profit company and the final condition (Condition C) is that the employment is one from which the earner receives no earnings other than sums paid to the earner in respect of expenses which are paid by reason of the employment (*SI 2001/1004, Sch 3, Pt VIII, para 3A*);
- with effect in relation to expenses incurred on or after 6 April 2014, a payment of, or a contribution towards, the expenses of the earner's employment to the extent that those expenses are travel expenses which are exempt from income tax by virtue of *ITEPA 2003,*

s 241B (where a directorship is held as part of a trade or profession) (*SI 2001/1004, Sch 3, Pt VIII, para 3B*);

- with effect in relation to expenses incurred on or after 6 April 2014, a payment of, or a contribution towards, the expenses of the earner's employment to the extent that those expenses are travel expense deductible for income tax purposes in accordance with *ITEPA 2003, s 340A* (travel between linked employments) (*SI 2001/1004, Sch 3, Pt VIII, para 3C*);
- a payment of, or a contribution towards, the expenses of the earner's employment to the extent that those expenses relate to travel at the start and finish of an overseas employment and are deductible for income tax purposes by virtue of *ITEPA 2003, s 341* or would be so deductible if conditions B and C in that section were omitted and the earnings of the employment were subject to income tax as employment income (*SI 2001/1004, Sch 3, Pt VIII, para 4*);
- a payment of, or contribution towards, the expenses of the earner's employment to the extent that they relate to travel between employments where the duties of the employment are performed abroad and are deductible under *ITEPA 2003, s 342*, or would be so deductible if conditions E and F were omitted from that section and the earnings from the employment were subject to income tax as employment income (*SI 2001/1004, Sch 3, Pt VIII, para 4A*);
- so much of the earner's earnings that equal the included amount in *ITEPA 2003, s 370* in respect of travel costs and expenses in relation to the employee's travel where the duties are performed or the amount that would be the included amount within that section if the earner were resident and ordinarily resident in the UK (*SI 2001/1004, Sch 3, Pt VIII, para 4B*);
- so much of the earner's earnings that equal the included amount in *ITEPA 2003, s 371* in respect of the travel costs and expenses of the employee's visiting spouse, civil partner or children where the duties of the employment are performed abroad or the amount that would be the included amount under that section if the earner were resident and ordinarily resident in the UK (*SI 2001/1004, Sch 3, Pt VIII, para 4C*);
- so much of an employed earner's earnings as equals the amount of the deduction permitted for foreign accommodation and subsistence costs and expenses of an overseas employment under *ITEPA 2003, s 376* or the amount which would be deductible if the earnings of the employment were charged to income tax as employment income under *ITEPA 2003* (*SI 2001/1004, Sch 3, Pt VIII, para 4D*);
- so much of an employed earner's earnings as equal the aggregate amount of the deductions permitted for income tax purposes in relation to the

travel costs and expenses of a non-domiciled employee or employee's spouse, civil partner or children where the duties are performed in the UK under *ITEPA 2003, s 373, 374* or which would be so permitted if the earnings of the employment were subject to tax as employment income under *ITEPA 2003* (*SI 2001/1004, Sch 3, Pt VIII, para 5*); and

- a payment of, or contribution towards, expenses in relation to the travelling expenses of mainland transfers of offshore oil and gas workers where such a payment or contribution is exempt from income tax by virtue of *ITEPA 2003, s 305* (*SI 2001/1004, Sch 3, Pt VIII, para 6*).

Cars, vans, cycles and other vehicles and associated payments

3.69 The following payments are not taken into account when computing earnings for Class 1 National Insurance purposes:

- a payment by way of a discharge of a liability of an employee in connection with a taxable car or van or an exempt heavy goods vehicle which is exempt from income tax by virtue of *ITEPA 2003, s 239(1), (2)*, unless (with effect from 6 April 2018) the payment is made pursuant to an optional remuneration arrangement (*SI 2001/1004, Sch 3, Pt VIII, para 7*);
- to the extent that it would otherwise be earnings, the amount of a qualifying mileage allowance payment in respect of qualifying vehicles other than cars calculated as set out at **3.32**, unless with effect from 6 April 2018, the payment is made pursuant to an optional remuneration arrangement (*SI 2001/1004, Sch 3, Pt VIII, para 7A*);
- to the extent that it would otherwise be earnings, the qualifying amount of a mileage allowance payment in respect of a cycle (calculated by applying the formula in **3.32** using for R the rate approved for cycles under *ITEPA 230(2)*, currently 20p per mile) (*SI 2001/1004, Sch 3, Pt VIII, para 7B*);
- to the extent that it would otherwise be earnings, the qualifying amount of a passenger payment (calculated by applying the formula in **3.32** and using for R the rate approved for passenger payments under *ITEPA 2003, s 234*, currently 5p per mile) (*SI 2001/1004, Sch 3, Pt VIII, para 7C*);
- a payment by way of the provision of car fuel for private motoring in a company car, charged to tax by virtue of *ITEPA 2003, s 149* (*SI 2001/1004, Sch 3, Pt VIII, para 7D*) (but note this is within the Class 1A charge: see Chapter 4);
- a payment by way of the provision of van fuel which is chargeable to income tax by virtue of *ITEPA 2003, s 160* (*SI 2001/1004, Sch 3, Pt VIII, para 7E*) (but note this is within the Class 1A charge: see Chapter 4);

- a payment of, or a contribution towards, the provision of car parking facilities at or near the earner's place of employment which would be exempt from income tax by virtue of *ITEPA 2003, s 237* (*SI 2001/1004, Sch 3, Pt VIII, para 8*).

Other expenses and allowances of the employment

3.70 The following expenses and allowances of employment are disregarded from the computation of earnings for Class 1 National Insurance purposes:

- any amount which is exempt from tax under *ITEPA 2003, s 289A* (exemption for qualifying paid and reimbursed expenses) (*SI 2001/1004, Sch 3, Pt VIII, para 8A);*
- with effect from 6 April 2020, a payment to a person who holds a voluntary office in respect of expenses which is exempted from income tax under *ITEPA 2003, s 229B (SI 2001/1004, Sch 3, Pt VIII, para 8B)*;
- any specific and distinct payment of, or contribution towards, expenses which an employed earner actually incurs in carrying out the duties of the employment (other than mileage allowance payments in excess of the qualifying amount) (*SI 2001/1004, Sch 3, Pt VIII, para 9*);
- a payment of, or a contribution towards meeting, a person's liability for council tax or water or sewerage charges in respect of accommodation occupied by him and provided for him for reason of his employment and where the provision of such accommodation is exempt for income tax purposes by virtue of *ITEPA 2003, s 99, 100* (*SI 2001/1004, Sch 3, Pt VIII, para 10*);
- (Northern Ireland only) a payment of, or a contribution towards meeting a person's liability for rates or water or sewerage charges in respect of accommodation occupied by him and provided for him by reason of his employment if, by virtue of *ITEPA 2003, ss 99, 100* (accommodation provided for performance of duties or as a result of a security threat), he is not liable for tax in respect of the provision of that accommodation (*SI 2001/1004, Sch 3, Pt VIII, para 11);*
- a payment by way of a foreign service allowance for Crown Service employees which is not regarded as income for any income tax purposes by virtue of *ITEPA 2003, s 299* (*SI 2001/1004, Sch 3, Pt VIII, para 12*);
- a payment by the Secretary of State for Defence designated as an Operational Allowance under Royal Warrant made under the *Armed Forces Act 2006, s 333* made to a member of Her Majesty's forces (*SI 2001/1004, Sch 3, Pt VIII, para 12A*);

- a payment designated as Council Tax Relief under Royal Warrant made under the *Armed Forces Act 2006, s 333* made to a member of Her Majesty's forces (*SI 2001/1004, Sch 3, Pt VIII, para 12B*);
- with effect from 6 April 2012, a payment designated as a Continuity of Education Allowance under Royal Warrant made under the *Armed Forces Act 2006, s 333* made to or in respect of members of the armed forces of the Crown (*SI 2001/1004, Sch 3, Pt VII para 12C*);
- with effect from 2 July 2019, a payment of armed forces accommodation allowances in respect of which no liability to tax arises under *ITEPA 2003*;
- a payment by way of an allowance to a person in the service of the Commonwealth War Graves Commission or the British Council paid with a view to compensating him for the extra cost of living outside the UK in order to perform the duties of the employment (*SI 2001/1004, Sch 3, Pt VIII, para 13*);
- a payment of, or a contribution towards, expenses incurred in providing an employee with medical treatment (including all forms of treatment for, and procedures for diagnosing any physical or mental ailment, infirmity or defect) outside the UK (including providing for an employee to be an in-patient) in a case where the need for the treatment arises while the employee is outside the UK for the purposes of performing the duties of the employment or providing insurance for the employee against the cost of such treatment (*SI 2001/1004, Sch 3, Pt VIII, para 14*);
- with effect from 1 January 2015, a payment or reimbursement in respect of recommended medical treatment in respect of which no liability to income tax arises by virtue of *ITEPA 2003, s 320C* (*SI 2001/1004, Sch 3, Pt VIII, para 14A*);.
- a payment in respect of daily subsistence allowances paid by the European Commission to persons whose services are made available to the Commission by their employers under the detached national experts scheme which is exempt from income tax by virtue of *ITEPA 2003, s 304* (*SI 2001/1004, Sch 3, Pt VIII, para 15*);
- with effect from 6 April 2011, a payment in respect of subsistence allowances paid by a specified body of the EU located in the UK to persons who because of their expertise in matters relating to the subject matter of the functions of the body are seconded to the body by their employers. The EU bodies located in the UK specified for these purposes are The European Medicines Agency, The European Police College and The European Banking Authority (*SI 2001/1004, Sch 3, Pt VIII, para 15A*);
- with effect from 28 February 2011, a payment in respect of accommodation expenses of MPs which is exempt from tax by virtue of *ITEPA 2003, s 292* (*SI 2001/1004, Sch 3, Pt VIII, para 16(a)*);

- with effect from 28 February 2011, a payment in respect of overnight expenses of other elected representatives which is exempt from tax by virtue of *ITEPA 2003, s 293* (*SI 2001/1004, Sch 3, Pt VIII, para 16(b)*);
- with effect from 28 February 2011, a payment in respect of UK travel and subsistence expenses of MPS, which is exempt from tax by virtue of *ITEPA 2003, s 293A* (*SI 2001/1004, Sch 3, Pt VIII, para 16(c)*);
- with effect from 1 September 2013, a payment in respect of UK travel expenses or other elected representatives which is exempt from tax by virtue of *ITEPA 2003, s 293B* (*SI 2001/1004, Sch 3, Pt VIII, para 16(ca)*);
- with effect from 28 February 2011, a payment in respect of European travel expenses of MPs and other representatives which is exempt from tax by virtue of *ITEPA 2003, s 294* (*SI 2001/1004, Sch 3, Pt VIII, para 16(d)*); and
- with effect from 6 April 2016, a payment to which no liability to income tax arises by virtue of *ITEPA 2003, s 259A* (*SI 2001/1004, Sch 3, Pt VIII, para 17*).

Incentives by way of securities

3.71 The following payments by way of securities, restricted securities and restricted interests in securities and gains arising from them are disregarded in the computation of earnings for Class 1 National Insurance purposes by virtue of the *Social Security (Contributions) Regulations 2001* (*SI 2001/1004*), *Sch 3, Pt IX*:

- a payment by way of a right to acquire securities (*SI 2001/1004, Sch 3, Pt IX, para 3*);
- a payment by way of an allocation of shares in priority to members of the public in respect of which no liability to income tax arises by virtue of *ITEPA 2003, s 542* (*SI 2001/1004, Sch 3, Pt IX, para 5*);
- a payment that is deducted from the earnings of the employment under a partnership share agreement (within the meaning of *ITEPA 2003, Sch 2, para 44*) forming part of a share incentive plan (*SI 2001/1004, Sch 3, Pt IX, para 6*);
- a payment by way of shares under a share incentive plan (within the meaning of *ITEPA 2003, Sch 2) (SI 2001/1004, Sch 3, Pt IX, para 7*);
- a payment by way of the acquisition (including the acquisition pursuant to an employment-related securities option) of securities, interests in securities or securities options in connection with the employed earner's employment if, or to the extent that, what is acquired is not a readily convertible asset (*SI 2001/1004, Sch 3, Pt IX, para 7A*);

- a payment by way of the acquisition of restricted securities or a restricted interest in securities where those securities are, or that interest is, employment-related if no charge to income tax arises under *ITEPA 2003, s 425* other than by *s 425(2)*, unless an election has been made under *ITEPA 2003, s 425(3) (SI 2001/1004, Sch 3, Pt IX, para 9*);
- a gain realised by the exercise (in whole or in part) of a right obtained before 6 April 1999 to acquire shares in a body corporate (unless falling within the exclusion at **3.67**) but only to the extent that the gain realised consists of the shares acquired (*SI 2001/1004, Sch 3, Pt IX, para 16*);
- a gain realised by the exercise of a replacement right to acquire shares in a body corporate where the original right was satisfied, provided that the exclusion at **3.67** does not apply and, in respect of the transaction through which the replacement right was obtained, A is not substantially greater than R, where A is the market value of the shares which may be obtained by the exercise of the right acquired on that occasion less any consideration which would have to be given on that occasion by and on behalf of the earner (disregarding any restriction on its exercise) and R is the market value of the shares subject to the right assigned or released on that occasion, immediately before that occasion, less any consideration which would have been required to be given by or on behalf of the earner for the exercise of that right, disregarding any restriction on its exercise. Where the transaction involves only a partial replacement of an earlier right, R is proportionately reduced (*SI 2001/1004, Sch 3, Pt IX, para 16A*).

The disregards listed in the last two bullets of the list above do not apply to a payment that is made on or after 10 April 2003, which would otherwise fall to be disregarded where the market value of the shares has increased by more than 10% by things done on or after 6 April 1999, otherwise than for genuine commercial reasons. Things done otherwise than for genuine commercial reasons would include anything that is done as part of a scheme or arrangement, of which the main purpose, or one of the main purposes, is the avoidance of tax or National Insurance contributions or any transaction between companies which, at the time of the transaction, are members of the same group on terms which are such as might be expected to be agreed between persons acting at arm's length (but excluding a payment for group relief within the meaning of *ICTA 1988, s 402(6)*) (*SI 2001/1004, Sch 3, Pt IX, para 17*).

Payments made to internationally mobile employees

3.72 With effect from 6 April 2015, certain payments made to internationally mobile employees are disregarded in the calculation of earnings for Class 1 National Insurance purposes (*SI 2001/1004, Sch 3, Pt IX, para 18*). The amount disregarded is the total of the instalments which satisfy any of the following conditions on the day that the instalment is paid:

- the instalment does not give rise to a liability to pay earnings-related contributions because the employed earner does not fulfil the prescribed conditions as to residence and presence in Great Britain or Northern Ireland set out in *SI 2001/1004, reg 148*;
- the instalment does not give rise to a liability to pay earnings-related contributions because the employed earner is determined to be only subject to the legislation of another EEA State or Switzerland by virtue of *Regulation EC 883/2004 Title II* or *Regulation EC 987/2009 Title II*; or
- the instalment does not give rise to a liability to pay earnings-related contributions because the employed earner is determined to be subject only to the legislation of a country outside the UK, pursuant to an Order made under *SSAA 1992, s 179*.

For the purposes of the calculation of the disregarded amount, amounts that count as employment income under *ITEPA 2003, Pt 7, Ch 2–5* are treated as having been paid in equal instalments on each day of the relevant period, determined in accordance with *ITEPA 2003, s 41G*.

Miscellaneous payments

3.73 The following miscellaneous payments are disregarded in computing earnings for Class 1 National Insurance purposes by virtue of the *Social Security (Contributions) Regulations 2001* (*SI 2001/1004*), *Sch 3, Pt X*:

- a payment on account of a person's earnings in respect of which his employment as an employed earner which comprises or represents and does not exceed sums which have previously been included in his earnings for the purposes of his assessment of earnings-related contributions (*SI 2001/1004, Sch 3, Pt X, para* 2);
- an amount (A) which represents, arises or derives from wholly or part from an amount (B) included as earnings under *SI 2001/1004, reg 22B* (disguised remuneration: see **3.30**) except to the extent that (A) exceeds (B) (*SI 2001/1004, Sch 3, Pt X, para 2A*);
- a payment by way of the discharge of any liability for secondary contributions which have been transferred from the secondary contributor to the employed earner by an election made jointly by them under *SSCBA 1992, Sch 1, para 3B* (*SI 2001/1004, Sch 3, Pt X, para 3*);
- a payment by way of incidental expenses, in whatever form, to the extent that it is charged to income tax by virtue of *ITEPA 2003, s 200A*. Amounts in excess of the permitted maximum (£5 per night for stays in

the UK and £10 per night for stays abroad) are included within earnings unless the payment is by way of a benefit in kind. (*SI 2001/1004, Sch 3, Pt X, para 4*);

- a payment of, or in respect of, a gratuity or offering which is not made directly or indirectly by the secondary contributor and does not comprise or represent sums previously paid to the secondary contributor and the secondary contributor does not allocate the payment directly or indirectly to the earner (*SI 2001/1004, Sch 3, Pt X, para 5*);
- any payment by way of a redundancy payment (*SI 2001/1004, Sch 3, Pt X, para 6*);
- a sickness payment paid from funds for making such payments (of a type mentioned in *SSCBA 1992, s 4(1)*: see **3.25**) to the extent that they are attributable to contributions to those funds by the employed earner (*SI 2001/1004, Sch 3, Pt X, para 7*);
- a payment in respect of travelling and subsistence during public strikes which is not charged to tax by virtue of *ITEPA 2003, s 245* (*SI 2001/1004, Sch 3, Pt X, para 8(a)*);
- a payment in respect of transport between home and work for disabled employees which is not charged to tax by virtue of *ITEPA 2003, s 246* (*SI 2001/1004, Sch 3, Pt X, para 8(b)*);
- a payment in respect of transport home either as a result of late working or the failure of car sharing arrangements which is not charged to tax by virtue of *ITEPA 2003, s 248* (*SI 2001/1004, Sch 3, Pt X, para 8(c)*);
- a payment in respect of accommodation outgoings of ministers of religion not charged to tax by virtue of *ITEPA 2003, s 290A* (*SI 2001/1004, Sch 3, Pt X, para 8(d)*);
- a payment in respect of allowances paid to ministers of religion in respect of accommodation outgoings not charged to tax by virtue of *ITEPA 2003, s 290B* (*SI 2001/1004, Sch 3, Pt X, para 8(e)*);
- a payment in respect of a suggestion scheme award not charged to tax by virtue of *ITEPA 2003, s 321* (*SI 2001/1004, Sch 3, Pt X, para 8(f)*);
- an amount equal to the VAT charged where goods and services are supplied by an earner in employed earner's employment and the earnings paid in respect of that employment include remuneration for the supply of those goods and services and VAT is chargeable on that supply (*SI 2001/1004, Sch 3, Pt X, para 9*);
- a payment in respect of employee liabilities and indemnity insurance which is deductible from general earnings for income tax purposes by virtue of *ITEPA 2003, s 346* (*SI 2001/1004, Sch 3, Pt X, para 10*);
- a payment of, or a contribution towards, any fee, contribution of annual subscription to a professional body, learned society etc which is

deductible from general earnings for income tax purposes by virtue of *ITEPA 2003, ss 343* and *344* (unless provided pursuant to an optional remuneration arrangement) (*SI 2001/1004, Sch 3, Pt X, para 11*);

- a payment of a fee in respect of employment as a minister of religion that does not form part of a stipend or salary paid in respect of that employment (*SI 2001/1004, Sch 3, Pt X, para 13*);
- a payment in lieu of coal or smokeless fuel if the employee is a colliery worker or a former colliery worker, providing that the amount of coal or fuel in respect of which the payment is made does not substantially exceed the amount reasonably required for personal use. It is assumed that this condition is met unless the contrary is shown (*SI 2001/1004, Sch 3, Pt X, para 14*);
- with effect from 26 July 2001, a payment made by an issuer of charge cards, cheque guarantee cards, credit cards or debit cards as a reward to an individual who assists in identifying or recovering lost or stolen cards in the course of his employment as an employed earner, together with any income tax paid by the issuer for the purposes of discharging any liability of the individual to income tax on the payment (*SI 2001/1004, Sch 3, Pt X, para 15*);
- with effect from 17 December 2002, a payment made in accordance with regulations made under the *Education Act 2002, s 186* in respect of the repayment, reduction or extinguishing of the amount payable in respect of a student loan and a payment for the purpose of discharging any liability of the earner to income tax for any tax year where income tax is chargeable in respect of such a payment and the payment is made for the purposes of discharging the income tax liability itself (*SI 2001/1004, Sch 3, Pt X, para 16*);
- with effect from 1 September 2003, a payment by way of income on a notional payment which the employer must account for under *ITEPA 2003, s 710* (*SI 2001/1004, Sch 3, Pt X, para 17*);
- with effect from 6 April 2008, other than in Northern Ireland, any In-Work Emergency Discretion Fund payment made to a person pursuant to arrangements made by the Secretary of State under the *Employment and Training Act 1973* (*SI 2001/1004, Sch 3, Pt X, para 18*);
- with effect from 6 April 2008, in Northern Ireland only, any In-Work Emergency Fund payment made to a person pursuant to arrangements made by the Department of Economic Development under the *Employment and Training Act (Northern Ireland) 1950, s 1* (*SI 2001/1004, Sch 3, Pt X, para 19*);
- with effect from1 July 2008, other than in Northern Ireland, any Up-Front Childcare Fund payment made pursuant to arrangements made by the Secretary of State under the *Employment and Training Act 1973, s 2* (*SI 2001/1004, Sch 3, Pt X, para 20*);

- with effect from 27 October 2008, other than in Northern Ireland, any Better off in Work Credit payment made pursuant to arrangements made by the Secretary of State under the *Employment and Training Act 1973, s 2* (*SI 2001/1004 Sch 3, Pt X, para 21*);
- with effect from 22 February 2011, a payment of a fee in respect of an application to join the scheme administered under the *Protection of Vulnerable Groups (Scotland) Act 2007, s 2* (*SI 2001/1004 Sch 3, Pt X, para 22*);
- with effect from 10 June 2013, the fee for an updating certificate by virtue of the *Police Act 1997, s 116(4)(b), (5)(b)* (*SI 2001/1004 Sch 3, Pt X, para 23(1)*);
- the fee for criminal record certificates (paid under the *Police Act 1997, s 113A(1)(b)*), the fee for enhanced criminal record certificates (paid under the *Police Act 1997, s 113B(1)(b)*, the fee for criminal record certificates: Crown employment (paid under the *Police Act 1997, s 114(1)(b)*) and the fee for enhanced criminal record certificates; judicial appointments and Crown employment (paid under the *Police Act 1997, s 116(1)(b)* where the application is made at the time as an application under *s 116A(4)* or *(5)* of that Act for the certificate to be subject to up-to-date arrangements (*SI 2001/1004 Sch 3, Pt X, para 23(2)*);
- with effect from 1 September 2013, a payment, or reimbursement, in accordance with the *Employment Rights Act 1996, s 205A(7)* of any reasonable costs of obtaining relevant advice in relation to a proposed employee shareholder agreement (*SI 2001/1004, Sch 3, Pt X, para 24*);
- with effect for the tax year 2014/15 and subsequent tax years, any payment made by an employer to an employed earner which represents the amount on which Class 1 or Class 1A contributions are payable by a limited liability partnership in respect of that earner by virtue of the *Social Security Contributions (limited Liability Partnership) Regulations 2014, regs 3, 4* (*SI 2001/1004, Sch 3, Pt X, para 25*).

Certain payments by trustees disregarded in the computation of earnings

3.74 Any payment or part of a payment that is made by trustees before 6 April 1990, the amount of which is, or may be dependent upon, the exercise by the trustees of a discretion or the performance by them of a duty arising under the trust and which not being a sickness payment by virtue of *SSCBA 1992, s 4(1)* (see **3.33**) is treated as remuneration derived from an employed earner's employment is disregarded in the computation of earnings for Class 1 National Insurance purposes if either of the conditions set out below is met (the *Social Security (Contributions) Regulations 2001* (*SI 2001/1004*), *reg 26(1)*).

The first condition is satisfied if the trust, under which the payment is made, was created before 6 April 1985 (*SI 2001/1004, reg 26(2)*).

The second condition is satisfied if:

- the trust under which the payment is made was created on or after 6 April 1985;
- that trust took effect immediately on the termination of a trust created before 6 April 1985;
- the person to whom the payment is made was either a beneficiary under an earlier trust or would have been such a beneficiary if, while the earlier trust was subsisting, he or she had held the employment in respect of which the payment is made; and
- there were, or are, payments under the earlier trust which in the case of payments made on or after 6 October 1987 are payments made in circumstances to which the above apply.

Payments to directors disregarded in the computations of earnings

3.75 A payment by a company to, or for the benefit of, a director of that company in respect of any employed earner's employment of that director with that company and in respect of which one of the conditions below is satisfied is disregarded in the computation of earnings for Class 1 National Insurance contributions (the *Social Security (Contributions) Regulations 2001 (SI 2001/1004), reg 27(1)*).

The first condition (*SI 2001/1004, reg 27(2)*) is satisfied if:

- the director is a partner in a firm carrying on a profession;
- being a director of a company is a normal incident of membership of that profession and of membership of the firm of the director;
- the director is required by the terms of his partnership to account to his firm for the payment; and
- the payments form an insubstantial part of that firm's gross returns.

The second condition (*SI 2001/1004, reg 27(3)*) is satisfied if:

- the director was appointed to that office by a company having the right to do so by virtue of its shareholding in, or an agreement with, the company making the payment;
- by virtue of an agreement with the company that appointed him, the director is required to account for the payment to that company; and
- the payment forms part of the profits brought into charge to corporation tax or income tax of the company that appointed the director.

The third condition (*SI 2001/1004, reg 27(4)*) is satisfied if:

- the director was appointed to that office by a company other than a company making the payment;
- by virtue of an agreement with the company that appointed him, the director is required to account for the payment to that company;
- the payment forms part of the profits brought into charge to corporation tax if the company that appointed the director; and
- the company that appointed the director is not one which the director has, or any person connected with the director has, or the director and any persons connected with him together have, control.

Earnings normally paid after pensionable age

3.76 Where in a year in which an earner attains pensionable age, a payment of earnings is made to the earner before the date on which he reaches pensionable age but which would normally be paid in a later year, no primary Class 1 liability arises in respect of those earnings (*SI 2001/1004, reg 28*).

However, if earnings are paid after the date on which pensionable age is attained but would normally be paid before that date, the exception from primary Class 1 contributions does not apply (*SI 2001/1004, reg 29*).

Coronavirus home office expenses

3.77 For a temporary period, an amount which represents the reimbursement of coronavirus related home office expenses is disregarded in the computation of earnings (*Social Security Contributions (Disregarded Payments) (Coronavirus) Regulations 2020, SI 2020/525*).

For the purposes of the disregard, 'coronavirus related home office expenses' are expenses incurred in respect of the equipment where:

- that equipment was obtained for the sole purpose of enabling the employee to work from home as a result of the coronavirus outbreak; and
- the provision of the equipment would have been exempt from tax under *ITEPA 2003, s 316* if it had been provided directly to the employed earner by or on behalf of the secondary contributor.

The disregard applies on a statutory basis in respect of payments made on or after 11 June 2020 until the end of the 2020/21 tax year. However, HMRC have confirmed that they will apply the disregard on a concessionary basis from 16 March 2020 to 11 June 2020. Thus, employed earners who purchased equipment to work at home at the start of the lockdown and were reimbursed prior to 11 June 2020 will also benefit from the disregard.

Separate regulations, the *Social Security (Disregarded Payments) Coronavirus Regulations 2021 (SI 2021/242), reg 3(2)* apply the disregard for the 2021/22 tax year.

NHS track and trace support payments

3.78 NHS track and trace support payments of £500 may be paid by a local authority to individuals in England who are on low income and who are unable to work because they are required to self-isolate, either because they have tested positive for Coronavirus or because they have been in close contact with someone who has tested positive for Coronavirus. The *Social Security Contributions (Disregarded Payments) (Coronavirus) (England) Regulations 2020 (SI 2020/1065)* provide for the payments to be disregarded in the calculation of earnings for Class 1 National Insurance purposes.

Coronavirus tests

3.79 A payment that is made to an employed earner in respect of the cost of a coronavirus test taken or to be taken by that employed earner is disregarded in calculation of the earner's earnings for the purposes of earnings-related contributions. The payment is also disregarded in the computation of Class 1A National Insurance contributions (*Social Security Contributions) (Disregarded Payments) (Coronavirus) (No 2) Regulations 2020 (SI 2020/1523)*). Separate regulations, the *Social Security (Disregarded Payments) Coronavirus Regulations 2021 (SI 2021/242), reg 3(3)*, apply the disregard for the 2021/22 tax year.

Payments of earnings to directors

3.80 Although the same rules apply to directors as to other employees in determining what should and should not be included in gross pay for Class 1 National Insurance purposes, there are some payments that are unique to directors and in respect of which the following rules apply.

For these purposes, 'director' means (*Social Security (Contributions) Regulations 2001 (SI 2001/1004) reg 1*:

- in relation to a company whose affairs are managed by a board of directors or similar body, a member of that board or similar body;
- in relation to a company whose affairs are managed by a single director or similar person, that director or person; and

- any person in accordance with whose directions or instructions the company's directors (as defined above) are accustomed to act (but excluding any person on whose advice the directors act where that advice is given in a professional capacity only).

HMRC guidance on the treatment of payments made to directors can be found in booklet CA44, *National Insurance for Company Directors*, the latest edition of which is available to download from the gov.uk website (see www.gov.uk/government/publications/ca44-national-insurance-for-company-directors).

Fees and bonuses

3.81 The general rule is that when fees and bonuses are voted to directors, the fees and bonuses are added to all other earnings paid in the annual earnings period and National Insurance contributions are assessed on the total.

However, there are exceptions to this general rule and these are outlined below.

Payments made in advance or in anticipation of voting

3.82 Payments that are made in advance or in anticipation of the voting of fees or bonuses are earnings for National Insurance contributions. Class 1 National Insurance contributions are due at the time that the payments are made.

If contributions have not been paid at the time the payment was made (for example if the primary threshold had not been reached) National Insurance contributions are due at the time the fees or bonuses are voted.

If the fees or bonuses voted are less than the advance or anticipatory payments and National Insurance contributions were paid at the time that the payments were made, no further National Insurance contributions are due at the time of the vote.

If the fees or bonuses are waived or refunded wholly or partially to the company after they have been voted, National Insurance contributions are due on any advance or anticipatory payments and the balance of any fees and bonuses.

Directors' accounts

3.83 A director may have an account with the company, such as a loan account or a current account.

Class 1 National Insurance contributions are due when fees and bonuses are voted and credited to the account and are calculated using the rates applying at the time of the vote.

However, no Class 1 National Insurance liability arises when the director withdraws money from the account, provided that the account is in credit.

However, if the account goes overdrawn or the amount by which it is overdrawn increases, a Class 1 National Insurance liability arises in respect of the overdrawn amount or the increase in the overdrawn amount, unless the withdrawal is made in anticipation of payments (such as dividends) which are not earnings for Class 1 National Insurance purposes.

In the event that the director uses his or her account with the company to settle personal bills, a National Insurance liability will arise if the account goes overdrawn and the debiting of the account is made in anticipation of a payment that is earnings (such as fees or a bonus). Class 1 National Insurance contributions are due in this situation on the overdrawn amount, or the increase in the overdrawn amount, as appropriate. In calculating the liability, the rates applying at the time that the account is debited should be used.

No Class 1 National Insurance liability arises if the account becomes overdrawn or further overdrawn on the payment of a personal bill and the debit is made in anticipation of a payment that is not earnings (such as dividends).

If withdrawal of funds to pay personal bills triggers the overdraft or increase in the overdraft but the director does not normally receive advance or anticipatory payments, the withdrawal does not give rise to a Class 1 National Insurance liability, unless the company authorises the overdraft. This can be done either in writing or verbally by the other directors agreeing that they know about the overdraft.

Fees voted to a future period

3.84 If fees are voted to a future period, the Class 1 National Insurance liability arises when the fees are made available to the director.

Repayment of loans

3.85 In the event that a director lends money to the company, any repayment of that loan does not constitute earnings for Class 1 National Insurance purposes. This means that no Class 1 National Insurance contributions are due on the repayment.

Company pension

3.86 If a director receives a pension from the company, that pension is not earnings for Class 1 National Insurance purposes. However, normal rules apply to fees, bonuses and salary paid after the director has retired.

If the director is above pension age, no primary Class 1 contributions are due on payments of earnings, although the secondary Class 1 liability remains.

What to include in gross pay for National Insurance purposes: HMRC guidance

3.87 The rules on what constitutes earnings are complicated and are not always easy to apply in practice. The position is further complicated by the fact that the same rules do not always apply for National Insurance and PAYE purposes. HMRC booklet CWG2, *Employer's Further Guide to PAYE and NICs* contains guidance to help employers decide whether they need to include a particular payment within gross pay for National Insurance purposes. Items included within gross pay for National Insurance purposes are liable for Class 1 National Insurance contributions. The latest edition of the booklet is available to download from the gov.uk website (see www.gov.uk/government/publications/cwg2-further-guide-to-paye-and-national-insurance-contributions). Chapter 5 of the 2020/21 edition sets out what to include and exclude in gross pay for National Insurance purposes.

Guidance on earnings for Class 1 National Insurance purposes can also be found in HMRC's National Insurance Manual at NIM02000ff.

EARNINGS PERIODS

Concept of earnings period basis

3.88 Unlike PAYE, the liability for Class 1 National Insurance contributions is not computed on a cumulative basis. Instead, the liability is computed separately for each earnings period without any reference to earnings in any previous earnings periods in the tax year. The earnings in each earnings period are aggregated and the liability is computed by reference to total earnings in the earnings period.

Thus, in order to compute the Class 1 National Insurance liability correctly, it is necessary first to identify the appropriate earnings period and then to compute the earnings for that earnings period.

Normally, the earnings period is the regular interval between which payments are made. However, where the employee is not paid at regular intervals, special rules are needed to determine the earnings period.

Special rules also apply in relation to directors to prevent manipulation of the earnings period rules to reduce the amount of National Insurance payable (see **3.97**). Under these rules, directors have an annual earnings period.

HMRC guidance on the earnings period rules can be found in the HMRC publication CWG2, *Employer's Further Guide to PAYE and NIC*. The latest edition is available on the gov.uk website at www.gov.uk/government/publications/cwg2-further-guide-to-paye-and-national-insurance-contributions.

> **Focus**
>
> Class 1 National Insurance contributions are contributed on a non-cumulative basis for each earnings period. Directors have an annual earnings period.

Employees paid at regular intervals

3.89 Where the employee is paid at a regular interval, determining the earnings period is straightforward. The earnings period corresponds with the regular payment period, so that if the employee is paid weekly, the earnings period is a week, if the employee is paid monthly, the earnings period is a month and so on.

The following tables illustrates the corresponding earnings period for various regular pay intervals.

Pay interval	Earnings period
Weekly	Weekly
Fortnightly	Two weekly
Four weekly	Four weekly
Monthly	Monthly
Quarterly	Quarterly
Half-yearly	Half yearly
Yearly	Yearly

Example 3.7—Determining earning periods

Ben is paid weekly every Thursday. His earning periods are weekly.

If an employee is paid at regular intervals, but the date on which the payment is made changes, the employee should be treated as being paid at regular intervals but National Insurance contributions should be worked out on each payment, even if two or more payments are made in the same earnings period.

Employees not paid at regular intervals but treated as being paid at regular intervals

3.90 Where the payment is not made at a regular interval, but there is a regular pattern covering the period for which the payment is made, the earnings period corresponds with that regular pattern. For example, if an employee is paid monthly on the last Friday of the month, for some months the payment interval will be four-weekly and for other months it will be five-weekly.

If the contract shows the pay as a monthly amount, the earnings period is treated as a month, irrespective of the fact that not all the earnings periods in the tax year will be the same length.

Employees paid at irregular intervals

3.91 Determining the earnings period is more complicated where the employee is not paid at regular intervals. The general rule when an employee is paid irregularly is that the earnings period is the period that the payment covers or one week, whichever is longer.

In the event that it is not practicable to determine the earnings period in this way, the earnings period is taken to be from the date of the previous payment to the date of the current payment or, if the employee is new, the date from which the employment began to the date of the first payment.

An earnings period cannot be less than a week. If the rules outlined above give a period of less than a week, the earnings period is taken to be one week.

It should be noted that if the employee is paid in irregular or unequal payments and it is determined that this practice avoids National Insurance contributions, HMRC can direct that NICs are worked out on a different basis (see **3.96**).

Employees with more than one set of regular payments

3.92 It may be that an employee is paid more than one set of regular payments, each with a different (but regular) payment interval. An example would be an employee who receives a salary each month and commission each quarter. In this scenario, the employee receives both regular monthly and regular quarterly payments.

In a situation such as this, the rule is that the earnings period is the shorter of the regular intervals. In the example cited above, this would be a month. The payments received in that period are added together and Class 1 National Insurance contributions are worked out on the total.

Example 3.8—Determining the earnings period: more than one regular payment of earnings

Oliver is paid a monthly salary of £5,000 on the last Friday of each month. He is also paid commission on a quarterly basis.

In September 2021, Oliver receives his regular salary of £5,000 and commission of £2,000. His Class 1 National Insurance liability is calculated on the total payments in the month of £7,000 using a monthly earnings period of September 2021.

However, it should be noted that where there is more than one regular pay interval and HMRC determine that most of the earnings are paid by reference to the longer pay interval, they may direct the employer to work out the National Insurance contributions due by reference to the longer pay interval.

If the employer is directed to use an annual earnings period, the earnings period for the remainder of the tax year will be the number of weeks left in that tax year at the time that the direction is made.

New starters

3.93 An employee may start work part way through the normal pay interval. When making the first payment of earnings to a new starter, Class 1 National Insurance contributions are calculated by reference to what will be the normal pay interval for the employment. This rule applies even if the interval between the start date and the first pay day is less than the normal earnings period.

Example 3.9—Determining the earnings period for new starters: scenario 1

An employee starts work on 9August 2021. His contract states that he will be paid monthly on the last Friday of the calendar month. His first pay day is 31 August 2021.

Although the employee has not worked the full month, an earnings period of one month is used to work out the Class 1 National Insurance contributions due in respect of the payment of earnings made on 31 August 2021.

However, if the first payment to the employee spans more than two earnings periods in the same tax year, the earnings should be worked out separately for each of those earnings periods.

Example 3.10—Determining the earnings period for new starters: scenario 2

An employee starts work on 9 August 2021. His contract states that he will be paid on the last Friday of the month, but the employee is not paid for the first time until 24 September 2021. The employee is paid £5,000 of which £4,000 relates to September 2021 and £1,000 relates to August 2021.

The payment must be split and the NICs worked out separately. The employee is treated as if he had been paid £1,000 in August and £4,000 in September. A monthly earnings period is used in each case.

In the event that the interval between the employee starting work and the first pay day spans two or more earnings periods, which fall in different tax years, the same rule applies. The payment is split and the NICs are worked out separately for each period. However, in working out the Class 1 National

Insurance contributions due, the rates and limits at the time the payment was actually made should be used (i.e. those for the new tax year).

Similar rules apply when an employee leaves the employer's employment.

Unusual pay day

3.94 An employee may occasionally be paid on a day other than the normal pay day, for example because the usual pay day falls on a bank holiday. If this situation arises, the procedure depends on whether the actual date of payment and usual date of payment fall in the same tax year. If they do, the rule is to treat the payment made at a different time as if it had been made on the usual pay day and work out NICs by reference to the normal earnings period. If the actual date and usual date fall in different tax years, the actual payment date is used, unless the normal payment date was a non-banking day.

If the usual payment day is a non-banking day (Saturday, Sunday or a bank holiday) and the payment is made early or late as a result, the payment is treated as being made on the usual payment date.

If a payment made early or late is paid at the same time as another regular payment of earnings (for example a weekly paid employee is paid two weeks' earnings together), the Class 1 National Insurance contributions should be worked out separately on each payment.

Abnormal pay practices

3.95 It is possible to reduce the overall Class 1 National Insurance contributions payable by manipulating the timing and amount of earnings paid. Where HMRC consider that abnormal pay practices have been followed, they have the power (by virtue of the *Social Security (Contributions) Regulations 2001* (*SI 2001/1004*), *reg 30*) to determine the contributions due as if the abnormal pay practice had not been followed and instead the earner had been paid in accordance with a practice that was normal for the employment in question.

An abnormal pay practice is a practice in the payment of earnings that is abnormal for the employment in question.

Because directors have greater scope to influence the time and manner of payments made to them, special earnings period rules apply to directors. These are outlined at **3.96**.

> **Focus**
>
> Anti-avoidance provisions apply to target attempts to avoid/reduce the amount of National Insurance payable by manipulating the timing and the amount of payments.

Practices designed to reduce liability

3.96 The non-cumulative nature of earnings for National Insurance purposes means that it is possible to manipulate earnings to reduce the overall Class 1 National Insurance bill. For example, by paying very little earnings in one earnings period and larger payments in another earnings period, the overall Class 1 National Insurance bill may be lower than if regular payments are made. The following example illustrates this.

Example 3.11—Making irregular payments to reduce liability

John is paid £3,000 each month. For September and October 2021, his Class 1 National Insurance liability in each month is £264.36 (12% (£3,000 – £797)). This gives a combined primary Class 1 liability for the two months of £528.72.

However, if instead John was paid £700 in September and £5,300 in October his primary Class 1 National Insurance liability would be as follows:

September – no primary Class 1 National Insurance contributions are due as earnings for the month of £700 are below the monthly primary threshold for 2021/22 of £797.

October – Primary Class 1 National Insurance contributions due are £429.26 ((12% (£4,189 – £797)) + (2% (£5,300 – £4,189))).

The combined primary Class 1 contributions payable for September and October are now £429.26.

By making uneven payments, the primary Class 1 National Insurance bill for April and May is reduced from £528.72 to £429.26, a saving of £99.46. This is achieved by moving earnings from the 12% rate to the 2% rate.

Not surprisingly HMRC are not happy with this and legislation exists to counter the practice.

The *Social Security (Contributions) Regulations 2001* (*SI 2001/1004*), *reg 31* contain powers such that where a practice exists as to the making of irregular or unequal payments for the purpose of reducing or avoiding National Insurance contributions, HMRC may make a direction to secure the contributions that would have been due had that practice not been followed.

To prevent directors manipulating their earnings to reduce their National Insurance liability, special earnings period rules apply to directors. These are set out at **3.97**.

Directors' earnings periods

3.97 The scope of a director to influence the time and amount of payments of earnings is considerably greater than for the average employee. As illustrated at Example 3.11 it is possible to reduce the overall National Insurance bill by making uneven payments of earnings. The non-cumulative nature of National Insurance contributions makes it possible to manipulate earnings to reduce the overall amount payable by taking advantage of the lower rate of primary Class 1 contributions payable once the upper earnings limit has been reached. A person who is paid £3,000 each month of the year will pay considerably more in primary contributions than someone who is paid £400 for 11 months and £31,600 for one month, even though their total earnings for the year are the same.

To counter this, directors have an annual earnings period (the *Social Security (Contributions) Regulations 2001* (*SI 2001/1004*), *reg 8*). This means that regardless of the interval at which payments are made to the director throughout the tax year, the National Insurance liability is worked out on an annual basis using the total earnings in the year and the annual limits.

Where the director is appointed after the start of the tax year, a pro-rata earnings period applies. Where a pro-rata annual earnings period applies, the lower earnings limit, primary threshold and upper earnings limit are proportionately reduced when calculating the primary Class 1 National Insurance contributions due.

However, if the director is a director at the start of the tax year and resigns part way through the tax year, the earnings period is not proportionately reduced. However, for any subsequent tax year where he or she receives earnings other than as a director, the annual earnings period rules do not apply.

For administrative ease, National Insurance contributions can be worked out in the same way as for other employees on the earnings paid for each pay period, with payments being made on account of the final liability throughout the year (see **3.116**). A recalculation on an annual basis is performed when the last payment is made and any outstanding National Insurance due is paid at that time.

The calculation of Class 1 National Insurance contributions on directors' earnings is explained in more detail at **3.115**.

Focus

Directors have an annual earnings period for Class 1 National Insurance. However, to spread the liability more evenly, the liability can, if preferred, be calculated for each pay period as for other employees, performing an annual recalculation in the last period of the tax year.

3.98 The definition of 'director' is wide and extends beyond someone registered as a director with Companies House. For these purposes (and by virtue of the *Social Security (Contributions) Regulations 2001* (*SI 2001/1004*), *reg 1(2)*) a director means:

- in relation to a company whose affairs are managed by a board of directors or similar body, a member of that board or similar body;
- in relation to a company whose affairs are managed by a single director or similar person, that director or person; and
- any person in accordance with whose directions or instructions the company's directors (as defined above) are accustomed to act.

However, a person giving advice in a professional capacity is not treated as a director.

AGGREGATION OF EARNINGS

Overview of the aggregation rules

3.99 Class 1 National Insurance contributions are not payable until the primary threshold is reached. Potentially, the overall National Insurance bill could be reduced by fragmenting a job to take advantage of multiple NIC-free bands. This is illustrated by the following example.

Example 3.12—Aggregation of earnings

Molly has a job which pays her £2,000 a month. In 2021/22 she pays primary Class 1 National Insurance contributions each month of £144.36 (12% (£2,000 – £797)).

Her employer decides to split her job into two separate jobs. She is paid £800 a month for one job and £1,200 a month for the other. For each job she is able to earn up to the monthly primary threshold of £797 per month before paying any National Insurance contributions.

In respect of job 1, in 2021/22 she pays primary Class 1 National Insurance contributions each month of £0.36 (12% (£800 – £797)).

In respect of job 2, in 2021/22 she pays primary Class 1 National Insurance contributions each month of £48.36 (12% (£1,200 – £797)).

By splitting her job, her primary Class 1 liability is reduced from £144.36 per month to £48.72 (£0.36 + £48.36) per month, a saving of £95.64 (£797 @12%), achieved as a result of the availability of a second NIC-free band for earnings up to the primary threshold (£797 per month for 2021/22).

Clearly, HMRC are not going to allow jobs to be split just to reduce the amount of National Insurance contributions payable. The aggregation of earnings rules exist to counter this practice and require the earnings from two or more jobs to be aggregated when certain conditions apply. These are examined at **3.100**.

Requirement to aggregate

3.100 Where an employee has more than one job it may be necessary to aggregate the earnings from those jobs for the purposes of calculating the Class 1 National Insurance liability (*SSCBA 1992, Sch 1, para 1*). Whether it is necessary to aggregate will depend of the relationship between the employers.

If the employee has one or more jobs and the employers are not associated, the earnings are not aggregated and the Class 1 National Insurance liability is computed separately for each job. This means that the primary and secondary thresholds remain available in respect of each job. Consequently the employee will pay less National Insurance than if he or she had one job with the same total earnings.

However, if the employers are carrying on business in association with each other, the earnings from each job must be added together and the Class 1 National Insurance liability computed on the total unless it is not practicable to do so (see **3.101**). This is to prevent associated employers splitting jobs to reduce the National Insurance bill.

Employers are considered to be carrying on a business in association if:

- their businesses serve a common purpose; and
- to a significant degree they share such things as accommodation, personnel or customers.

If the employee has two or more jobs with the same employer, the earnings from each job in the earnings period must be added together and National Insurance contributions calculated by reference to the total earnings, unless such aggregation is not reasonably practicable (see **3.101**).

HMRC guidance on the aggregation of earnings can be found in their National Insurance Manual at NIM 10000ff.

Example 3.13—Requirement to aggregate earnings

Julia has one job with X Ltd in which she earns £2,000 a month. She also has a job with Y Ltd earning £1,500 a month.

X Ltd and Y Ltd are both owned by Z Ltd. The businesses both operate in the marketing consultancy sector and operate out of the same building. They are considered to be associated.

Consequently, unless aggregation is not reasonably practicable, the earnings from both jobs must be added together and the Class 1 liability for the month computed on Julia's total earnings of £3,500.

In the event that an employee has two or more jobs with different employers but receives a single payment for those jobs and the employers are carrying on business in association with each other, the Class 1 National Insurance liability is computed on the total payment by the employer who makes the payment of earnings. However, if the employers are not carrying on business in association with each other, each employer must pay Class 1 National Insurance contributions on their share of the payment.

Exception from the requirement to aggregate

3.101 Employers are relieved from the requirement to aggregate earnings from two or more jobs where aggregation would normally be required if it is not reasonably practicable to aggregate.

The phrase 'not reasonably practicable to aggregate' is not defined in the legislation. However, guidance on when HMRC will accept that aggregation not to be reasonably practicable is found in booklet CWG2, *Employer's Further Guide to PAYE and NICs*, which is available on the Gov.uk website at www.hmrc.gov.uk/government/publications/cwg2-further-guide-to-paye-and-national-insurance-contributions and in HMRC's National Insurance Manual at NIM10009.

For example, HMRC may accept that aggregation is not practicable if the employers operate a computerised payroll that is unable to perform an aggregated calculation and the calculation would have to be performed manually. However, if this is claimed as a reason for not aggregating, the employer may be required to demonstrate this to be the case.

Where an employer claims that it is not reasonably practicable to aggregate earnings, the onus is on the employer to show this to be the case, taking into account the costs, resources and effects of aggregation on running the business. In deciding if the test has been met, HMRC will consider the following:

- is it a fact that the payroll software cannot aggregate;
- is the payroll software provided by an external supplier or by an internal IT section;
- does the software supplier provide an update package that includes aggregation;
- if the calculation has to be performed manually, what are the costs;
- how many employees are potentially affected; and
- has there been a material change in the labour force since the decision to not aggregate was taken.

In relation to the issue of whether it is 'reasonably practicable' to aggregate earnings, the case of *Mailer v Austin Rover Group* [1989] 2 All ER 1087 determined that:

- 'reasonably practicable' was narrower than 'physically possible';

- risk has to be measured against the cost of removing it; and
- account has to be taken of the likelihood of the risk.

In commenting on the principles established in this case, HMRC note (in their National Insurance Manual at NIM10009) that:

> 'Taking the principles in order:
>
> - It is always possible to aggregate but that is not the test. And the "separately calculated" provision is not failed merely because it is the same employer or payroll system.
> - Costs to the employer are not just financial. Time, effort and the effect on the business have to be considered because the weight of the cost of compliance should not be disproportionate to the loss of National Insurance contributions and benefit entitlement.
> - *Mailier* and other cases are generally considering whether there is a duty to guard against unknown and unexpected events. It is the Department's view that employers have a very limited argument on the third bullet point because aggregation is a known and recurring event. However, that is not enough to negate any informed judgement by an employer that aggregation is not reasonably practicable.

The cases consider the balance between risk on one hand and the sacrifices necessary for averting the risk on the other. Basically, an employer needs to balance his employee's interests against his own costs. It is very important that the consequences for the primary contributor are considered, especially the low paid, because of the potential loss of benefits and pension rights.

The employer can only make an informed decision if all the facts are established because 'reasonably practicable' is related to the individual circumstances. The evidence is that employers with computerised payrolls are the ones who find difficulty in complying with the need to aggregate. However, the existence of such a payroll is not enough evidence that aggregation is not practicable. Manual or other fixes will have to be considered and costed especially when there will be similar risks in future years if aggregation is not achieved and the employer will have to revisit the issue.

The Department takes account of the following points when comparing the costs of aggregation against the risks to contributors:

- Is it a fact, rather than an assumption, that payroll software cannot aggregate earnings?
- Is the payroll software an outside package, tailored package, provided by an internal IT section or able to be upgraded by internal resources? Has the payroll system been changed? If so, why was an aggregation requirement not part of the new specification?
- Does the provider of an outside or tailored package give an update service that includes aggregation? Is it possible to upgrade or would the

employer have to buy a new system? What are the costs of upgrading the software? Is there a dedicated internal IT team that might be able to provide it cheaply subject to competing claims for their services?

- If the work has to be carried out manually what are the costs? Does the employer already have a manual support resource for payroll glitches, urgent payments and so on? Would new staff be required? What is entailed in staff years in manually calculating the NICs, which takes into account that experience will reduce the need for the initial, possibly untrained, resource?
- How many employees are potentially affected? What is the total number of employees on the payroll? Do employees have similar pay periods? Is aggregation a continuing requirement or a one-off consideration because of a particular project or task? What are the amounts of NICs at stake and the effect on the NIF and primary contributors? How does this compare to the costs of compliance?
- Has there been a material change in the labour force since the decision not to aggregate was taken? Or a material change in the state benefits that aggregation could bring (State Second Pension may be relevant here).'

ANNUAL MAXIMUM AND DEFERMENT

Annual maximum for primary Class 1 National Insurance contributions

3.102 There is a cap on the contributions payable by any employed or self-employed earner in any one tax year. This is known as the annual maximum. However, there is no maximum limit on the contributions payable by a secondary contributor.

It may be necessary to consider the annual maximum for Class 1 contributions if an employed earner has two or more jobs or if an employed earner is simultaneously self-employed.

The annual maximum for Class 1 National Insurance contributions purposes is calculated in accordance with the *SSCBA 1992, s 19(2)* and the *Social Security (Contributions) Regulations 2001* (*SI 2001/1004*), *reg 21* as follows:

Step one

Calculate 53 × (UEL – PT)

Where:

UEL is the weekly upper earnings limit and PT is the weekly earnings threshold for primary Class 1 National Insurance purposes.

Step two

Multiply the result of step 1 by 12%.

Step three

Add together, in respect of all the employed earner's employments, so much of the earnings in each of those employments as exceeds the primary threshold and does not exceed the upper earnings limit.

Step four

From the sum produced in step 3, subtract the amount found by the formula in step 1.

Step five

If the result found by step 4 is a positive value, multiply it by 2%.

If the result is nil or a negative value, it is treated for the purposes of step 8 as nil.

Step six

Add together, in respect of all the employed earner's employments, so much of the earnings in each of those employments as exceeds the upper earnings limit.

Step seven

Multiply the sum produced in step 6 by 2%.

Step eight

Add together the amounts produced by steps 2, 5 and 7.

The result of step 8 is the annual maximum subject to the following qualifications.

Where the earner pays primary contributions on band earnings at a rate of less than 12% because the earner is either in a contracted-out employment or a married woman with a valid reduced rate election, for the purposes of computing the annual maximum, a rate of 12% is used at step 2 of the calculation.

Example 3.14—Annual maximum on primary Class 1 contributions

Mark has two jobs in 2021/22. The jobs are not related. He earns £60,000 from one job and £18,000 from the other job.

The maximum amount of primary Class 1 National Insurance contributions that he is liable to pay in 2021/22 is as follows:

Step 1

The primary threshold for 2021/22 is £184 per week and the upper earnings limit is £967 per week.

53 × (UEL – PT) = 53 × (£967 – £184) = 53 × £783 = £41,499.

Step 2

£41,499 × 12% = £4,979.88.

Step 3

For 2021/22 the annual primary threshold is £9,568 and the annual upper earnings limit is £50,270.

Earnings exceeding the primary threshold and not exceeding the upper earnings limits are (£18,000 – £9,568) + (£50,270 – £9,568) = £8,432 + £40,702 = £49,132.

Step 4

£49,132 – £41,499 = £7,633.

Step 5

£7,633 × 2% = £152.66.

Step 6

Earnings exceeding the upper earning limit

£60,000 – £50,270 = £9,730.

Step 7

£9,730 × 2% = £194.60.

Step 8

£4,979.88. + £152.66 + £194.60 = £5,327.14.

Therefore the maximum primary Class 1 National Insurance contributions that Mark is liable to pay in respect of his jobs is £5,327.14.

Focus

The amount of primary Class 1 contributions payable by an individual for a tax year where that individual has more than one job is subject to a cap – the annual maximum. There is, however, no cap on secondary contributions.

Deferment

3.103 If in any tax year, where an employed earner has two or more employed earner's employments it may be possible to defer the payment of primary contributions in respect of one or more jobs. This will be possible where the contributions payable will exceed the annual maximum. Applying for a deferment removes the need to pay the contributions initially and subsequently to claim a repayment for those contributions paid in excess of the annual maximum after the year end.

The extent to which deferment is possible will depend both on the number of employments and the level of earnings in those employments. For 2021/22, a person who has two employments, where earnings in one of those employments is at least equal to the upper earnings limit of £967 per week (£4,189 per month), will be able to defer contributions in respect of the other employment.

If for 2021/22 the employee has three employments and earnings from at least one of those employments is £967 per week for each week of the tax year (or £4,189 each month), deferment is permitted in respect of the remaining employments. Alternatively, where the combined earnings from two of those employments are at least equal to the upper earnings limit plus the primary threshold, which for 2021/22 is £1,151 per week (£967 + £184) or £4,986 (£4,189 + £797) per month for each week/month of the tax year, deferment is permitted in respect of the remaining employment.

For any number of employments, if the earnings from one employment are at least equal to the upper earnings (£967 per week, £4,189 per month for 2021/22) deferment is permitted in respect of the other employments. However, if the earnings from all jobs are less than the UEL, deferment may still be possible if the earnings criterion is met.

The earnings criterion is found by applying the following formula:

$$UEL + (E-1)\ WPT$$

Where:

- UEL is the weekly upper earnings limit (£967 for 2021/22);
- WPT is the weekly primary threshold (£184 for 2021/22); and
- E is the number of employments from which earnings are taken into account in satisfying the earnings criterion.

If the earnings criterion is met, Class 1 contributions may be deferred in respect of the employments whose earnings were not taken into account in satisfying the earnings criterion.

The following table summarises the earning criterion which must be met for value of E from 1 to 10 for 2021/22:

E **Number of employments for which earnings are taken into account**	**UEL + (E–1) WPT** **Maximum weekly earnings from those employments for deferment to be permitted in respect of remaining employments (2021/22)**
1	£967
2	£1,151
3	£1,335
4	£1,519
5	£1,703

E **Number of employments for which earnings are taken into account**	**UEL + (E–1) WPT** **Maximum weekly earnings from those employments for deferment to be permitted in respect of remaining employments (2021/22)**
6	£1,887
7	£2,071
8	£2,255
9	£2,439
10	£2,623

Example 3.15—Deferment

Sarah has four jobs in 2021/22. Her weekly earnings in respect of them are as follows:

Job	**Weekly earnings**
1	£750
2	£160
3	£420
4	£250

Her earnings do not equal or exceed the upper earnings limit in respect of any job. Therefore she must satisfy the earnings criteria for deferment to be permitted.

In respect of jobs 1 and 3, her earnings are £1,170 per week. This means the earnings criterion where E = 2 of £1,151 per week is met. She can therefore apply for deferment in respect of jobs 2 and 4.

Where a deferment is granted the employed earner is still liable to pay primary contributions at the additional rate of 2% on earnings from employments in respect of which deferment has been granted. This is because earnings over the upper earnings limit attract a primary Class 1 National Insurance liability at the additional primary rate (2% for 2021/22).

Deferment is not normally granted in the year in which state pension age is reached, although HMRC will consider a deferment if the earner can show that he or she expects to pay maximum contributions by the time that state pension age is reached.

Applying for a deferment

3.104 A deferment is not granted automatically and must be applied for. The application can be made online or by post (on form CA72A) and should be done before the start of the tax year to which it relates, although HMRC will accept the application until 14 February in the tax year to which it relates. HMRC publish guidance notes on the deferment process. Guidance on the deferment process and links to the online application and detailed guidance notes can be found on the gov.uk website at www.gov.uk/government/publications/national-insurance-application-for-deferment-of-payment-of-class-1-national-insurance-contributions-ca72a.

Applications from third parties (such as an accountant or tax adviser) can only be accepted with the earner's written consent.

The application should ideally be submitted before the start of the tax year to which it relates so that the deferment can be in place from the start of the tax year. However, deferment applications for employed taxpayers for 2021/22 will be accepted until 14 February 2022. Applications received between 14 February 2022 and 5 April 2022 will only be considered with the agreement of the deferred employer. If the application is not made in time, it may be possible to apply for a refund for contributions paid in excess of the annual maxima (see **3.28**).

If HMRC agree to the deferment application HMRC will issue a deferment certificate CA2700 which they will send to the relevant employers. Where an employer receives a deferment certificate they should deduct primary Class I National Insurance contributions at a rate of 2% on all earnings above the primary threshold. Where deferment has been granted, HMRC will check that sufficient primary Class 1 National Insurance contributions have been paid in the year. In the event that they have not, the earner will be asked to pay the shortfall. The following year, if HMRC consider it appropriate, they will write and invite the earner to renew the deferment application before the start of the new tax year.

If HMRC reject the deferment application they will advise the earner in writing and explain why the application was not successful.

If the deadline for applying for a deferment is missed and the contributor has two or more jobs and has overpaid Class 1 National Insurance, they can apply to HMRC for a refund of the overpaid contributions (see **3.134**).

Focus

Where an individual has more than one job, it may be possible to apply to defer the payment of primary contributions in respect of one or more job. Where contributions are deferred, National Insurance is payable at the 2% rate rather than at 12%. Deferment prevents the need to pay main rate contributions initially and reclaim them if the annual maximum is exceeded.

State pension age and deferment

3.105 HMRC do not normally allow deferment of Class 1 National Insurance contributions in the tax year in which the contributor reaches state pension age. However, a deferment will be considered if the contributor can demonstrate that by the time that they reach state pension age, they expect to have paid maximum Class 1 contributions for the year. This may be the case if a person has several employments and their birthday is near the end of the tax year or where the contributor is a director of a company with an annual earnings period.

CONTRACTING OUT

What was contracting out?

3.106 Contracting-out came to an end on 5 April 2016.

Under the state pension scheme that applies to individuals who reached state pension age before 6 April 2016, there are two elements to the state pension – the basic state pension and the second state pension (S2P). The basic state pension is a flat rate pension that is payable to anyone who has paid sufficient National Insurance contributions or has sufficient National Insurance credits when they reach state pension age. The second state pension (formerly known as SERPS (state earnings-related pension) is paid in addition to the basic state pension and is dependent on the National Insurance contributions paid prior to reaching state pension age. The two-tier state pension is replaced by a single-tier state pension for those who reach state pension age on or after 6 April 2016.

Under the two-tier state pension system applying to those who reached state pension age before 6 April 2016, it was possible to opt out of the second state pension and instead choose to top up the basic state pension by means of a private pension scheme. This is known as contracting-out. It is not possible to build up further entitlement to the second state pension after 5 April 2016 and contracting-out for salary-related (defined benefit) schemes came to an end on that date. Contracting-out on a defined contribution basis (money purchase plans) came to an end on 5 April 2012.

A person who contracted out of the second state pension does not receive a second state pension. Instead they made their own arrangements to top up the basic state pension. Consequently they were not required to contribute to the second state pension scheme. Therefore, where an employed earner chose to contract out of the second state pension through an occupational pension scheme, both the employer and the employee paid a lower rate of National Insurance contributions. The National Insurance contribution reduction was given by way of a contracted-out rebate. The rebate was paid to compensate for the giving up of the right to the second state pension. The amount of the rebate and the way in which it is given depended on the nature of the scheme through which the employee contracts out. From 6 April 2012 until 5 April 2016 rebates were only payable in respect of COSR scheme. No rebates are payable after 5 April 2016 as contracting-out came to an end on that date.

Prior to 6 April 2012 it was also possible to contract out via a personal or stakeholder pension. Where this route was taken, the employee and the employer continued to pay full rate National Insurance contributions. However, to compensate for the forfeited second state pension, HMRC paid money directly into the employee's pension scheme. These contributions to the pension scheme are known as minimum contributions and comprised a rebate of National Insurance contributions paid and tax relief on the employee's share of the rebate.

Where a person reaches state pension age on or after 6 April 2016 and had contracted-out prior to that date, the period for which the contributor was contracted-out is taken into account in calculating the foundation amount for calculation of the single-tier state pension.

Single-tier state pension

3.107 The single-tier state pension is payable to those who reach state pension age on or after 6 April 2016 and whose contribution record is sufficient. Individuals who reached state pension age prior to 6 April 2016 continue to receive the basic state pension and, where applicable, the earnings related state pension. A person needs 35 qualifying years to receive a full single-tier state pension, and at least ten qualifying years to receive a reduced single-tier state pension.

CALCULATING CLASS 1 NATIONAL INSURANCE CONTRIBUTIONS

Overview of the calculation of Class 1 National Insurance contributions

3.108 The Class 1 National Insurance liability is generally calculated using the exact percentage method. While this can be performed manually, in most cases the calculation is performed using a software package or using one of the free calculators or the downloadable Basic PAYE Tools provided by HMRC. Software packages generally use the exact percentage method. The introduction of real time information (RTI) for PAYE, under which employers are required to report pay and deduction information to HMRC electronically each time that an employee is paid, requires the use of payroll software and as a result it is rare for National Insurance to be performed manually. However, understanding the manual calculation is a good way to get to grips with how National Insurance contributions are calculated.

HMRC still produce National Insurance tables which can be used to calculate National Insurance contributions using the tables method, although the introduction of RTI means that manual methods of calculation are now largely redundant. The tables are discussed further at **3.110**.

When working out the primary Class 1 National Insurance liability it is vital that the correct rates or tables are used as the relevant rate will vary depending whether the employee is over pension age or whether the employed earner is a married woman with a valid reduced rate election (see **3.110**). It is therefore important that RTI software packages are kept up to date and updated each year and that the correct National Insurance category letter is used to ensure that contributions are calculated correctly.

Where the employed earner is a director, it is necessary to re-compute the liability on an annual basis at the end of the tax year as directors have an annual earnings period for Class 1 National Insurance purposes (see **3.98**). The calculation of directors' National Insurance contributions is examined further at **3.115**.

The National Insurance employment allowance was introduced with effect from 2014/15 onwards. Where the employer qualifies for the allowance, it is available to offset against the employer's Class 1 National Insurance liability. Where the allowance is available, contributions for the earnings period are worked out in the usual way (as indicated in the examples that follow) and the allowance is deducted from the total employer's Class 1 liability for the period to the extent that it remains available. The allowance is set at £4,000 for 2021/22. For further details on the employment allowance, see **3.13**.

Focus

Liability to Class 1 National Insurance contributions is calculated almost universally using the exact percentage method; this is the method used by software packages. Although HMRC continue to produce tables for manual calculations, these are largely redundant as calculation tools.

Exact percentage method

3.109 The exact percentage method is the more accurate of the two methods and is the method generally used by payroll software packages. The exact percentage method works by applying the relevant National Insurance rate to the earnings attracting liability at that rate.

Where the exact percentage method is used, the calculations should be rounded to the nearest penny (with amounts of a halfpenny or less being disregarded) (the *Social Security (Contributions) Regulations 2001* (*SI 2001/1004, reg 12*). Contributions at the normal rate and the contracted-out rate should be calculated separately.

No primary Class 1 National Insurance liability arises until earnings reach the lower earnings limit. No actual contributions are payable on earnings between the lower earnings limit (£120 per week for 2021/22) and the primary threshold (£184 per week for 2021/22), but such earnings are liable to contributions at a notional zero rate which acts to preserve entitlement to the basic state pension and contributory pension for those whose earnings fall within this band. Earnings between the primary threshold and upper earnings limit (£967 per week for 2021/22) are liable to contributions at the main rate of 12% for 2021.22. National Insurance contributions are payable at the additional rate of 2% on earnings in excess of the upper earnings limit (£967 per week for 2021/22).

A married woman with a valid reduced rate election (see **3.112**) pays reduced rate contributions (5.85% for 2021/22) on earnings between the primary threshold and upper earnings limit. If the employed earner has earnings above the upper earnings limit (£967 per week for 2021/22), primary Class 1 National Insurance contributions are payable at the additional rate of 2% irrespective of the rate paid on earnings between the primary threshold and upper earnings limit.

As far as secondary contributions are concerned, if the employed earner is a married woman with a reduced rate election, secondary contributions are payable at the main rate of 13.8% on all earnings above the secondary threshold (£170 per week for 2021/22). However, where the employee is under the age of 21 (see **3.9**) or an apprentice under the age of 25 (see **3.10**) secondary contributions are payable at a zero rate on earnings below, respectively, the upper secondary threshold for under-21s (set at £967 per week for 2021/22) or the apprentice upper secondary threshold (AUST), also set at £967 per week for 2021/22. From 6 April 2021, employers are also eligible for relief from secondary contributions on the earnings of armed forces veterans up to the upper secondary threshold of £967 per week. However, contributions must be paid as normal for 2021/22 on earnings in excess of the upper secondary threshold of £170 per week as the relief is given retrospectively from 6 April 2022 (see **3.11**).

Example 3.16—Calculating Class 1 contributions using the exact percentage method: earnings below UEL – employee aged over 21

Richard is paid weekly. In one week in 2021/22 he had earnings of £400. Richard is 45. Using the exact percentage method, the associated primary and secondary Class 1 National Insurance liability is calculated as follows:

Primary Class 1 National Insurance contributions

(£400 – £184) × 12% = £25.92

Secondary Class 1 National Insurance contributions

(£400 – £170) × 13.8% = £31.74

Example 3.17—Calculating Class 1 contributions using the exact percentage method: earnings below UEL – employee aged under 21

Jake is paid weekly. In one week in 2021/22 he had earnings of £400. Jake is 19. Using the exact percentage method, the associated primary and secondary Class 1 National Insurance liability is calculated as follows:

Primary Class 1 National Insurance contributions

(£400 – £184) × 12% = £25.92

Secondary Class 1 National Insurance contributions

As Jake is under 21 and his earnings are below the upper secondary threshold for under 21s of £967 per week, no secondary contributions are payable in respect of his earnings of £400.

Example 3.18—Calculating Class 1 contributions using the exact percentage method: earnings above the UEL – employee aged over 21

Karen is paid weekly. She is 51. In one week in 202/21 she had earnings of £1,200. Using the exact percentage method, the associated primary and secondary Class 1 National Insurance liability is calculated as follows:

Primary Class 1 National Insurance contributions

((£967 – £184) × 12%) + (£1,200 – £967) × 2%)) = £98.62

Secondary Class 1 National Insurance contributions

(£1,200 – £170) × 13.8% = £142.14

Example 3.19—Calculating Class 1 contributions using the exact percentage method: earnings above the UEL and Upper Secondary Threshold for Under 21s – employee aged under 21

Georgia is paid weekly. In one week in 2021/22 she had earnings of £1,200. Georgia is 19. Using the exact percentage method, the associated primary and secondary Class 1 National Insurance liability is calculated as follows:

Primary Class 1 National Insurance contributions

((£967 – £184) × 12%) + ((£1,200 – £967) × 2%) = £98.62

Secondary Class 1 National Insurance contributions

As Georgia is under 21, secondary contributions are only payable to the extent that her earnings exceed the upper secondary threshold for under 21s of £967 per week. Secondary contributions on earnings between the secondary threshold and upper secondary threshold for under 21s are payable at a zero rate. The secondary liability is therefore as follows:

((£967 – £170) @ 0%) + ((£1,200 – £967) @ 13.8%) = £32.15

Tables method

3.110 The tables method is a manual method and provides an alternative to the exact percentage method. It relies on the use of a series of ready reckoner tables. Use of the tables method is permitted by the *Social Security (Contributions) Regulations 2001* (*SI 2001/1004*), *reg 12(2)*. This method is now rarely used in practice, however, the tables are still published.

Different tables exist for different circumstances and it is important that the correct tables are used. The most commonly-used table is Table A which is used for employed earners aged 16 and above and below pension age.

The tables are contained within various booklets. The booklets and associated tables for 2021/22 are as follows.

Table Letter	Used for	Booklet contained within
A	Standard rate contribution	CA38
B	Married women and widows not contracted out of the second state pension who hold a valid reduced-rate election (CA4139, CF383, CF380A)	CA41
C	Employer only contributions for employees who are over state pension age for whom a valid certificate CA4140 or CF384 is held	CA41
G	Foreign-going mariners and deep sea fishermen – apprentices under age 25	CA42
H	Apprentices under 25	CA38
J	Employee for whom a deferment certificate (CA2700) is held	CA38
M	Employees aged under 21	CA38
P	Foreign-going mariners and deep sea fishermen – employee under 21 who has a deferment	
Q	Foreign-going mariners and deep sea fishermen – employee has a deferment	CA42
R	Foreign-going mariners and deep sea fishermen – standard-rate contributions	CA42
T	Foreign-going mariners and deep sea fishermen – reduced-rate contributions	CA42
W	Foreign-going mariners and deep sea fishermen – employees over state pension age, employer-only contributions	CA42
Y	Foreign-going mariners and deep sea fishermen – standard rate employee under 21	
Z	Employees aged under 21 for whom a deferment certificate (CA2700) is held	CA38

A flowchart showing which Table to use is included in Booklet CA38.

If the employee is authorised to pay his or her own contributions and is in a not contracted-out employment, Table A or B in booklet CA40 should be used.

The latest editions of the tables are available to download from the gov.uk website. Paper copies can be ordered from the employer orderline by calling 0300 123 1074.

The table letter used must be recorded on the employee's deductions working sheet (P11 or equivalent). It is important that the correct table letter is used to ensure that the payroll software package deducts the correct amount of National Insurance.

Using the tables to calculate contributions

3.111 The tables method to calculate National Insurance contributions is largely redundant following the introduction of RTI (which necessitates the use of payroll software in order to meet the RTI filing requirements). However, employers who are exempt from online filing or who are unable to file payroll information online may use the tables to calculate National Insurance contributions manually.

If the National Insurance tables are used to calculate Class 1 National Insurance contributions, the first step is to ensure that the correct table is being used. As well as the different tables for the different table letters, within each table letter there are different tables for weekly-paid and monthly-paid employees.

If the employee earns between the lower earnings limit and the upper earnings limit, the contributions payable are simply found by looking up the relevant earnings in the far left-hand column of the table and simply copying the figures from the tables onto the P11. If the actual earnings are not shown, the nearest lowest figure should be used. Column 1e contains employer's contributions, column 1f, the employee's contributions and the far right column the total of the employer's and employee's contributions. The final column is for information only and does not appear on the P11. Although no actual contributions are payable on earnings between the lower earnings limit and the primary threshold, where the employee earns at or above the lower earnings limit entries are required on the P11 and for this reason the table starts at earnings equal to the lower earnings limit rather than the primary threshold.

If the employee has earnings in excess of the upper earnings limit, the calculation of National Insurance contributions using the tables is a two-stage process. The first stage is to find the contributions on earnings at the upper earnings limit as described above. The contributions due on earnings above the upper earnings limit are found using the additional gross pay table. It is simply a case of subtracting the upper earnings limit (£962 for 2020/21) from the actual earnings and looking up the remainder in the left-hand column of the additional gross pay table and reading across the entries for columns 1e, 1f and for the total contributions. These should be added to the contributions on earnings at the upper earnings limit taken from the standard table to find the contributions due on the earnings and the entries that need to be made on the P11. If the exact amount is not shown in the additional gross pay table, entries are added together to make the required figure.

Example 3.20—Calculating Class 1 National Insurance contributions using the tables method: weekly paid employee

John is an employee. He is 43. The correct National Insurance table to use is Table A. He is paid weekly and for one week in 2021/22 he is paid £200. The entries from weekly Table A are as follows:

Earnings up to and including UEL	Earnings at Lower Earnings Limit (LEL)	Earnings above LEL, up to and including Primary Threshold (PT)	Earnings above PT, up to and including the UEL	Employer's contributions due on all earnings above the ST	Employee's contributions due on earnings above the PT	Total of employer's contributions (information only)
	1a	1b	1c	1d	1e	
£200	£120.00	£64.00	£16.00	£4.21	£1.98	£6.19

The tables method shows primary contributions of £1.98 and secondary contributions of £4.21 to be due.

Married women and widows with reduced-rate elections

3.112 A woman who was married before 6 April 1977 could elect to pay reduced contributions (the *Social Security (Contributions) Regulations 2001* (*SI 2001/1004*), *regs 127–131*). The election had to be made before 12 May 1977. Where a married woman or widow holds a valid certificate of election (form CA4139, CF383 or CF380A) she is entitled to pay primary Class 1 National Insurance contributions at a reduced rate on earnings between the primary threshold and the upper earnings limit. For 2020/21, the reduced rate is 5.85%. A married woman or widow with earnings above the upper earnings limit pays contributions at the standard additional rate of 2% on those earnings.

Secondary contributions are payable at the standard rate and are unaffected by the election.

A married woman paying reduced-rate contributions cannot contract out of the second state pension. Where such an election is in force the woman does not build up benefit and pension entitlement by virtue of her own contributions.

Example 3.21—Reduced rate election

Rita holds a valid reduced rate election. She is not in a contracted-out employment and is paid weekly. In 2021/22 she had earnings of £1,000 a week and is paid weekly.

Rita pays primary Class 1 contributions at the reduced rate of 5.85% on earnings above £184 per week up to £967 per week. She pays primary contributions at the additional rate of 2% on earnings above £967 per week. She is liable to pay primary Class 1 contributions of £46.47 ((5.85% (£967 – £184)) + (2% (£1,000 – £967)) on her earnings.

Her employer pays secondary contributions at secondary rate of 13.8% on earnings above £170 per week. Secondary contributions payable are £114.54 (13.8% (£1,000 – £170)).

Cessation of the election

3.113 The election ceases to have effect if any of the following events occur:

- for two consecutive years the woman has had earnings below the lower earnings limit and has not been self-employed during that period;
- the woman's marriage ends either as a result of divorce or annulment. The certificate ceases to have effect from the date of the decree absolute or the date of the annulment;
- the woman gives notice that she wishes the election to be revoked;
- the woman is a widow who ceases to qualify for widow's benefit and who does not remarry before the end of the tax year;
- contracted-out primary contributions are paid in error at the full rate for a year and the woman chooses to continue to pay the full-rate contributions in the following tax year; or
- not contracted-out contributions are paid at the full rate in error and the woman decides to continue to pay such contributions and informs HMRC of her decision and does not claim a refund of any full-rate contributions paid nor pay any further reduced-rate contributions.

Revoking the election

3.114 A woman with a reduced-rate election can revoke that election by giving notice in writing to HMRC. The revocation takes effect from the end of the week in which the notice is given or such later week as may be specified in the revocation notice.

In certain cases it may be beneficial for a woman to revoke a reduced-rate election.

Where a reduced-rate election is in force, the woman does not build up benefit entitlement by reference to her own contributions. Instead her benefit entitlement is dependent on her husband's contributions. However, since 6 April 2000 where an employed earner has earnings between the lower earnings limit and primary threshold, benefit entitlement is preserved by means of notional contributions at a zero rate. This means that if a married woman with a reduced-rate election has earnings in this band, she would be able to build up her own benefit entitlement without having to actually pay any National Insurance contributions. Therefore, it may be worthwhile considering revoking the election where earnings fall within this band. The issue of whether such a revocation will be beneficial will depend on current and future earnings. Those considering whether such a revocation will be beneficial can contact HMRC to discuss their personal situation prior to making the decision.

Calculating directors' National Insurance contributions

3.115 As discussed at **3.97,** directors are subject to an annual (or pro-rata annual) earnings period to prevent them reducing their overall National Insurance liability by controlling the timing and amount of payments of earnings during the tax year (the *Social Security (Contributions) Regulations 2001* (*SI 2001/1004*), *reg 8*). This has an impact on how directors' Class 1 National Insurance contributions are calculated.

The annual earnings basis rules mean that payments to the director earlier in the tax year are taken into account when calculating the National Insurance contributions due on a particular payment of earnings. The calculation effectively operates on a cumulative basis in a similar way to PAYE.

The director does not pay any Class 1 National Insurance contributions on his or her earnings until his or her cumulative earnings reach the primary threshold. He or she then pays Class 1 National Insurance contributions at the main rate (or contracted-out rate as appropriate) until cumulative earnings reach the upper earnings limit. Thereafter, Class 1 contributions are payable at the additional rate of 2%.

The calculation of secondary contributions works in a similar way. If the director is aged 21 or over, no secondary Class 1 National Insurance contributions are due until earnings in the tax year reach the secondary threshold. If the director is under 21, no secondary contributions are due until the director's earnings exceed the upper secondary threshold for under 21s. Likewise, if the director is an apprentice under the age of 25, no secondary contributions are payable under earnings that exceed the apprentice upper secondary threshold (AUST). Thereafter, secondary Class 1 contributions are payable at the secondary rate of 13.8%.

Example 3.22—Annual earnings period for directors

William is a company director. He is aged 35. For 2021/22 he receives payments of earnings as follows:

Month	Payment of earnings
April 2021 (month 1)	£2,000
May 2021 (month 2)	£20,000
September 2021 (month 6)	£50,000
March 2022 (month 12)	£10,000

The annual earnings limits for 2021/22 are as follows:

Lower earnings limit	£6,240
Primary threshold	£9,568
Secondary threshold	£8,840
Upper earnings limit	£50,270
Upper secondary threshold for under 21s	£50,270
Apprentice upper secondary threshold	£50,270

His National Insurance contributions for 2021/22 calculated using an annual earnings period are as follows:

For 2021/22, the annual primary threshold is £9,568, the annual secondary threshold is £8,788 and the annual upper earnings limit is £50,270.

Month 1

Earnings to date (£2,000) are less than both the primary of £9,568 and the secondary threshold of £8,840. Therefore no primary or secondary Class 1 National Insurance contributions are due on the payment of £2,000 in April 2021.

Month 2

Earnings to date in tax year are £22,000 (£2,000 + £20,000). This is above the annual primary threshold but below the annual upper earnings limit.

National Insurance contributions due on earnings of £22,000 are as follows:

Primary contributions: (£22,000 – £9,568) × 12% = £1,491.84

As no primary Class 1 contributions have been paid so far in the tax year, primary Class 1 contributions of £1,491.84 are deducted from the payment of earnings of £20,000 in May 2021.

Secondary contributions: (£22,000 – £8,840) × 13.8% = £1,816.08

As no contributions have been paid to date in the tax year, the secondary contributor must pay secondary Class 1 contributions of £1,816.08 on the payment of earnings of £20,000 in May 2021.

Month 6

Earnings to date in the tax year are £72,000 (£2,000 + £20,000 + £50,000)

National Insurance contributions due on earnings of £72,000 are as follows:

Primary contributions: ((£50,270 – £9,568) × 12%) + (£72,000 – £50,270) × 2%) = £5,318.84

William has already paid primary Class 1 contributions of £1,491.84 on earnings paid earlier in the tax year. Consequently, he must pay primary Class 1 contributions of £3,827 (£5,318.84 – £1,491.84) on the payment of £50,000 in September 2021.

Secondary contributions: (£72,000 – £8,840) × 13.8% = £8,716.08

Secondary Class 1 contributions already paid on earnings paid earlier in the tax year are £1,816.08 Therefore secondary Class 1 contributions payable in respect of the payment of earnings of £50,000 on September 2021 are £6,900.00 (£8,716.08 – £1,816.086). Note, as earnings earlier in the year have already exceeded the secondary threshold, this is simply £50,000 @ 13.8%.

Month 12

As earnings previously in the tax year have exceeded the upper earnings limit, the payment of £10,000 in March 2022 attracts primary Class 1 contributions at the additional rate of 2%. The primary Class 1 contributions payable are thus £200 (£10,000 × 2%).

Secondary contributions are payable at the rate of 13.8%, giving a liability of £1,380 (£10,000 × 13.8%).

Contributions payable for the year on total earnings of £82,000 (£2,000 + £20,000 + £50,000 + £10,000) are as follows:

Primary contributions: ((£50,270 – £9,568) × 12%) + ((£82,000 – £50,270) × 2%) = £5,518.84 (£1,491.84 + £3,827 + £200)

Secondary contributions: (£82,000 – £8,840) × 13.8% = £10,096.08 (£1,816.08 + £6,900 + £1,380)

Applying an annual earnings basis means that the director's National Insurance liability is not spread evenly throughout the year. No contributions are payable at the start of the year until the primary threshold is reached, the director then suffers a high National Insurance burden as all earnings attract contributions at the main rate until the upper earnings limit is reached. The burden then drops significantly once the upper earnings limit is reached.

To alleviate the problems associated with this and to spread the National Insurance liability more evenly throughout the tax year, alternative assessment arrangements can be operated instead.

Alternative assessment arrangements

3.116 HMRC operate alternative assessment arrangements for the payment of directors' National Insurance contributions. Under these arrangements, the director's earnings period remains an annual one, but payments on account of the final liability are made throughout the year. The payments of account are calculated on a non-cumulative basis using the actual payment interval in the same way as for other employees. The liability is recomputed when the final payment is made and outstanding National Insurance paid.

Example 3.23—Company directors: alternative assessment arrangements

Helen is a company director. She is 47. Her National Insurance contributions for 2020/21 are assessed using the alternative assessment arrangements.

During 2021/22, Helen is paid £3,000 each month. She is also paid a bonus of £30,000 in September 2021 and £40,000 in March 2022.

The National Insurance contributions payable on account in months 1 to 11 are as follows:

Month	Payment	Primary Class 1 NICs	Secondary Class 1 NICs
1 (April 2021)	£3,000	£264.36 ((£3,000 – £797) × 12%)	£312.29 ((£3,000 – £737) × 13.8%)
2 (May 2021)	£3,000	£264.36 ((£3,000 – £797) × 12%)	£312.29 ((£3,000 – £737) × 13.8%)
3 (June 2021)	£3,000	£264.36 ((£3,000 – £797) × 12%)	£312.29 ((£3,000 – £737) × 13.8%)
4 (July 2021)	£3,000	£264.36 ((£3,000 – £797) × 12%)	£312.29 ((£3,000 – £737) × 13.8%)
5 (August 2021	£3,000	£264.36 ((£3,000 – £797) × 12%)	£312.29 ((£3,000 – £737) × 13.8%)
6 (September 2021)	£33,000	£983.26 ((£4,189 – £797) × 12%) + ((£33,000 – £4,189) × 2%)	£4,452.29 ((£33,000 – £737) × 13.8%)
7 (October 2021)	£3,000	£264.36 ((£3,000 – £797) × 12%)	£312.29 ((£3,000 – £737) × 13.8%)
8 (November 2021)	£3,000	£264.36 ((£3,000 – £797) × 12%)	£312.29 ((£3,000 – £737) × 13.8%)
9 (December 2021)	£3,000	£264.36 ((£3,000 – £797) × 12%)	£312.29 ((£3,000 – £737) × 13.8%)
10 (January 2022)	£3,000	£264.36 ((£3,000 – £797) × 12%)	£312.29 ((£3,000 – £737) × 13.8%)

Month	Payment	Primary Class 1 NICs	Secondary Class 1 NICs
11 (February 2022)	£3,000	£264.36 ((£3,000 – £797) × 12%)	£312.29 ((£3,000 – £737) × 13.8%)
TOTAL	£63,000	£3,628.86	£7,575.19

As the payment intervals are monthly, the monthly limits are used in calculating the payments on account of earnings (primary threshold of £797 and the secondary threshold of £737 and upper earnings limit £4,189).

When the final payment is made in March 2022 (month 12) it is necessary to re-compute the liability on an annual basis using the annual thresholds (primary threshold of £9,568 and secondary threshold of £8,840 and the upper earnings limit £50,270).

Total payments in the tax year are £106,000 ((£3,000 × 12) + £30,000 + £40,000)

National Insurance contributions due for the year on earnings of £106,000

Primary contributions: ((£50,270 – £9,568) × 12%) + (£106,000 – £50,270) × 2%) = £5,998.87.

Total primary Class 1 contributions paid on account in months 1 to 11 inclusive are £3,628.86. Therefore primary contributions deducted from the earnings of £43,000 (salary of £3,000 plus bonus of £40,000) payable in March 2022 are £2,370.014 (£5,998.87 – £3,628.86).

Secondary contributions: (£106,000 – £8,840) × 13.8% = £13,408.08

Total secondary Class 1 contributions paid on account in months 1 to 11 inclusive are £7,575.19. Secondary contributions payable in respect of the payment of earnings of £43,000 in March 2022 are therefore £5,832.89 (£13,408.08 – £7,575.19).

Further guidance on directors' National Insurance contributions is available in HMRC booklet CA44, *National Insurance for Company Directors*, (which is available to download from the gov.uk website www.gov.uk/government/publications/ca44-national-insurance-for-company-directors).

Focus

Directors have an annual earnings period for Class 1 National Insurance. The liability can be calculated on a cumulative basis (as for PAYE) by reference to the annual rates and limits from the start of the tax year, although this means that the liability is not spread evenly throughout the year, even where the director is paid the same each month. To avoid this, the contributions can instead be calculated initially according to the pay period, as for other employees. Where this method is chosen, it is necessary to recalculate the liability on an annual basis for the final payment of the year, and pay any balance owing. It will be necessary to select which basis you want to use in your RTI software package.

SALARY SACRIFICE ARRANGEMENTS

Overview of salary sacrifice arrangements

3.117 A salary sacrifice arrangement is one where an employee gives up some of his or her cash salary in return for a non-cash benefit. Prior to 6 April 2017, salary sacrifice arrangements were very beneficial from both a tax and National Insurance perspective if the employee swaps cash salary for a benefit that is exempt from tax and National Insurance as this will save tax and both employer and employee National Insurance contributions. However, new valuation rules were introduced from 6 April 2017 which resulted in the tax and National Insurance exemptions being lost when a benefit is provided under a salary sacrifice arrangement or where a cash alternative is offered unless the benefit in question is pensions or pension advice, childcare, cycles or cyclists' safety equipment or ultra-low emission cars. Where an arrangement is in place at 5 April 2017, the exemptions were preserved until 6 April 2018 for most benefits and until 6 April 2021 where the arrangements relate to living accommodation, school fees or cars that are not ultra-low emission cars. For National Insurance purposes, the alternative valuation rules override the earnings disregard where an exemption would otherwise be in point. Where benefits are made available under an optional remuneration arrangement and the alternative valuation rules apply, the amount that is treated as earnings is the relevant amount. This is the higher of salary foregone (or cash alternative offered, as relevant) and the amount otherwise treated as earnings (ie the cash equivalent value).

However, even where an exemption is not in point, swapping cash salary for a benefit in kind can be beneficial from a National Insurance angle. Payments of salary and wages attract a liability to Class 1 National Insurance contributions and as such both employer and employee contributions are payable. By contrast, most taxable benefits in kind attract a liability to Class 1A rather than Class 1 contributions. As the Class 1A charge is an employer-only charge, moving liability from Class 1 to Class 1A will save employee contributions. If the employee's earnings are below the upper earnings limit, this will save 12%. If earnings exceed the upper earnings limit, the saving will be 2%.

To the extent that a salary sacrifice arrangement remains worthwhile, where one is implemented, it is important that the arrangement is effective (see **3.119**) and that all parties understand the implications of the arrangement, particularly if the sacrifice causes earnings to drop below the lower earnings limit (£120 for 2021/22).

The charge to Class 1A National Insurance contributions is discussed in Chapter 4.

Effective salary sacrifice arrangements

3.118 The benefit of salary sacrifice arrangements was greatly reduced from 6 April 2017 as the majority of tax and National Insurance exemptions are lost where a benefit is made available via a flexible remuneration arrangement such as a salary sacrifice scheme. However, there are still National Insurance savings to be had by moving the liability from Class 1 to Class 1A and saving employee contributions. For HMRC to regard a salary sacrifice arrangement as effective and to calculate National Insurance and tax by reference to the new arrangements, the contractual right to cash pay must be reduced. This means that the potential future remuneration must be given up before it is treated as received for tax or National Insurance purposes. Further, the true construction of the revised contractual arrangement must be that the employee is entitled to lower cash remuneration and a benefit.

HMRC do not accept that a salary sacrifice arrangement is effective if the employee continues to be entitled to the higher level of remuneration and rather than give up salary in exchange for the benefit, the employee has merely asked the employer to apply a portion of the salary in the acquisition of the benefit. This distinction is important as if HMRC do not accept that the salary has been given up, they will charge tax and National Insurance as if the employee has continued to receive the higher salary. This will mean that any savings from swapping salary to a benefit that is exempt from National Insurance (and/or tax) or within the charge to Class 1A rather than to Class 1 is lost.

Consequential effects of salary sacrifice arrangements

3.119 Reducing cash salary can have a number of knock-on effects, particularly where earnings are around the lower earnings level. In using salary sacrifice arrangements to reduce tax and National Insurance payable, the consequential effects should also be considered in evaluating whether the swap is worthwhile.

Entitlement to statutory payments (statutory sick pay, statutory maternity pay, statutory adoption pay, statutory paternity pay, statutory shared parental pay and statutory parental bereavement pay) is contingent on the employee having average weekly earnings at least equal to the lower earnings limit for National Insurance purposes (£120 per week for 2021/22). Where cash salary drops below this level, entitlement to statutory payments may be lost.

Even where earnings remain above the lower earnings limit, the amount of statutory payment payable may also be affected. This is particularly true as regards payments of statutory maternity pay for the first six weeks which is at a rate of 90% of average weekly earnings.

Reducing earnings below the lower earnings limit will adversely affect the employee's contribution record and may reduce entitlement to the basic state pension and to contributory benefits.

If the employee contributes to a pension scheme, particularly if the level of contributions is a percentage of earnings, reducing salary will affect pension contributions which in turn may affect the pension ultimately payable.

Where a salary sacrifice arrangement is introduced, cash pay cannot fall below the level of the National Living Minimum Wage, set at £8.91 per hour from 1 April 2021 or, where the employee is under the age of 25, the National Minimum Wage appropriate to the employee's age.

Entering into a salary sacrifice arrangement can also affect tax credits that are payable.

> **Focus**
>
> Changes to the treatment of salary sacrifice arrangements from 6 April 2017 seriously curtailed the benefits associated with using them. Although there are savings to be had from shifting the National Insurance liability from Class 1 to Class 1A, they are unlikely to be significant enough to justify the use of such an arrangement. Salary sacrifice arrangements are now only really viable for a limited range of benefits.

COLLECTING AND RECORDING CLASS 1 NATIONAL INSURANCE CONTRIBUTIONS

Overview of collection provision

3.120 The provisions governing the collecting, recording and reporting of National Insurance contributions are found in the *Social Security (Contributions) Regulations 2001* (*SI 2001/1004*), *Sch 4*).

As far as Class 1 National Insurance contributions are concerned, the provisions largely mirror those applying for PAYE purposes and the relevant provisions of the *Income Tax (Pay As You Earn) Regulations 2003* (*SI 2003/2682*) are imported into the social security legislation and contained within *SI 2001/1004, Sch 4, Pt 1*.

Collection of primary contributions from the employee

3.121 The liability for the payment of primary contributions lies 'in the first instance' with the secondary contributor (*SSCBA 1992, Sch 1, para 3(1)*). However, the primary contributions are recovered from the employee via deduction from the payment of earnings to which they relate.

Where earnings are aggregated for the purposes of computing the National Insurance liability (see **3.99**), the associated liability may be deducted from any of the earnings so aggregated (*SI 2001/1004, Sch 4, para 7*).

Any primary contributions that are paid by the secondary contributor are deemed to have been paid by the earner (*SSCBA 1992, Sch 1, para 3(1)*). However, the secondary contributor is entitled to recover those contributions from the earner (*SSCBA 1992, Sch 1, para 3(2)*).

Liability for secondary contributions

3.122 Secondary contributors must pay secondary contributions on payments of earnings made to an employed earner.

Where the employer is entitled to the employment allowance (see **3.13**), this is deducted from the secondary liability for the tax month or quarter prior to paying the contributions over to HMRC.

The liability for secondary contributions can only be transferred to the employed earner in very limited circumstances, as can the right to recover such contributions from the employee. These are discussed at **3.131**.

Recording Class 1 National Insurance contributions

3.123 Certain records must be maintained for Class 1 National Insurance purposes. By law, the employer is entitled to maintain a deductions working sheet (form P11 or equivalent) for each employee. This will generally be maintained electronically via the employer's payroll software package. As far as National Insurance contributions are concerned, the regulations require that the information listed below must be recorded each time a payment of earnings is made (the *Social Security (Contributions) Regulations 2001* (*SI 2001/1004*), *Sch 4, para 7(13)*).

- date of the payment (relevant week or month number);
- earnings up to and including the current lower earnings limit where earnings exceed that limit;
- earnings which exceed the current lower earnings limit but do not exceed the current primary threshold;
- earnings which exceed the current primary threshold but which do not exceed the current upper earnings limit;
- the sum of all primary Class 1 contributions and all secondary Class 1 contributions payable on the earnings; and
- the primary contributions and secondary contributions payable on the employee's earnings.

Details of statutory payments (statutory sick pay, statutory maternity pay, statutory paternity pay, statutory adoption pay and statutory shared parental pay must also be recorded.

Retention of records

3.124 An employer is required to keep and preserve all contribution records that are not required to be sent to HMRC for not less than three years after the end of the tax year to which they relate (the *Social Security (Contributions) Regulations 2001 (SI 2001/1004) Sch 4, para 26*). The records may be kept in any form and by any means.

For these purposes, 'contribution records' are wage sheets, deductions working sheets and other documents and records relating to:

- the calculation or payment of earnings to the employer's employees or the amount of earnings-related contributions;
- the amount of Class 1A and Class 1B contributions payable by the employer; and
- any information about the amounts of Class 1A and Class 1B contributions payable by the employer.

Where a joint election has been made to transfer some or all of the secondary liability to the employee (see **3.120**), the employer must maintain (*Sch 4, para 8*):

- a copy of the election;
- a copy of the notice of approval issued by HMRC;
- the name and address of the secondary contributor who has entered into the agreement;
- the name of the employed earner; and
- the employed earner's National Insurance number,

throughout the period for which the election is in force and also for six years after the end of that period (*Sch 4, para 26(3)*).

Payment of contributions to HMRC

3.125 The secondary contributor must pay over primary and secondary Class 1 National Insurance contributions to HMRC. The payment is made together with payments of PAYE, student loan deductions and, where relevant, deductions from subcontractors. Payment is normally made on a monthly basis. However, if the employer has average monthly payments in respect of PAYE deductions, National Insurance contributions, student loan deductions and deductions from subcontractors of less than £1,500, payment can be made quarterly.

The tax month ends on the 5th of the month. Where payment is made quarterly, the quarters end on 5 July, 5 October, 5 January and 5 April.

Where payment is made electronically, cleared funds must reach HMRC within 17 days of the end of the tax month or quarter (i.e. by 22nd of the month). If payment is not made electronically, the cleared funds must reach HMRC within 14 days of the end of the tax month or quarter (i.e. 19th of the month). Large employers (employers with 250 employees or more) must make their payments electronically. Interest is charged on payments made late.

The National Insurance contributions due for the month or quarter is the total of all employees' (primary Class 1) and employer's (secondary Class 1) contributions for the month or quarter, less any statutory sick pay that the employer is entitled to recover and any statutory maternity pay, statutory paternity pay or statutory adoption pay that and, where relevant, the NIC compensation, the employer is entitled to recover. This is added to the PAYE due for the month and the quarter and paid over to HMRC.

Where payment is not made electronically, it must be accompanied by a payslip from booklet P30BC. It is not necessary to show the split between PAYE and NIC when making the payment to HMRC.

Mistakes in the amount paid over to HMRC that are made in the tax year can be corrected in a subsequent payment in the same tax year.

Penalties are charged when payments of PAYE and NIC are made late on more than one occasion during the tax year. The penalty is a percentage of the tax and NIC paid late and the penalty rate depends on the number of occasions in the tax year on which payment is made late.

The penalty is levied in-year on a quarterly basis.

Number of occasions on which payment made late in the tax year	**Penalty rate**
1	No penalty as long as the payment is not more than six months late.
2, 3 or 4	1%
5, 6 or 7	2%
8, 9 or 10	3%
11 or more	4%

An additional penalty of 5% is charged if a monthly or quarterly payment remains outstanding after six months and a further penalty of 5% applies if payment has not been made after 12 months.

Focus

It is important to have procedures in place for ensuring that payments of PAYE and NIC are made on time each month. Late payments attract interest, and penalties are charged if payment is made late on more than one occasion in the tax year.

In-year reporting under RTI

3.126 Provisions governing the reporting requirements under RTI for National Insurance purposes are contained in the *Social Security (Contributions) Regulations 2001 (SI 2001/1004)*, as amended by the *Social Security (Contributions) (Amendment No. 3) Regulations 2012 (SI 2012/821)*.

The information that a real time information employer (i.e. one within RTI) must send to HMRC in relation to payments made to their employers and the associated Class 1 National Insurance contributions is set out in *SI 2001/1004 regs 21A* to *21F*.

The regulations require that each time an employee for whom an employer is required to maintain a deductions working sheet is paid, the employer must deliver a real time return to HMRC (the *Social Security (Contributions) Regulations 2001 (SI 2001/1004) reg 21A*). The return must be made using an approved method of electronic communication. Where at any particular time a payment is made to more than one employee, the return must include information in respect of each employee to whom a payment is made. Where the employer operates more than one payroll and payments are made to one or more employee on each payroll, the employer must make a real time information return in respect of each payroll.

The information that must be contained within a real time information return is set out in the *Social Security (Contributions) Regulations 2001(SI 2001/1004) Sch 4A*.

The return must include the employer's HMRC office number, the employer's PAYE reference and the employer's accounts office reference. It must also include the following information about the employee:

- employee's name;
- employee's date of birth;
- employee's current gender;
- if known, the employee's National Insurance number or otherwise the employee's address; and
- the number used by the employer to identify the employee (and where this is different from the number used on a previous return, an indication of the number previously used).

As far as National Insurance contributions are concerned, the return must contain the following information (the *Social Security (Contributions) Regulations 2001 (SI 2001/1004) Sch 4A, paras 3–12*):

- amount of the payment included in the employee's earnings for the purposes of determining the amount of earnings-related contributions;
- the number of earnings periods to which the payment relates;

- where applicable, whether earnings from more than one employment have been aggregated;
- the relevant category letter (or letters, as appropriate);
- if the employee is a director, whether the employer has used an annual earnings period;
- if the employee is a director who was appointed in the year and a pro-rata earnings period is used, the week of appointment; and
- for each category letter, the total amount of secondary Class 1 contributions payable on the employee's earnings in the earnings period in which the return is made, the total amount of secondary Class 1 contributions payable on the employee's earnings in the year to date, the total amount of primary Class 1 contributions payable on the employee's earnings in the earnings period in which the return is made and the total amount of primary Class 1 contributions payable on the employee's earnings in the year to date.

If earnings are to be aggregated, details of category letters and primary and secondary contributions need only be provided when the final payment in the earnings period is made.

In the event that the employee is in a contracted-out employment at any time in the tax year, the employer must also provide the relevant contracting-out certificate number as part of the final return for the tax year.

Where in the earnings period the employee has received statutory sick pay, statutory maternity pay, statutory paternity pay, statutory adoption pay, shared parental pay or statutory parental bereavement pay, the return must also include the total amount paid in the current employment in the year to date. Where additional statutory paternity pay is paid, the name and National Insurance number of the mother or adopter of the child, as appropriate, must also be included in the return.

A real time information return must also include details of amounts recovered under the statutory sick pay percentage threshold scheme or small employers' compensation scheme and also details of amounts covered by the regional employers' contributions holiday for new businesses (see **3.114**). Employers eligible for the employment allowance must claim this via their RTI software.

If after making a return the employer discovers an error, the error must be corrected in the first return which is made after the discovery of the error. Previous year errors can now be corrected by submitting a revised Full Payment Submission (FPS). Where an error is discovered after 19 April, it can also be corrected using an Earlier Year Update (the *Social Security (Contributions) Regulations 200, (SI 2001/1004, Sch 4, reg 21E*). The return must be made as soon as possible after the discovery of the error.

The main return under RTI is the full payment submission (FPS). A FPS detailing pay and deductions must be made each time an employee is paid and must be submitted at or before the payment is made to the employee. A penalty is charged where RTI returns are submitted late in more than one tax month in the tax year. The penalty depends on the number of employees in the PAYE scheme, as shown in the table below. However, it should be noted HMRC allow a three-day period of grace before charging a penalty (although this is a concession not an extension to the filing deadline and employers who routinely file in this window may receive a penalty).

Number of employees	Monthly penalty
1 to 9	£100
10 to 49	£200
50 to 249	£300
250 or more	£400

If the returns are submitted over three months late, an additional penalty of 5% of the tax and National Insurance that should have been reported is also charged.

If an employer does not make any payments in the tax month the employer must submit an employer payment submission (EPS) instead of a FPS. The EPS acts as a nil return. In the event that the employer receives funding from HMRC, an EPS must be submitted in addition to an FPS.

Focus

Timely reporting is essential under RTI as penalties are levied where reports are made late for more than one month in the tax year. Although a concessionary three-day period of grace is allowed, this should be for emergencies only. Penalties will be charged if reports are routinely filed within this window.

Year-end procedures under RTI

3.127 Under real time information (RTI) employers are required to submit pay and deductions information to HMRC progressively throughout the tax year at or before payment is made to the employee. At the end of the year, the employer must comply with the RTI end-of-year procedures.

In the last pay period of the year, the employer must submit the Full Payment Submission (FPS) or Employer Payment Summary (EPS) as normal, but must indicate on the submission that it is the final submission for the year. If the employer submits FPSs for weekly and monthly payrolls, the last FPS is the last one submitted in the tax year, regardless of whether it relates to the weekly or monthly payroll. If no payments are made in the final pay period in the year, the employer must submit an EPS indicating that no payments are due in the final pay period and that the EPS is the final submission for the tax year.

The final submission must be made on or before 19 April after the end of the tax year. Where the final submission is made by means of the FPS, this must be made at or before the last payment is made to an employee in the tax year. Where the submission is made by the EPS, this must be done by 19 April. HMRC will accept a FPS after 19 April 2019. Corrections found after 19 April can also be made on an Earlier Year Update (EYU). Penalties are charged at a rate of £100 per 50 employees for each month or part month that the submission remains outstanding after 19 May.

The employer must supply the employee with a P60 (certificate of pay and tax deducted for the tax year) by 31 May following the end of the tax year.

Form P60

3.128 Employers (regardless of whether or not they are reporting in real time) must give all employees employed on 5 April a certificate of pay and tax deducted (form P60) by 31 May after the end of the tax year. Form P60 can be given to employees electronically.

Certificate of employer's liability to pay contributions after inspection of documents

3.129 Following an inspection, HMRC may seek to recover contributions due from the employer. As a result of information obtained following an inspection of an employer's records in accordance with *FA 2008, Sch 36*, an officer of HMRC may prepare a certificate showing the amount of earnings-related contributions which it appears to HMRC that the employer is liable to pay, excluding any amount paid as compensation under the statutory sick pay and statutory maternity pay schemes, for the tax year or years covered by the inspection, or the amount of any Class 1B National Insurance contributions which it appears that the employer is liable to pay, together with any earnings related and/or Class 1B contributions that have not been paid (the *Social Security (Contributions) Regulations 2001 (SI 2001/1004), Sch 4, para 26A*).

Unless the contrary is proved, the certificate is treated as sufficient evidence that the employer is liable to pay the contributions due. Thus, where the employer believes the liability to be less than that shown in the certificate, the onus is on the employer to prove that this is the case.

Recovering secondary contributions from employees in limited circumstances

Joint agreements

3.130 There is a general prohibition on the recovery of secondary Class 1 National Insurance contributions from the employee (*SSCBA 1992, Sch 1, para 3A*). However, this prohibition is lifted in certain limited circumstances.

By virtue of *SSCBA 1992, Sch 1, para 3A*, it is possible for the employer and employee to enter into a joint agreement which allows the secondary contributor to recover (whether by deduction or otherwise) the whole or any part of the secondary Class 1 contributions which are payable in respect of the earner's earnings and which are subject to the agreement.

Such an agreement can only be made in respect of the secondary Class 1 liability arising in connection with earnings that:

- relate to the charge on certain post-acquisition events in relation to restricted securities and which are chargeable to income tax by virtue of *ITEPA 2003, s 426*;
- relate to the charge on certain post-acquisition events in relation to convertible securities and which are charged to income tax by virtue of *ITEPA 2003, s 438*; and
- comprise a share option gain (calculated in accordance with *ITEPA 2003, s 479*) chargeable to income tax by virtue of *ITEPA 2003, s 476*.

Where an agreement is made to recover the secondary Class 1 contributions from the employee, the liability to pay the contributions remains with the secondary contributor.

An agreement can also be made in certain circumstances where the liability is retrospectively imposed.

Elections

3.131 It is also possible, again in limited circumstances, for the employer and employee to elect for some or all of the secondary liability to the employee (*SSCBA 1992, Sch 1, para 3B*). As with recovery by agreement (see **3.130**) an election can only be made in respect of earnings that:

- relate to the charge on certain post-acquisition events in relation to restricted securities and which are chargeable to income tax by virtue of *ITEPA 2003, s 426*;
- relate to the charge on certain post-acquisition events in relation to convertible securities and which are charged to income tax by virtue of *ITEPA 2003, s 438*; and

- comprise a share option gain (calculated in accordance with *ITEPA 2003, s 479*) chargeable to income tax by virtue of *ITEPA 2003, s 476*.

The election must be made in the prescribed form and contain information prescribed in the *Social Security (Contributions) Regulations 2001* (*SI 2001/1004*), *Sch 5*. Model elections are available to download from the HMRC website. These are contained in Employment Related Securities Manual at ERSM170750.

The election may be refused or withdrawn by HMRC. Otherwise, once made, it remains in force until:

- it ceases to have effect in accordance with its terms;
- it is revoked jointly by both parties; or
- notice is given by the earner to the secondary contributor terminating the election.

The election may also be made in certain circumstances where a permitted liability is imposed retrospectively.

In April 2016 HMRC published a consultation document, the purpose of which is to gather evidence on whether there is still a need for NIC elections. Views were also sought on the potential consequences of removing the ability to make an NIC election. It should be noted that HMRC have no plans to remove NIC agreements (see **3.126**). In October 2016 HMRC confirmed that employer National Insurance contributions arising in connection with employee shares schemes could continue to be formally transferred to the employee on the making of a joint election.

Correction of errors

3.132 The mechanism for correcting Class 1 NIC errors depends whether the error is discovered before the end of the tax year in which it was made or in a subsequent tax year.

If the mistake in the amount of National Insurance contributions deducted from an employee is discovered during the tax year, it can usually be put right within that tax year. Where possible, the mistake should be corrected in the week or month in which it is discovered. Where too much National Insurance has been deducted from an employee's pay, the overpayment should be refunded to the employee on the next pay day.

The position on recovering underpayments from employees is slightly more complicated and is described at **3.134**

Recovering underpayments from employees

3.133 The general rule is that where the secondary contributor makes an error resulting in an underpayment of primary Class 1 National Insurance contributions, the employer must pay the amount due as a result of that error to HMRC. However, where the error was made 'in good faith' the employer can recover the amount of the underpayment from the employee.

An error is 'made in good faith' if it occurred at the time that the earnings were paid and at that time the employer was genuinely unaware of the error. HMRC cite the following examples of errors that would be regarded as having been made in good faith:

- using out of date National Insurance percentage rates, limits or thresholds;
- deducting the wrong Class of National Insurance contributions, for example paying Class 1A contributions instead of Class 1 contributions on an item;
- deducting the wrong category of National Insurance contributions, for example deducting contracted-in National Insurance contributions instead of not contracted-out contributions;
- arithmetical errors where either manual calculations were performed or where payroll data was input incorrectly;
- delays in notifying changes of an employee's circumstances to the payroll department.

Where the error was made in good faith, the underpayment can be recovered from the employee by deductions from earnings subject to adherence to conditions as to the amount of the recovery and the timescale for making the recovery.

As regards the amount that can be recovered from a payment of earnings, this cannot exceed the normal primary Class 1 National Insurance liability on those earnings.

Example 3.24—Recovering underpayments from employees (1)

Susan is a monthly paid employee. She is paid £2,000 each month in 2021/22. As a result of an error made in good faith, her employer failed to deduct primary contributions of £200 from her earnings.

Her employer can recover the underpayment from Susan, but the recovery is limited to the amount of primary National Insurance contributions payable on the earnings from which recovery is to be made.

As Susan is paid £2,000 per month, she must pay primary contributions of £144.36 (12% (£2,000 – £797)) each month (2021/22 figures) on those earnings. Consequently, recovery is limited to £144.36 in any month.

Her employer can recover £144.36 in the month in which the mistake was discovered (meaning Susan suffers a deduction of £288.72 in that month). The balance of £55.64 (£200 – £144.36) cannot be recovered in that month and must be recovered the following month.

As regards the time limit for making the recovery, the employer has the remainder of the tax year in which the error was discovered and all of the following year in which to make the recovery. This means the earlier in the tax year that the error is discovered, the longer the potential recovery period.

Example 3.25—Recovering underpayments from employees (2)

An employer discovers in August 2021 that an error in good faith has led to an underpayment of primary Class 1 National Insurance contributions. The employer has until 5 April 2023 in which to recover the underpayment from the employee.

The employer must ensure that the payments due to HMRC are made at the correct time and that the correct position is shown on the year-end returns, even if amounts have yet to be recovered from the employee.

If an employee receives a payment knowing that the employer deliberately failed to deduct a primary contribution that was due, HMRC can make a direction to recover that contribution from the employee.

Refunds of contributions paid in error

3.134 If an employed earner pays Class 1 National Insurance contributions in excess of the maximum for that year (see **3.102**), he or she may apply for a refund of so much of those contributions as exceeds the annual maximum (the *Social Security (Contributions) Regulations 2001* (*SI 2001/1004*), *reg 52*). This may be the case where an application for deferment was not made or was made late.

An application for a refund must be made in writing to:

HM Revenue and Customs
National Insurance Contributions and Employer Office
BX9 1AN

The application should be made as soon as possible after the end of the tax year and should be supported by evidence of contributions paid in the year (such as payslips or P60s). There is no time limit for claiming a refund of contributions paid in excess of the annual maxima.

HMRC produce a tool which can be used to determine when a National Insurance refund is due and the procedure for claiming it. The tool is available on the gov.uk website.

Interest and penalties

3.135 Interest is charged on Class 1 National Insurance contributions paid late (the *Social Security (Contributions) Regulations 2001* (*SI 2001/1004*),

Sch 4, para 17). The interest is charged in year, running from the date the payment was due to HMRC until the date that the liability is settled. Penalties are charged when PAYE and NIC are paid late on more than one occasion in the tax year (see **3.117**). This applies equally to RTI and non-RTI employers. The penalty is currently levied after the end of the tax year. The penalties are levied in-year on a quarterly basis.

Late filing penalties also apply to RTI returns filed late. The first default in the year will not attract a penalty and the number of defaults is capped at one per month regardless of the number of submissions made in that month. A three-day period of grace is allowed before a penalty is charged. The penalties are charged in-year on a quarterly basis.

If interest is charged as a result of an official error that interest is refunded (the *Social Security (Contributions) Regulations 2001* (*SI 2001/1004*), *Sch 4, para 18*).

Interest is also paid on refunds of contributions. The interest runs from the payment date of 19 April following the tax year until the date that the refund is made (the *Social Security (Contributions) Regulations 2001* (*SI 2001/1004*)).

Penalties are charged for late and incorrect year-end returns and also for a failure to make a return electronically where one was required to be made in this way.

A cross-tax penalty regime applies in respect of errors in tax returns where the return was due on or after 1 April 2009 in relation to a return period starting on or after 1 April 2009. This applies to incorrect RTI returns from 6 April 2013. The inaccuracy penalty regime is discussed at **1.16**.

Liability of directors for company contributions

3.136 Provisions exist which allow the unpaid contributions relating to a company to be transferred to a director of that company where the debt is due to the fraudulent or negligent behaviour of some of all of the directors (*SSAA 1992, s 121C*). The provision targets 'phoenix directors' who incur large debts as a result of non-payment, liquidate the company protected by the limited liability status and then start a new company debt-free.

Where debts are transferred to the directors personally under these provisions, the director has a right of appeal on the grounds that he or she did not act fraudulently or negligently.

Debts of managed service companies

3.137 In certain circumstances HMRC may recover the contribution debts of managed service companies from relevant third parties (the *Social Security (Contributions) Regulations 2001* (*SI 2001/1004*), *Sch, 4, Pt 3A*).

Only relevant contribution debts can be transferred to the relevant third party. A relevant contribution debt is one which satisfies one of the conditions A to E below (*SI 2001/1004, Sch 4, para 29B*).

Condition A is met if a decision has been made in accordance with the *Social Security (Transfer of Functions etc) Act 1999, s 8* that an amount of Class 1 National Insurance contributions are due in respect of a qualifying period and any part of that amount has not been paid within 14 days from the date on which the decision became final and conclusive.

Condition B is met if an employer delivers a return at the end of the 2007/08 or later tax year showing an amount of total contributions deducted by the employer for that tax year. HMRC prepare a certificate showing how much of the contributions included in that return remain unpaid and those contributions are still unpaid 14 days from the date on which the certificate was prepared.

Condition C is met if HMRC prepare a certificate showing the amount of contributions that the employer is liable to pay for a qualifying period and any part of that amount is unpaid 14 days after the date on which the certificate is prepared.

Condition D is met if HMRC serve a notice of a specified amount of earnings-related contributions payable by the employer which requires payment of Class 1 contributions which they consider the employer is liable to pay and any part of that amount is unpaid 14 days after the date on which the certificate is prepared.

Condition E is met if a certificate is prepared following the inspection of the employer's records showing an amount of contributions which it appears that the employer is liable to pay. HMRC make a written demand for payment of those contributions and any part of that amount is unpaid 14 days after the date on which the written demand for payment was made.

If the managed service company has a relevant contribution debt and HMRC consider that all or part of that debt cannot be recovered from the managed service company within a reasonable period, the debt can be recovered from:

- a director or other office holder or associate of the managed service company;
- the managed service company provider;
- a person who, directly or indirectly, has encouraged or been actively involved in the provision by the managed service company of the services of the individual; or
- a director or other office holder or an associate of a person (other than an individual) who falls within the preceding two bullets.

The debt is transferred by way of a transfer notice. Broadly, this must be issued within 12 months of the debt becoming a relevant contribution debt. Payment of the debt must be made within 30 days of the date on which the transfer notice is served (*SI 2001/1004, Sch 4, para 29F*).

A right of appeal exists against the issue of a transfer notice (*SI 2001/1004, Sch 4, para. 29G*). The appeal must be lodged within 30 days of the date on which the transfer notice was issued.

Security for the payment of Class 1 contributions

3.138 HMRC can ask an employer to provide security for the payment of earnings-related contributions where they consider this necessary for the protection of Class 1 contributions (the *Social Security (Contributions) Regulations 2001 (SI 2001/1004) Sch 4, Pt 3B*).

Security can be required from the employer or from a director, company secretary, any similar officer or any person purporting to act in such a capacity in relation to the employer. Where the employer is a limited liability partnership, security can be sought from a member of that partnership. HMRC can require that a person give security of a specified value or that security is given by more than one person, who are treated as being jointly and severally liable for that security.

Where a security is required, HMRC will give notice to the person or persons from whom security is sought specifying the value of security to be given, the manner in which the security is to be given, the date by which it is to be provided and the period of time for which it is required. The date for the provision of the security cannot be less than 30 days after the date on which notice is given. The employer has a right (under *FA 2009, Sch 56, para 10(1)*) to request that payment of the security be deferred.

Once security has been provided the employer can request a reduction in the value of the security held by HMRC if circumstances have changed due to hardship of the person who is no longer a person from whom security can be sought. A reduction can also be sought if there has been a significant reduction in the number of employed earners or if the employer has ceased to be an employer. Where such a request is made, HMRC must let the employer know the outcome of the request.

The employer has a right of appeal against the requirement to provide security. Where security has been given, a right of appeal also exists against a rejection of an application for a reduction in security or the amount of reduction given where this is smaller than requested. Notice of the appeal must be given within 30 days and must state the grounds of the appeal.

Failure to comply with a notice to provide security or further security constitutes an offence. A person found guilty of such an offence is liable on summary conviction to a fine not exceeding level 5 on the standard scale.

HMRC guidance on the use of the power to request security for PAYE and NIC is available on the gov.uk website (see www.gov.uk/government/publications/securities-in-respect-of-paye-and-national-insurance-contributions). The guidance makes it clear that the power will be used to tackle the handful of employers who deliberately try and defraud the government, for example, by deliberately choosing not to pay, by engaging in phoenixism, running up large PAYE and NIC debts and penalties and failing to respond to HMRC's attempts to contact them. The amount of security required is calculated on a case-by-case basis depending on the amount at risk and on the previous behaviour of the employer and other risks.

The security will normally be in the form of either a cash deposit from the business or the director, held by HMRC or paid into a joint account held by the taxpayer and HMRC or in the form of a bond from an approved financial institution which is payable on demand.

PLANNING POINTS

3.139

- When structuring a remuneration package consider whether the elements are 'earnings' for National Insurance purposes. Payments that are outside the definition of earnings do not attract a liability to Class 1 National Insurance contributions (although a liability to Class 1A may arise).
- Where payments are made to employees as a result of the Covid-19 pandemic, check whether they benefit from the temporary disregards for reimbursed home working equipment and Coronavirus antigen tests.
- Claim the employment allowance where this is available. For 2021/22, the allowance is set at £4,000, but its availability is restricted to employers whose secondary Class 1 liability in the previous tax year was less than £100,000. The allowance is not available to companies with one employee where that employee is also a director. It is not given automatically and must be claimed. Anti-avoidance provisions apply.
- Although the benefits of salary sacrifice arrangements were considerably reduced from 6 April 2017 onwards, it is still possible to benefit from National Insurance savings by using a salary sacrifice arrangement by moving the liability from Class 1 on cash earnings to Class 1A on benefits in kind and saving employee contributions (but beware of potential implications of reducing cash salary on entitlement to pension, benefits and statutory payments).
- In a family company situation, consider paying dividends rather than salary to save National Insurance contributions. However, where the employment allowance is available, it is generally efficient to pay a salary equal to the personal allowance as the additional primary contributions payable on salary in excess of the primary threshold are offset by the associated corporation tax deduction.
- Consider timing of payments and use of earnings period rules to reduce overall NIC burden (but beware anti-avoidance provisions on manipulation of earnings period rules).

- Less National Insurance is payable if earnings are spread over several jobs than earned from the same job, but be aware of when aggregation of earnings is required.
- Where a person has more than one job, it may be possible to defer liability in respect of one or more employments.
- Directors should consider using the alternative arrangements to enable their NIC liability to be spread more evenly throughout the year as compared to strict application of the annual earnings period rules.
- Where services are provided through an intermediary, be aware of IR35 rules and situations where a deemed payment of attributable earnings may arise.
- Ensure that returns are made in a timely fashion and reasonable care is taken to ensure errors are not made to ensure penalties are not incurred unnecessarily.
- Ensure National Insurance contributions are paid over to HMRC on time to avoid interest charges and penalties.

Chapter 4

Class 1A National Insurance contributions

SIGNPOSTS

- Class 1A National Insurance contributions are employer-only National Insurance contributions payable on most taxable benefits in kind (see **4.1**).
- The Class 1A rate is the same as the secondary Class 1 rate – 13.8% for 2021/22 (see **4.2**).
- A Class 1A charge arises where the liability conditions are met (see **4.3**).
- The legislation provides for exclusions from the Class 1A charge, including those where a Class 1 liability exists to prevent a double charge (see **4.4**).
- The way in which a benefit is provided to an employee will have an impact on the National Insurance liability that arises (see **4.18**).
- From 6 April 2020, the Class 1A charge is extended to taxable termination payments in excess of £30,000 and to sporting testimonial payments in excess of the £100,000 lifetime tax-free limit (see **4.22** and **4.23**).
- The Class 1A charge is calculated by reference to the cash equivalent value of taxable benefits provided to employees (see **4.24**).
- The employer must report the Class 1A liability on form P11D(b) by 6 July following the end of the tax year to which it relates (see **4.39**).
- Class 1A contributions are payable by 22 July after the end of the tax year where payment is made electronically, or by 19 July otherwise (see **4.40**).

OVERVIEW OF CLASS 1A NATIONAL INSURANCE CONTRIBUTIONS

Nature of Class 1A National Insurance contributions

4.1 Class 1A National Insurance contributions are employer-only contributions charged on most taxable benefits in kind provided to employees.

The Class 1A charge was introduced with effect from 6 April 1991. Initially the charge only applied in respect of company cars and fuel provided for private motoring in such cars. However, it was extended to most taxable benefits in kind from 6 April 2000. From 6 April 2020, the Class 1A charge was extended further, and from that date it applies to taxable termination payments in excess of the £30,000 tax-free threshold and to sporting testimonials in excess of the £100,000 lifetime limit.

The benefits code in its entirety applies to all employees regardless of their earnings rate and consequently the Class 1A charge applies in respect of all taxable benefits provided to employees (unless within the charge to Class 1 or 1B or otherwise exempt from Class 1A). For 2015/16 and earlier tax years, no Class 1A liability arose in respect of benefits provided to lower paid employees earning at a rate of less than £8,500 a year, even if those benefits were taxable.

Payment of Class 1A contributions does not confer any benefit entitlement on the employee to whom the benefits giving rise to the Class 1A charge are provided.

The main charging provision for the Class 1A charge is found in *SSCBA 1992, s 10*, with *SSCBA 1992, s 10ZA* and *10ZB* covering the provision of benefits in kind and non-cash vouchers by a third party. The Treasury is given the power (by *SSCBA 1992, s 10ZC*) to provision as is expedient for Class 1A purposes in consequence of the making of relevant retrospective tax legislation. The *Social Security (Contributions) Regulations 2001* (*SI 2001/1004*) specify exemptions from the Class 1A charge (see **4.12**) and also set the framework for the payment and collection of Class 1A contributions (see **4.33**).

HMRC publish a guidance booklet on Class 1A National Insurance contributions. Booklet CWG5 *Class 1A National Insurance contributions on benefits in kind – a guide for employers* is available on the gov.uk website at www.gov.uk/government/publications/cwg5-class-1a-national-insurance-contributions-on-benefits-in-kind.

Guidance on the Class 1A charge can also be found in HMRC's National Insurance Manual at NIM13000ff. HMRC Manuals are available on their website (see www.hmrc.gov.uk/manuals).

> **Focus**
>
> Class 1A contributions are employer-only contributions – there is no employee Class 1A liability.

Rate of Class 1A National Insurance contributions

4.2 Class 1A National Insurance contributions are employer-only contributions which are payable at the Class 1A rate. The Class 1A rate for

2021/22 is 13.8%, which is the same as the main secondary rate for Class 1 contributions.

> **Focus**
>
> The rate of Class 1A National Insurance is the same as the secondary Class 1 rate.

LIABILITY TO CLASS 1A NATIONAL INSURANCE CONTRIBUTIONS

Liability conditions

4.3 For a Class 1A National Insurance liability to arise, various liability conditions must be met (*SSCBA 1992, s 10*). The conditions are that:

- the benefit must be from, or by reason of, an employee's employment and must be chargeable to income tax as general earnings under the *Income Tax Earnings and Pensions Act 2003* (see **4.5);**
- the employment is relevant employment (see **4.6**);
- the earnings are not liable to Class 1 National Insurance contributions (see **4.9**);
- the earnings are not specifically excluded from the Class 1A charge (see **4.11ff**).

From a practical perspective, if an employer is required to complete at least one P11D or payrolls benefits in kind, it is likely that a Class 1A National Insurance liability will arise.

The benefits code now applies in its entirety to all employees (subject to an exception for lower paid ministers of religion) regardless of their earnings rate. This means that employers are required to pay Class 1A National Insurance contributions on all taxable benefits provided to employees, unless the benefit is specifically exempted or within the Class 1 charge.

From 6 April 2020, Class 1A National Insurance contributions also apply to taxable termination payments in excess of the £30,000 tax-free threshold and to sporting testimonials in excess of the £100,000 lifetime limit. However, rather than being included in the Class 1A liability reported on the P11D(b) after the year end, Class 1A contributions on termination payments and sporting testimonials must be reported to HMRC under real time information and pay over to HMRC with PAYE and Class 1 contributions for the month.

If the tax on an item that would normally attract a Class 1A National Insurance charge is settled by means of a PAYE settlement agreement, Class 1B National Insurance contributions are payable in place of the Class 1A liability that would otherwise arise. Class 1B National Insurance contributions are discussed in Chapter 5.

Does a Class 1A National Insurance liability on a benefit in kind arise?

4.4 The following questions should be asked to work out whether a Class 1A liability arises in respect of a benefit in kind:

Question 1

Have benefits been provided to employees by reason of their employment which are chargeable to income tax?

If the answer to this question is 'no', no Class 1A National Insurance contributions are due.

Question 2

Is the employment an 'employed earner's employment' (ie is the recipient an employee)?

If the answer is 'no', no Class 1A contributions are due.

Question 3

Are Class 1 National Insurance contributions due on the benefit?

If the answer is 'yes', no Class 1A contributions are due.

Question 4

Is the benefit included within a PAYE Settlement Agreement?

If the answer is 'yes', no Class 1A contributions are due.

Question 5

Is the benefit provided for business use only, or is the primary use for business purposes where any private use is not significant?

If the answer to this question is 'yes', no Class 1A contributions are due.

Question 6

Is the benefit excluded from the Class 1A charge?

If the answer is 'yes', no Class 1A contributions are due.

Is the item chargeable to income tax?

4.5 A Class 1A National Insurance liability can only arise if the benefit in kind is chargeable to income tax as general earnings (as defined in *ITEPA 2003, s 7(3)) (SSCBA 1992, s 10(1)(a))*.

This means that if there is no income tax liability there can be no Class 1A National Insurance liability. Consequently, a benefit in kind which is exempt from income tax is not liable to Class 1A National Insurance contributions.

The general disregard from earnings for payments in kind for Class 1 purposes (see **3.43**) means that, in the majority of cases, if a benefit is exempt from tax and therefore outside the charge to Class 1A National Insurance contributions, it will escape contributions liability altogether. However, some payments in kind remain in the Class 1 net (see **3.42**).

> **Focus**
>
> The benefit must be taxable for a Class 1A charge to arise – if there is no tax liability, there is no Class 1A liability.

Is the employment a relevant employment?

4.6 A Class 1A liability on a benefit in kind arises only if the earnings in question are from a relevant employment (*SSCBA 1992, s 10(1)(a)*).

A relevant employment is one which is both an employed earner's employment and the employment is an employment other than a lower paid employment as a minister of religion.

The definition of a relevant employment limits the Class 1A liability to benefits and expenses provided to the employed. This means that no Class 1A liability can arise in respect of the self-employed.

Importance of the P11D

4.7 The P11D is the starting point for the calculation of Class 1A National Insurance contribution on benefits in kind.

All taxable benefits provided to employees (and directors) must be returned on the P11D to the extent that they have not been payrolled or included within a PAYE Settlement Agreement.

However, both benefits and expenses returned on the P11D and those that are payrolled are taken into account in computing the Class 1A liability.

> **Focus**
>
> The P11D is key in working out the Class 1A liability. However, where benefits have been payrolled, these too must be taken into account in working out the Class 1A charge.

Directors

4.8 The provision of a taxable benefit in kind to a director will an associated Class 1A National Insurance charge as for other employees.

A director is defined as:

- in relation to a company whose affairs are managed by a board of directors or similar body, a member of that board or similar body;
- in relation to a company whose affairs are managed by a single director or similar person, that director or person;
- in relation to a company whose affairs are managed by the members themselves, a member of the company.

A 'director' also includes anyone in accordance with whose direction or instructions the directors, as defined above, are accustomed to act. For a person to be regarded as a director, it is not necessary for that person to have 'director' in their job title. Similarly, the mere fact that someone is called a director will not automatically mean that they are a director for these purposes. A director is simply someone who falls within one or more of the above definitions.

A person is not regarded as a director for the purposes of the benefits in kind legislation if he or she is 'outside the scope'. A director will be 'outside the scope' if he or she does not have a material interest in the company and either the director is a full-time working director or the company is a charity or non-profit making concern.

For these purposes, a director has a material interest if he or she is able to control, either directly or indirectly, 5% of the company's share capital. In the case of a close company, a person has a material interest if he or she possesses or is entitled to acquire, such rights as would, in the event of a winding up of the company or in any other circumstances, give entitlement to more than 5% of the assets that would then be available for distribution among the participators. In determining whether the director has holdings of 5% or more, and thus a 'material interest', the holdings of any associates must be taken into account.

A 'full-time working director' is one who is required to devote substantially the whole of his or her time to the service of the company in a managerial or technical capacity.

If a taxable benefit is provided to a director who is 'outside the scope', a Class 1A liability will still arise if the director is provided with taxable benefits.

Are the earnings liable to Class 1 National Insurance contributions?

4.9 To prevent a dual contribution liability, a Class 1A charge will not arise if the benefit in kind already attracts a Class 1 National Insurance liability.

Under the Class 1 National Insurance legislation, there is a general disregard for payments in kind (see **3.42**) which prevents a Class 1 National Insurance liability from arising on the majority of benefits in kind and paves the way for the Class 1A charge. However, some payments in kind are excluded from the disregard and kept within the Class 1 net (see **3.44–3.46**). Such earnings are therefore outside the scope of the Class 1A charge.

HMRC booklet CWG5, *Class 1A National Insurance contributions of benefits in kind – a guide for employers* includes a chart summarising the National Insurance treatment of common benefits in kind. The booklet is available to download from the gov.uk website at www.gov.uk/government/publications/cwg5-class-1a-national-insurance-contributions-on-benefits-in-kind.

> **Focus**
>
> A Class 1A liability will not arise if the benefit is within the Class 1 charge – the Class 1 charge takes priority.

Is the benefit excluded from the Class 1A charge?

4.10 Certain benefits in kind are specifically excluded from the Class 1A charge. The *Social Security (Contributions) Regulations 2001* (*SI 2001/1004*), *reg 40* prescribes general earnings in respect of which Class 1A contributions are not payable. These are discussed in detail at **4.11ff**.

Items exempt from tax, covered by an extra-statutory concession or by a dispensation or included within a PAYE settlement agreement are not liable to Class 1A National Insurance contributions.

EXCLUSIONS FROM THE CLASS 1A CHARGE

Overview of items excluded from the Class 1A charge

4.11 The *Social Security (Contributions) Regulations 2001* (*SI 2001/1004*), *reg 40* sets out those categories of general earnings in respect of which a Class 1A National Insurance contribution is not payable. These items are examined at **4.12ff**.

Also excluded from the Class 1A charge are:

- items which are not chargeable to income tax as general earnings (see **4.5**);
- items exempt from tax by virtue of an extra-statutory concession (see **4.16**); and
- items included within a PAYE settlement agreement in respect of which a Class 1B National Insurance liability arises instead (see Chapter 5):
- items provided for business use but no significant private use is allowance (see **4.20**); and
- items already liable for Class 1 (see Chapter 3).

Exempt benefits are outside the scope of the Class 1A charge.

General earnings excluded from the Class 1A charge

4.12 The following items of general earnings are specifically excluded from the Class 1A National Insurance charge by virtue of the *Social Security (Contributions) Regulations* 2001 (*SI 2001/1004*), *reg 40*:

- a payment by way of any benefit pursuant to a registered pension scheme to which the provisions on authorised pensions and lump sums in *FA 2004, s 204(1)*, the provision on the taxation of benefits under registered pension schemes in *FA 2004, Sch 31* and the provision in unauthorised payments in *FA 2004, s 208* or *s 209* apply (*SI 2001/1004, reg 40(2)(a)*);
- a payment by way of an employer's contribution to a pension scheme that is eligible for migrant member relief by virtue of *FA 2004, Sch 33, para 2* or one that is eligible for transitional relief under the *Taxation of Pension Schemes (Transitional Provisions) Order 2006* (*SI 2006/572*), *art 15(2)* (*SI 2001/2004, reg 40(2)(a)*);
- a payment by way of an employer's contribution to a pension scheme established by a government outside the UK for the benefit of its employees or primarily for their benefit and any benefit referable to such a contribution, whenever made (*SI 2001/1004, reg 40(2)(a)*);
- a payment by way of benefits from a pension scheme which are referable to contributions made before 6 April 2006, provided that *ITEPA 2003, s 386* (which dealt with the charge on payments to non-approved retirement benefit schemes) does not apply to those contributions by virtue of *ITEPA 2003, s 390* (*SI 2001/1004, reg 40(2)(a)*);
- a payment by way of benefits subject to the unauthorised payment charged, imposed by *FA 2004, s 208* as applied to a relevant non-UK scheme by virtue of *FA 2004, Sch 31, para 1* (*SI 2001/1004, reg 40(2)(a)*);
- a payment by way of relevant benefits (within the meaning of *ICTA 1988, s 612*) pursuant to an unapproved retirement benefits scheme and attributable to payments prior to 6 April 1998 (*SI 2001/1004, reg 40(2)(a)*);
- a payment by way of any benefit pursuant to an unapproved retirement benefits scheme that is attributable to payments on or after 6 April 1998 and before 6 April 2006 and which have previously been included in a person's earnings for the purposes of the assessment of his or her liability for earnings-related contributions (*SI 2001/1004, reg 40(2)(a)*);
- a payment to a pension scheme that is afforded relief from taxation by virtue of *art 25(8)* of the Convention set out in the Schedule to the *Double Taxation Relief (Taxes on Income) (France) Order 1968* (*SI 1968/1869*), *art 17A* of the Convention set out in the Schedule to the *Double Taxation Relief (Taxes on Income) (Republic of Ireland)*

Order 1976 (*SI 1976/2151*), *art 27(2)* of the Convention set out in the Schedule to the *Double Taxation Relief (Taxes on Income) (Canada) Order 1980* (*SI 1980/709*), *art 28(3)* of the Convention set out in the Schedule to the *Double Taxation Relief (Taxes on Income) Denmark Order 1980* (*SI 1980/2960*), *art 17(3)* of the Convention set out in the Schedule to the *Double Taxation Relief (Taxes on Income) (South Africa) Order 2002* (*SI 2002/2138*) or *art 17(3)* of the Convention set out in the Schedule to the *Double Taxation Relief (Taxes on Income) (Chile) Order 2003* (*SI 2003/3200*) (*SI 2001/1004, reg 40(2)(a)*);

- a payment by way of benefits pursuant to an employer-financed pension only scheme or a pension pursuant to an employer-financed pension only scheme to which *SI 2001/1004, Sch 3, para 10* (see **3.57**) applies (*SI 2001/1004, reg 40(2)(a)*);
- a payment by way of an employer's contribution to a superannuation fund to which *ICTA 1988, s 615(3)* applies and a payment by way of an annuity paid by such a fund (*SI 2001/1004, reg 40(2)(a)*);
- a payment made to an employed earner receiving full-time instruction at a university, technical college or similar educational establishment provided that the employed earner has enrolled at the educational establishment for a course lasting at least one academic year at the time the payment is made, the employed earner is required to attend the course for an average of 20 weeks in the academic year, the academic establishment is open to members of the public generally and offers more than one course of practical or academic instruction, the educational establishment is not run by the secondary contributor or by a trade organisation of which the secondary contributor is a member and the total amount payable to the earner does not exceed the specified amount (£15,480 for the academic year beginning on 1 September 2007 and subsequent academic years) (*SI 2001/1004, reg 40(2)(ab)*);
- a payment by way of, or a contribution towards, the expenses of the earner's employment to the extent that those expenses relate to travel at the start and finish of an overseas employment and are deductible for tax purposes in accordance with *ITEPA 2003, s 341*, or would be so deductible if conditions B and C in that section were omitted and the earnings of the employment were subject to income tax as employment income (*SI 2001/1004, reg 40(2)(b)*);
- so much of an employed earner's earnings as equal the aggregate of the amount deductible under *ITEPA 2003, ss 373, 374* in respect of the travel costs and expenses of a non-domiciled employee or the employee's spouse, civil partner or child where the duties are performed in the UK or would be so permitted if the earnings of the employment were subject to tax as employment income under *ITEPA 2003* (*SI 2001/1004, reg 40(2)(b)*);
- a payment by way of an allowance to a person in the service of the Commonwealth War Graves Commission or the British Council paid

with a view to compensating him for the extra cost of living outside the UK in order to perform the duties of his employment (*SI 2001/1004, reg 40(2)(b)*);

- a payment by way of a right to acquire securities (*SI 2001/1004, reg 40(2)(c)*);
- a payment by way of an allocation of shares in priority to members of the public in respect of which no liability to income tax arises by virtue of *ITEPA 2003, s 542* (*SI 2001/1004, reg 40(2)(c)*);
- a payment deducted from the earnings in respect of a partnership share agreement within a share incentive plan (*SI 2001/1004, reg 40(2)(c)*);
- a payment by way of an award of shares under a share incentive plan (*SI 2001/1004, reg 40(2)(c)*);
- a payment by way of the acquisition of securities, interests in securities or securities options in connection with the employed earner's employment if, or to the extent, that what is acquired is not a readily convertible asset (*SI 2001/1004, reg 40(2)(c)*);
- a payment of, or in respect of, a gratuity or offering which is not made, directly or indirectly by the secondary contributor and does not comprise or represent sums previously paid by the secondary contributor or which is not allocated, directly or indirectly, by the secondary contributor and, if made by a person who is connected to the secondary contributor, is made in recognition for personal services rendered to the connected person by the earner or by another earner employed by the same secondary contributor and is similar in amount to that which might reasonably be paid to a person who is not so connected or the person making the payment does so in his capacity as tronc master, provided that the payment is not made by a trustee holding property for persons including the earner (*SI 2001/1004, reg 40(2)(d)*);
- the amount equal to the VAT where goods and services are supplied by an earner in his or her employment, earnings are paid to, or for the benefit of, the earner in respect of that employment and those earnings include remuneration for the supply of those goods and services and VAT is chargeable on that supply (*SI 2001/1004, reg 40(2)(d)*);
- a payment of, or contribution towards any fee, contribution or annual subscription which is deductible for tax purposes under *ITEPA 2003, ss 343, 344* (*SI 2001/1004, reg 40(d)*);
- a payment of a fee in respect of employment as a minister of religion which does not form part of the stipend or salary paid in respect of that employment (*SI 20011004, reg 40(2)(d)*); and
- a payment made by the issuer of charge cards, cheque guarantee cards, credit cards or debit cards as a reward to an individual who assists in

identifying or recovering lost or stolen cards in the course of his or her employment as an employed earner, together with any income tax paid by the issuer for the purpose of discharging any liability of the individual to income tax on the payment (*SI 2001/1004, reg 40(2)(d)*).

The above items are also taken outside the Class 1 National Insurance net by virtue of the *Social Security (Contributions) Regulations 2001* (*SI 2001/1004*) *Sch 3* (see **3.43ff**). Consequently, no National Insurance liability arises in respect of them.

Travel expenses

4.13 Also excluded from the Class 1A charge is a payment of, or a contribution towards, qualifying travel expenses that the holder of an office or employment is obliged to incur and pay as the holder of that office or employment. Likewise, any specific and distinct payment of, or a contribution towards, expenses that an employed earner actually incurs in carrying out his or her employment (other than mileage allowance payments in excess of the approved amount) is outside the Class 1A charge (*SI 2001/1004, reg 40(3)*).

NHS track and trace support payments

4.14 NHS track and trace support payments of £500 are made to eligible individuals on low income who are unable to work because they are required to self-isolate, either because they have tested positive for Coronavirus or because someone they know has tested positive for Coronavirus. The *Social Security Contributions (Disregarded Payments) (Coronavirus) (England) Regulations 2020 (SI 2020/1065), reg 3* provides for NHS track and trace support payments to be specifically excluded from the Class 1A charge.

Items not charged to tax by virtue of an extra-statutory concession

4.15 The final category of general earnings excluded from the Class 1A charge by virtue of the *Social Security (Contributions) Regulations 2001* (*SI 2001/1004*), *reg 40* is items exempt from income tax by virtue of the following extra-statutory concessions (*SI 2001/1004, reg 40(7)*):

- ESC A11: residence in the UK – year of commencement or cessation of residence;
- ESC A37: tax treatment of directors' fees received by partnerships and other companies;
- ESC A56: benefits in kind: tax treatment of accommodation in Scotland provided for employees;

- ESC A91: living accommodation provided by reason of employment; and
- ESC A97: Jobmatch programme.

Cars made available for disabled earners only for business and home to work travel

4.16 No Class 1A liability arises in respect of the provision of a car to a disabled earner if the following conditions are met (the *Social Security (Contributions) Regulations 2001* (*SI 2001/1004*), *reg 38*):

- the car is made available to an earner who is disabled;
- the car is made available to the earner by reason of his employment;
- the car is made available on account of the earner's disability for the purposes of, or for purposes which include assisting, the earner's travelling between the earner's home and place of employment;
- the terms on which the car is made available to the earner prohibit private use other than by the earner to whom it is made available and in travelling between the earner's home and work; and
- no prohibited private use has been made of the car in the year.

PAYE settlement agreements

4.17 A PAYE settlement agreement (PSA) is a voluntary agreement between the employer and HMRC under which the employer agrees to pay the tax due on certain benefits in kind provided to employees. PAYE settlement agreements can only be used to meet the tax liability on benefits that are minor, given on an irregular basis or provided in circumstances in which it is impracticable to apply PAYE, report the benefit on form P11D or to apportion a shared benefit between employees.

From a National Insurance perspective, items included within a PAYE settlement attract a liability to Class 1B National Insurance contributions in place of the Class 1 or Class 1A charge that would otherwise arise (*SSCBA 1992, s 10(6)*). Thus, no Class 1A liability arises in respect of an item included within a PSA.

Class 1B National Insurance contributions are discussed in Chapter 5.

> **Focus**
>
> Where the benefit is included within a PAYE Settlement Agreement, a Class 1B liability arises in place of the Class 1 liability that would otherwise arise.

EFFECT OF METHOD OF PROVIDING BENEFITS ON LIABILITY

Impact of way in which benefits are provided on NIC charge

4.18 The way in which a benefit is provided to an employee can determine whether any associated National Insurance liability is to Class 1 or Class 1A. This will affect the amount of National Insurance payable as Class 1A contributions are payable only by the employer, whereas both employees and employers are liable to pay Class 1 National Insurance contributions.

If the employer provides the employee with benefits, such as medical insurance or the use of a company car, the liability is generally to Class 1A. However, if the employer provides the employee with cash with which to buy the benefit, the cash so provided remains liable to Class 1 National Insurance contributions as for any other payment of earnings.

Similarly, the liability is to Class 1 if the employer meets a personal liability of an employee. For example, if the employee takes out a contract of private medical insurance and the employer either pays the bill on the employee's behalf or reimburses the employee, the amount paid or reimbursed is treated as earnings and is liable to Class 1 National Insurance contributions

However, if the employer takes out a contract to provide private medical insurance cover to employees, the associated benefits falls within the Class 1A charge.

As there is no employee liability under Class 1A, it makes sense wherever possible to structure benefit provision so that it falls within the Class 1A net rather than within the Class 1 liability. As a general rule, this will mean providing the employee with the benefits itself, rather than meeting or reimbursing the cost of a benefit that an employee has acquired himself.

> **Focus**
>
> It is important to recognise that providing the benefit has different National Insurance implications to providing the employee with the cash to cover the cost of the benefit. The former is within the Class 1A charge, and as such the liability is only on the employer, whereas the latter is within the Class 1 charge, giving rise to a liability on both the employee and the employer.

Salary sacrifice arrangements

4.19 Benefits in kind may be made available to an employee under a salary sacrifice arrangement. The employer and employee agree that the employee will give up cash salary in return for a non-cash benefit. To be regarded as effective by HMRC, the employee must not be able to revert back to the higher salary at will.

From 6 April 2017 the advantages of salary sacrifice arrangements are seriously curtailed. From that date, unless the benefit is one of a limited range of benefits, the associated tax and National Insurance are lost where the benefit is made available via a salary sacrifice or flexible benefits arrangement or where a cash alternative is made available and new valuation rules apply under which the taxable amount and the amount for National Insurance purposes is the higher of the salary foregone and the cash alternative and the cash equivalent calculated by applying normal rules. The new valuation rules do not apply to the following benefits (in respect of which any associated exemptions are preserved):

- pension savings;
- employer-provided pension advice;
- childcare and childcare vouchers;
- cycles and cyclists' safety equipment under cycle to work schemes; and
- ultra-low emission cars.

Transitional rules apply to arrangements in existence at 5 April 2017, in respect of which the start date for the new rules is the earlier of the date on which the contract end, is modified or renewed, and 6 April 2021 where the benefit taken in exchange is a car (other than an ultra-low emissions car) living accommodation or school fees, and 6 April 2018 in all other cases.

Prior to the introduction of these rules, a salary sacrifice arrangement could be particularly worthwhile where the benefit received in exchange for the reduction in salary is exempt from tax and National Insurance, such as childcare vouchers up to the exempt amount. The employee saves tax and National Insurance and the employer also saves secondary Class 1 National Insurance contributions.

A salary sacrifice arrangement can still be beneficial where the benefit taken in exchange is not exempt from tax and National Insurance as swapping cash earnings for a non-cash benefit will generally move the National Insurance charge from Class 1 to Class 1A. As Class 1A is an employer-only charge this will have the effect of saving employee Class 1 contributions. This remains the case beyond April 2017 and as such as salary sacrifice arrangement can still be beneficial in saving employee National Insurance contributions. However, from that date, for most benefits in kind provided via an optional remuneration arrangement, the amount on which National Insurance is calculated is the relevant amount (ie the higher of the cash equivalent value and the cash foregone). Consequently, salary sacrifice arrangements should be used with care as a means of mitigating National Insurance.

Care should also be taken when entering into a salary sacrifice arrangement as reducing cash earnings can affect the employee's pension and benefit entitlement. Particular care is needed if the sacrifice reduces earnings below the lower earnings limit (£120 per week for 2020/21) as this will adversely affect entitlement to statutory payments and will also affect the employee's contribution record and may impact on his or her entitlement to the state pension. It is important to ensure that the employee continues to be paid at least the National Living Wage or, where the employee is under the age of 25, the National Minimum Wage appropriate to the employee's age.

> **Focus**
>
> The benefit of salary sacrifice schemes was seriously curtailed from 6 April 2017. However, there can be National Insurance savings from providing a benefit via a salary sacrifice arrangement, as the liability moves from Class 1 to Class 1A, saving employee National Insurance contributions.

Benefits provided for business use

4.20 From 6 April 2016, a tax exemption applies in respect of paid and reimbursed expenses that would be fully deductible if the expense were paid by the employee. Benefits and expenses that fall within the terms of the exemption are also exempt from National Insurance. The rules for calculating the Class 1A charge in relation to mixed use benefits are discussed at **4.21**.

The tax legislation (in *ITEPA 2003, s 316*) also provides an exemption from tax for benefits provided to employees on the employer's business premises to enable the employee to carry out the duties of his or her employment. The exemption remains available where there is some private use of the accommodation, supplies or services, provided that the private use is not significant. As such benefits are exempt from tax, no Class 1A liability arises.

The tax exemption also applies to benefits provided away from the employer's premises where the sole purpose of their provision is to enable the employee to fulfil the duties of his or her employments. Examples would include the provision of a fax machine or computer to enable the employee to work from home. Again, the exemption is not lost as a result of private use provided that the private use is insignificant. As no tax liability arises where this condition is met, no Class 1A liability arises either.

> **Focus**
>
> Where a benefit is provided wholly for business use, or where any private use is insignificant, no Class 1A liability arises.

Mixed use benefits

4.21 In some situations a benefit may be provided for both business and private use. Where the private use is significant, the exemption outlined at **4.20** is not in point.

In most cases, where a benefit is provided for business and private use, Class 1A National Insurance contributions are payable on the full amount of the benefit. As with other benefits, the amount taken into account in the Class 1A calculation is the cash equivalent returned on the P11D.

However, if the employee makes good the cost of any private use, no tax liability, and consequently no Class 1A National Insurance liability, arises.

Care must be taken where there is mixed use and the employee is entitled to a deduction in respect of the business element only. Following the enactment of *ITEPA 2003* there was confusion whether the *SSCBA 1992, s 10(7)*, as amended to reflect *ITEPA 2003*, actually replicated the previous position in which deductions were disregarded where there was only partial business use, such that the Class 1A charge was based on the full amount of the benefit as reported on the P11D. The legislation was amended from 6 April 2007 to clarify that this was indeed the case.

The legislation, as amended from 6 April 2007, makes it clear that deductions for *ITEPA 2003, ss 363–365* are disregarded in computing the Class 1A liability. Hence, the deductions do not reduce the Class 1A liability, which is based on the full value reported on the P11D. This situation may arise if, for example, an employer provides the employee with a phone at home for both business and private calls, the contract for which is in the employer's name. Unless the employee meets the cost of all private calls and the line rental in full, the employer must return the benefit on the P11D. The employee can claim a corresponding deduction for the business calls on his or her tax return. As the line rental is not used wholly, exclusively and necessarily for business purposes, no deduction is available in respect of business portion. The Class 1A liability is based on the value reported on the P11D. There is no adjustment to Class 1A calculation for the deduction in respect of business calls. The position is illustrated by way of the following example.

Example 4.1—Class 1A liability and mixed use benefits

An employer provides an employee with a landline telephone at his home to enable him to make works calls from home, which comprise a necessary part of his job. The employer contracts with the phone company as regards the provision of the phone. The phone is also available for the employee's private use and the employee is not required to make good the cost of the private calls.

The line rental is £180 a year. Total calls in the year are £600, of which £390 relate to business calls.

The employer returns a taxable benefit of £780 on the P11D. The employee claims a deduction of £390 in relation to the business calls.

However, the amount returned on the P11D (£780) is taken into account in calculating the Class 1A liability. There is no adjustment in respect of the business calls.

In the event that a benefit is only available to an employee for private use for part of the tax year, this will be reflected in the benefit in kind calculation.

This may arise where, for example, an employee has the private use of a yacht for one week a year. The Class 1A charge is based on the cash equivalent of the benefit as calculated for tax purposes and returned on the P11D or payrolled.

Termination payments

4.22 From 6 April 2020, Class 1A National Insurance contributions apply to taxable termination payments in excess of £30,000. The charge, which was given legislative effect by the *National Insurance Contributions (Termination Awards and Sporting Testimonials) Act 2019, s 1* is imposed by *SSCBA 1992, s 10(1A)*. The charge applies where a termination award is treated as employment income of an earner by *ITEPA 2003, s 403* and the earner is chargeable to income tax on that amount.

The tax treatment of termination payments was reformed from 6 April 2018. Where an employment is terminated on or after that date, the approach is to compare the termination award to what is known as the 'post-employment notice pay' (PENP). The PENP is broadly the pay that the employee would have received had he or she worked their notice period. The termination award is taxed as earnings up to the level of the PENP and liable to Class 1 (employer and employee) National Insurance contributions. To the extent that the termination award exceeds the PENP, it is taxed as a termination payment, the first £30,000 of which is tax-free. Certain payments, such as redundancy pay, are always taxed as termination payments rather than earnings, regardless of whether the total termination award is more than the PENP; however, such payments count towards the £30,000 tax-free limit.

To avoid a double charge, no Class 1A liability arises on earnings that are subject to a Class 1 charge. Payments made on termination that are taxed as earnings do not attract a Class 1A charge as these are within the charge to Class 1.

Where a Class 1A charge arises in respect of a taxable termination payment in excess of the £30,000 tax-free threshold, the liability is reported to HMRC via real time information and paid with PAYE and Class 1 National Insurance for that period, rather than being included within the P11D calculation and paid after the end of the tax year.

Sporting testimonials

4.23 As From 6 April 2020, Class 1A National Insurance contributions apply to taxable sporting testimonial payments in excess of the £100,000 tax-free lifetime limit.

Legislation which took effect from 6 April 2018 confirmed that non-contractual, non-customary sporting testimonials are taxable to the extent that they exceed a £100,000 lifetime tax-free allowance. The Class 1A liability on sporting testimonials will apply where a tax charge applies.

The Class 1A charge will fall on the sporting testimonial committee and it will be the responsibility of the sporting testimonial committee to report and pay the Class 1A liability to HMRC. The liability will be reported and paid via the PAYE/RTI process, rather than through the P11D(b) process. However, if the sportsperson is provided with a taxable benefit during his or her sporting testimonial year, such as a company car, the usual Class 1A process will apply to the benefit in kind, which should be paid and reported by the sporting testimonial committee via the P11D(b) process.

Legislative effect is given to the Class 1A charge on sporting testimonials in excess of £100,000 by new *SSCBA 1992, s 10ZBA*, as inserted by the *National Insurance Contributions (Termination Payments and Sporting Testimonials) Act 2019, s 3*.

EMPLOYEES ABROAD

Class 1A liability in respect of benefits provided to employees abroad

4.24 Benefits in kind may be provided to employees whilst they are working aboard. They may also be provided for use by the employee's family whilst the employee is working abroad or left available for use by the employee on his or her return to the UK.

The extent to which a Class 1A National Insurance liability arises in respect of employees going abroad to work or coming from abroad to work in the UK depends on whether the benefit is chargeable to tax as general earnings under *ITEPA 2003* and whether the employer is liable to secondary Class 1 National Insurance contributions for any part of the tax year for which the benefit was provided. For a Class 1A National Insurance liability to arise, both of these conditions must be met.

When a person's liability to pay Class 1 National Insurance contributions whilst abroad comes to an end, the liability to Class 1A National Insurance contributions in respect of benefits in kind provided to that person also comes to an end, This may mean that the Class 1A National Insurance liability ends part way through a tax year. In this situation an adjustment is needed when calculating the Class 1A National Insurance liability. The benefit is treated as being unavailable for the part of the year after the date on which the Class 1 National Insurance liability is ceased. Any adjustment should be made using the adjustment facility on the P11D(b) on a pro rata basis to reflect the number of days on which the benefit is treated as being unavailable by virtue of the ending of the Class 1 liability.

The National Insurance treatment of workers going to and coming from abroad is discussed fully in Chapter 9.

CALCULATING THE CLASS 1A CHARGE

Earnings attracting the Class 1A charge

4.25 The starting point of the Class 1A charge on benefits in kind is to determine that earnings in respect of which Class 1A contributions are liable. These are the benefits as returned on the P11D and those which have been payrolled. The figure is computed at employer-level, rather than for each individual employee.

The legislation provides that Class 1A contributions are payable on so much of the general earnings from the relevant employment 'that are left out of account' in the computation of earnings for Class 1 purposes (*SSCBA 1992, s 10(1)(c)*). This is subject to the proviso that Class 1A contributions are not payable if Class 1B contributions are payable instead by virtue of the inclusion of the emolument in a PAYE settlement agreement (*SSCBA 1992, s 10(6)*: see **4.15**).

The earnings figure for Class 1A purposes is also adjusted to take account of items that are not liable to the Class 1A charge (see **4.11ff**).

From 6 April 2020, a Class 1A National Insurance liability arises on taxable termination payments in excess of the £30,000 threshold and sporting testimonial payments in excess of £100,000. Where such a liability arises, it is dealt with separately from any Class 1A National Insurance contributions on benefits in kind and not included in the P11D(b) calculation.

Focus

The starting point for the P11D calculation is the cash equivalent values reported on the P11Ds. The values that need to be taken into account are those entered in boxes with a `Class 1A' indicator. Where benefits have been payrolled, the cash equivalent of payrolled benefits must also be taken into account. The calculation is performed on the P11D(b).

Class 1A charge computed before excluded deductions

4.26 When computing the earner's emoluments for the purposes of computing the Class 1A liability, no account is taken of the following deductions (*SSCBA 1992, s 10 (7), (7B)*):

- deductions for employee's expenses (other than a limited deduction for agency fees paid by entertainers;
- deductions from benefits code earnings permitted by *ITEPA 2003, ss 363–365*; or
- deductions for earnings representing benefits or reimbursed expenses.

The Class 1A charge is computed before taking account of these deductions. The exception to this rule is where the deduction is at least equal to the cash equivalent of the benefit (i.e. the benefit is used only for business purposes) (*SSCBA 1992, s 10(7A)*).

Class 1A charge based on taxable values of benefits in kind

4.27 The practical effect of the legislation is that the Class 1A charge is based on the taxable value of those benefits and expenses falling within the Class 1A net. This will be the cash equivalent value or, where provision is made under an optional remuneration arrangement, such as a salary sacrifice arrangement, the relevant value. The taxable value is the measure of the benefit for income tax purposes and is the value returned on the P11D or, where benefits are payrolled, the payrolled amount. Unless specific provisions apply to determine the calculation of the cash equivalent value for a particular benefit, as is the case for cars, living accommodation, car fuel and beneficial loans, for example, the cash equivalent value is simply the cost to the employer, less any amounts made good by the employee.

Alternative valuation rules apply from 6 April 2017 onwards to most benefits which are made available as part of an optional remuneration arrangement, such as a salary sacrifice arrangement, or where a cash alternative is offered instead. Under the rules, the value of benefits provided in this way is the relevant amount. This is broadly the higher of the cash equivalent value computed under normal rules and the cash foregone or cash alternative offered. For commentary on salary sacrifice arrangements, see **4.19.**

Computation at employer level

4.28 The Class 1A charge is an employer only charge. It is levied on the cash equivalent value of taxable benefits provided to all employees regardless of their earnings rate (subject to the exemption for lower-paid ministers of religion).

Therefore, it is not necessary to work out the Class 1A charge associated with particular benefits provided to particular employees. The computation is a global computation based on the total value of taxable benefits provided by the employer to employees that fall within the scope of the Class 1A charge.

From 6 April 2020, a Class 1A liability arises on taxable termination payments and taxable sporting testimonial payments. Where such a charge arises, it is computed and dealt with separately from any Class 1A National Insurance liability on benefits in kind.

Benefits reported on the P11D

4.29 The starting point of the calculation of the Class 1A liability on benefits in kind is form P11D, which is the return of expenses and benefits. To aid the calculation of the Class 1A charge, the cash equivalent values which need to be taken into account in the calculation are highlighted on form P11D by means of brown boxes with a Class 1A indicator.

The employer will need the P11Ds for all employees and directors for the tax year in question in order to work out the Class 1A contributions payable.

Payrolled benefits

4.30 Employers have the option to deal with the tax on most benefits in kind via the payroll in a process known as `payrolling' rather than return those benefits to HMRC on form P11D. Under payrolling, the cash equivalent of the benefit is treated like extra annual salary paid to the employee evenly throughout the year on the employee's normal pay day. It is possible to payroll all benefits in kind with the exception of employer-provided living accommodation and low-interest and interest-free loans. However, to payroll benefits for a particular year, the employer must register with HMRC to do so before the start of the tax year. HMRC are not able to process requests to payroll in year. Once benefits have been registered for payrolling, they remain registered unless the employer deregisters them. This must be done before the start of the tax year for which it is to have effect.

Where benefits have been payrolled, the cash equivalent of those benefits must be taken into account in calculating the Class 1A charge.

Using form P11D(b) to calculate the Class 1A charge on benefits in kind

4.31 Form P11D(b) is a dual-purpose form. It is the employer's declaration that all required P11D forms have been submitted to HMRC. It is also the statutory Class 1A return. In its role as the Class 1A return, section 1 of the form contains a proforma Class 1A computation.

The Class 1A charge is computed as follows:

Step one

Add together the total of the entries in the brown Class 1A indicator boxes on all P11D forms for the tax year.

Step two

Add together the cash equivalent values of payrolled benefits

Step three

Add together the Step 1 and Step 2 figures

This figure should be entered in Box A on form P11D(b).

Step four

Multiply by the Class 1A rate as shown in Box B on form P11D(b). For 2017/18 and 2018/19 this is 13.8%.

Step five

Enter the result of step two (Box A entry multiplied by Class 1A rate in Box B) in Box C. This is the employer's Class 1A liability for the year.

Where a payroll software package or HMRC's expenses and benefits returns online service is used to complete expenses and benefits returns, the Class 1A calculation is performed programmatically.

Where paper forms are submitted, the calculation can be performed manually as outlined above.

Example 4.2—Calculating the Class 1A liability on benefits on kind

An employer provides taxable benefits to a number of employees and directors. For 2020/21, the total cash equivalent value of benefits shown in the brown Class 1A boxes on forms P11D is £40,000. The employer also payrolls benefits with a cash equivalent value of £10,000.

The total cash equivalent value of taxable benefits provided to employees in 2020/21 is £50,000.

The employer's Class 1A liability for 2019/20 is £6,900 (£50,000 × 13.8%).

Form P11D(b) can be completed online or on a paper form which can be downloaded from the gov.uk website: see www.gov.uk/government/publications/paye-end-of-year-expenses-and-benefits-p11db.

Adjustments to the Class 1A charge on benefits in kind

4.32 In certain situations it may be necessary to adjust the total benefits liable to Class 1A contributions as computed in accordance with **4.30** above.

Where it is necessary to adjust the value of the benefits taken from the P11Ds and shown in Box A in section 1 of the P11D(b), the employer should not complete Box C in section 1. Section 4 should be completed instead.

Adjustments may be necessary if:

- substitute P11D forms are used or P11D information is submitted in list format and the substitute forms or lists do not identify the items subject to Class 1A National Insurance contributions;
- a benefit is shown on the P11D as liable to Class 1A contributions, but the cash equivalent value shown for tax purposes has already had tax deducted from it;

- the employer has taken over an existing business and the previous employer has either paid Class 1A National Insurance contributions in respect of employees who left before the date of the transfer or would have been due to pay the Class 1A National Insurance contributions;
- the employer finds an error in the amount of Class 1A National Insurance contributions previously calculated and reported; or
- a benefit has been reported on the P11D that is fully matched by a deduction for tax purposes.

The adjustment process, as set out in section 4 of form P11D(b) is as follows:

Step one

Enter the figure from Box A in section 1 in Box A in section 4. This is the total cash equivalent value of all benefits provided to P11D employers and directors as computed by adding together the cash equivalents shown in the Class 1A boxes on all of the employer's P11Ds for the tax year in question plus the cash equivalent of any payrolled benefits.

Step two

Add any amounts not included in Box A on which Class 1A National Insurance contributions are due. The entry should be made in Box B in section 4 and a description given in the box provided.

Step three

Deduct any amounts included in box A on which Class 1A National Insurance contributions are not due. The entry should be made in Box C and a description given in the box provided.

Step four

Enter the revised total value of benefits on which Class 1A National Insurance contributions are due in Box D. This is the total of Box A plus Box B minus Box C.

Step five

Calculate the Class 1A charge. This is the Box D figure multiplied by the Class 1A percentage as shown in Box E (13.8%). The result is entered in Box F, which shows the Class 1A contributions payable by the employer for the year.

Example 4.3—Calculation of Class 1A liability: adjustment of benefit values

An employer's P11Ds shows total benefits liable to Class 1A National Insurance contributions of £30,000 for 2021/22. The employer also payrolls benefits with a value of £15,000, which are not reported on the P11D.

It is therefore necessary to adjust the value of benefits liable to Class 1A contributions when calculating the Class 1A liability.

Benefits attracting Class 1A contributions as shown on P11Ds (Box A)	£30,000
Amounts not included in Box A on which Class 1As are due (Box B)	£15,000
Amounts included in Box A on which Class 1As are not due (Box C)	
Revised total of benefits on which Class 1A contributions are due (box D)	£45,000
Class 1 percentage (Box E)	13.8%
Class 1A NICs payable (£29,400 × 13.8%) (Box F)	£6,210.00

Rounding

4.33 When calculating the Class 1A charge, the figures are rounded to the nearest penny, with amounts of less than a halfpenny being ignored (the *Social Security (Contributions) Regulations 2001* (*SI 2001/1004*), *reg 39*).

Multiple employments and shared benefits

4.34 In the event that an employed earner is provided with a benefit in kind by virtue of more than one employment held by him or her, the liability for the associated Class 1A charge is shared by the relevant secondary contributors (the *Social Security (Contributions) Regulations 2001* (*SI 2001/1004*), *reg 36*). This applies regardless of whether the employments are with the same or different employers.

The amount payable by each employer is found by deducting an amount equal to the fraction:

$$\frac{X - 1}{X}$$

as multiplied by the Class 1A charge from the Class 1A charge (as normally computed), where X is the number of employments in respect of which the benefit is provided.

The adjustment also applies where a benefit is provided to two or more employed earners concurrently by reason of their respective employments with the same employer.

Example 4.4—Calculating the Class 1A liability: more than one employment in the same group

Greg has two employments. The employments are with two separate companies within the same group. He is provided with one company car in respect of both employments. For 2020/21 the car has a cash equivalent value of £4,000.

The normal Class 1A charge would be £552 (£4,000 × 13.8%). To avoid a double charge each employer would pay £276, being £552 – (£552 × ½).

Calculating the Class 1A charge on taxable termination payments

4.35 From 6 April 2020, a Class 1A National Insurance liability arises on taxable termination payments in excess of the £30,000 tax-free threshold. The charge is at the Class 1A percentage (13.8% for 2020/21) and is applied to the amount of the termination treated as employment income by virtue of *ITEPA 2003, s 403* to the extent that it exceeds £30,000.

Calculating the Class 1A charge on sporting testimonial payments

4.36 From 6 April 2020, a Class 1A National Insurance liability arises on sporting testimonial payments to the extent that they exceed the tax-free lifetime limit of £100,000. The charge is at the Class 1A percentage (13.8% for 2021/22) and is applied to the amount of the sporting testimonial to the extent that the total amount exceeds £100,000.

BENEFITS PROVIDED BY A THIRD PARTY

Awards by third parties

4.37 The NIC treatment of awards by a third party depends on the type of award and whether the employer has arranged its provision with the third party.

The employer is responsible for meeting the reporting requirements and paying any NIC due where the employer arranges for the employees to receive an award from a third party which attracts a Class 1A NIC liability or where a third party provides employees with an award that attracts a Class 1 liability (*SSCBA 1992, s 10ZA*).

However, if the third party provides an award that is liable to Class 1A NICs and the employer has not arranged its provision, it is the third party rather than the employer who is responsible for reporting details of the award and paying the associated Class 1A contributions due.

Where a third party provides an employee with a cash payment, a cash voucher or a benefit that normally attracts a Class 1 liability, the award will attract a Class 1 liability.

Where the award takes the form of a taxable benefit provided to a P11D employee or a director or a non-cash voucher, the award will attract a Class 1A liability.

Some awards from small parties, such as small gifts (value of less than £250 in the tax year) are exempt from tax and NICs.

> **Focus**
>
> Where benefits are provided by a third party, the Class 1A liability will depend on who arranged the provision; if the employer arranges for the benefit to be provided, the liability falls on the employer, but if the employer had no involvement in its provision, the third party provider is liable.

Meaning of 'arranged'

4.38 The liability for any Class1A contributions arising in respect of benefits and awards made by a third party depends on whether the employer has 'arranged' the provision of the benefit or the award (*SSCBA 1992, s 10ZA*).

An employer is regarded as having 'arranged' the provision of the award if the employer has taken an active part in its provision. Examples include the employer asking the third party to make the award or meeting some of the costs.

However, HMRC do not regard an employer as having 'arranged' an award if the involvement is limited to providing the third party with a list of employees.

Non-cash vouchers

4.39 The rules on the incidence of Class 1A National Insurance in respect of benefits provided by third parties (see **4.38**) also apply in respect of the provision of a non-cash voucher by a third party (*SSCBA 1992, s 10ZB*). The provisions also apply in relation to non-cash vouchers provided by third parties to P9D employees.

The treatment of non-cash vouchers for NIC purpose differs depending on whether the vouchers are provided by an employer (or by a third party under an arrangement with the employer) or independently by a third party. Where the liability falls on the employer, the charge is to Class 1, However, where the liability falls on the third party, the charge is to Class 1A.

COLLECTION OF CLASS 1A NATIONAL INSURANCE CONTRIBUTIONS

Reporting requirements

4.40 The way in which Class 1A National Insurance contributions are notified to HMRC depends on whether the charge arises in respect of benefits in kind or, with effect from 6 April 2020, on taxable termination or sporting testimonial payments.

Where an employer provides taxable benefits in kind to employees, a Class 1A National Insurance liability will arise in respect of those benefits in kind. An employer must notify HMRC of the liability for Class 1A National Insurance contributions on forms P11D(b), which is both the employer's declaration that all required forms P11D have been submitted to HMRC and also the employer's statutory Class 1A return.

Form P11D(b) must reach the employer no later than 6 July following the end of the tax year to which it relates (the *Social Security (Contributions) Regulations 2001* (*SI 2001/1004*), *reg 80*). This is the same date by which expenses and benefits returns P11D and P9D must reach HMRC. Thus the return for 2021/22 must reach HMRC by 6 July 2022.

Form P11D(b) can be filed electronically using HMRC's PAYE Online service. Expenses and benefits forms, including form P11D(b), can also be submitted electronically using HMRC's Online Expenses and Benefits Service. However, there is no obligation to file electronically and paper forms can be sent if preferred.

Where, from 6 April 2020, a Class 1A National Insurance liability arises on a taxable termination payment in excess of the £30,000 threshold, the employer must notify HMRC on the Full Payment Submission via real time information. Payment of the liability is made as for PAYE and Class 1 National Insurance contributions.

Likewise, where from 6 April 2020, a Class 1A National Insurance liability arises on a taxable termination payment in excess of the tax-free lifetime limit of £100,000, the sporting testimonial committee must notify HMRC via real time information and pay the liability as for payments of PAYE and Class 1 National Insurance contributions. However, if the sportsperson also receives benefits in kind during their testimonial year, for example a company car, the usual Class 1A reporting process for benefits in kind applies, and the benefit should be reported to HMRC on form P11D(b).

Focus

The deadline for submission of Form P11D(b) – the Class 1A return – is 6 July following the end of the tax year to which it relates.

Due date for payment of Class 1A National Insurance contributions

4.41 The date by which Class 1 National Insurance contributions are due for payment depends on whether they relate to benefits in kind or, from 6 April 2020, to taxable termination payments or taxable sporting testimonials.

To the extent that they relate to benefits in kind, Class 1A National Insurance contributions must be paid by 22 July following the end of the tax year to which they relate where payment is made electronically. If payment is made by cheque, an earlier deadline of 19 July applies (the *Social Security (Contributions) Regulations 2001* (*SI 2001/1004*), *reg 71*).

Where from 6 April 2020 onwards a Class 1A National Insurance liability arises on taxable termination payments or taxable termination payments, the liability must be paid by the 22nd of the month in which the tax month in which the payment was made ends if payment is made electronically, or by the 19th of that month where payment is made by cheque. Payment is made to HMRC with and as for PAYE and Class 1 National Insurance contributions for that month.

> **Focus**
>
> Class 1A contributions are payable by 22 July following the end of the tax year to which they relate if payment is made electronically, or by 19 July otherwise. Interest is charged on late payments.

Interest on Class 1A contributions

4.42 Interest is charged on Class 1A National Insurance contributions paid late. The interest runs from the due date to the date when payment is actually made (the *Social Security (Contributions) Regulations 2001* (*SI 2001/1004*), *reg 76*).

If interest has been paid on a Class 1A liability and either that interest is found not to be due or the Class 1A liability in respect of which it was paid is returned to the employer or repaid, the interest will also be repaid (the *Social Security (Contributions) Regulations 2001* (*SI 2001/1004*), *reg 78*).

If the interest is charged as a result of an official error by HMRC, that interest will also be repaid (the *Social Security (Contributions) Regulations 2001* (*SI 2001/1004*), *reg 79*).

Interest is also paid on refunded Class 1A contributions. The interest runs from the later of 19 April after the end of the tax year and the actual date of payment until the date on which the repayment is made (the *Social Security (Contributions) Regulations 2001* (*SI 2001/1004*), *reg 77*). As the due date for payment of Class 1A contributions (see **4.43**) falls after 19 April, the interest period will generally run from the date of payment until the date on which the repayment is made.

Penalties

4.43 Penalties may be charged in respect of a late and/or incorrect P11D(b).

Where contributions are underpaid as a result of an incorrect P11D(b), a maximum penalty of up to 100% of the contributions underpaid may be charged (the *Social Security (Contributions) Regulations 2001* (*SI 2001/1004*), *reg 81*). The penalty must be levied within six years of the making of the return, or, if later, within three years of the final determination of the Class 1A liability. The penalty is mitigable.

Penalties may also be charged for a failure to make a return by the due date. The maximum penalty depends on the number of earners in respect of whom Class 1A contributions are payable (the *Social Security (Contributions) Regulations 2001* (*SI 2001/1004*), *reg 81(4)*). The penalty is charged for each month that the failure to make the return continues as follows:

- £100 where the number of earners in respect of whom Class 1A contributions are payable is 50 or less; and
- £100 for each 50 earners in respect of whom Class 1A contributions are payable, plus an additional £50 where that number is not a multiple of 50.

The penalty is capped at the amount of the Class 1A contributions due.

The penalty regime for errors in tax returns (see **1.15**) does not apply for Class 1A purposes.

Focus

Care should be taken to ensure that the P11D(b) is correct and filed on time as penalties may be charged for late or incorrect returns.

Set-off against Class 1 contributions

4.44 If an employer has paid a Class 1A contribution that he was not liable to pay, the employer can deduct that contribution from a payment of secondary Class 1 contributions that he is liable to (the *Social Security (Contributions) Regulations 2001* (*SI 2001/1004*), *reg 83*). The set-off can only be made for income tax periods in the same tax year.

Security for amounts of Class 1A contributions

4.45 HMRC have the power to ask the employer to provide security or further security for amounts of Class 1A National Insurance contributions where they consider it necessary to protect revenue.

The provisions on the power to require security set out at **3.141** in relation to Class 1 National Insurance contributions apply also to Class 1A contributions (the *Social Security (Contributions) Regulations 2001 (SI 2001/1004), reg 83A*).

Cessation of trade

4.46 Special provisions apply in relation to Class 1A National Insurance contributions if the business ceases during the tax year.

In the event that the trade ceases during the tax year, within 12 days of the end of the month in which cessation occurred the employer must record on the deductions working sheet (P11) the category letter Y and the amount of Class 1A contributions payable.

Class 1A contributions, together with Class 1 contributions and PAYE tax due, should be sent to the employer's HMRC Accounts Office within 14 days of the end of the month in which the cessation occurred (or 17 days of the end of the final tax month where the payment is made electronically) (the *Social Security (Contributions) Regulations 2001* (*SI 2001/1004*), *reg 73*). Where the final income tax month is a month starting on 6 April, 6 May or 6 June, the employer must also pay any Class 1A contributions due in respect of the immediately preceding tax year.

Details of the Class 1A contributions due for the final year should be returned on the P11D(b) for that year.

Transfer or succession of business

4.47 Where there is a transfer or succession of the business and some employees employed by the old employer cease to be employed by the new employer before the date of the transfer, the old employer must account and pay any Class 1A National Insurance contributions relating to benefits provided to the employees no longer employed after the transfer (the *Social Security (Contributions) Regulations 2001* (*SI 2001/1004*), *reg 72*). The Class 1A contributions must be paid within 14 days of the end of the relevant final tax month, unless payment is made electronically, in which case the deadline for payment is 17 days from the end of the final tax month. If the final tax month is one beginning on 6 April, 6 May or 6 June, any Class 1A contributions relating to the previous tax year must also be paid.

Responsibility for dealing with Class 1A contributions in respect of benefits provided to employees transferred to the new employer rests with the new employer and the associated Class 1A National Insurance liability must be retuned on the P11D(b) of the new employer. Normal return and payment deadlines apply.

Powers to make provisions in consequence of retrospective tax legislation

4.48 The Treasury has the power (in *SSCBA 1992, s 10ZC*) to make provisions in relation to Class 1A National Insurance contributions in consequence of any relevant retrospective tax provision that is made at or before such regulations are made or which may be passed or made after that time. For these purposes, 'relevant retrospective tax provisions' are provisions that have retrospective effect and affect the amount of general earnings charged to tax as employment income.

However, any regulations made under these provisions cannot impose a liability to pay Class 1A contributions or increase the amount of Class 1A contributions payable. However, these provisions are without prejudice to any liability to pay a Class 1A contribution that arises by virtue of any relevant retrospective tax provision or any powers conferred by other provisions.

RECORD KEEPING

Records required for Class 1A purposes

4.49 An employer is required to keep documents or records relating to Class 1A National Insurance contributions for three years after the end of the year in which the contribution became payable. Class 1A National Insurance contributions for 2021/22 are payable by 22 July 2022 (or by 19 July 2022 if not paid electronically). The contributions in respect of 2021/22 are due in the 2022/23 tax year. Thus records and documents relating to 2020/21 Class 1A National Insurance contributions must be kept until at least 5 April 2026 (the *Social Security (Contributions) Regulations 2001, SI 2001/1004, Sch 4, para 26*). The records can be kept in any form and by any means.

The record-keeping requirement extends to documents and records relating to the amount of any Class 1A National Insurance contributions and any information about the amounts of Class 1A contributions.

The Class 1A charge on benefits in kind follows the P11D, the records required to enable the Class 1A liability to be computed are essentially those that are needed to enable the P11D to be completed. These include:

- details of all benefits provided to employees;
- dates of provision;
- cash equivalent of those benefits (and such information as is necessary to enable cash equivalent to be computed, such as cost of benefit, etc);
- for cars, details of make and model, list price, list price of accessories, CO2 emission, periods of unavailability.

It is also necessary to keep records of payrolled benefits. Sufficient records must also be kept to enable any adjustments that may be required in the computation of the Class 1A charge to be made.

From 6 April 2020, a Class 1A liability also arises on taxable termination payments in excess of the £30,000 exemption and also on sporting testimonials in excess of the lifetime allowance of £100,000. Sufficient records should be kept to identify where a liability arises and to calculate that liability.

PLANNING POINTS

4.50

- The Class 1A charge applies to taxable benefits provided to all employees, regardless of the earnings rate of the employee.
- The way in which benefits are provided will impact on the National Insurance liability. Providing the benefit direct to the employee rather than by giving them cash from which to buy the benefit will generally give rise to a Class 1A charge rather than a Class 1 charge, thereby saving employee contributions.
- Any contract for the provision of the benefit should be between the employer and the benefit provider. If the contract is between the employee and the provider and the employer either reimburses the expenditure or pays the bill on the employee's behalf, the liability is to Class 1 rather than to Class 1A, with the result that employee contribution will also be due.
- Although the attractiveness of salary sacrifice schemes was reduced from 6 April 2017, it is still possible to enjoy employee National Insurance savings by moving the liability from Class 1 to Class 1A, saving employee contributions, by providing the benefit rather than the cash to buy the benefit. However, the savings are unlikely to be significant and care must be taken by using salary sacrifice arrangements.
- Ensure returns are correct and are filed by the due date to avoid penalties.
- Ensure the Class 1A liability is paid on time as interest is charged where payment is made late.

Chapter 5

Class 1B National Insurance contributions

SIGNPOSTS

- Class 1B contributions are employer-only contributions payable on items included within a PAYE Settlement Agreement in place of the Class 1 or Class 1A liability that would otherwise arise (see **5.1**).
- The Class 1B rate is the same as the secondary Class 1 rate – 13.8% for 2021/22 (see **5.2**).
- A PAYE Settlement Agreement is an arrangement with HMRC which allows the employer to meet the tax and National Insurance obligations in respect of the benefits included in the agreement on the employee's behalf (see **5.5**).
- A PAYE Settlement Agreement cannot be used for all benefits, only those meeting certain conditions (see **5.6**).
- Class 1B National Insurance contributions are due by 22 October after the end of the tax year to which they relate, or by 19 October otherwise (see **5.14**).

OVERVIEW OF CLASS 1B NATIONAL INSURANCE CONTRIBUTIONS

Nature of Class 1B National Insurance contributions

5.1 Class 1B National Insurance contributions are employer-only contributions that are payable in respect of items included within a PAYE settlement agreement (PSA) in place of the Class 1 or Class 1A liability that would otherwise arise. Class 1B National Insurance contributions are also payable on the income tax payable under the PSA.

The charging provision for Class 1B contributions is *SSCBA 1992, s 10A*. Regulations (the *Social Security (Contributions) Regulations 2001* (*SI 2001/1004*), *reg 42* provide for certain persons to be excepted in prescribed circumstances from the liability to pay Class 1B National Insurance contributions (see **5.10**).

Class 1B National Insurance contributions are payable with the tax due under a PAYE settlement agreement in a lump sum (see further **5.14**). Where payment is made electronically, cleared funds must reach HMRC by 22 October after the end of the tax year to which the PSA relates. If payment is made by cheque it must reach HMRC by 19 October after the end of the tax year to which the PSA relates.

Liability to Class 1B National Insurance contributions only arises if the employer is resident, present or has a place of business in Great Britain or Northern Ireland at the time that the contributions are payable. However, while the contributions may be paid voluntarily if this condition is not met, there is little benefit in doing so. Class 1B contributions do not confer any benefit entitlement.

Focus

Class 1B National Insurance contributions are employer-only contributions payable in respect of items included within a PSA in place of the Class 1 or Class 1A liability that would otherwise arise.

Class 1B percentage

5.2 Class 1B National Insurance contributions are levied at the Class 1B percentage. This is a percentage rate equal to the secondary rate of Class 1 National Insurance contributions (*SSCBA 1992, s 10A(6)*).

For 2021/22, the Class 1B percentage is 13.8%.

Focus

The Class 1B rate is the same as the secondary rate of Class 1 National Insurance contributions – 13.8% for 2021/22.

Statutory payments and PSAs

5.3 Entitlement to statutory payments (statutory sick pay (SSP), statutory maternity pay (SMP), statutory paternity pay (SPP), statutory adoption pay (SAP), statutory shared parental pay (ShPP) and statutory parental bereavement pay (SPBP)) depends, amongst other things, on the employee having average weekly earnings at least equal to the lower earnings limit for Class 1 National Insurance purposes.

If the inclusion of an item within a PSA means that the employee's average weekly earnings drops below the lower earnings limit (£120 for 2021/22), without special rules, the employee would lose entitlement to statutory payments. To prevent employees being disadvantaged in this way, the average earnings calculation for statutory payments purposes is performed as if the items were not included within the PSA (see also HMRC's National Insurance Manual at NIM18160).

This places a requirement on the employer to:

- track the payments to the individual which have been dealt with under the PSA and which would otherwise have attracted a liability to Class 1;
- recalculate the gross earnings for SSP, SMP, SPP, SAP, ShPP or SPBP purposes by taking into account the earnings included within the PSA; and
- determine whether on this basis the employee's earnings satisfy the average earnings condition needed to qualify for entitlement to statutory payments.

> **Focus**
>
> To prevent employees using entitlement to statutory payments, the calculation of average earnings is made as if items have not been included in the PSA where their inclusion causes average earnings to drop below the lower earnings limit.

Residence and presence conditions

5.4 The residence and presence conditions prescribed by the *Security (Contributions) Regulations 2001* (*SI 2001/1004*), *reg 145, 146* (see **9.17**) apply for Class 1B National Insurance purposes. Consequently:

- an employer is only liable to pay Class 1B National Insurance contributions if that employer is resident or present in, or has a place of business in, Great Britain or Northern Ireland when the contributions become payable, but
- the employer may pay Class 1B National Insurance contributions voluntarily if they wish, even if they do not satisfy the residence and presence conditions which apply to liability.

An employer is not liable to pay Class 1B National Insurance contributions in relation to any employee who is working for them, but who is not ordinarily resident or employed in Great Britain or Northern Ireland until that employee has been in Great Britain or Northern Ireland for a continuous period of 52 weeks.

Conversely, an employer who has a place of business in Great Britain or Northern Ireland will remain liable to pay Class 1B National Insurance contributions for the first 52 weeks during which an employee, who is ordinarily resident in

Great Britain or Northern Ireland, is employed by the employer outside Great Britain or Northern Ireland.

For the importance of residence and presence conditions generally, see further **9.16**ff.

PAYE SETTLEMENT AGREEMENTS

Purpose of a PAYE settlement agreement

5.5 A PAYE settlement agreement (PSA) is an arrangement with HMRC that allows the employer to meet the tax and National Insurance liability in respect of certain benefits and expenses on the employee's behalf. This enables the employee to receive the benefit or expense free of tax and National Insurance contributions. It also simplifies matters for the employer from an administrative viewpoint as the tax and National Insurance are paid together in a single lump sum after the end of the tax year.

From a National Insurance perspective, Class 1B National Insurance contributions are payable on items included within the PSA that would otherwise attract a liability to Class 1 or Class 1A National Insurance contributions. Class 1B contributions are also payable on the income tax charged under the PSA, as the tax paid on the employee's behalf is itself a benefit. The income tax liability is calculated on the grossed up value of the benefits to reflect this.

Where a PSA is in place, the employer does not need to return items covered by the agreement on forms P11D at the end of the year or payroll them. Where an item within a PSA would otherwise attract a Class 1 National Insurance liability, that item is disregarded when calculating earnings for Class 1 National Insurance purposes.

Once agreed, the PSA remains an enduring agreement until circumstances change. There is no need to renew it each year, although it is prudent to check that it remains valid and make any changes that may be required.

> **Focus**
>
> A PSA enables the employer to settle the tax and National Insurance liability on items included within the agreement on the employee's behalf. Where an agreement is in place, the National Insurance liability is to Class 1B, rather than to Class 1 or Class 1A.

Scope of a PAYE settlement agreement

5.6 A PSA cannot be used for all types of expenses and benefits and an item can only be included within a PSA if it meets certain conditions. These are set out in Statement of Practice 5/96.

The first condition is that the item is either a taxable benefit provided or made available by reason of the employee's employment with the employer or is an expense paid to such an employee.

The second condition is that expenses or benefits are:

- minor as regards the amount of the sums paid or the type of benefit provided or made available;
- irregular as regards the frequency with which, or the times at which, the sums are paid or the benefit made available;
- paid in circumstances where deduction of tax by reference to the tax tables is impracticable; or
- in the case of a benefit that is provided or made available to a number of employees on a shared basis, apportionment of the benefit between the employees is impracticable.

These conditions prevent the use of a PSA in respect of cash payments, such as payments of salary, wages, bonuses or round sum allowances, or in respect of many of the major benefits commonly provided, such as company cars.

During the Covid-19 pandemic, a PSA could be used where employees provide benefits and expenses to employees to, say, assist them working from home, the provision of which is not exempt from tax and National Insurance.

> **Focus**
>
> A PSA cannot be used to meet the employee's tax and National Insurance liability for all benefits and expenses. It is only suitable for those meeting the conditions set out above.

Minor items

5.7 An item can be included within a PSA if it is minor in value. Statement of Practice 5/96 gives the following examples of items qualifying on this basis:

- long service awards not qualifying for exemption from tax;
- incentive awards;
- reimbursement of late night taxi fares home not qualifying for exemption from tax;
- reimbursement of personal incidental expenses outside the tax-free limit;
- a present for an employee in hospital;
- staff entertainment, for example a ticket to Wimbledon;
- use of company van;
- use of a pool car where conditions for exemption are not met;

- telephone bills; and
- gift vouchers and small gifts.

However, it should be noted that the introduction of the trivial benefits exemption with effect from 6 April 2016 has reduced the need to include minor items with a PSA as many of them will fall within the terms of the exemption, which applies to items costing not more than £50 (capped at £300 per tax year in respect of the provision of minor items to directors of close companies and their families).

> **Focus**
>
> The introduction of the trivial benefits exemption has taken most items falling in the `minor' category outside the tax charge; consequently a PSA is no longer needed in most cases to deal with minor items.

Irregular items

5.8 An item can also be included within a PSA if it is paid irregularly to an employee. In deciding whether an item is paid 'irregularly' HMRC will take into account the nature of the item, the normal frequency of the payment and how often it was given to the individual employee in question.

Statement of Practice 5/96 cites the following examples of items that would qualify for inclusion with a PSA on the grounds of irregularity:

- occasional attendance at an overseas conference where the expenses are not tax deductible;
- the expenses of a spouse occasionally accompanying an employee on a business trip abroad;
- the occasional use of a holiday flat;
- one-off gifts that are not minor.

> **Focus**
>
> A PSA can be used for one-off and occasional items, but not for those provided regularly unless they qualify under another head.

Impracticability

5.9 The final route by which an item might qualify for inclusion within a PSA is that it is impracticable to operate PAYE on the item or to determine the amount of a shared benefit that should be apportioned to each employee.

To meet this condition the employer would be expected to demonstrate that it would not be possible to apply PAYE or to apportion the benefit without a disproportionate amount of effort or record keeping taking account of the value of the item concerned, the number of employees and the nature of the items involved.

Statement of Practice 5/96 lists the following examples of items that might qualify for inclusion within a PSA on grounds of impracticability:

- free chiropody care;
- hairdressing services;
- shared use of a firm's bus to work;
- Christmas parties and similar entertainment provided by the employer which are outside the tax exemption;
- cost of shared taxis home not satisfying the tax exemption; and
- shared cars.

EXCLUSIONS FROM THE CLASS 1B CHARGE

Exception from Class 1B liability

5.10 In certain circumstances, the employer is excepted from the liability to pay Class 1B National Insurance contributions in respect of employees who remain subject to the social security arrangements of a country other than the UK (the *Social Security (Contributions) Regulations 2001* (*SI 2001/1004*), *reg 42*). The exception from liability applies where:

- the employee is subject to the social security arrangements of a country which is another European Economic Area member state; or
- the employee is subject to the social security arrangements of a country that has a reciprocal agreement with the UK.

Where the exception applies, the employer can, if the employer so wishes, pay Class 1B contributions voluntarily.

Although there is no benefit in paying Class 1B National Insurance contributions voluntarily as they do not confer any benefit entitlement, from a practical perspective, depending on the composition of the workforce and the value of the expenses and benefits involved, it may be cheaper to pay the Class 1B contributions than to incur administrative costs involved in isolating those employees falling within the exception.

PSA entered into after start of the tax year

5.11 In a case where a PSA has been entered into after the start of the tax year and before the PSA was entered into, Class 1 National Insurance contributions were due on an item included within the PSA, there is no liability to Class 1B contributions in respect of this item (*SSCBA 1992, s 10A(5)*). This prevents a double contribution liability from arising (see also timing issues at **5.17**).

> **Focus**
>
> It should be noted that it is not necessary to renew the PSA each year. Once agreed, it is an enduring agreement unless circumstances change. It should, however, be reviewed annually to ensure it remains valid and current.

CALCULATING CLASS 1B CONTRIBUTIONS

Working out the Class 1B liability

5.12 Class 1B National Insurance contributions are payable on:

- the value of items included within a PSA that would otherwise give rise to a Class 1 or Class 1A liability; plus
- the total amount of tax payable by the employer under the PSA.

The Class 1B liability is found by applying the Class 1B percentage (13.8% for 2019/20 and 2020/21) to the sum of these amounts.

It should be noted the total tax payable under the PSA attracts a Class 1B National Insurance liability regardless of whether some of the items on which the tax is payable are items that would not attract a Class 1 or Class 1A liability if they were outside the PSA.

Example 5.1—Calculating the Class 1B liability

Diamond Ltd enters into a PSA in respect of a ball to celebrate the company's ten-year anniversary. The ball has a cost of £250 per head and as such falls outside the tax exemption for Christmas parties and similar annual functions.

Had the employer not agreed the PSA with HMRC, the provision of the benefit would have attracted a Class 1A National Insurance liability in respect of P11D employees and directors.

The total cost of the function is £50,000. The tax payable under the PSA is £20,000. Class 1B National Insurance contributions are calculated as follows:

Value of items included within the PSA otherwise attracting a liability to Class 1 or Class 1A contributions	£50,000
Tax payable under the PSA	£20,000
Total value on which Class 1B contributions are payable	£70,000
Class 1B contributions @ 13.8%	£9,660

Thus, the Class 1B liability in respect of the PSA is £9,660.

It should be noted that because Class 1B contributions are also payable on the tax due under the PSA, the employer's Class 1B liability will be higher than the Class 1A liability replaced (in this case £6,900 being £50,000 @13.8%). However, where the item would be otherwise liable to Class 1 contributions, the Class 1B contributions replace both the employer and employee Class 1 contributions, which may reduce the overall NIC bill.

Where benefits provided to Scottish taxpayers are included in a PSA, the tax payable is worked out using the Scottish rates of income tax. Similarly, where benefits are provided to Welsh taxpayers, the Welsh rates of income tax should be used (although for 2021/22 these are aligned with the rest of the UK excluding Scotland).

Focus

As Class 1B contributions are also payable on the tax paid on the employee's behalf, the Class 1B liability is higher than the Class 1A liability it replaced.

Rounding

5.13 The Class 1B National Insurance liability is calculated to the nearest penny with amounts of halfpenny or less being ignored and other amounts being rounded up to the nearest whole penny (the *Social Security (Contributions) Regulations* 2001 (*SI 2001/1004*), *reg 41*).

COLLECTION AND REPORTING

Due date for payment of Class 1B National Insurance contributions

5.14 Class 1B National Insurance contributions are due by 22 October following the end of the tax year if payment is made electronically. Cleared funds must reach HMRC's account by this date. However, there is an earlier deadline if payment is made by cheque and the cheque must reach the Accounts Office no later than 19 October. Class 1B National Insurance contributions are payable together with the tax due under the PSA in a single payment.

Where a PSA is agreed, HMRC will issue the employer with a 'notice to pay', form P630 and a payment slip. This will be issued once the tax due under the PSA has been agreed with the inspector. The employer must then calculate the Class 1B National Insurance contributions due and, if not paid electronically, send the payment and the payslip to the collector of taxes.

Where the due date for payment falls on a weekend, payment must be sent so that it reaches HMRC or, if paid electronically, cleared funds must reach HMRC's account, by the last banking day before the deadline.

> **Focus**
>
> Class 1B National Insurance contributions are payable by 22 October after the end of the tax year to which they relate where payment is made electronically; or by 19 October otherwise. Late payments attract interest.

Interest

5.15 Interest is charged on Class 1B National Insurance contributions paid late. The interest period runs from the due date until the date on which the liability is actually paid.

Overpayment of Class 1B contributions is unlikely. However, should this occur, interest is paid on the overpayment. The interest period runs from the date on which the payment was made until the date that the overpayment is refunded. Any overpaid Class 1B contributions would normally be set against Class 1 or Class 1A liabilities before a repayment is made.

Penalties

5.16 There are no specific penalty provisions in respect of Class 1B National Insurance contributions.

However, the inaccuracy penalty regime outlined at **1.15** applies for Class 1B purposes.

TIMING CONSIDERATIONS

Time limits for agreeing a PSA

5.17 A PSA can be agreed at any time up until 6 July following the tax year to which it relates. This is the deadline for submitting P11Ds and P9Ds, so basically the PSA must be agreed before the benefits and expenses are reported to HMRC on form P11D.

Thus, the deadline for agreeing a PSA for 2021/22 is 5 July 2022.

It is not necessary to agree a PSA each year, as once agreed the PSA is an enduring agreement unless circumstances change. However, where circumstances change, any amendments must be made to the PSA before 6 July after the end of the year to which it relates.

> **Focus**
>
> It is not necessary to agree a PSA each year – once agreed it remains in place for subsequent years unless circumstances change. However, it is important to check each year that the PSA remains valid and update it if necessary.

Potential NIC problems if PSA agreed after the start of the tax year

5.18 Where a PSA is in force, Class 1B National Insurance contributions are payable on items included within the PSA that would otherwise attract a Class 1 or a Class 1A National Insurance liability. Once a PSA has been set up, it remains in place until revoked by the employer or HMRC – it is not necessary to renew it each year, although it is prudent to check that it is still required and that the circumstances on which it is based remain unchanged.

If a PSA is agreed after the start of the tax year and includes items that normally attract a Class 1 liability, the Class 1 liability may have already been paid when the PSA is agreed. If the Class 1B contributions are worked out in the normal way, a double contributions liability would arise in respect of those items on which Class 1 contributions have been paid. As noted at **5.11**, Class 1B contributions are not payable on items on which Class 1 contributions have already been paid. It is important to be aware of this and to adjust the computation accordingly to avoid paying both Class 1 and Class 1B.

The Class 1B liability only replaces Class 1 or Class 1A contributions that have not yet become due for payment. If the PSA is agreed later than the due date for the Class 1 or Class 1A liability, the original liability will stand.

Example 5.2—Class 1B liability: effect on Class 1 contributions where PSA agreed after the start of the tax year

A PSA is agreed for the first time on 25 August 2021, applying from the 2021/22 tax year. The PSA includes items that would normally be liable for Class 1 National Insurance contributions.

The due date for Class 1 contributions is the 22nd of the month if paid electronically (or 19th of the month if paid by cheque). Class 1 contributions for the month to 5 August 2021 are due by 22 August 2021 if paid electronically (or by 19 August 2021 if paid by cheque).

The Class 1 contributions due for the month to 5 August 2021 should have been paid prior to the PSA being entered into on 25 August 2021. Thus Class 1B contributions are only due for 2021/22 on those items from 6 August 2021 to 5 April 2022 that would otherwise give rise to a Class 1 liability and which are included in the PSA from 25 August 2021.

(See also HMRC's National Insurance Manual at NIM18110).

Example 5.3—Class 1B liability: effect on Class 1A contributions where PSA agreed before Class 1A liability falls due

A PSA is entered into on 2 May 2022, applying from the 2021/22 tax year. The PSA includes items that would normally be chargeable to Class 1A National Insurance contributions. Although this is after the end of the 2021/22 tax year, the Class 1A National Insurance liability does not fall due until 22 July 2022 if paid electronically, which is after the date on which the PSA is agreed. Consequently, Class 1B contributions for 2021/22 are due for the whole year on the items within the PSA that would otherwise attract a Class 1A liability.

RECORDS

Record-keeping requirements

5.19 An employer is required to keep records and documents relating to Class 1B National Insurance contributions for at least three years from the end of the tax year in which the contributions became payable (the *Social Security (Contributions) Regulations 2001 (SI 2001/1004) Sch 4, para 26*). Class 1B contributions for 2021/22 are payable by 22 October 2022 if paid electronically (or by 19 October 2022 if paid by cheque). The payment date falls in the 2022/23 tax year. Thus records and documents relating to Class 1B National Insurance contributions for 2021/22 must be kept until at least 5 April 2026.

The records and documents can be kept in any form and by any means.

The documents and records that are required to be kept are those relating to the amount of Class 1B contributions payable and any information about those contributions. This will include details of the items included within the PSA, whether those items would otherwise be liable to Class 1 or Class 1A contributions, the cash equivalent value of those items and the tax payable under the PSA.

PLANNING POINTS

5.20

- Where items that would otherwise attract a liability to Class 1 National Insurance contributions are included within a PAYE settlement agreement, the employee's NIC liability is reduced as no primary contributions are payable.
- It is not necessary to set up a new PSA each year – it is an enduring agreement remaining in place until revoked by the employer or HMRC. However, it is prudent to check each year that the circumstances on which it is based remain unchanged and that it is still required.
- As Class 1B National Insurance contributions are payable on the tax on items included within the PAYE settlement agreement, the Class 1B liability is higher than the Class 1A liability it replaces as the tax paid on the employee's behalf represents a further benefit liable to Class 1B National Insurance contributions.

- Class 1B National Insurance contributions are paid in October after the end of the tax year, whereas Class 1A contributions are due three months earlier, in July. Consequently, the Class 1B charge offers a cash flow advantage over the Class 1A charge. Where items attracting a Class 1 liability are included within a PSA, a greater cashflow benefit is achieved as the Class 1 contributions are payable monthly (or quarterly for certain smaller employers).
- To ensure primary Class 1 National Insurance savings are realised, a new PAYE settlement agreement should ideally be concluded before the start of the tax year as the Class 1B charge can only replace Class 1 contributions on items included within the agreement to the extent that those contributions have not already fallen due.
- Class 1B National Insurance contributions should be paid by the due date to avoid interest charges arising.

Chapter 6

Class 2 National Insurance contributions

SIGNPOSTS

- Class 2 National Insurance contributions are flat-rate contributions payable by the self-employed (see **6.1**).
- The self-employed continue to pay Class 2 contributions as the proposed abolition has been put on hold (see **6.2**).
- A Class 2 liability arises where earnings from self-employment exceed the small profits threshold (see **6.3**).
- A person must notify HMRC of their self-employment. This can be done in various ways (see **6.6**).
- A Class 2 contribution is payable for each week of self-employment in the tax year at the Class 2 weekly rate –£3.05 per week for 2021/22 (**6.09**).
- Class 2 contributions currently provide the mechanism by which a self-employed earner builds up his or her contributions record (see **6.11**).
- Stopping payment of Class 2 contributions during the Covid-19 pandemic may have implications on your contributions record (see **6.35**).

OVERVIEW OF CLASS 2 NATIONAL INSURANCE CONTRIBUTIONS

Nature of Class 2 National Insurance contributions

6.1 Class 2 National Insurance contributions are flat-rate contributions payable by the self-employed and are currently the mechanism by which the self-employed accrue benefit entitlement (see **6.11**). The self-employed also pay Class 4 contributions by reference to their profits (see Chapter 8).

Class 2 National Insurance contributions are specified in terms of a weekly rate (see **6.9**). Different rates apply to share fishermen and volunteer development workers (see **6.25**).

The liability to Class 2 National Insurance contributions is imposed by *SSCBA 1992, s 11* and the *Social Security (Contributions) Regulations 2001* (*SI 2001/1004*).

> **Focus**
>
> Class 2 contributions are flat rate weekly contributions payable by the self-employed, and currently the mechanism by which the self-employed build up their contributions record.

Proposed reform of National Insurance regime for the self-employed

6.2 Proposed reforms to the National Insurance regime for the self-employed have been placed on hold. Under the proposed reforms, Class 2 National Insurance contributions were to have been abolished from 6 April 2019 (one year later than originally planned), and Class 4 National Insurance contributions were to have been reformed from the same date to provide the mechanism by which the self-employed earn entitlement to the state pension and contributory benefits.

However, the government announced on 6 September 2018 that the abolition of Class 2 contributions (and the associated reforms to Class 4) would now not take place during the life of what was then the current Parliament. Consequently, Class 2 contributions remain in place, and the self-employed continue to pay Class 2 and Class 4 contributions.

In a written statement to Parliament, the U-turn was attributed to concerns on the impact of the measure on self-employed earners with low earnings (who can opt to pay Class 2 contributions voluntarily rather than Class 3, which are considerably more expensive). However, the government confirmed their commitment to simplifying the tax system for the self-employed and are to keep the issue under review 'in the context of the wider tax system and the sustainability of public finance'.

Self-employed earners with earnings above the small profits threshold continue to pay Class 2 National Insurance contributions, while those with profits below the small earnings threshold can, if they so wish, opt to pay Class 2 contributions voluntarily to preserve their contributions record (see **6.20**). This is a significantly cheaper option than paying voluntary Class 3 contributions.

> **Focus**
>
> Proposed reforms to the National Insurance regime for the self-employed under which Class 2 contributions were to have been abolished from 6 April 2019 have not gone ahead. The self-employed continue to pay Class 2 contributions.

Liability for Class 2 National Insurance contributions

6.3 A liability to Class 2 National Insurance contributions arises if an earner is in self-employment in the relevant tax year and the earner has relevant profits equal or exceeding the small profits threshold for that year (*SSCBA 1992, s 11(1), (2)*). The small profits threshold is set at £6,515 for 2021/22. Relevant profits for the purposes of determining whether a Class 2 liability arises are profits from the self-employment in respect of which Class 4 contributions are payable (or would be payable if those profits exceeded the lower profits limit for Class 4 purposes) (*SSCBA 1992, s 11(3)*).

Grants received by self-employed earners under the Self-Employment Income Support Scheme (SEISS), payable where a self-employed person's business has been adversely affected by the Covid-19 pandemic, are included in working out profits and will be taken into account in determining whether earnings from self-employment exceed the small profits threshold.

Where a liability to Class 2 National Insurance contributions arises, the self-employed earner is liable to pay a Class 2 contribution for each week on that tax year that he or she is in self-employment. Consequently, contributions are payable for a week in which the earner is on holiday. However, if the earner is incapable of work, for example due to sickness, he or she may be excepted from liability (see **6.13**). During the Covid-19 pandemic, a self-employed earner may be prevented from working, for example. During this time, the earner may be excepted from liability to pay Class 2 contributions. However, in deciding whether to cease paying Class 2 contributions for periods when they were unable to work, consideration should be given to the impact on their contribution record (see **6.35**).

The Class 2 liability is an annual liability which is computed retrospectively by reference to the number of weeks in which the earner was self-employed during the tax year.

Class 2 contributions are not payable for any week before that in which the earner attains the age of 16 or after that in which the earner attains pensionable age (*SSCBA 1992, s 11(7)*).

The number of hours worked in a week is also irrelevant in determining the Class 2 National Insurance liability. A person must pay a full week's contributions even if he or she only works one day a week. However, a liability only arises if the earnings from self-employment in the year equal or exceed the small profits threshold. The nature of self-employment is such that there may be weeks when the earner does not actually have any work. This may be particularly so if the work is seasonal in nature. However, if the self-employed person remains available for work and is looking for work, the Class 2 liability continues, even if no actual work is undertaken. However, the liability will cease when the self-employment ceases, for example if the business is discontinued.

Example 6.1—Liability for Class 2 contributions

Rob is a self-employed gardener. In 2021/22 he takes two weeks' holiday in August 2021, a week's holiday at Christmas and a week's holiday in September 2020. He earns no money while he is on holiday.

Due to the nature of his business, he has no work for one week in November 2021 and also for two weeks in January 2022. However, he remains available for work for both of these weeks.

Despite the fact that Rob does not work and does not earn for seven weeks during the 2021/22 tax year his liability is computed by reference to the full tax year and he is liable to pay Class 2 contributions of £158.60 (52 x £3.05) for 2021/22.

The liability for Class 2 contributions only applies to a self-employed person who is normally resident in Great Britain or who has resided in Great Britain for 26 of the 52 weeks preceding the contribution week in question (the *Social Security (Contributions) Regulations 2001* (*SI 2001/1004*), *reg 145(1)(d)*) (see further **9.17**). However, this rule is modified in relation to share fishermen (see **6.25**) and volunteer development workers (see **6.26**).

If a person is simultaneously employed and self-employed, he or she will be liable for both Class 1 and Class 2 contributions (and also Class 4 contributions on profits). However, there is an annual maximum which limits the total contributions payable (see **6.28**).

HMRC have confirmed that the liability to pay Class 2 contributions extends to sleeping and inactive partners and also that they are eligible to seek exception. Sleeping or inactive partners who were not already paying Class 2 contributions were required to do so from April 2013. However, a salaried partner of a limited liability partnership who is treated as an employee is liable to Class 1 National Insurance contributions rather than to Class 2 and Class 4.

Notifying liability to pay Class 2 National Insurance contributions

6.4 When a person starts to work in a self-employed capacity, he or she must inform HMRC of this fact. A person who fails to register as self-employed within the required time frame may be charged a penalty (the *Social Security (Contributions) Regulations 2001* (*SI 2001/1004*), *reg 87, 87A, 87AA*).

New businesses can register for self-assessment at www.gov.uk/register-for-self-assessment/self-employed. The Class 2 registration is undertaken at the same time as registering for business taxes.

Notification of commencement of Class 2 liability

6.5 The regulations provide that where a person commences or ceases to be a self-employed earner on or after that date, that person must immediately notify HMRC either by approved electronic means or in writing of the date on which the self-employment commenced or ceased (the *Social Security (Contributions) Regulations 2001 (SI 2001/1004), reg 87AA*). This can be done in various ways (see **6.6**).

A person is treated as having notified HMRC immediately where notification is made within such further time as HMRC may allow (*regs 87A(4), 87AA(4)*).

Procedure for notifying self-employment

6.6 There is a single registration process effective for both tax and National Insurance purposes. The Class 2 liability is triggered when a person registers as self-employed.

Registration can be done in various ways:

- online on the HMRC website (www.gov.uk/register-for-self-assessment/self-employed);
- by telephone by calling HMRC's Newly Self-Employed Helpline on 0300 200 3504; or
- by completing application form CWF1 online if the self-employed earner has previously filed a tax return but is doing different work from that done previously (see www.gov.uk/register-for-self-assessment/self-employed).

To register as self-employed, the following information is required:

- name;
- address;
- contact phone number;
- National Insurance number;
- date of birth;
- most recent tax reference if previously self-employed;
- date self-employment started;

- nature of the business;
- business phone number if different from contact phone number;
- position in business;
- whether the registrant has any business partners and if so, their names and addresses and National Insurance numbers (business partners must also register in their own right);
- if joining an existing business, the tax reference for that business.

In the event that the self-employed person expects to do all his or her work for one person, that person's name must also be supplied. In this scenario, the self-employed person should ensure that they are really self-employed rather than an employee (see also **2.5ff**).

The registration process should be completed no later than 5 October in the tax year after that in which the self-employment started. Thus a person who commences self-employment in the 2021/22 tax year must register with HMRC no later than 5 October 2022.

> **Focus**
>
> A newly self-employed person must notify HMRC that they are self-employed. This can be done by registering online for self-assessment and should be done no later than 5 October after the end of the tax year in which the self-employment commenced.

Start of self-employment

6.7 A person's liability to Class 2 contributions is calculated by reference to the number of weeks in the tax year for which the earner was self-employed. This includes weeks when the person was on holiday or had no work as the self-employment is regarded as continuing during such periods. However, it will not always be clear when the self-employment actually starts as setting up a new business often involves a long preparatory period. Consequently, it will not always be clear on how many weeks' self-employment the liability for the first tax year's contributions should be based.

As far as the legislation is concerned, a self-employed earner is defined (in *SSCBA 1992, s 2(1)(b)*) as

> 'a person who is gainfully employed in Great Britain other than in employed earner's employment (whether or not he is also employed in such employment)'.

Therefore, for a person to be a self-employed earner, the employment must be 'gainful'. What constitutes a 'gainful' employment is not specified in the legislation, but based on case law, HMRC regard an employment as being 'gainful' when it is run with a view to making à profit or if the person is paid for the goods or services provided regardless of whether there was any intention of earning from money from the venture.

From a practical perspective, the self-employment can generally be regarded as starting from the day that the person is open for trade and is aiming to make money from the business venture.

Notifying cessation of liability to Class 2 contributions

6.8 A person is also required to notify HMRC if they cease to be liable to pay Class 2 National Insurance (as will be the case where the self-employment ceases) or they cease to become entitled to pay Class 2 National Insurance (the *Social Security (Contributions) Regulations 2001 (SI 2001/1004), reg 87AA*).

Rate of Class 2 National Insurance contributions

6.9 Class 2 National Insurance contributions are flat-rate contributions specified by means of a weekly rate.

For 2021/22, the rate is set at £3.05 per week. There is no liability if earnings from self-employment for that year are below the small profits threshold, set at £6,515 for 2021/22.

Special rates of Class 2 National Insurance contributions apply to share fisherman (see **6.25**) and to volunteer development workers (see **6.26**).

For 2021/22, the rate for share fishermen is set at £3.70 per week and the rate for volunteer development workers is set at £6 per week. The rates applying for earlier years are set out in Appendix 4.

Focus

The Class 2 rate for 2021/22 is £3.05 per week. Higher rates are payable by share fishermen and volunteer development workers, reflecting different benefit entitlements.

Contribution week

6.10 Class 2 National Insurance contributions are payable for each contribution week that the earner is self-employed and not excepted from liability. A contribution week is a period of seven days staring at midnight between Saturday and Sunday (the *Social Security (Contributions) Regulations* 2001 (*SI 2001/1004*), *reg 1*).

Benefit entitlement and Class 2 National Insurance contributions

6.11 Class 2 National Insurance contributions earn self-employed people the right to a state pension and to a range of contributory benefits. Payment of Class 2 contributions 'buys' entitlement to the basic state pension or single-tier state pension (depending on the date on which the contributor reaches state pension age), contribution-based employment and support allowance, maternity allowance and bereavement allowance. The benefits conferred by Class 2 contributions are not identical to those conferred by Class 1 contributions payable by the employed earners as Class 2 contributions do not count towards contribution-based jobseeker's allowance in the way that Class 1 contributions do. The exception to this is in the case of share fishermen and volunteer development workers who pay a slightly higher rate of Class 2 National Insurance contribution which buys them entitlement to contributory jobseeker's allowance (see **6.28**).

Class 2 National Insurance contributions provide self-employed people with the opportunity to accrue benefit entitlement for a low contribution cost.

The self-employed also pay Class 4 National Insurance contributions by reference to the profits from the self-employment. Class 4 contributions do not currently confer any benefit entitlement on the self-employed.

For further details of the benefit rights attaching to the payment of Class 1 National Insurance contributions, see **1.28**.

Focus

Payment of Class 2 contributions is the mechanism by which the self-employed earn entitlement to the state pension and contributory benefits.

EXCEPTIONS FROM THE LIABILITY TO CLASS 2 NATIONAL INSURANCE CONTRIBUTIONS

Overview of exceptions

6.12 The *Social Security (Contribution) Regulations 2001* (*SI 2001/1004*) set out the circumstances in which a self-employed earner may be excepted from liability to Class 2 contributions for a contribution week (see **6.13**).

It should be noted that no Class 2 liability arises if profits from the self-employment are below the small profits threshold for the tax year. For 2021/22, it is set at £6,515. Married women and widows with valid reduced-rate elections may also be excepted from the liability to pay Class 2 National Insurance contributions (see **6.19**).

Volunteer development workers who are self-employed earners are excepted from the liability to pay standard Class 2 National Insurance contributions but may instead pay special Class 2 National Insurance contributions (the *Social Security (Contributions) Regulations 2001* (*SI 2001/1004*), *reg 151*) (see **6.26**).

> **Focus**
>
> A liability to pay Class 2 contributions arises only if profits exceed the small profits threshold, set at £6,515 for 2021/22. Where profits are below this level, the self-employed earner is not obliged to pay Class 2 but can choose to do so voluntarily. This offers a cheap option for securing a qualifying year.

Exceptions by virtue of incapacity

6.13 A self-employed earner is excepted from paying a Class 2 National Insurance contribution for any contribution week (the *Social Security (Contributions) Regulations 2001* (*SI 2001/1004*), *reg 43(1)*):

- in respect of the whole of which the earner is in receipt of incapacity benefit;
- in respect of the whole of which the earner is in receipt of the employment and support allowance;
- throughout the whole of which the earner is incapable of work;
- in respect of which the earner is in receipt of maternity allowance;
- throughout the whole of which he is undergoing imprisonment or detention in legal custody; or
- in respect of any part of which the earner is in receipt of carer's allowances or an unemployability supplement.

Similarly, Class 2 contributions are not payable by anyone under 16 or over state pension age.

Share fishermen are excepted from liability to Class 2 National Insurance contributions in respect of a week in which they are in receipt of incapacity benefit or are entitled to a contribution-based jobseeker's allowances or, but for a failure to satisfy the contribution conditions for that benefit, would be so entitled (the *Social Security (Contributions) Regulations 2001* (*SI 2001/1004*) *reg 125(1)(e)* modifying *reg 43(1)(a)* in the case of share fishermen). For further details on special Class 2 National Insurance contributions payable by share fishermen, see **6.25**.

In determining if the above conditions are met for the entire contribution week Sunday is generally disregarded. However, where a self-employed earner objects to working on a specific day other than Sunday on religious grounds and does not object to working on a Sunday, that specific day is disregarded instead of Sunday (the *Social Security (Contributions) Regulations 2001* (*SI 2001/1004*), *reg 43(2)*).

Where a self-employed earner is excepted from paying a Class 2 contribution for a contribution week by virtue of these provisions, the earner can, if he so wishes, pay the Class 2 contribution for that week voluntarily to maintain his or her contribution record (see also voluntary Class 2 contributions at **6.20**).

Small profits threshold

6.14 No liability to Class 2 National Insurance contributions arises if profits from the self-employment are below the small profits threshold. The small profits threshold is set at £6,515 for 2021/22. Where profits are below this level, the exception from liability is given automatically – there is no need to apply for an exception certificate.

> **Focus**
>
> An automatic exception from paying Class 2 contributions arises if earnings are below the small profits threshold; although a self-employed earner with profits below this level can choose to pay Class 2 contributions voluntarily.

Earnings for small profits threshold purposes

6.15 No liability to Class 2 National Insurance contributions arises if relevant profits from the self-employment do not exceed the small profits threshold. This is set at £6,515 for 2021/22.

Relevant profits are the profits from the self-employment in respect of which Class 4 National Insurance contributions are payable (or would be payable if those earnings exceeded the lower profits limit for Class 4 National Insurance purposes) (*SSCBA 1992, s 11(3)*).

Impact of low earnings on earner's contribution record

6.16 No liability to Class 2 contributions arises if earnings are below the small profits threshold. However, a failure to pay Class 2 contributions may adversely affect the earner's contribution record, unless he pays Class 1 or Class 3 contributions instead.

Consequently, the self-employed earner may wish to pay voluntary contributions to protect his contributions records. This will cost £3.05 per week for 2021/22. By contrast, Class 3 voluntary contributions cost £15.40 per week for 2021/22, and as such are significantly more expensive.

Plans to abolish Class 2 National Insurance contributions from 6 April 2019 have been put on hold. Consequently, the opportunity to pay Class 2 rather than Class 3 contributions remains available.

See **6.22** for the extended window of opportunity to pay Class 2 contributions voluntarily.

> **Focus**
>
> The decision not to go ahead with the abolition of Class 2 contributions means that it remains possible for a self-employed earner with profits below the small profits threshold to take advantage of the opportunity to pay Class 2 contributions voluntarily – costing only £3.05 per week for 2021/22 compared to £15.40 per week for Class 3 contributions.

Married women and widows with reduced-rate elections

6.17 Married women and widows who hold a valid reduced-rate election (see **3.111**) and who are self-employed do not have to pay Class 2 National Insurance contributions (the *Social Security (Contributions) Regulations 2001* (*SI 2001/1004*), *reg 127(3)(b)*). However, such women are still liable to pay Class 4 National Insurance contributions by reference to their profits.

VOLUNTARY PAYMENT OF CLASS 2 NATIONAL INSURANCE CONTRIBUTIONS

Why pay voluntary Class 2 National Insurance contributions?

6.18 Payment of Class 2 National Insurance contributions confers entitlement to the state pension and other contributory benefits (see **6.11**) on the self-employed earner.

Where a self-employed earner has no liability to pay Class 2 contributions because his or her profits from the self-employment are below the small profits threshold or the earner is excepted from liability as a result of any of the reasons listed at **6.13**, consideration should be given as to whether it is worthwhile to pay the Class 2 contributions voluntarily. A person who is entitled to pay Class 2 National Insurance contributions but who is not liable or who is excepted from liability retains entitlement to pay the contributions voluntarily if he or she so wishes (the *Social Security (Contributions) Regulations 2001* (*SI 2001/1004*), *regs 43(3), 46*).

Paying Class 2 National Insurance contributions voluntarily will enable the self-employed earner to maintain his or her contributions record and entitlement to contributory benefits. As Class 2 contributions are set at a lower rate than Class 3 contributions (£3.05 per week for 2021/22) for Class 2 contributions as opposed to £15.40 for 2021/22 for Class 3 National Insurance contributions), paying Class 2 contributions voluntarily where the earner is self-employed is a considerably cheaper option than paying Class 3 contributions.

However, in deciding whether it is necessary to pay voluntary Class 2 contributions, the self-employed earner should consider whether such contributions are necessary. This will depend on the individual's own contribution record, details of which can be obtained from HMRC. If the self-employed earner will have sufficient contributions to earn a full state pension, paying Class 2 contributions voluntarily is unlikely to be worthwhile. To qualify for the full single-tier pension, a person needs 35 qualifying years; a minimum of ten qualifying years is needed for a reduced single-tier pension.

The decision not to proceed with the abolition of Class 2 contributions means that the option for self-employed earners with low earners to pay Class 2 contributions voluntarily remains available. Where it is beneficial to pay Class 2 contributions voluntarily, the self-employed may wish to take this opportunity to build up their contributions record in this way.

Focus

Where a self-employed earner has earnings below the small profits threshold, contributions can be paid voluntarily. While this option remains available it offers a cheap way to secure a qualifying year. However, the self-employed earner should first check his or her contributions record; if they already have sufficient qualifying years for the full state pension (currently 35 years), there is no need to pay a voluntary contribution.

Payment of voluntary Class 2 contributions by person employed abroad

6.19 In certain circumstances voluntary Class 2 National Insurance contributions may be paid by a person going to a country outside the EEA which is not covered by a reciprocal agreement (see Chapter 9 for commentary on international issues). To qualify for payment of voluntary Class 2 National Insurance contributions, the person must have been ordinarily gainfully employed abroad before leaving Great Britain or Northern Ireland and meet the following conditions (which also apply for Class 3 purposes):

- the person has lived in Great Britain or Northern Ireland at any time for a continuous period of three years; or
- has paid at least 156 contributions into that scheme before April 1975; or
- in at least three tax years from April 1975, has paid contributions that give an earnings factor of at least 50 times the lower earnings limit up to April 1978 or 52 times the lower earnings limit from April 1978;

(the *Social Security (Contributions) Regulations 2001* (*SI 2001/1004*), *reg 147*).

However, if the person has paid Class 1 National Insurance contributions for the first 52 weeks of employment abroad, HMRC will accept the application to pay voluntary contributions regardless of whether the above conditions are met (see HMRC's National Insurance Manual at NIM 33603).

Paying voluntary Class 2 contributions to secure a state pension

6.20 The date on which a person reaches state pension age and the state pension for which they will be eligible determines how many qualifying years are required for a full state pension and consequently, depending on the person's contributions record, whether making voluntary contributions is worthwhile.

The single-tier state pension is paid to those who reach state pension age on or after April 2016. A person will need 35 years' contributions to be eligible for the full single-tier state pension. The contributions must be paid in the claimant's own right. A person who reaches state pension age on or after April 2016 and who will not have 35 qualifying years otherwise may wish to consider paying Class 2 contributions voluntarily if they are eligible to do so. However, if a person will have 35 qualifying years without making voluntary contributions, paying Class 2 contributions voluntarily will not enhance their pension.

Where state pension age is reached on or after 6 April 2016 a minimum of ten qualifying years is needed for a person to be eligible to receive a pension. If a person has some qualifying years, but less than ten, it may be worth paying voluntary Class 2 contributions where possible to increase the number of qualifying years to at least ten in order to secure a state pension.

Focus

A person needs 35 qualifying years for the full single-tier state pension, and at least 10 for a reduced pension. Paying Class 2 voluntarily may be worthwhile in order to secure entitlement to the state pension.

Voluntary Class 2 contributions not paid within the permitted period

6.21 Where a self-employed earner is not liable to pay Class 2 National Insurance contributions (see **6.12ff**) but is entitled to do so and voluntary contributions have not been paid in the permitted period, HMRC may agree to extend the time limit for paying the contributions if they are satisfied that:

- the failure to pay was attributable to the contributor's ignorance of error; and
- that ignorance or error was not the result of the contributor's failure to exercise due care and diligence,

(the *Social Security (Contributions) Regulations 2001* (*SI 2001/1004*), *reg 61*).

The legislation does not define ignorance or error, so they take their ordinary everyday meanings. In the absence of ignorance or error, the time limits for paying voluntary Class 2 National Insurance contributions cannot be extended.

If the voluntary contributions have not been paid due to ignorance or error, HMRC must also be satisfied that the contributor exercised due care and diligence. In determining if this is the case, they will take account of:

- the steps that the contributor took to maintain his or her contribution record;
- whether they have been warned previously of the consequences of late payments; and
- the contributor's ability to understand their obligation to pay Class 2 National Insurance contributions, taking account of their age, health and intelligence.

The case of *Mrs Adedolapo Fehinola Adojutelegan v Derek Clark (Officer of the Board)* SpC 430/04 is cited by HMRC (see HMRC's National Insurance Manual at NIM23005) as an example of a case where ignorance or error has been accepted but due care and diligence have not been exercised.

Voluntary contributions 2006/07 to 2015/16 – extended time limit for persons reaching state pension age on or after 6 April 2016

6.22 A person who will reach pension age on or after 6 April 2016 (and who therefore will receive the new single-tier state pension) and who is entitled but not liable to pay a Class 2 contribution in respect of one or more of the tax years 2007/08 to 2015/16 (under *SI 2001/1004 reg 46* or *s 147(1)(a)*) and who had not paid such a contribution prior to 18 April 2013, may pay such a contribution in the period beginning on 6 April 2013 and ending on 5 April 2023. The contribution is payable at the 2012/13 rate of £2.65 per week where it is paid in respect of 2006/07 to 2010/11. For 2011/12 to 2015/16 the contribution is paid at the rate applying for the relevant year (the *Social Security (Contributions) Regulations 2001, SI 2001/1004, reg 61B*). Where the contribution is paid on or after 6 April 2019 but before 6 April 2023, it is paid at the highest Class 2 rate in force in the period from the year to which the contribution relates to the year in which it is paid.

To qualify for entitlement to the full single-tier pension a person needs 35 qualifying years compared to the 30 needed for the full basic state pension payable to those who reached state pension age before 6 April 2016. The ability to make contributions for eligible years until 5 April 2023 provides the opportunity to boost the single-tier state pension in a low cost manner.

Focus

A limited window is available in which to pay voluntary Class 2 contributions for past years to build up entitlement to the single-tier state pension.

Death of contributor

6.23 In the event that a self-employed earner who is entitled but not liable to pay Class 2 National Insurance contributions dies before those contributions are paid, those contributions may be paid on his or her behalf subject to the same provisions as regard to payment had the earner not died (the *Social Security (Contributions) Regulations 2001, SI 2001/1004, reg 62*).

SPECIAL CLASS 2 NATIONAL INSURANCE CONTRIBUTIONS

Special Class 2 rates

6.24 In addition to the standard rate of Class 2 National Insurance contributions payable by most self-employed earners, there are two categories of earners who pay Class 2 National Insurance contributions at a higher rate. Special Class 2 rates apply to share fishermen (see **6.25**) and to volunteer development workers (see **6.26**).

For 2021/22 the rates are as follows:

Special Class 2 rate for share fishermen	£3.70 per week
Special Class 2 rate for volunteer development workers	£6.00 per week

The rates for earlier years are set out in Appendix 4.

Share fishermen

6.25 Share fishermen pay a higher rate of Class 2 National Insurance contributions to enable them to earn entitlement to contribution-based jobseeker's allowance. Standard Class 2 National Insurance contributions do not count towards this benefit as it is not generally payable to the self-employed.

For 2021/22, the share fishermen rate is £3.70 and the standard Class 2 rate is £3.05. A share fisherman is defined in the regulations (*SI 2001/1004, reg 115*) as a person who:

- is ordinarily employed in the fishing industry, otherwise than under a contract of service, as the master or a member of the crew of any UK fishing vessel within the meaning of the *Merchant Shipping Act 1995, s 1*, manned by more than one person, and who is remunerated in respect of that employment in whole or in part by a share of the profits or gross earnings of the fishing vessel; or
- has ordinarily been so employed, but who by reason of age or infirmity ceases to be so employed and becomes ordinarily engaged in employment ashore in the UK, otherwise than under a contract of service, making or

mending any gear appurtenant to a UK fishing vessel or performing other services ancillary to or in connection with that vessel and is remunerated in respect of that employment in whole or in part by a share of the profits or gross earnings of that vessel and has not ceased to be ordinarily engaged in such employment.

The special rules apply only to share fishermen who are employed under a contract for services. Share fishermen employed under a contract of service are within the rules applying to mariners (see **9.44**).

The fact that a share fisherman may spend his time outside the territorial waters of the UK does not preclude a liability to Class 2 National Insurance contributions from arising. The legislation (*SI 2001/1004*, *reg 125(a)*) specifically provides for a share fisherman to be regarded as a self-employed earner irrespective of the fact that the employment may not be in the UK.

Focus

Share fishermen pay a higher rate of Class 2 contribution to secure entitlement to contribution-based jobseekers allowance.

Volunteer development workers

6.26 A special rate of Class 2 National Insurance contributions also applies to volunteer development workers. Such workers are not required to pay standard Class 2 National Insurance contributions but can opt to pay a special rate of Class 2 National Insurance contributions in order to maintain their contribution record. For 2021/22, the rate for volunteer development workers is £6 per week. A volunteer development worker is defined in the legislation as a person certified as such and who is:

- ordinarily resident in Great Britain or Northern Ireland; and
- is employed outside the UK;

(the *Social Security (Contributions) Regulations 2001* (*SI 2001/1004*), *reg 149*).

A volunteer development worker is treated as being a self-employed earner to the extent that he or she is not regarded as an employed earner for Class 1 National Insurance purposes, irrespective of the fact that the self-employment is outside the UK (*SI 2001/1004*, *reg 150*).

The volunteer development worker provisions except a volunteer development worker from the liability to pay standard Class 2 National Insurance contributions. However, such a worker is entitled to pay Class 2 National Insurance contributions at the special rate for volunteer development workers (*SI 2001/1004*, *reg 151*). Thus payment of special Class 2 National Insurance contributions for volunteer development workers is optional not compulsory. The special rate is set at 5% of the lower earnings limit for the tax year in question (*SI 2001/1004, reg 152(b)*). Thus, for 2021/22 the rate is £6 per week, being 5% of the lower earnings limit for 2021/22 of £120 per week

Contributions paid by volunteer development workers at the special rate allow the worker to maintain his or her contribution records while working abroad.

For details of the collection procedures applying the case of special Class 2 National Insurance contributions payable by volunteer development workers, see **6.25**.

> **Focus**
>
> Volunteer development workers can choose to pay Class 2 contributions at the special rate of £6 per week for 2021/22 to maintain their contributions record. Payment is optional rather than compulsory.

ANNUAL MAXIMUM

Annual maximum

6.27 Where an earner is simultaneously employed and self-employed, there is a limit on the total amount of Class 1 and Class 2 National Insurance contributions payable for a particular year. This is known as the annual maximum.

The annual maximum is calculated by reference to a formula set out in the *Social Security (Contributions) Regulations 2001* (*SI 2001/1004*), *reg 21*. The calculation is set out at **3.99**.

Any contributions paid in excess of the maximum may be refunded (see **6.35**).

PAYMENT AND COLLECTION OF CLASS 2 NATIONAL INSURANCE CONTRIBUTIONS

Methods of paying Class 2 contributions

6.28 Class 2 contributions are collected through the self-assessment process, with contributions due no later than 31 January after the end of the tax year to which they relate. This means that contributions for 2021/22 are due by 31 January 2023.

The legislation also permits the deduction of Class 2 National Insurance contributions from certain pensions or allowance payable by the Secretary of State (*SSCBA 1992, Sch 1, para 10*). Pensions from which contributions may be deducted are listed in the *Social Security (Crediting and Treatment of Contributions and National Insurance Numbers) Regulations 2001* (*SI 2001/769*), *reg 10*.

Unpaid Class 2 contributions may be collected via the PAYE system by an adjustment to the employee's tax code where the self-employed earner is also an employed earner.

Separate collection arrangements apply in respect of special Class 2 National Insurance contributions payable by volunteer development workers (see **6.31**).

> **Focus**
>
> Class 2 contributions are collected through the self-assessment system with income tax and Class 4 contributions. However, unlike Class 4 contributions, they are not taken into account in calculating payments on account.

Class 2 National Insurance payment deadlines

6.29 Class 2 contributions are payable under self-assessment. Contributions for 2021/22 are due by 31 January 2023. Class 2 contributions (unlike Class 4) are not taken into account in working out payments on account for self-assessment purposes.

Collection of unpaid Class 2 National Insurance contributions via PAYE code

6.30 HMRC are able to collect unpaid Class 2 National Insurance contributions via the PAYE system through an adjustment in the earner's tax code where the self-employed earner with unpaid Class 2 contributions is also an employed earner. If an earner does not want the unpaid contributions to be collected in this way, the outstanding liability must be paid in full.

Collection of special Class 2 National Insurance contributions from volunteer development workers

6.31 Separate collection arrangements apply in relation to the optional Class 2 contributions payable by volunteer development workers.

A volunteer development worker wishing to pay special Class 2 National Insurance contributions must complete an application form (CF83) and send it to his or her employing organisation. The employing organisation will act as agent for the payment of the Class 2 National Insurance contributions (HMRC's National Insurance Manual NIM 34050).

For commentary on volunteer development workers, see **6.25**.

Late paid Class 2 National Insurance contributions

6.32 Class 2 National Insurance contributions that are paid late may have to be paid at a rate higher than that applying at the time when the contributions were due. The rate at which the contributions are paid will depend on when the payment is made and the reason for the late payment (*SSCBA 1992, s 12(3)*).

Class 2 National Insurance contributions are payable at the rate prevailing in the contribution week to which they relate if they are paid between the original due date and the end of the tax year following that for which they were due.

Example 6.2—Class 2 contributions paid late

Class 2 National Insurance contributions for 2020/21 were due to be paid by 31 January 2022, but were paid late in March 2022. As the payment was made before the first anniversary of the end of the tax year for which they were due (ie by 5 April 2022) the contributions are payable at the 2021/22 rate of £3.05 per week.

However, if payment is made later than the first anniversary of the end of the tax year to which it relates, the contributions are payable at the highest rate applying in the period from the week in which they were due to the date on which the contribution was paid. However, this rule does not apply and contributions are not payable at a rate higher than the rate applying in the week for which they were due if:

- the failure to pay the contributions on time was due to the contributor's ignorance or error; and
- that ignorance or error was not caused by the contributor failing to exercise due diligence,

(the *Social Security (Contributions) Regulations 2001* (*SI 2001/1004*), *reg 65*).

Class 2 National Insurance contributions are payable at the rate applying at the time a request for payment is made if such a request is made within the last month of a tax year and the contributions are paid within one month of that request (the *Social Security (Contributions) Regulations 2001* (*SI 2001/1004*), *reg 64*).

Interest is not charged on late paid Class 2 National Insurance contributions.

Focus

Where Class 2 contributions are paid late, the rate at which they are paid will depend on whether they are paid within a year of the due date. Where paid outside this time, they may be payable at a higher rate than that for the year to which they relate.

Late paid volunteer development worker contributions

6.33 Where a volunteer development worker pays a contribution for a week that falls within an earlier year than the one in which it is paid, the worker is entitled to pay the contribution at the rate prevailing in the week in respect of which it is paid (the *Social Security (Contributions) Regulations 2001* (*SI 2001/1004*), *reg 153(1), (2), (3)*).

Example 6.3—Contributions paid late by a volunteer development worker

A volunteer development worker pays a special Class 2 National Insurance contribution in respect of a week falling within the 2020/21 tax year. The contribution is made in June 2021 (ie in the 2021/22 tax year). The contribution is therefore paid at the 2021/22 rate of £6.00 per week.

However, if the payment is made after the end of the year immediately following the contribution year and the weekly rate of contribution payable by volunteer development workers is different from that applying in the week to which the contribution relates, the contribution must be paid at the highest rate applying in the period from the week for which it was due to the date on which it was paid (the *Social Security (Contributions) Regulations 2001* (*SI 2001/1004*), *reg 153(4)*).

Refunds of Class 2 contributions

6.34 Class 2 National Insurance contributions paid in excess of the annual maximum can be refunded. Class 2 contributions are refunded ahead of Class 1 contributions. Contributions made in error may also be refunded.

Applications for refunds must be made online or by post using the form available on the gov.uk website (see www.gov.uk/government/publications/national-insurance-application-for-a-refund-of-class-2-national-insurance-contributions-ca8480).

It is not possible to apply for a refund of voluntary Class 2 contributions.

COVID-19 PANDEMIC

Impact of the Covid-19 pandemic on Class 2 contributions

6.35 A liability for Class 2 National Insurance contributions arises for 'each week of the year that the earner is in the employment' if profits from the self-employment are more than the small profits threshold for the relevant tax year, which for 2021/22 is £6,515 (*SSCBA 1992, s 11*). During the Covid-19 pandemic lockdown, many self-employed people were not allowed to work. For some, such as those in the leisure and hospitality sector this remained the case for several months. Arguably, no liability to Class 2 contributions arises for those weeks where the self-employed earner was not allowed to work.

Further, profits may decline significantly as a result of the pandemic and where profits fall below the small profits threshold of £6,515 for 2021/22, the self-employed earner is not liable to pay Class 2 National Insurance contributions for 2021/22. However, if a grant has been received under the Self-Employment Income Support Scheme, that must be taken into account in computing the profits for determining whether a liability exists.

If, as a result of the Covid-19 pandemic, a self-employed earner is not obliged to pay Class 2 National Insurance contributions for some weeks or at all for 2021/22, consideration should be given whether contributions should be paid voluntarily to maintain the contributions record (see **6.18**).

If the business ceases as a result of the pandemic, the earner will need to notify HMRC that their liability to Class 2 contributions has ceased (see **6.8**). Where the business is interrupted but continues, this is not necessary and consideration should be given whether it is beneficial to continue to pay Class 2 contributions during the interruption period.

PLANNING POINTS

6.36

- The planned abolition of Class 2 contributions has been put on hold. The self-employed continue to pay Class 2 (and Class 4) contributions.
- On starting self-employment, it is important that HMRC are notified. Self-employed earners can register online for Class 2 National Insurance contributions at the same time as registering for self-assessment. This must be done by 5 October following the end of the tax year in which self-employment commenced.
- Where an entitlement but not a liability to pay Class 2 National Insurance contributions arises, consider paying Class 2 contributions voluntarily to maintain pension and benefit entitlement as this is considerably cheaper than paying Class 3 National Insurance contributions. However, consideration should be given as to whether it is necessary to make voluntary contributions or whether the contributor will have a full contributions record without paying voluntary contributions. The number of qualifying years needed for a full state pension will depend on the date on which state pension age is reached.
- Where a person will reach state pension age on or after 6 April 2016 and is eligible to pay Class 2 contributions for one or more years in the period 2007/08 to 2015/16 but had not done so by 18 April 2013, the earner can make contributions in respect of eligible years until 5 April 2023 to boost his or her single-tier state pension. This may be worthwhile.

- If a person's earnings from self-employment are less than the small profits threshold (£6,515 for 2021/22) no Class 2 contributions are payable. However, consideration should be given to paying the contributions voluntarily where this is necessary to maintain pension and benefit entitlement.
- The Covid-19 pandemic may impact an earner's liability to pay Class 2 contributions. Where the earner is not liable to pay Class 2 contributions for 2021/22, considerations should be given as to whether it advisable to pay them voluntarily.

Chapter 7

Class 3 and Class 3A National Insurance contributions

SIGNPOSTS

- Class 3 contributions are voluntary contributions which can be paid in order to make up shortfalls in a contribution record (see **7.1**).
- Class 3 contributions are payable at a weekly rate, set at £15.40 per week for 2021/22 (see **7.2**).
- Payment of Class 3 contributions is contingent on the associated eligibility conditions being met (see **7.4**).
- Before paying Class 3 contributions, consideration should be given as to whether the payment is worthwhile (see **7.13**).
- To qualify for a full single-tier state pension, 35 qualifying years are needed. Extended time limits apply for those reaching state pension age on or after 6 April 2016 in which to pay contributions for 2006/07 to 2015/16 (see **7.23**).
- Class 3 contributions paid late may be payable at a higher rate than that for the year to which they relate (see **7.25**).
- Class 3A contributions were payable during a limited window to enable those who reached state pension age before 6 April 2016 to enhance their state pension. The payment window has now closed (see **7.33**).

OVERVIEW OF CLASS 3 NATIONAL INSURANCE CONTRIBUTIONS

Nature of Class 3 National Insurance contributions

7.1 Class 3 National Insurance contributions are voluntary contributions which a contributor may choose to pay in order to make up shortfalls in his or her contribution record and to protect benefit entitlement. As the contributions are voluntary, there is no liability to pay Class 3 contributions.

The single-tier state pension is payable to people who reach state pension age on or after 6 April. A person needs 35 qualifying years in order to receive the full single-tier state pension. By contrast, a person who reached state pension age between 6 April 2009 and 5 April 2016 needed 30 qualifying years to receive the full basic state pension. The impact of the introduction of the single-tier pension on the need to pay voluntary Class 3 contributions is discussed further at **7.14**.

In determining whether it is necessary to pay voluntary contributions, account should also be taken of any National Insurance credits received (see **1.29**). If credits are being received, it is not normally possible to pay voluntary contributions.

In deciding whether it is worthwhile paying voluntary contributions, it is also beneficial to consider whether a person has the option to pay voluntary Class 2 contributions (see **6.17**) as this is a much cheaper way of building up qualifying years.

Although Class 3 National Insurance contributions are voluntary contributions, they can only be paid by eligible persons. The eligibility conditions are outlined at **7.4** below. Rules introduced by the *Pensions Act 2008* allow some people to buy up to an additional six years of voluntary Class 3 National Insurance contributions to enhance their basic state pension entitlement. These rules are discussed further at **7.12**.

A person who reached state pension age before 6 April 2016 had the option of making a Class 3A contribution to enhance their state pension. However, the window for making a Class 3A contribution closed on 5 April 2017. Class 3A contributions are discussed further at **7.35**.

Class 3 National Insurance contributions are specified by means of a weekly rate (see **7.2**).

Where for 2021/22 a person would not otherwise have paid sufficient contributions for the year to be a qualifying year as a result of the Covid-19 pandemic, consideration could be given to paying voluntary Class 3 contributions to make up the shortfall so that the year is a qualifying year. However, if the earner is self-employed, paying Class 2 contributions voluntarily is a cheaper option (see **7.17**).

The right to pay Class 3 National Insurance contributions is given by virtue of *SSCBA 1992, s 13*. Further provisions governing the payment of Class 3 National Insurance contributions are contained in the *Social Security (Contributions) Regulations 2001* (*SI 2001/1004*), *Pt VIII*.

> **Focus**
>
> Class 3 contributions are voluntary contributions which can be paid to make up a shortfall in the contributions record. However, before paying a Class 3 contribution, consideration should be given as to whether this will be worthwhile.

Rate of Class 3 National Insurance contributions

7.2 Class 3 National Insurance contributions are specified by means of a weekly rate. For 2021/22, the Class 3 rate is £15.40 per week. The rates applying for earlier years are set out in Appendix 5.

> **Focus**
>
> Class 3 contributions are payable at a weekly rate, set at £15.40 per week for 2021/22.

Class 3 National Insurance contributions and benefit entitlement

7.3 Class 3 National Insurance contributions are paid to make up a shortfall in the contributor's contribution record in order to preserve benefit entitlement. Class 3 contributions count towards the contributions conditions for the following benefits:

- state pension;
- bereavement payment;
- bereavement allowance; and
- widowed parent's allowance.

ELIGIBILITY TO PAY CLASS 3 NATIONAL INSURANCE CONTRIBUTIONS

Eligibility conditions

7.4 Although Class 3 National Insurance contributions are voluntary contributions, they can only be paid by those eligible to do so. Eligibility to pay Class 3 National Insurance contributions is dependent on the following conditions being met:

- the person is aged 16 or over;
- the person satisfies the conditions as to residence or presence in Great Britain or Northern Ireland;
- the person complies with the conditions relating to methods and time of payment (see **7.17ff**); and
- the person's earnings factor derived from Class 1 National Insurance contributions treated as paid or credited and/ or Class 2 National Insurance contributions paid and/or Class 3 National Insurance contributions paid or credited is less than the qualifying earnings factor.

Where these conditions are met, a person is eligible to pay Class 3 National Insurance contributions for a particular year in order to acquire a qualifying earnings factor for that year (*SSCBA 1992, ss 13, 14*). Such contributions may only be paid to satisfy the contribution conditions for benefit entitlement purposes (*SSCBA 1992, s 13(1)*).

The eligibility conditions for Class 3 contributions do not require a person to be under state pension age. However, the contributions must be paid in respect of a year before state pension age was reached (see also **7.6**). Where a person is nearing state pension age is it advisable to seek a pension forecast in order to assess whether paying such contributions is worthwhile (see **7.11**).

A person is not eligible to pay Class 3 contributions if that person is a married woman or widow who has chosen to pay reduced rate contributions (see **3.114**) for the whole of the tax year for which that person wishes to pay voluntary Class 3 contributions.

A person who is eligible to pay Class 3 National Insurance contributions also has the right to pay additional Class 3 National Insurance contributions in certain cases (see **7.12**).

Persons who reached state pension age before 6 April 2016 were, for a limited window only, able to pay voluntary Class 3A contributions to enhance their state pension (see **7.35**). The payment window closed on 5 April 2017.

Focus

Although Class 3 contributions are voluntary contributions, they can only be paid if the associated eligibility conditions are met.

Earnings factors

7.5 Broadly, a person's earnings factor is used as a measure for entitlement to benefits. The earnings factor is derived from earnings paid in, or from earnings credited and from Class 2 paid and Class 3 contributions paid or credited. A person's earnings factor is capped at 58 times the upper earnings limit for that year. For a year in respect of which contributions have been paid to count for benefit entitlement purposes, the earnings factor for that year must be at least equal to the qualifying earnings factor. Where this is not the case HMRC will notify the contributor that there is a shortfall (see **7.15**).

Voluntary contributions (Class 3 or Class 2: see **7.7**) can be paid to make up the shortfall and turn the earnings factor for the year into a qualifying earnings factor.

The legislation governing earnings factors is found in *SSCBA 1992, ss 22–24* and the *Social Security (Earnings Factor) Regulations 1979* (*SI 1979/676*).

Residence and presence conditions

7.6 A person who is otherwise eligible to pay Class 3 National Insurance contributions (see **7.4**) must satisfy certain conditions as regards residence and presence conditions in Great Britain or Northern Ireland in order to be allowed to make such contributions (the *Social Security (Contributions) Regulations 2001* (*SI 2001/1004*), *reg 48(1), 145(1)(e)*).

The residence and presence conditions are that the person:

- is resident in either Great Britain or Northern Ireland throughout the relevant tax year; or
- has arrived in either Great Britain or Northern Ireland during the relevant tax year and is liable, or has been liable, to pay Class 1 or Class 2 National Insurance contributions for an earlier period in the relevant tax year; or
- has arrived in either Great Britain or Northern Ireland during the relevant tax year and was either ordinarily resident in either of those countries throughout the whole tax year, became ordinarily resident during the course of the relevant tax year, or,
- although not ordinarily resident, has arrived in Great Britain or Northern Ireland in the relevant tax year or the previous tax year and has been continuously present for 26 complete contribution weeks.

In a case where a person arrived in the previous tax year, voluntary contributions can only be paid in respect of the relevant tax year and not the previous tax year (unless the residence and presence conditions are met for that year).

For the meaning of ordinarily resident, see **9.9** and for details on the rules governing the payment of voluntary Class 3 National Insurance contributions for periods abroad, see **9.23**).

Precluded Class 3 National Insurance contributions

7.7 The regulations preclude the payment of Class 3 National Insurance contributions in certain circumstances (the *Social Security (Contributions) Regulations 2001* (*SI 2001/1004*), *reg 49*). A person is not entitled to pay Class 3 National Insurance contributions where:

- in respect of any year if that person would, but for the payment of such a contribution, be entitled to be credited with a contribution;
- in respect of any year in which the aggregate of his or her earnings factors derived from earnings in respect of which primary Class 1 contributions payable at the main primary percentage have been paid, credited earnings or Class 2 or Class 3 contributions paid or credited is less than 25 times the lower earnings limit and either the period has passed within which Class 3 contributions can be treated as paid for the year under the *Social Security (Crediting and Treatment of Contributions*

and National Insurance Numbers Regulations 2001 (*SI 2001/769*), *reg 4* or he or she has sooner, in accordance with the *Social Security (Contributions) Regulations 2001* (*SI 2001/1004*), *reg 56* applied for the return of any Class 3 National Insurance contributions paid in respect of that year;

- in respect of any year in which the aggregate of his or her earnings factors derived from earnings in respect of which primary Class 1 contributions, payable at the main primary rate, have been paid, credited earnings or Class 2 or Class 3 contributions paid or credited is more than 25 times the lower earnings limit but less than the qualifying earnings factor and either the period has passed within which Class 3 contributions can be treated as paid for the year under the *Social Security (Crediting and Treatment of Contributions and National Insurance Numbers Regulations 2001* (*SI 2001/769*), *reg 4* or he or she has sooner, in accordance with the *Social Security (Contributions) Regulations 2001* (*SI 2001/1004*), *reg 56* applied for the return of any Class 3 National Insurance contributions paid in respect of that year;
- in respect of any year if it causes the aggregate earnings factors derived from earnings in respect of which primary Class 1 contributions payable at the main primary rate have been paid, credited earnings, or Class 2 or Class 3 contributions paid or credited to exceed the qualifying earnings factor by an amount which is more than half that year's lower earnings limit; or
- in respect of any year in which the person attains 17 or 18 years of age if in an earlier year he or she has satisfied the first condition for retirement pension or widow's pension or widowed mother's allowance.

However, a person is entitled to pay Class 3 National Insurance contributions (regardless of whether any of the circumstances listed in the first three bullets above apply) if payment of such a contribution would enable that person to satisfy the first condition for retirement pension or widowed mother's allowance, widowed parent's allowance, bereavement allowance or widow's pension or the contribution condition for bereavement payment or widow's payment and the relevant condition was not satisfied at the beginning of the year.

Acquired gender

7.8 A person is not generally entitled to pay a Class 3 National Insurance contribution in respect of a year in which he or she attains pensionable age. However, this rule is relaxed where the person in question is a transsexual to whom a full gender recognition certificate has been issued, provided age 60 has been attained and the acquired gender is male. Such a person is not precluded from paying Class 3 National Insurance contributions for the year in which the person attains age 60, any subsequent year before that in which the full gender recognition certificate is issued and the year in which the full gender recognition certificate is issued. This allows payment to be made for the years for which the person was precluded from paying contributions by having reached pensionable age as a woman, but for which pensionable age had not yet been reached as a man (the *Social Security (Contributions) Regulations 2001* (*SI 2001/1004*), *reg 49(2B), (2C)*).

Transfers to the European Communities' pension scheme

7.9 A person employed by European Community institutions can transfer their rights to a state pension to the Pension Scheme of the European Communities' Institution (PSEC). Making such a transfer would create a gap in the home country contribution record for the period for which the transfer was made. To prevent entitlement to two pensions (UK state pension and PSEC pension) from arising, a person is precluded from paying Class 3 National Insurance contributions for the period covered by the transfer to the PSEC. The gap in the contributor's contribution record created by the transfer cannot be filled by payment of Class 3 National Insurance contributions (the *Social Security (Contributions) Regulations 2001* (*SI 2001/1004*), *reg 49A*).

Married women with reduced-rate elections

7.10 A married woman with a valid reduced-rate election (see **3.112**) is not eligible to pay Class 3 National Insurance contributions.

Autocredits and voluntary contributions

7.11 Autocredits were credits given to people approaching state pension age. They were made available from 6 April 1983 to men for the tax year of their 60th birthday and the following four tax years if they have not paid enough Class 1 contributions to give a qualifying year or are self-employed and have a valid small earnings exception certificate and are resident in Great Britain for more than 182 days in the tax year. Autocredits are not awarded in the year in which a man reaches age 75 or a subsequent tax year. Autocredits reflected the differering state pension ages of men and women.

As a result of the equalisation of state pension age from 2010, autocredits have now been phased out. Women did not receive the credits for the years between the year in which they reach the age of 60 and that in which they reach their state pension age. From April 2010, men only received credits from the year in which they reach the state pension age of a woman born on the same day. For example, a woman born between 6 October and 5 November 1950 reaches state pension age on 6 May 2011. A man born between these dates was given autocredits for the four years from 2011/12 to 2013/14.

The last year for which autocredits were given was 2018/19 (see further HMRC National Insurance Manual at NIM41245).

Men who were entitled to autocredits did not need to pay voluntary Class 3 contributions for the years for which autocredits were given. However, a man who has reached the state pension age of a woman born on the same day and who has not gained entitlement to a full basic state pension may pay voluntary Class 3 contributions if he has been absent from Great Britain for more than 182 days in a tax year and was not entitled to autocredits as a result. However, voluntary contributions cannot be paid if they are not needed for pension entitlement. Consequently, a state pension forecast should be obtained before deciding whether to pay voluntary contributions.

ADDITIONAL CLASS 3 NATIONAL INSURANCE CONTRIBUTIONS

Right to pay additional Class 3 contributions

7.12 Legislation introduced by the *Pensions Act 2008* and contained now within *SSCBA 1992, s 13A* allowed certain people to buy up to an additional six years of voluntary contributions to enhance their basic state pension entitlement. These contributions are in addition to those permitted within normal time limits. The window for making the contributions has now expired.

An eligible person was entitled (subject to any conditions set out in regulations made by the Treasury) to pay Class 3 National Insurance contributions in respect of a missing year. For these purposes, a missing year is a year that is not earlier than 1975/76 in respect of which a person would be eligible to pay a Class 3 contribution but for a time limit on the payment of that contribution. The time limits for payment of Class 3 National Insurance contributions are discussed at **7.19ff**.

For the purposes of entitlement to pay additional Class 3 National Insurance contributions, a person was an eligible person if he or she met certain conditions.

The first condition is that the person attained pensionable age during the period beginning on 6 April 2008 and ending on 5 April 2015. The second condition is that there are at least 20 tax years each of which is a qualifying year or one which is covered in full by Home Responsibilities Protection (see **1.32**). A year that meets these conditions is one to which the following applies:

- a person has been paid or credited with contributions that are of a relevant class for the purposes of *SSCBA 1992, Sch 3, para 5, 5A* or credited, in respect of 1987/88 or a subsequent tax year with earnings and in the case of that year, the earnings factor is not less than the qualifying earnings factor for the year; or
- in the case of a person who will attain pensionable age before 6 April 2010, the year is one in which the person was precluded from regular employment by responsibilities at home.

For these purposes, the earnings factor, in the case of 1987/88 or any subsequent year is that which is derived from so much of a person's earnings as did not exceed the upper earnings limit and upon which such of the contributions paid or credited are primary Class 1 National Insurance contributions that were paid or treated as paid or earnings credited and any Class 2 or Class 3 contributions for the year. For years before 1987/88, the earnings factor is that which is derived from contributions of a relevant class paid or credited for that year.

If the person attained pensionable age before 6 April 2010 (i.e. between 6 April 2008 and 5 April 2010), a third eligibility condition applied. This is that the person had, in respect of any one tax year before that in which he or she attains pensionable age, actually paid contributions that are of the relevant class for pension entitlement and for that year, the earnings factor is not less than the qualifying earnings factor for that year.

Additional Class 3 National Insurance contributions could be paid for a maximum of six years (*SSCBA 1992, s 13A (3)*). They had to be paid before the end of the period of six years from the date on which a person attains pensionable age. The latest date by which they could be paid was 5 April 2021 where a person attained pensionable age on 5 April 2015.

Example 7.1—Time limit for paying voluntary contributions

Barbara attained pension age on 3 January 2015. She is eligible to pay additional Class 3 National Insurance contributions in respect of missing years. The additional contributions had to be paid no later than 2 January 2021.

Additional Class 3 National Insurance contributions are payable at the rate in force at the time when the contribution is paid. Therefore additional contributions that were payable in 2020/21 in respect of a missing year were payable at the 2020/21 rate of £15.30 per week, regardless of the rate prevailing for the missing year. The annual cost for a missing year 'bought' in 2020/21 was £795.60 for the full year (£15.30 × 52 weeks).

The ability to pay additional Class 3 National Insurance contributions allowed those who met the eligibility conditions to get a second bite at the cherry.

In deciding whether to pay additional Class 3 contributions, the same considerations applied as regards payments of standard Class 3 contributions. These are discussed at **7.13**.

It should be noted that a person could not pay additional Class 3 National Insurance contributions under *SSCBA 1992, s 13A* if they were within the time limits for paying normal Class 3 National Insurance contributions under *SSCBA 1992, s 13* (see **7.18ff**).

Married women with a reduced rate election (see **3.116**) could not pay additional Class 3 contributions whilst that election is in force.

> **Focus**
>
> A limited window existed for those who reached state pension age before 6 April 2016 (and after 5 April 2008) to pay additional contributions for a missing year, as long as the person has at least 20 qualifying years. The contributions had to be paid within six years from the date on which state pension age was attained, and at the rate for the year in which the contributions were paid.

DECISION TO PAY CLASS 3 NATIONAL INSURANCE CONTRIBUTIONS

Is payment of voluntary contributions worthwhile?

7.13 Class 3 National Insurance contributions are voluntary contributions paid to top up a person's contribution record where there are gaps to enable that person to qualify for the basic state pension or the single-tier pension, depending on the date on which they reach state pension age, and other contributory benefits.

It is not necessary for every year from age 16 to pensionable age to be a qualifying year. Therefore if a person only has a few non-qualifying years, benefit entitlement is unlikely to be adversely affected. As such it is not likely to be worthwhile paying voluntary contributions for the few non-qualifying years.

Before paying any Class 3 National Insurance contributions a pension forecast should be obtained from HMRC to enable an informed decision to be made. This can be obtained online: see www.gov.uk/check-state-pension.

The single-tier state pension is payable to people who reach state pension age on or after 6 April 2016. A person needs 35 qualifying years in order to receive the full single-tier state pension, rather than the 30 needed for the full basic state pension payable to those who reached state pension age before 6 April 2016. Further, a person needs a minimum of ten years' contributions to receive a reduced single-tier pension and only contributions made in the individual's own right, rather than by a spouse, count. This may mean that paying voluntary contributions may be worthwhile. A person who reached state pension age between 6 April 2010 and 5 April 2016 needed 30 qualifying years in order to qualify for the full basic state pension. A person who reached state pension age before 6 April 2016 was, for a limited period, able to top up his or her contribution record by making a Class 3A contribution (see **7.35**) instead or as well as making voluntary Class 3 contributions. A limited window existed for paying further voluntary contributions where state pension age was attained before 6 April 2016 (see **7.12**).

In deciding whether to make voluntary contributions it is necessary to have regard to individual circumstances and the date on which state pension age is reached as this will determine the number of qualifying years that are needed to qualify for either the basic state pension or the single-tier state pension, as appropriate.

A person may receive a letter from HMRC (see **7.16**) advising that he or she has a contribution shortfall for a particular tax year. The receipt of such a notice does not mean that Class 3 National Insurance contributions should be paid. It simply informs the recipient that a particular year is not a qualifying year. Again, it is necessary to assess whether the payment of such contributions is worthwhile and whether it will improve entitlement to the state pension and other benefits.

The cost of the additional contributions may be difficult to justify in terms of the increased pension that they buy and a person may prefer to save or invest the funds elsewhere. If a person has earnings from self-employment and is eligible but is not liable to pay Class 2 National Insurance contributions, it may be better to pay voluntary Class 2 National Insurance contributions rather than paying Class 3 National Insurance contributions as the rate of Class 2 contributions is much lower than the Class 3 rate. This is explored further at **7.17**.

Focus

Before paying a Class 3 contribution consideration should be given to whether this is worthwhile and to the return received on the contribution, and whether a better return could be received elsewhere. A person should also consider whether the option to pay Class 2 voluntarily is available, as this is much cheaper than Class 3.

Impact of the payment of Class 3 National Insurance contributions on entitlement to the single-tier state pension

7.14 The single-tier state pension is payable where a person reaches state pension age on or after 6 April 2016. A person needs 35 qualifying years to be eligible for the full single-tier state pension. Also, a person needs at least 10 qualifying years in order to receive a reduced single-tier pension. A person who does not have 10 qualifying years may want to make voluntary contributions so that they have enough to receive a reduced state pension.

If a person will not have 35 qualifying years by the time that they reach state pension age, it may be worthwhile paying Class 3 contributions to increase their eventual state pension. This may be even more worthwhile if a person has less than 10 years. However, it should be noted where a person is eligible but not required to pay Class 2 contributions, paying voluntary Class 2 contributions instead of Class 3 contributions represents a cheaper option (see **7.17**).

Where state pension age is reached on or after 6 April 2016, assuming that the person has the required minimum ten qualifying years needed to qualify for the single tier state pension, each additional year will increase the pension payable by 1/35th. For 2021/22, the single tier state pension is £179.60 per week, and an additional year is worth £5.13 per week, meaning that a person would need to receive the state pension for at least three years for the payment of voluntary contributions for a year to be worthwhile.

Focus

In deciding whether Class 3 contributions are worthwhile consideration should be given to the number of qualifying years that the person currently has, the number that they will have after paying the contributions, and the difference this will make to their state pension, if any.

Deficiency notices

7.15 National Insurance contributions paid are credited to the contributor's National Insurance account on the National Insurance Recording System (NISR 2). HMRC perform a scan of NISR 2 approximately 18 months after the end of the tax year to identify those contributors with a contributions shortfall for the year in question. This may arise if an employee has not paid National Insurance contributions or received a National Insurance credit for each week in the tax year, for example, because the person has had a break in employment or a career break or because their earnings in at least one week of the tax year were below the lower earnings limit. A person who is self-employed may have a shortfall if they have not paid a Class 2 contribution for one or more weeks in the tax year or if their earnings for a particular year were below the small profits threshold.

The contributor is sent a letter (a 'deficiency notice') which gives details of the shortfall and the amount that the contributor needs to pay to make the year qualify for the purposes of entitlement to the basic State Pension. There are different versions of the letter (CA8334) depending on whether the person is in the UK or abroad.

The purpose of the exercise is to alert contributors to the fact that they have a contributions shortfall for a particular tax year and to enable them to pay voluntary Class 3 National Insurance contributions to make up the shortfall if they so wish. The notice also allows those who believe that they have paid sufficient contributions and who consider the information held by HMRC to be wrong, to advise HMRC of that fact and for the issue to be resolved.

Where a person chooses to pay Class 3 National Insurance contributions following the issue of a deficiency notice, the contributions must be paid within the normal time limits (see **7.19**).

If a deficiency notice is received at a time when the contributor was in receipt of one of the following benefits:

- incapacity benefit;
- industrial injuries benefit included as an unemployability supplement;
- jobseekers allowance;
- maternity allowance; or severe disablement allowance,

HMRC advise the recipient to contact their local jobcentre plus.

In the event that a deficiency notice is received which the recipient believes to be incorrect, he or she should contact HMRC's Deficiency Notice Helpline on 0300 200 3503.

Checking your National Insurance record

7.16 A person can check their National Insurance record to see if they have any gaps. This will enable a decision to be made as to whether it is necessary or worthwhile to pay voluntary Class 3 National Insurance contributions to plug any gaps in the record in order to qualify for a state pension or a better state pension. There are various ways in which a person can check their contributions record. This can be done (see www.gov.uk/check-state-pension). A person can also check their contribution record by calling HMRC's National Insurance Helpline on 0300 200 3500 or by writing to HMRC at the following address:

National Insurance contributions and Employers Office
HM Revenue and Customs
BX9 1AN

The statement will show National Insurance payments and credits. It will also identify gaps in payment and credits that mean a year is not a qualifying year. Where voluntary contributions can be paid to fill in the gaps, the statement will show the cost of paying those contributions.

A statement cannot be requested for the current or the previous tax year. Instead contributors wishing to find out about current or recent gaps should contact the Future Pension Centre, either by completing the online enquiry form, by telephone (0345 3000 168) or by writing to:

Pension Service 9
Mail Handling Site A
Wolverhampton
WV98 1LU

HMRC also produce an online state pension calculator which will calculate when a person will reach state pension age and provide them with an estimate of their basic state pension in today's prices. The calculator can be viewed on the Gov.uk website at www.gov.uk/calculate-state-pension.

Class 3 versus voluntary Class 2

7.17 Where a person is self-employed and not liable but entitled to pay Class 2 contributions (for example, because that person has earnings below the small profits thresholds limit (see **6.17**) or by reasons of incapacity (see **6.16**)) and that person wishes to pay voluntary contributions to make up a contribution shortfall, it is cheaper to pay voluntary Class 2 National Insurance contributions rather than paying Class 3 National Insurance contributions. For 2021/22, the Class 2 rate is £3.05 per week and the Class 3 rate is £15.40 per week. Therefore, paying Class 2 voluntarily where eligible to do so rather than Class 3 will save £12.35 per week in 2021/22.

A further benefit in paying voluntary Class 2 contributions rather than Class 3 contributions is that Class 2 contributions count for entitlement to incapacity benefit, whereas Class 3 contributions do not.

Thus a self-employed person who is entitled but not obliged to pay Class 2 National Insurance contributions is advised to make up a contributions shortfall by paying voluntary Class 2 National Insurance contributions rather than by paying Class 3 National Insurance contributions.

Further details on the payment of voluntary Class 2 National Insurance contributions are given in the commentary at **6.22ff**.

> **Focus**
>
> Where a person is eligible but not liable to pay Class 2 contributions because their earnings from self-employment are below the small profits threshold (£6,515 for 2021/22), it is much cheaper to pay Class 2 contributions voluntarily than pay Class 3.

NOTIFICATION REQUIREMENTS

7.18 A person who wishes to pay Class 3 National Insurance contributions must notify HMRC of the date on which they wish to start paying contributions (the *Social Security (Contributions) Regulations 2001 (SI 2001/1004), regs 87, 87A, 87AA*). Notification must be made in writing or by an approved electronic means.

Likewise, where a person wishes to cease paying Class 3 contributions, he or should must notify HMRC of the date on which they wish payment of such contributions to cease. Again, notification must be made in writing or by an approved electronic means.

A person paying Class 3 contributions must also notify HMRC immediately of any change of address (the *Social Security (Contributions) Regulations 2001 (SI 2001/1004), reg 88*).

As Class 3 contributions are voluntary contributions, penalties are not imposed for a failure to notify.

PAYMENT OF CLASS 3 NATIONAL INSURANCE CONTRIBUTIONS

Methods of paying Class 3 National Insurance contributions

7.19 The method for paying Class 3 National Insurance contributions depends whether the payment is made in arrears in response to a deficiency notice or whether the contributor has notified in advance of an intention to pay Class 3 National Insurance contributions where it is apparent that the earnings factor for the year will be below the qualifying level. This would be the case, for example, where the contributor is not working and not entitled to contribution credits.

If a person is sent a deficiency notice (see **7.15**), the notice will contain instructions on how to pay. Although payment can be made by cheque, HMRC recommends that payment is made electronically.

Payment of Class 3 National Insurance contributions can also be made by monthly direct debit, quarterly, or by means of a one-off payment. Payment cannot be made quarterly by direct debit – where the quarterly payment option is chosen, the contributor will be sent a bill in July, October, January and April.

A person wishing to pay Class 3 applications by direct debit must complete form CA5603. This is available to download from the HMRC website at www.hmrc.gov.uk/nic/ca5603.pdf.

Where payment is made by direct debit, Class 3 contributions are paid monthly in arrears. The direct debit is collected on the second Friday of the month. The number of weeks' contributions payable depends on the number of Sundays in the preceding month. This means that for some months, four weeks' contributions are payable and for other months five weeks' contributions are due. Where payment is made by direct debit, the payment will appear on the contributor's bank statement as' HMRC NI – DD'.

HMRC advise that anyone wishing to set up a direct debit for the collection of Class 3 National Insurance contributions should allow 21 days for it to become effective. However, HMRC will write to the contributor to confirm the date on which the first payment will be taken. Collection normally starts in May. Payments will appear on the contributor's bank statement as 'HMRC NI DD'.

Authority for collection by direct debit is given by the *Social Security (Contributions) Regulations 2001* (*SI 2001/1004*), *reg 90*.

A person who wishes to pay Class 3 National Insurance contributions quarterly must do so by quarterly payment request. The quarterly payment request arrangements are prescribed in the *Social Security (Contributions) Regulations 2001* (*SI 2001/1004*) *reg 89*.

A person wishing to pay by quarterly payment request should contact the National Insurance Deficiency Helpline on 0300 200 3503 to set up an account. Once this has been done HMRC will issue a payment request with a payslip and unique reference for each quarter setting out how much should be paid.

A quarterly payment request is issued within 14 days of the end of each contribution quarter which shows the number of weeks' Class 3 National Insurance contributions payable for that quarter. The contribution quarters are periods of not less than 13 weeks commencing with the first day of the first, fourteenth, twenty-seventh or fortieth contribution week in any year (*SI 2001/1004, reg 89(7)*). Payments in response to a quarterly payment request can be made by a variety of methods, including:

- internet or telephone banking;
- Bank Giro;
- at the post office; or
- by post.

Where payment is made by telephone or internet banking, payment should be made to the following bank account:

Sort code	08 32 20
Account number	12001004
Account name	HMRC NICO Telephone Banking

Where payment is made in response to a quarterly payment request, the reference number shown on the payslip should be used. Where payment is made in response to a deficiency notice, the reference shown on the form should be used. In each case the reference is 18 characters long and should be entered without spaces.

Where payment is made by Bank Giro, the HMRC payslip should be used. To allow for delays in bank processing, HMRC recommend allowing at least three working days for the payment to reach HMRC.

Payment can also be made at a Post Office by cheque, credit or debit card.

HMRC regard payments made by Bank Giro or at a Post Office as being made electronically.

Although HMRC recommend that payment is made by internet or telephone banking, Bank Giro or at a Post Office, it is also possible to pay Class 3 contributions by cheque through the post. Cheques should be made payable to 'HM Revenue and Customs only' followed by the 18-digit Class 3 reference number and accompanied by the HMRC payslip. Neither the cheque nor the payslip should be folded, nor should they be held together with a paper clip or staple. HMRC recommend that at least three working days are allowed for the payment to reach them.

Further guidance on paying Class 3 National Insurance contributions is available on the Gov.uk website at www.gov.uk/pay-voluntary-class-3-national-insurance. Where Class 3 contributions are paid late, they may be payable at a rate higher than the original rate (see **7.24**).

Time limits for paying Class 3 National Insurance contributions

7.20 Class 3 National Insurance contributions are due within 42 days of the end of the tax year to which they relate (the *Social Security (Contributions) Regulations 2001* (*SI 2001/1004*), *reg 48(3)(a)*). However, they may be paid at a later date as long as they are paid before the end of the sixth tax year following the year in respect of which they relate (the *Social Security (Contributions) Regulations 2001* (*SI 2001/1004*), *reg 48(3)(b)(i)*). The limits may be extended in certain circumstances (see **7.21** and **7.23**).

The normal payment deadlines for years for which contributions can still be paid within normal limits are shown in the table below.

Tax year with gap in National Insurance contributions	**Deadline for payment of voluntary Class 3 contributions**
2015/16	5 April 2022
2016/17	5 April 2023
2017/18	5 April 2024
2018/19	5 April 2025
2019/20	5 April 2026
2020/21	5 April 2027
2021/22	5 April 2028

In the event that the Class 3 National Insurance contributions relate to a tax year which included a period of at least six months of full-time education, full-time apprenticeship or training (provided that the earnings were below the lower earnings limit for the year), the Class 3 National Insurance contributions must be paid before the end of the sixth year in which the education, apprenticeship, training ended (the *Social Security (Contributions) Regulations 2001* (*SI 2001/1004*), *reg 48(3)(b)(ii), (iii)*). The same rule applies where the contributions relate to a tax year that included a period of at least six months' imprisonment in legal custody. The six-month period can span two tax years.

If Class 3 National Insurance contributions are paid within the time limits but after the due date for benefit purposes, they will normally only count for benefit purposes from the date that they are actually paid (see HMRC's National Insurance Manual at NIM25027).

> **Focus**
>
> The normal window for payment of Class 3 National Insurance contributions is six years from the end of the tax year for which the contribution is payable.

Extended time limits

7.21 The time limits for paying Class 3 National Insurance contributions (as set out at **7.20**) may be extended if the contribution was paid late as a result of ignorance or error or the contributor was given misleading advice. Special rules also applied in respect of the years 1993/04 to 2007 where National Insurance credits were awarded wrongly during a period of sickness, unemployment or while attending an approved training course.

A consequence of the move to the single-tier state pension, which applies to those reaching state pension age on or after 6 April 2016, is that a person needs 35 qualifying years to qualify for the full single-tier state pension and at least 10 qualifying years to be eligible for a state pension. Persons who reached state pension age between 6 April 2010 and 5 April 2016 only needed 30 qualifying years for a full basic state pension. To enable those reaching state pension age on or after 6 April 2016 to meet the new qualifying conditions, time limits for paying Class 3 contributions for 2006/07 to 2015/16 have been extended (see **7.23**).

> **Focus**
>
> A limited window is available to allow those who reached state pension age on or after 6 April 2016 to pay additional Class 3 contributions to boost their state pension.

Extended time limits – contribution paid late due to ignorance or error

7.22 In the case of contributions paid late due to ignorance or error, two tests must be met for HMRC to grant an extension to the payment deadline. These are set out in the *Social Security (Contributions) Regulations 2001* (*SI 2001/1004*), *reg 50*.

The first test is that the failure was due to the contributor's ignorance and error. If this is the case, the contributor must also satisfy the second test, which is that the ignorance or error was not as a result of his or her failure to exercise due diligence.

In deciding if these tests are met, HMRC give 'ignorance' and 'error' their normal everyday meaning. In the absence of ignorance or error, there is no case for extending the time limits. Where HMRC accept that there is ignorance or error, the next stage is to determine whether the contributor acted with due care and diligence. This is something of a subjective test, but guidance as to HMRC's interpretation of the phrase can be found in their National Insurance Manual at NIM25031. In assessing whether the contributor took due care and diligence, HMRC take account of what steps the contributor took to maintain his or her contribution record, including what questions they asked and what information they were given and also the contributor's age, health and intelligence.

Where HMRC are satisfied that both these tests are met, the Class 3 National Insurance contributions may be paid at such later time as HMRC allow.

Where contributions are paid late through ignorance or error, those contributions may be treated as having been paid at an earlier date where this is necessary for entitlement to a contributory benefit (the *Social Security (Contributions) Regulations 2001* (*SI 2001/1004*), *reg 6*).

The time limits may also be extended if the contributor has been given misleading advice or guidance by HMRC or other government agency or department. Where it is accepted that this is the case, the contributor will be put back in the position that he or she would have been in had the misleading advice not been given.

Extended time limits for 2006/07 to 2015/16 for person reaching state pension age on or after 6 April 2016

7.23 Under the single-tier state pension, which applies to those reaching state pension age on or after 6 April 2016, a person needs 35 qualifying years to qualify for the full single-tier state pension and at least 10 qualifying years to be eligible for a reduced state pension. Those reaching state pension age between 6 April 2010 and 5 April 2016 only needed 30 qualifying years for a full basic state pension. To enable those reaching state pension age on or after 6 April 2016 to meet the new qualifying conditions, time limits for paying Class 3 contributions for 2006/07 to 2015/16 have been extended. The extended time limit applies in respect of Class 3 contributions payable for one or more of the tax years 2006/07 to 2015/16 where a person who will reach state pension age on or after 6 April 2016 was entitled (under *SI 2001/1004, reg 48*) to pay a Class 3 contribution for one or more of those years but the contribution had not been paid by 18 April 2013 (the *Social Security (Contributions) Regulations 2001 (SI 2001/1004), reg 50C*). Unless state pension age is reached between 6 April 2016 and 5 April 2017, the contribution can be paid at any time in the period from 6 April 2013 to 5 April 2023. Where state pension age is reached on or after 6 April 2016 but before 6 April 2017, the period for paying the contribution runs from 18 April 2013 to 5 April 2023.

Contributions paid on or after 6 April 2019 are payable at the rate applying in the year in which the payment is made (*SI 2001/1004, reg 50C(6)*).

> **Focus**
>
> The number of qualifying years needed for the full single-tier state pension is 35, compared to 30 for the basic state pension payable to those who reached state pension age before 6 April 2016. Extended time limits are available for those reaching state pension age on or after 6 April 2016 to pay Class 3 contributions for 2006/07 to 2015/16 in order to boost their state pension.

Time limits for paying additional Class 3 contributions

7.24 A person who is outside the normal time limits (as extended where appropriate) for paying standard Class 3 contributions and who meets the eligibility conditions for paying additional Class 3 National Insurance contributions (see **7.12**) can pay additional Class 3 contributions in respect of up to six missing years.

The contributions must be paid within six years of the date on which that person reaches pensionable age (*SSCBA 1992, s 13A(4)*).

Thus a person who reaches pension age on 17 June 2017 has until 16 June 2023 to pay additional Class 3 contributions.

Consequences of paying Class 3 National Insurance contributions late

7.25 Where a Class 3 National Insurance contribution is paid late, the contribution may be payable at a rate higher than that prevailing in the contribution year to which it relates. However, if the Class 3 National Insurance contribution is paid before the end of the tax year but one following that to which it relates, it is paid at the rate prevailing in the contribution year (*SSCBA 1992, s 13(4), (6)*).

In the event that a Class 3 National Insurance contribution is paid after the end of the next tax year but one following the contribution year and the rate of Class 3 National Insurance contribution at the time of payment is different from that for the contribution year, the Class 3 National Insurance contribution is payable at the highest rate in the period from the contribution year to the date of payment (*SSCBA 1992, s 13(6)*). This rule is waived where contributions are paid late as a result of ignorance or error (see **7.24**), in relation to the years 1996/97 to 2001/02 inclusive where late payment resulted from delays in issuing deficiency notices, in respect of the years 1993/94 to 2007/08 where credits were wrongly awarded as a result of official error or in respect of the years 2006/07 to 2015/16 where a person reaches state pension age on or after 6 April 2016 and had not paid the contribution by 18 April 2013 (see **7.28**).

Example 7.2—Rate of late paid Class 3 contributions

A contributor pays a Class 3 National Insurance contribution in respect of 2015/16. The payment is made on 2 May 2021.

The payment is made within the six-year limit (ie by 5 April 2021), but after the end of the tax year but one following the end of the contribution year. The contribution was paid in 2020/21 and must be paid at the highest rate prevailing in the period from 2014/15 to 2020/21.

The rates for those years are as follows:

Year	Class 3 rate (£ per week)
2021/22	£15.40
2020/21	£15.30
2019/20	£15.00
2018/19	£14.65
2017/18	£14.25
2016/17	£14.10
2015/16	£14.10

The contributions paid for 2015/16 on 2 May 2021 are payable at the rate of £15.40 per week (the rate for 2020/21) as this is the highest rate prevailing in the period starting with the contribution year and ending with the date of payment.

Focus

Where a Class 3 contribution is paid late, it may be payable at a rate higher than that for the year to which it relates, notwithstanding that the contribution is made within normal time limits.

Rate of contributions paid late through ignorance or error

7.26 The time limits for paying Class 3 National Insurance contributions may be extended where HMRC are satisfied that the contributions are paid late as a result of ignorance or error and that the ignorance or error was not caused by the contributor failing to show due care and diligence (see **7.22**).

Where these tests are met, the rules governing payment of Class 3 contributions at a rate higher than that prevailing in the contribution year (see **7.27**) do not apply. Instead the contribution is payable at the original rate for the contribution year (the *Social Security (Contributions) Regulations 2001* (*SI 2001/1004*), *reg 65*).

Example 7.3—Contributions paid late through ignorance or error

Assume the facts are as in Example 7.2 above, but that HMRC are satisfied that the Class 3 contribution was paid late as a result of ignorance or error which did not arise from the failure of the contributor to exercise due care and diligence.

As a result, the Class 3 National Insurance contributions are payable at the original rate for 2015/16 of £14.10 per week.

Normal time limits expired

7.27 Where the time limits for paying contributions have expired, those who meet the eligibility conditions for additional Class 3 contributions as set out at **7.12** effectively got a second chance to make up contributions for missing years.

Where these conditions were met, contributions for up to six missing years can be paid up until the end of the period of six years from the date on which the person attained pensionable age.

The contributions were payable at the rate in force at the time when the contribution is paid, regardless of the rate prevailing for the missing year.

Rate of contribution for 2006/07 to 2015/16 where person reaches state pension age on or after 6 April 2016

7.28 As noted at **7.23**, as a result of the increase in the number of qualifying years needed for the single-tier state pension, persons who reach state pension age on or after 6 April 2016 have a longer period in which to make voluntary contributions for the years from 2006/07 to 2015/16 to the extent that those contributions had not already been paid before 18 April 2013.

Where the contribution was paid before 6 April 2019, if it relates to the tax years 2006/07 to 2009/10, it was payable at the 2012/13 rate of £13.25 per week, whereas if the contribution is for the year 2010/11 to 2015/16, it was payable at the rate applying for the year to which it relates. Contributions paid on or after 6 April 2019 are payable at the rate applying in the year in which the payment is made (*SI 2001/1004, reg 50C(6)*). Thus, contributions paid in 2021/22 are paid at the 2021/22 rate of £15.40 per week.

Focus

Where a contribution is paid by a person reaching state pension age on or after 6 April 2016 within the extended time limits in order to increase the number of qualifying years that they have, the rate at which the contribution is paid will depend on when payment is made.

Class 3 National Insurance contributions paid within one month of notification of arrears

7.29 In the event that HMRC issue a notice requesting payment of a Class 3 National Insurance contribution within the last month of a tax year and the payment of that contribution is made within one month of the request for payment, but in the following tax year, the Class 3 contribution due is calculated as if it were paid on the last day of the tax year in which the request for payment was made (the *Social Security (Contributions) Regulations 2001* (*SI 2001/1004*), *reg 65*).

Payment of Class 3 National Insurance contributions following the death of a contributor

7.30 Class 3 National Insurance contributions may be paid on behalf of a deceased contributor if, immediately before the contributor's death, he or she was entitled to pay such contributions. Where payments are made by a third party on a deceased contributor's behalf, as regards time limits and rates of payments, the same rules apply as would apply if the contributions had been paid by the contributor (the *Social security (Contributions) Regulations 2001 (SI 2001/1004), reg 62).*

Payment of Class 3 National Insurance contributions after issue of a gender recognition certificate

7.31 A gender recognition certificate issued under the *Gender Recognition Act 2004* allows a person's acquired gender to be recognised for legal purposes. As a result, a person may be entitled to pay contributions where, under their previous gender, they were ineligible to do so having reached pensionable age.

Where such a certificate has been issued, any Class 3 National Insurance contributions that are payable in respect of the tax year of issue and the following tax year are payable at the rate for the tax year to which the contribution relates (the *Social Security (Contributions) Regulations 2001* (*SI 2001/1004*), *reg 65B*).

Return of precluded Class 3 National Insurance contributions

7.32 If a person has paid Class 3 National Insurance contributions that he or she was not entitled to pay, those contributions can be repaid. However, repayment is not automatic and the contributor must apply to HMRC for a refund (the *Social Security (Contributions) Regulations 2001* (*SI 2001/1004*), *reg 56*).

A refund can be claimed online at www.gov.uk/claim-national-insurance-refund.

CLASS 3A NATIONAL INSURANCE CONTRIBUTIONS

Nature of Class 3A National Insurance contributions

7.33 Class 3A National Insurance contributions were introduced in October 2015 and were available for a limited period to those who reached state pension age before 6 April 2016. In most cases, the payment window ended on 5 April 2017.

The purpose of the Class 3A scheme is to enable those who have not been able to build up much additional pension and who reach state pension age prior to the introduction of the single-tier pension to boost their income. The legislation governing the eligibility to pay Class 3A National Insurance contributions is contained in *SSCBA 1992, ss 14A, 14B and 14C*. The rate of Class 3A contributions is set out in the *Social Security Class 3A Contributions (Units of Additional Pension) Regulations 2014 (SI 2014/3240)*.

People who paid Class 3A contributions will receive extra additional state pension (S2P or SERPS) in return. The rate of Class 3A contributions depended on the age of the contributor at the date on which the payment is made. The table published as Appendix 6 shows the amount that must be paid for each additional pension unit of £1 per week. A person who is age 70 at the time of payment will need to make a payment of £779 to increase their pension by £1 per week. This means that at current levels they will need to continue to live and draw the state pension until they are 85 in order to break even. A person can pay Class 3A contributions to increase their basic state pension by up to a maximum of £25 per week.

The collection of Class 3A contributions will be administered by HMRC. The additional pension earned as a result of payment of Class 3A contributions will be paid by the Department for Work and Pensions who will revise the contributor's state pension award to reflect the contribution.

Focus

The window for paying a Class 3A contribution has now closed.

Eligibility to pay Class 3A National Insurance contributions

7.34 An eligible person was entitled to pay a Class 3A National Insurance contribution in return for a unit of additional pension (*SSCBA 1992, s 14A*). The right to pay a Class 3A contribution applied from 12 October 2015 and the contribution had to be paid before the cut-off date. This was normally 5 April 2017. However, a later cut-off date applied where the end of the 30 day period beginning on the day on which a person was sent information on Class 3A contributions in response to a request for information made on or before 5 April 2017 fell after 5 April 2017.

A person was eligible to pay a Class 3A contribution if that person is entitled to a Category A, Category D retirement pension or graduated retirement benefit or has deferred entitlement to a Category A, Category D retirement pension or graduated retirement benefit. The amount of the contribution needed to buy a unit of additional pension is set out by the Treasury in regulations. A table showing the amount of contribution required depending on the age of the contributor at the time the Class 3A contribution is paid is set out as Appendix 6.

A person could make a Class 3A contribution on more than one occasion, but could not obtain more than the maximum number of units of additional pension. The maximum number is specified in regulations and is set at 25 (the *Social Security Class 3A Contributions (Units of Additional Pension) Regulations 2014 (SI 2014/3240), reg 3*). Each additional unit is set at £1 (*SI 2014/3240, reg 4*). This means that the maximum by which a person could increase their state pension by the payment of Class 3A contributions is £25 per week.

The Treasury has the power (in *SSCBA 1992, s 14C*) to make regulations which change who is eligible to pay Class 3A contributions, to remove the option for people to pay Class 3A contributions and to amend the substantive provisions.

Refund of Class 3A National Insurance contributions

7.35 The Treasury has the power to make regulations to provide for a Class 3A contribution to be repaid in certain circumstances (*SSCBA 1992, s 14B*). Such regulations may make provision about applications for repayment and other procedural matters. Where a Class 3A contribution is repaid, the contributor is treated as never having added the additional unit of pension in respect of that contribution. Any benefit paid by reference to the unit of additional pension relating to the repaid contribution may be recovered by deducting them from the repayment of that contribution.

PLANNING POINTS

7.36

- Voluntary contributions can be made to enhance a person's state pension. Class 3 contributions can be paid to make up a shortfall in a person's contributions record.
- Before paying voluntary Class 3 National Insurance contributions determine if such contributions are actually needed. A person who reached state pension age on or after 6 April 2016 needs 35 qualifying years for the full single-tier state pension and 10 years to receive any state pension.
- In deciding whether to pay voluntary contributions it is necessary to evaluate whether the return is worthwhile.

- If a person is eligible but not liable to pay Class 2 National Insurance contributions, it is considerably cheaper to pay Class 2 contributions voluntarily (at £3.05 per week for 2021/22) than to pay Class 3 contributions (at £15.40 per week for 2021/22). Class 2 contributions also confer better benefit entitlement.
- Where a decision is made to pay Class 3 contributions, if possible the contributions should be made before the end of the tax year following that for which the contributions are payable. Delaying payment beyond this date may mean that the contributions are payable at a higher rate than that in force for the year to which they relate.
- Where the payment deadline is missed, those people eligible to pay additional class 3 contributions get a second chance to top up their contribution record. Contributions for up to six missing years can be paid any time up to six years from the date on which the person reaches state pension age.
- Those reaching state pension age on or after 6 April 2016 have until 5 April 2023 to make voluntary contributions for the years 2006/07 to 2015/16 to the extent that these were not paid prior to 18 April 2013. Consideration should be given as to whether this is necessary to improve or secure their single-tier state pension.

Chapter 8

Class 4 National Insurance contributions

SIGNPOSTS

- Class 4 contributions are payable by the self-employed by reference to their profits (see **8.1**).
- Liability for Class 4 contributions arises in respect of a trade, profit or vocation to the extent that those profits exceed the lower profits limit (see **8.2**).
- Class 4 contributions are payable at the main rate of 9% on profits between the lower profits limit and the upper profits limit, and at the additional rate of 2% on profits in excess of the upper profits limit (see **8.3**).
- The profits on which Class 4 contributions are based are those computed as for tax purposes (see **8.5**).
- Certain persons are excepted from liability to Class 4, including those under the age of 16 and those who have reached state pension age (see **8.8**).
- Where a person is simultaneously employed and self-employed, they may pay Class 1, Class 2 and Class 4 contributions. A cap, the annual maximum, places a limit on the amount of Class 4 contributions payable for an earner for a year (see **8.21**).
- Class 4 contributions are collected under the self-assessment system with income tax and are payable by 31 January after the end of the tax year to which they relate. They are taken into account in working out payments on account (see **8.22**).
- Where a person receives a Self-employment Income Support Scheme grant during the Covid-19 pandemic, this must be taken into account in computing their profits for 2020/21 on which Class 4 contributions are payable (see **8.36**)

OVERVIEW OF CLASS 4 NATIONAL INSURANCE CONTRIBUTIONS

Nature of Class 4 National Insurance contributions

8.1 Class 4 National Insurance contributions are payable by the self-employed in addition to Class 2 National Insurance contributions (for which see Chapter 6). Employed earners pay Class 1 National Insurance contributions by reference to their earnings (see Chapter 3) and likewise self-employed earners pay Class 4 National Insurance contributions by reference to their profits. However, unlike Class 1 contributions, the payment of Class 4 contributions does not currently confer any benefit entitlement as this role is provided by the payment of Class 2 contributions, which are payable by the self-employed in addition to any Class 4 liability.

Proposals to reform the National Insurance regime for the self-employed have been put on hold. Consequently, Class 4 contributions continue to confer no benefit entitlement and act essentially like an additional tax on profits.

The Class 4 contribution liability is based on the profits of the trade, profession or vocation for the tax year in question, as computed for tax purposes in accordance with *ITTOIA 2005, Pt 2, Ch 2* (see **8.15**). No Class 4 contributions are payable until profits reach the lower profits limit for the year. Once this has been reached, Class 4 contributions are payable at the main Class 4 percentage on earnings between the lower profits limit and the upper profits limit and at the additional Class 4 percentage on profits in excess of the upper profits limit. In this way, the structure of Class 4 National Insurance contributions mirrors that applying for Class 1 purposes, although the rates are not the same.

Liability to Class 4 National Insurance contributions is imposed by *SSCBA 1992, s 15*. The *Social Security (Contributions) Regulations 2001* (*SI 2001/1004*), *Pt VIII* set out exceptions from the Class 4 charge (see **8.8**) and contain provisions governing the payment and administration of Class 4 National Insurance contributions (see **8.22**). Further guidance on Class 4 National Insurance contributions can be found on the Gov.uk website (www.gov.uk) and in HMRC's National Insurance Manual (see www.hmrc.gov.uk/manuals/nimmanual/index.htm).

> **Focus**
>
> Class 4 National Insurance contributions are payable by self-employed earners by reference to their profits. The payment of Class 4 contributions does not confer any pension or benefit entitlement.

Liability to Class 4 National Insurance

8.2 The liability to Class 4 National Insurance contributions is imposed by *SSCBA 1992, s 15* which provides for Class 4 National Insurance contributions to be payable for any tax year in respect of all profits which:

- are immediately derived from the carrying on or exercise of one of more trades, profession or vocations;
- are profits chargeable to income tax under *ITTOIA 2005, Pt 2 Ch 2* for the year of assessment corresponding to the tax year; and
- are not profits of a trade, profession or vocation carried out wholly outside the UK.

The liability for Class 4 National Insurance contributions falls on the person on whom the liability to income tax on those profits falls (*SSCBA 1992, s 15(2)*).

Where income tax is charged on a member of a limited liability partnership in respect of profits arising from the carrying on of a trade, profession or vocation by the limited liability partnership, Class 4 National Insurance contributions are payable by the members of the limited liability partnership in the same way that would be payable if the trade were carried on in partnership by the members. However, where a member of such a partnership is treated as an employed earner, his or her earnings are liable to Class 1 contributions rather than Class 4 (the *Social Security Contributions (Limited Liability Partnership) Regulations 2014 (SI 2014/3159)*; *SSCBA 1992, s 18A*).

If a trade is carried on by two or more persons jointly in partnership, the liability of any one of them in respect of Class 4 National Insurance contributions arises in respect of their share of the profits of the trade or profession. In computing the Class 4 liability, the person's share of partnership profits is aggregated with his or her share of the profits from any other trade, profession or vocation (*SSCBA 1992, Sch 2, para 4(1)*). Each partner is charged separately in respect of his or her Class 4 National Insurance contributions on partnership profits (*SSCBA 1992, Sch 2, para 4(2)*). HMRC have confirmed that the sleeping and inactive partners are liable to Class 4 National Insurance contributions and should account for them for 2013/14 and subsequent tax years.

The Class 4 charge is extended by *SSCBA 1992, s 18* to the earnings of employments that are treated by regulations made under *SSCBA 1992, s 18(2)* as being self-employments. Earners falling within this category are those deemed to be self-employed by the *Social Security (Categorisation of Earners) Regulations 1978 (SI 1978/1698)*, *Sch 1, Pt II* (see **2.38**), which includes examiners, moderators, invigilators and similar. Such persons are liable to pay special Class 4 National Insurance contributions, which are computed in the same way as standard Class 4 contributions. The charge is computed by reference to the earnings that would be earnings for Class 1 National Insurance purposes (see **3.8**), were the employment is not deemed to be self-employment by the regulations. Certain share fishermen are also liable to pay special Class 4 National Insurance contributions by virtue of the *Social Security (Contributions) Regulations 2001 (SI 2001/1004), reg 125(f)*. For more detailed commentary on special Class 4 National Insurance contributions, see **8.27**.

Certain persons are excepted from the liability to Class 4 National Insurance contributions by the *Social Security (Contributions) Regulations 2001* (*SI 2001/1004*), *Pt VIII* (see **8.8**).

> **Focus**
>
> The liability to pay Class 4 National Insurance contributions arises in respect of profits from a trade, profession or vocation.

Rates and limits for Class 4 National Insurance contributions

8.3 No Class 4 National Insurance contributions are payable until profits reach the lower profits limit. Class 4 contributions are then payable at the main Class 4 rate on profits between the lower profits limit and the upper profits limit. Once the upper profits limit has been reached, Class 4 National Insurance contributions are payable at the additional Class 4 rate on profits in excess of the upper profits limit.

The Class 4 National Insurance rates and limits applying for 2021/22 are as follows:

	2021/22
Lower profits limit	£9,568
Upper profits limit	£50,270
Main Class 4 rate (payable on profits between the lower profits limit and the upper profits limit)	9%
Additional Class 4 rate (payable on profits in excess of the upper earnings limit)	2%

The lower profits limit for Class 4 purposes is aligned with the primary earnings threshold applying for Class 1 National Insurance purposes and the upper profits limit for Class 4 National Insurance purposes is aligned with the upper earnings limit for Class 1 purposes.

At the time of the 2021 Budget, it was announced that the upper profits limit would remain at its 2021/22 level of £50,270 for tax years up to and including 2025/26.

The Class 4 rates and limits applying for earlier years are shown in Appendix 7.

Focus

There are two rates of Class 4 contribution. The main rate of 9% is payable on profits between the lower profits limit (£9,568 for 2021/22) and the upper profits limit (£50,270 for 2021/22), and at the additional rate of 2% on profits above the upper profits limit. No Class 4 liability arises if profits are below the lower profits limit.

Alignment of profits limits and tax thresholds

8.4 In accordance with measures introduced by the *National Insurance Contributions Act 2008*, the upper profits limit for Class 4 National Insurance purposes is fully aligned with the level at which higher rate tax becomes payable. For 2021/22, both the upper profits limit for Class 4 National Insurance purposes and the higher rate tax threshold for income tax purposes (for the UK excluding Scotland) are set at £50,270.

At the 2021 Budget, it was announced that the rate at which higher rate tax becomes payable and the upper profits limit would be frozen at £50,270 until April 2026 (remaining at the 2021/22 level for 2022/23, 2023/24, 2024/25 and 2025/26).

The Class 4 lower profits limit is aligned with the primary earnings threshold for Class 1 National Insurance purposes, such that the start point for earnings-related contributions payable by the employed and profit-related contributions payable by the self-employed is the same. The lower profits limit for Class 4 purposes is set at £9,568 for 2021/22, aligning with the primary threshold for Class 1 of £184 per week. Thus, the starting point for Class 1 and Class 4 National Insurance is lower than the personal allowance for tax purposes, which is set at £12,500 for 2020/21, although the government plans eventually to align the two.

Application of the Income Tax Acts

8.5 Class 4 National Insurance contributions are payable on the profits of the trade, profession or vocation as computed for tax purposes by the person liable for the tax on those profits. The tax rules are imported into the Class 4 regime by *SSCBA 1992, s 16*, which provides for all provisions of the Income Tax Acts, including in particular:

- provisions as to assessment, collection, repayment and recovery; and
- provisions on payment of tax (in *TMA 1970, Pt VA*) and on penalties (in *TMA 1970, Pt X);*
- provisions on penalties for failure to make returns (in *FA 2009, Sch 55*), penalties for failure to make payments on time (in *FA 2009, Sch 56)* and on dishonest conduct by tax agents (in *FA 2012, Sch 38*).

to apply with the necessary modifications in relation to Class 4 National Insurance contributions as if those contributions were income tax chargeable under *ITTOIA 2005, Pt 2, Ch 2* in respect of the profits of a trade, profession or vocation which is not carried on wholly outside the UK (*SSCBA 1992, s 16(1)*). The effect of this is that Class 4 National Insurance contributions for most practical purposes are treated in the same way as tax, with profits subject to broadly the same computational rules and Class 4 contributions collected as for tax via the self-assessment system and subject to the same payment deadlines.

This general rule is subject to:

- regulations (made under *SSCBA 1992, s 17(3)*) with regard to incidental matters arising out of the payment of Class 4 National Insurance contributions recovered by HMRC;
- regulations (made under *SSCBA 1992, s 17(4)*) providing for matters arising out of the deferment; and
- regulations for recovering Class 4 contributions (made under *SSCBA 1992, s 18*).

The applicability of the Income Tax Acts is also subject to the modifications set out in *SSCBA 1992, Sch 2*. These include the availability of reliefs in the computation of profits for Class 4 National Insurance purposes (see **8.17**), application of the rules to partnerships and trustees and the applicability of certain provisions of *TMA 1970*.

> **Focus**
>
> The profits on which the Class 4 liability is based are those as computed for income tax purposes.

Class 4 National Insurance contributions and benefit entitlement

8.6 Class 4 National Insurance contributions do not generate any entitlement to the state pension or to contributory benefits. The self-employed derive benefit entitlement from the payment of Class 2 National Insurance contributions. Class 4 National Insurance contributions are paid into the National Insurance fund and in this way help fund benefits.

Planned reforms to the National Insurance treatment of the self-employed which would have seen Class 2 abolished and Class 4 reformed so as to provide pension and benefit entitlement have been put on hold. Class 4 contributions continue to be payable on profits without conferring any benefit entitlement.

Class 2 National Insurance contributions are discussed in detail in Chapter 6.

> **Focus**
>
> The payment of Class 4 contributions does not confer any entitlement to benefits or to the state pension – this role is performed by Class 2.

Proposed reform of Class 4 National Insurance contributions

8.7 Proposals to reform the National Insurance regime, encompassing changes to the nature of Class 4 contributions, have been put on hold.

Under the proposed reforms, the self-employed would have paid a single class of National Insurance, Class 4, which would have been reformed so as to provide the mechanism by which the self-employed build up entitlement to contributory benefits and the state pension (having taken over that role from Class 2, which was to be abolished). The reformed Class 4 would have looked a lot like Class 1 contributions operated on an annual earnings basis.

Draft clauses to give statutory effect to the reformed Class 4 were published in December 2016. The draft legislation provided for the introduction of a new threshold – the Small Profits Limit (SPL) – which was to have been set at 52 times the lower earnings limit for the year in question. Under the proposals, contributions on profits between the SPL and the lower profits limit (LPL) would have been payable at a zero rate (in the same way as Class 1 contributions on earnings between the lower earnings limit and primary threshold are payable at a zero rate). This would have had the effect of bringing some self-employed earners within the proposed zero-rate band. The structure for reforming the Class 4 National Insurance contributions as outlined in the consultation document largely mirrored that for primary Class 1 National Insurance contributions where applied on an annual basis as for company directors.

However, as a result of the decision not to proceed with the reforms, the structure of Class 4 contributions for 2019/20 onwards remains unchanged.

The decision not to proceed with the abolition of Class 2 was attributed to the adverse effect the reforms would have on self-employed earners with low earnings who, had the reforms gone ahead, would no longer have been able to pay Class 2 contributions voluntarily and would have instead had to pay Class 3 contributions, which at £15.40 per week for 2021/22 compared to £3.05 per week for 2021/22 for Class 2, are considerably more expensive. However, in the written statement to Parliament announcing the decision not to proceed with the abolition of Class 2 contributions, the government stated that they remained committed to simplifying the tax system for the self-employed and 'will keep the issue under review in the context of the wider tax system and the sustainability of the public finance'.

It is likely that the need to sustain public finances and recover the revenue that would be lost from abolishing Class 2 contribution was at least partially behind the decision not to proceed with the planned reforms. At the time of the Spring 2017 Budget the government announced its intention to increase the main rate of Class 4 contributions from 9% to 10% from April 2018 and again to 11% from April 2019. Although the National Insurance Contributions (Rate Ceiling) Act 2015, which applied at that time prior to the 2017 General Election, did not apply to Class 4 contributions, providing the government with the flexibility (from legislative perspective) to increase the Class 4 rate, it was announced a week after the Budget (amid calls that the government had broken an election promise not to increase National Insurance contributions during the life of that Parliament) that the planned increases would not go ahead and the rate would remain at 9% for the remainder of the Parliament. However, the June 2017 General Election brought that Parliament (and the authority of the *National Insurance (Contributions) Rate Ceiling Act 2015*) to an end. The political sensitivities making it difficult to increase Class 4 contributions to recover the revenue that would be lost from abolishing Class 2 limit the opportunities for abolishing Class 2 whilst sustaining the public finances. It remains to be seen if, and when, National Insurance for the self-employed will be reformed and what any reforms will look like.

The enactment of the *Coronavirus Act 2020* (which enacts various measures of relevance to the Covid-19 pandemic) lifts the cap on the amount by which contributions can be increased. While this paves the way for possible National Insurance rises to meet some of the costs associated with the pandemic, it also creates the possibility of reinstating the reforms.

Focus

Under the proposed reforms to the National Insurance of the self-employed, Class 4 would have resembled primary Class 1 contributions more closely, with a notional zero rate applying where profits fall between the new small profits limit and the lower profits limit, allowing the self-employed with profits within this band to build up a contributions record for zero contribution cost, as for employed earners with earnings between the lower earnings limit and primary threshold. The planned reforms have been put on hold.

EXCEPTION FROM LIABILITY TO CLASS 4 NATIONAL INSURANCE CONTRIBUTIONS

Introduction to Class 4 exceptions

8.8 Certain persons are excepted from liability to Class 4 National Insurance contributions by virtue of the *Social Security (Contributions) Regulations 2001* (*SI 2001/1004*), *Pt VIII*. The regulatory exceptions are discussed at **8.9ff**.

Person over pensionable age

8.9 A person who is over pensionable age at the start of a tax year is excepted from liability to Class 4 National Insurance contributions by virtue of the *Social Security (Contributions) Regulations 2001* (*SI 2001/1004*), *reg 91(a)*. If a person attains pensionable age during the course of the tax year, they are liable for Class 4 National Insurance contributions for the whole of that year. The age at which a person attains pensionable age depends on their gender and their date of birth.

However, where a person registers a gender reassignment between the ages of 60 and 65 on the Transsexual Person's Register, that person is not liable for Class 4 National Insurance contributions if they were over pensionable age by reference to their gender at the start of that tax year. Liability for Class 4 National Insurance contributions in subsequent years depends on whether or not the person is over pensionable age by reference to his or her acquired gender (HMRC's National Insurance Manual at NIM24525).

> **Focus**
>
> Class 4 National Insurance contributions are no longer payable once a person reaches state pension age.

Persons under the age of 16

8.10 A person who is under the age of 16 at the start of the tax year may apply for exception from liability to Class 4 National Insurance contributions on profits for that year (the *Social Security (Contributions) Regulations 2001* (*SI 2001/1004*), *reg 93*).

If the application for exception is made before the start of the tax year to which it relates and HMRC are satisfied that the conditions for exception from liability are met (i.e. the person is under the age of 16 at the start of the tax year), they will issue a certificate of exception for that year. A certificate of exception will also be issued if the application is made after the start of the tax year but before Class 4 National Insurance contributions become due and payable. This effectively means that a person under the age of 16 on 6 April at the start of the tax year may apply for a certificate of exception for that year at any time before 31 January following the end of that tax year.

Where a certificate of exception has been issued, HMRC will not collect any Class 4 National Insurance contributions that would otherwise be payable on the profits for that tax year.

> **Focus**
>
> No liability for Class 4 contributions arises until a person has reached the age of 16 by the start of the tax year, even if they are making profits from self-employment.

Persons not resident in the UK

8.11 A person who for income tax purposes is not resident in the UK in the year of assessment is excepted from liability to Class 4 National Insurance contributions for that year by virtue of the *Social Security (Contributions) Regulations 2001* (*SI 2001/1004*), *reg 91(b)*.

Divers and diving supervisors

8.12 Where certain conditions are met, employment as a diver or diving supervisor is treated for income tax purposes as the carrying on of a trade in the UK (*ITTOIA 2005, s 15*). This is the case where:

- a person performs the duties of the employment as a diver or diving supervisor in the UK or in any areas designated by Order in Council under the *Continental Shelf Act 1964, s 1(7)*;
- the duties consist wholly or mainly of seabed diving activities; and
- any employment income from the employment would otherwise be chargeable to tax under *ITEPA 2003, Pt 2*.

For these purposes, seabed diving activities comprise taking part as a diver in diving operations concerned with the exploration or exploitation of the seabed, its subsoil and their natural resources and acting as a diving instructor in relation to any such diving operations.

Divers or diving instructors treated for income tax purposes as carrying on a trade (by virtue of *ITTOIA 2005, s 15*) are excepted from the liability to Class 4 National Insurance contributions by virtue of the *Social Security (Contributions) Regulations 2001(SI 2001/1004), reg 92*. Instead such divers remain within the Class 1 National Insurance net and are liable to pay Class 1 National Insurance contributions on their earnings.

Trustees

8.13 Class 4 National Insurance contributions are not payable in respect of profits assessed and charged on a person by virtue of *ITTOIA 2005, s 8* in his or her capacity as trustee under *SSCBA 1992, Sch 2, para 5(b)*).

Earnings from an employed earner's employments chargeable to tax as trading income

8.14 Employed earners are liable to Class 1 National Insurance contributions whereas self-employed earners are liable to Class 2 and Class 4 National Insurance contributions. Commentary on employment status can be found in Chapter 2.

Therefore, as a general rule, for any tax year in which an earner has earnings from employment which is an employed earner's employment and those earnings are chargeable to tax as trading income, the earner is excepted from liability to Class 4 National Insurance contributions on those earnings, provided an application for exception from liability is made (the *Social Security (Contributions) Regulations 2001* (*SI 2001/1004*), *reg 94*).

The application must be made before the start of the tax year to which it relates, or by such later time as allowed by HMRC. Where such an application is made, the person making the application is obliged to supply HMRC with such information as is necessary in order to determine whether the earner is entitled to the exception. The earner is not prohibited in applying for deferment of Class 4 National Insurance contributions pending the determination of the application for exception from liability.

The certificate may be revoked if the application contains erroneous information without which the certificate would not have been issued (the *Social Security (Contributions) Regulations 2001* (*SI 2001/1004*), *reg 97(4)*: see further **8.24**). Where the application is revoked, the contributor is liable to pay the contributions that would have been due had the certificate not been issued (the *Social Security (Contributions) Regulations 2001* (*SI 2001/1004*), *reg 98*).

The exception was widened from 2003/04 to apply to earnings from an employed earner's employment that are included within the calculation of profits chargeable to tax as trading income (the *Social Security (Contributions) Regulations 2001* (*SI 2001/1004*), *reg 94A*). In this case, it is not necessary to apply for the exception from Class 4 contributions. The exception is given automatically.

This exemption prevents earnings liable to Class 1 National Insurance contributions but which are included within the computation of profits for trading income purposes from suffering a further liability to Class 4 National Insurance contributions.

PROFITS FOR CLASS 4 NATIONAL INSURANCE PURPOSES

Class 4 National Insurance charge based on profits

8.15 Class 4 National Insurance contributions are payable in respect of the full amount of profits of any relevant trade, profession or vocation that is not carried on wholly outside the UK and which is chargeable to income tax under *ITTOIA 2005, Pt 2, Ch 2* (*SSCBA 1992, s 15(1)* and *Sch 2, para 2*). The computation for Class 4 National Insurance purposes is subject to a limited number of adjustments, predominantly in relation to reliefs, which are set out in *SSCBA 1992, Sch 2*.

In keeping with the link between tax and National Insurance for Class 4 purposes, the starting point of the computation of the Class 4 National Insurance liability is the profits of the trade, profession or vocation as computed for income tax purposes and returned on the earner's self-assessment return. In general, the profits on which the Class 4 National Insurance computation is based are those for the accounting year that ended in the tax year in question (the current year basis).

It should be noted that where the self-employed earner receives a grant under the Self-employment Income Support Scheme where their business has been adversely affected by the Covid-19 pandemic, that grant is taken into account in computing profits on which the Class 4 charge is based.

However, legislation introduced by the *National Insurance Contributions Bill 2021, cl 10* provides for self-isolation payments to be excluded from the computation of profits. Self-isolation payments are lump sum payments of £500 paid to provide financial support to eligible persons who are asked to self-isolate to help stop the spread of Coronavirus and who are unable to work from home and will suffer financial consequences as a result. The payments are made by local authorities, with separate schemes applying in England, Wales and Scotland. A separate exemption applies for Class 1 National Insurance purposes. The exemption applies for 2020/21 and subsequent tax years.

Example 8.1—Profits on which Class 4 liability based

Chris is a self-employed landscape gardener who has been in business for many years. He prepares his accounts to 31 December this year.

His income tax liability for 2021/22 is based on the accounts to 31 December 2021. The assessment is on a current year basis. This means that the profits assessed for the tax year are those for the accounting period ending in that tax year. The accounting year to 31 December 2021 is the year that ended in the 2021/22 tax year.

The Class 4 National Insurance liability is based on the same profits as the tax liability. Thus the Class 4 National Insurance liability for 2021/22 is based on the profits for the year ended 31 December 2020.

Different rules apply in the opening and closing years of a business for determining the basis period for a year of assessment. In the opening years of a business the basis periods are as follows:

Tax year	**Basis of assessment**
1 (year in which business starts)	Actual – profits from date of commencement to following 5 April
2	12 months to the accounting date or if the accounting date is less than 12 months from the date of commencement, first 12 months
3 and subsequent years	12 months to accounting date ending in year (current year basis)

In the final tax year, the profits assessed for the tax year are the actual profits from the start of the tax year to the date of cessation.

These rules are modified where the accounting date is changed.

The NIC rules mirror the tax rules. This means that the Class 4 National Insurance computation is based on the profits for the period that is the basis period for the income tax computation.

> **Focus**
>
> The Class 4 National Insurance rules follow the tax rules and the profits on which the Class 4 liability for a tax year is based are those assessed to tax in that year – normally those for the accounting period ending in that tax year.

Permitted deductions

8.16 For tax purposes, certain deduction are permitted in working out the taxable profit, on which income tax is payable. As far as permitted deductions are concerned, the National Insurance legislation does not exactly mirror the tax legislation. Some of the reliefs available for tax purposes are also allowed for National Insurance purposes, whereas others are specifically denied (see **8.18**). The rules governing deductibility of reliefs for Class 4 National Insurance purposes are set out in *SSCBA 1992, Sch 2*.

Relief for losses

8.17 For the purposes of computing the profits on which Class 4 National Insurance contributions are payable, the legislation (*SSCBA 1992, Sch 2, para 3(1)*) specifically permits relief for losses given under and in the manner provided by:

- *ITA 2007, s 64*, which provides for deduction of losses against general income in the loss making year, the previous tax year or both; and
- *ITA 2007, s 72*, which provides relief for losses in early years of a trade.

In each case, relief is only available in computing the profits liable for Class 4 National Insurance contributions if the loss arises from activities the profits of which would be brought into computation for the purposes of Class 4 National Insurance contributions.

Relief is also available when computing the profits for Class 4 National Insurance purposes for losses under and in the manner provided by:

- *ITA 2007, s 87*, which provides for the carry forward of losses against subsequent losses; and
- *ITA 2007, s 89*, which provides for the carry back of terminal losses.

Where a person claims loss relief for a tax year under any of the above provisions, the deduction is treated for the purposes of the charge to Class 4 National Insurance purposes as reducing that person's profits for any relevant trade, profession or vocation for that tax year. To the extent that losses remain unrelieved, they can be used to reduce the profits of subsequent years until the loss in extinguished. The loss must be used to reduce the first available profits (*SSCBA 1992, Sch 2 para 3(4)*).

It should be noted that where accounts are prepared on the cash basis, sideways loss relief and early years loss relief are not available.

Legislation introduced in the *Finance Act 2021, s 18* and *Sch 2* allows losses for 2020/21 and 2021/22 to be carried back against trading profits of the same trade for the previous three years (after any claim under *ITA 2007, s 64*) has been made. Losses are set against the trading profits of a later year before those of an earlier year. Where losses are carried back under the extended carry-back provisions, the Class 4 profits are correspondingly reduced.

Example 8.2—Impact of losses on Class 4 liability

Gillian runs a business as a self-employed photographer. She prepares accounts to 31 March each year. She also runs a second business as a self-employed beautician. The accounts for that business are also prepared to 31 March each year. The accounts for both businesses are prepared under the accruals basis.

The results of the two businesses for the years to 31 March 2021 and 31 March 2022 are as follows:

Business	**Year-end 31 March 2021**	**Year end 31 March 2022**
Photography	Profit of £2,000	Profit of £15,000
Beautician	Loss of (£4,000)	Profit of £1,000

The results for the year to 31 March 2021 form the basis of the Class 4 National Insurance computation for 2020/21 and the results for the year to 31 March 2022 form the basis of the Class 4 National Insurance computation for 2021/22.

The losses and profits on which Class 4 National Insurance contributions are charged for each of those years are as follows.

2020/21	**Profits for year**	**Loss carried forward**
Photography business: y/e 31/03/21	£2,000	
Less: relief for loss from beautician business	(£2,000)	£2,000
PROFITS LIABLE TO CLASS 4 NICS	Nil	

The loss from the beautician business is set against the profit from the photography business so as to reduce the profits to nil. No Class 4 National Insurance contributions are payable for 2019/20. The unutilised loss of £2,000 is carried forward to set against subsequent profits from self-employment.

2021/22	**Profit for year**	**Loss brought forward**	**Loss carried forward**
Photography business (y/e 31/03/22)	£15,000		
Beautician business	£1,000	£2,000	Nil
Less relief for loss brought forward	(£2,000)		
PROFITS LIABLE TO CLASS 4 NICs	£14,000		

The balance of the loss arising in the beautician business for the year ended 31 March 2021 is carried forward and relieved against the profits assessable in 2021/22 (ie those for year to 31 March 2022), reducing the profits on which Class 4 National Insurance contributions are payable for that year to £14,000.

Focus

Effect is given to relief for losses for Class 4 purposes where the profits are reduced for tax purposes as a result of loss relief. Thus, the profits liable to Class 4 National Insurance contributions are those on which the tax charge is based.

Relief for payments of interest

8.18 Relief for payments of interest that are allowable for tax purposes by virtue of *ITA 2007, s 383* are also allowed as a deduction from profits for Class 4 National Insurance purposes provided that they are incurred wholly and exclusively for the purposes of any relevant trade, profession or vocation (*SSCBA 1992, Sch 2, para 3(5)(b)*). Relief is given by way of deduction or set-off against profits chargeable to Class 4 National Insurance purposes in the year in which the payments are made. In the event that there are insufficient profits from which to deduct the interest payments, the excess is carried forward and deducted from the first available profits of a subsequent year.

The requirement that for a deduction to be allowed, the interest must be incurred wholly and exclusively for the purposes of a relevant trade, profession or vocation effectively means that the only interest payments deductible for tax purposes under *ITA 2007, s 383* which are also deductible for Class 4 National Insurance purposes are payments of interest on loans to buy plant and machinery for partnership use and payments of interest on loans to invest in a partnership. However, a deduction is not allowed for Class 4 purposes for interest on a loan to buy a partnership share from another partner (see HMRC's National Insurance Manual at NIM24605).

Where accounts are prepared using the cash basis, the deduction for interest is capped at £500.

Precluded deductions

8.19 Some reliefs and allowances that are available to reduce the profits on which income tax is charged are not similarly available to reduce the profits liable to Class 4 National Insurance contributions. By virtue of *SSCBA 1992, Sch 2, para 3(2)*, no relief is given in the computation of profits liable to Class 4 National Insurance contributions for:

- personal reliefs;
- payments of interest deductible under *ITA 2007, s 383* other than those incurred wholly and exclusively for the purposes of the business (see **8.17**);
- interest treated as a loss for the purposes of carry back or carry forward by virtue of *ITA 2007, ss 88, 94*;
- premiums or other consideration under annuity contracts and trust schemes; and
- personal pension contributions.

The non-deductibility of the above items, particularly personal reliefs, mean that if the self-employed person has no other sources of income, the profits on which Class 4 National Insurance contributions are payable will be higher than those on which tax is payable and Class 4 contributions may even be payable if there is no tax to pay. The lower profit limit for Class 4 National Insurance contributions, set at £9,658 for 2021/22 is lower than the personal allowance, set at £12,570 for 2021/22, and thus the Class 4 liability kicks in before the tax liability if the person's only income is that from self-employment.

Thus while the computation rules for Class 4 National Insurance purposes borrow from the tax rules, the profits charged to income tax and the profits on which the Class 4 National Insurance liability is based will not necessarily be the same.

> **Focus**
>
> The lower profits limit for Class 4 purposes is less than the personal allowance, so if a person has profits which fall between the lower profits limit and the personal allowance, assuming that they have no other income, they will have a liability to Class 4 National Insurance, but no tax liability.

CALCULATING THE CLASS 4 NATIONAL INSURANCE LIABILITY

Class 4 National Insurance computation

8.20 Class 4 National Insurance contributions are payable on the profits liable to Class 4 National Insurance purposes, as computed in accordance with the rules set out at **8.15ff**.

No Class 4 National Insurance contributions are payable unless profits exceed the lower profits limit for the tax year in question. For 2021/22 this is set at £9,568.

Class 4 National Insurance contributions are payable at the main Class 4 rate (9% for 2021/22) on such profits as exceed the lower profits limit (£9,568 for 2021/22) but which do not exceed the upper profits limit (£50,270 for 2021/22).

Class 4 National Insurance contributions are payable at the additional Class 4 rate (2% for 2021/22) on such profits as exceed the upper profits limit (£50,270 for 2021/22).

Example 8.3—Calculation of the Class 4 liability

Julian is a self-employed painter and decorator. He prepares accounts to 30 June each year. His profit for the year to 30 June 2021 (as adjusted for Class 4 National Insurance purposes) is £54,000.

His Class 4 National Insurance liability for 2021/22 (based on his profits for the year to 30 June 2021) is as follows:

On profits between the lower profits limit and upper profits limit ((£50,270 – £9,568) @ 9%)	£3.663.18
On profits above the upper profits limit ((£54,000 – £50,270) @ 2%)	£74.60
Class 4 National Insurance liability for 2021/22	£3,737.78

Julian is liable to pay Class 4 National Insurance contributions of £3,737.78 for 2021/22.

ANNUAL MAXIMUM

Annual maximum for Class 4 National Insurance purposes

8.21 A person who is concurrently employed and self-employed may be liable to Class 1, Class 2 and Class 4 National Insurance contributions. However, there is a cap, known as the annual maximum, on the amount of Class 4 National Insurance contributions payable by an earner for a tax year.

As Class 2 contributions are now determined retrospectively after the end of the tax year, it is no longer possible to apply for deferment of Class 4 contributions.

Contributions paid in excess of the maximum may be refunded (see **8.26**).

The calculation of the annual maximum applying for Class 4 National Insurance purposes is set out in the *Social Security (Contributions) Regulations 2001 (SI 2001/1004)*, *reg 100(3)* as follows:

Step one

Subtract the lower profits limit from the upper profits limit for the year.

Step two

Multiply the result of step one by 9%.

Step three

Add to the result of step two 53 times the weekly rate of the appropriate Class 2 National Insurance contribution.

Step four

Subtract from the result of Step three, the aggregate amount of any Class 2 National Insurance contributions and primary Class 1 National Insurance contributions paid at the main percentage rate.

The application of the following steps is determined by reference to the following three cases.

Case 1

If the result of this step is a positive value, and exceeds the aggregate of:

- primary Class 1 National Insurance contributions payable at the main percentage rate;
- Class 2 National Insurance contributions;
- Class 4 National Insurance payable at the main Class 4 percentage,

in respect of the earner's earnings, profits and gains for the year, the result of this step is the maximum amount of Class 4 National Insurance contributions payable.

Case 2

If the result of this step is a positive value, but does not exceed the aggregate mentioned in Case 1, the result of this step is the maximum amount of Class 4 National Insurance contributions payable.

Case 3

If the result of this step is a negative value, the maximum amount of Class 4 National Insurance contributions payable at the main Class 4 percentage rate is nil and the result of this step is treated as nil.

If Case 1 applies, steps five to nine do not apply.

If Case 2 or Case 3 applies, steps five to nine apply.

Step five

Multiply the result of step four by

$$\frac{100}{9}$$

Step six

Subtract the lower profits limit from the lesser of the upper profits limit and the amount of profits for the year.

Step seven

Subtract the result of step five from the result of step six.

If the result is a negative value, it is treated as nil.

Step eight

Multiply the result of step seven by 2%.

Step nine

Multiply the amount by which the profits and gains for the year exceed the upper profits limit for the year by 2%.

The maximum amount of Class 4 National Insurance contributions payable is:

- where Case 1 of step four applies, the result of that step; and
- where Case 2 or Case 3 of step four applies, the amount produced by adding together the result of steps four, eight and nine.

Where a person pays Class 1 primary contributions on earnings between the earnings threshold and the upper earnings limit at a rate that is less than the main primary Class 1 rate for the year, for example, because the person is a married woman with a valid reduced-rate election, for the purposes of the calculation, the main primary rate is used rather than the rate actually paid by the person (*SI 2001/1004*, *reg 100(4)*). This means that for 2020/21 the main rate of 12% is used in the calculation, regardless of the rate actually paid by the earner.

The Class 2 contributions rate used in the calculation is the appropriate rate for the earner in question. This is the standard Class 2 rate, unless the earner is a share fisherman or a volunteer development worker, in which case the rate is the special rate applying, respectively, to share fishermen and volunteer development workers.

Example 8.4—Calculating maximum Class 4 contributions payable

William is a self-employed personal trainer with profits of £58,000 for 2021/22 He is also employed on a part-time basis and earns £12,000 in 2021/22.

He pays Class 2 National Insurance contributions for 2021/22 of £3.05 per week.

The maximum Class 4 National Insurance contributions that William is liable to pay on the profits of his personal training business are found as follows:

Step one

Lower profits limit for 2021/22 is £9,568

Upper profits limit for 2021/22 is £50,270

Upper profits limit minus lower profits limit = £50,270 – £9,568 = £40,702

Step two

£40,702 × 9% = £3,663.18

Step three

Class 2 rate for 2021/22 is £3.05 per week.

53 × £3.05 = £161.65

£3,663.18 + £161.65= £3,824.83

Step four

Class 2 National Insurance contributions paid by William for 2021/22 are £158.60 (52 × £3.05)

Class 1 National Insurance contributions payable by William for 2021/22 at the main primary rate are £291.84 ((£12,000 – £9,568)) × 12%).

Aggregate of Class 2 National Insurance contributions and Class 1 National Insurance contributions payable at the main primary rate = £158.60 + £291.84 = £450.44

Step three result = £3,824.83

Step four result = £3,824.83 – £450.44 = £3.374.39

Aggregate of:

Primary Class 1 National Insurance contributions payable at the main rate	£291.84
Class 2 National Insurance contributions	£158.60
Class 4 National Insurance contributions payable at the main rate ((£50,270 – 9,568) × 9	£3,663.18
TOTAL	£4,113.62

The step four result (£3,824.83) is positive but does not exceed the aggregate of primary Class 1 National Insurance payable at the main rate, Class 2 National Insurance contributions and Class 4 National Insurance contributions payable at the main rate (£4,113.62). Therefore, Case 2 applies and the result of this step is the maximum amount of Class 4 National Insurance contributions payable at the main rate is £3,663.18 (9% × (£50,270 – £9,568)).

Step five

£3,663.18 × 100/9 = £40,702

Step six

Profits for the year are £58,000

Upper profits limit = £50,270

Lower profits limit = £9,568

Upper profits limit for year (lower than the profits for the year) minus lower profits limit = £50,270 – £9,568 = £40,702

Step seven

Step six result – step five result = £40,702 – £40,702 = nil.

Step eight

Nil

Step nine

(£58,000 – £50,270) × 2% = £154.60

Maximum Class 4 contributions for the year (found, as Case 2 applies, by adding together the results of steps four, eight and nine) is as follows:

Step four result	£3,824.83
Step eight result	Nil
Step nine result	£154.60
TOTAL	£3,979.43

Thus the maximum Class 4 National Insurance contributions payable by William for 2021/22 in respect of his personal training business are £3,979.43.

This can be compared to the Class 4 liability for 2021/22 if calculated in isolation of £3,817.78 ((£50,270 – £9,568) × 9%) + (£58,000 – £50,270) × 2%)).

If William pays Class 4 contributions as normal he will exceed the annual maximum for the year.

Focus

If a contributor is simultaneously employed and self-employed, paying Class 1, Class 2 and Class 4 contributions, check that the Class 4 liability does not exceed the annual maximum for Class 4.

PAYMENT AND COLLECTION OF CLASS 4 NATIONAL INSURANCE CONTRIBUTIONS

Application of the self-assessment system to collection of Class 4 National Insurance contributions

8.22 The link between income tax and Class 4 National Insurance contributions continues in relation to the payment and assessment of Class 4 National Insurance contributions.

Class 4 National Insurance contributions are collected through the self-assessment system in the same way as income tax. This means that the self-employed must self-assess their Class 4 National Insurance liability on the self-employment pages of the self-assessment tax return. Boxes 99 to 101 of the full supplementary self-employment pages provide for this. Where business turnover is less than the VAT registration threshold (£85,000 for 2021/22) the short self-employed supplementary pages can be completed instead of the full pages. Where these are used, the Class 4 liability does not need to be entered on the form. However, there are boxes to tick where the person is excepted from Class 4 National Insurance liability.

The deadline for submitting the self-assessment tax return depends on whether it is filed online or whether a paper return is filed. If the return is filed online, it must be filed by 31 January following the end of the tax year to which it relates. This means the deadline for filing the 2021/22 return is 31 January 2023. However, if a paper return is filed, an earlier deadline of 31 October after the end of the tax year applies. Thus a paper return for 2021/22 must be filed by 31 October 2022. Penalties are charged for returns filed late, including paper returns filed after 31 October. However, where the paper filing deadline is missed, no penalty is charged if the return is instead filed online by 31 January. Where the notice to deliver a tax return is dated less than three months before the normal filing date (ie after 31 July for paper returns or after 31 October for online returns) a later deadline of three months from the date of issue of the notice applies. The method by which the self-assessment return is filed does not affect the due date for payment of Class 4 National Insurance contributions (see **8.23**).

Penalties also apply in respect of errors in returns in accordance with the cross-tax penalty regime for inaccuracies in documents. Penalties chargeable under this regime are discussed at **1.17**.

> **Focus**
>
> Class 4 National Insurance contributions are collected through the self-assessment system with income tax, and the same filing and payment deadlines apply. Class 4 contributions are taken into account in working out payments on account.

Due dates for payment of Class 4 National Insurance contributions

8.23 Class 4 National Insurance contributions are payable with income tax due under the self-assessment system and the self-assessment due date of 31 January following the end of the tax year applies equally to Class 4 National Insurance contributions.

Under the self-assessment system, the taxpayer is required to make payments on account of his or her tax and Class 4 National liability, unless the total tax and Class 4 National Insurance bill is less than £1,000 or at least 80% of the tax payable is collected by deduction at source (such as under PAYE). Thus, unlike Class 2 contributions, Class 4 contributions are taken into account in determining whether payments on account are required, and where they are, the amount of each payment on account.

Where payments on account are required, these must be made by 31 January in the tax year and 31 July following the tax year. Each payment on account is one-half of the previous year's liability. A final balancing payment (where applicable) is due on 31 January following the end of the tax year. Where income falls the taxpayer can apply to reduce the payments on account. However, if they are reduced too much, interest is payable on the shortfall. Any balance which is due (ie where actual liability for the year exceeds the payments made on account) must be paid by 31 January after the end of the tax year

Interest may be charged on Class 4 National Insurance contributions paid late as for tax paid late under the self-assessment provisions in accordance with *TMA 1970, s 86* (applied by virtue of *SSCBA 1992, Sch 2, para 6(1)*).

Focus

Class 4 National Insurance contributions are payable by 31 January after the end of the tax year to which they relate. They are taken into account in calculating payments on account, and where a payment on account is due, payments must be made by 31 January in the tax year and 31 July after the tax year, with any balance being paid by 31 January after the end of the tax year.

Payment difficulties

Business Payment Support Service

8.24 HMRC's Business Payment Support Service was introduced to help businesses worried about being able to meet payments of tax and National Insurance. The service is designed to deal with new queries in respect of payments that are not already overdue. Different options are available to help those struggling to make payments that are already overdue.

The support line is open seven days a week and can be contacted on 0300 200 3835. Support line staff will review the circumstances pertaining to the case and discuss temporary options, such as arranging for payments to be made over a longer period. Where an arrangement is made with the Business Payment Support Service, HMRC do not charge an additional late payment surcharge. However, interest remains payable on any payments that are made after the due date.

To take advantage of the service, it is important that the support line is contacted and arrangements put in place before the payment falls due. In most cases it will be possible to agree payment arrangements promptly from the initial call, although more information may be required in more complicated cases.

To allow enquiries to be dealt with as efficiently as possible, the following information should be provided:

- tax reference;
- details of the tax and National Insurance that is subject to payment difficulties; and
- basic details of the business income and outgoings.

As Class 4 National Insurance is paid with tax in lump sums on 31 January and 31 July, cashflow difficulties may mean that businesses do not have the funds available to make the payments on the due date. Agreeing payment plans with HMRC allows the payment to be spread and in marginal cases may even save the business from failure. However, it is important that businesses anticipate difficulties and contact HMRC in a timely fashion so arrangements can be put in place before the payments become overdue. If HMRC think that the contributor can pay the bill on time, they will expect it to be paid and can take payment over the phone by debit and credit card. However, they may offer time to pay if they think that the contributor genuinely cannot pay in full on time but may be able to do so in the future. They will encourage the contributor to set up direct debit payments on agreed dates or may agree for payment to be made in instalments. Interest is charged on payments made late. Where arrangements are agreed it is important that payments under these arrangements are made on time. If payments are missed, HMRC may cancel the agreement and take legal action to recover the monies due.

When calling the Business Payment Support Service, HMRC will ask for information on income and expenditure, details of assets, such as savings and investments, and what action is being taken to enable payments to be met in the future. This information is needed to enable HMRC to assess the situation and to agree what action to take.

Further guidance on the Business Payment Support Service is available on the Gov.uk website.

Where a self-employed earner is facing financial difficulty due to the impact of the Covid-19 pandemic, they can defer the second payment on account for 2019/20, due by 31 July 2020. As long as it is paid with any balance of tax and National Insurance owing for 2019/20 by 31 January 2021, interest and penalties will not be charged.

HMRC are also operating a separate Coronavirus helpline for taxpayers who are unable to pay tax bills because of Coronavirus. The helpline can be contacted on 0800 024 1222. A webchat is also available.

Reallocation of Class 4 National Insurance contributions not due

8.25 Class 4 contributions that have been paid but which were not due may, in certain circumstances, be treated as payments on account of other contributions that may be due (the *Social Security (Contributions) Regulations 2001* (*SI 2001/1004*), *reg 101*). This only applies if:

- a certificate of exception is issued for the tax year for which payment of the Class 4 National Insurance contributions is made, or would have been issued had an application for its issue been made before the beginning of the year;
- the Class 4 National Insurance contributions are paid in error;
- the payment is in excess of that which is due from that earner for that year, or would have been so due had an application for exception been made before the beginning of the year; or
- the payment is in excess of the annual maximum for the year.

Alternatively, contributions paid and not due may be repaid if the relevant application is made (see **8.26**).

Repayment of Class 4 National Insurance contributions not due

8.26 If a person has paid Class 4 National Insurance contributions that are not due and wishes for them to be repaid rather than being treated as payments on account of other contributions, an application must be made for a repayment as repayment is not made automatically (the *Social Security (Contributions) Regulations 2001* (*SI 2001/1004*), *reg 102*). Where an application for repayment is made, the contributions are repaid to the earner unless the value of those contributions is less than 50 pence.

An application for repayment of contributions not due must be made in the period of five years beginning with 1 February in the year of assessment next following that in respect of which the payment was made or, if later, two years beginning with 6 April in the year of assessment next following that in which payment was made (the *Social Security (Contributions) Regulations 2001* (*SI 2001/1004*), *reg 102*).

Applications for refunds of National Insurance contributions can be made online using the tool at www.gov.uk/claim-national-insurance-refund. Refunds of Class 4 National Insurance contributions attract a repayment supplement. The repayment supplement is added to the National Insurance repaid.

SPECIAL CLASS 4 NATIONAL INSURANCE CONTRIBUTIONS

Nature of special Class 4 National Insurance contributions

8.27 Special Class 4 National Insurance contributions are payable by earners who are treated as self-employed and who would otherwise be employed earners (see **8.28**). The liability is imposed by the *Social Security (Contributions) Regulations 2001* (*SI 2001/1004*), *reg 103* by virtue of *SSCBA 1992, s 18*.

Special Class 4 National Insurance contributions are payable at the same rate as ordinary Class 4 National Insurance contributions (see **8.29**). However, they are imposed on earnings rather than profits (see **8.31**) and collected in a different way (**8.32**).

Liability for special Class 4 National Insurance contributions

8.28 Examiners, moderators and invigilators are deemed by regulations to be self-employed for National Insurance purposes (the *Social Security (Categorisation of Earners) Regulations 1978* (*SI 1978/1698*), *Sch 1, Pt II*). Such earners treated are liable to pay special Class 4 National Insurance contributions (the *Social Security (Contributions) Regulations 2001* (*SI 2001/1004*), *reg 103*; *SSCBA 1992, s 18*). Liability to special Class 4 National Insurance contributions is also extended to share fishermen by virtue of the *Social Security (Contributions) Regulations 2001* (*SI 2001/1004*), *reg 125(f)* to the extent that ordinary Class 4 National Insurance contributions are not collected in the normal way.

Rate of special Class 4 National Insurance contributions

8.29 Special Class 4 National Insurance contributions are payable at the same rate as ordinary Class 4 National Insurance contributions and follow the same structure (the *Social Security (Contributions) Regulations 2001* (*SI 2001/1004*), *reg 103(2)*).

No special Class 4 National Insurance contributions are payable until earnings reach the lower profits limit (£9,568 for 2021/22). Special Class 4 National Insurance contributions are then payable at the main Class 4 rate (9% for 2021/22) on earnings between the lower profits limit and the upper profits limit (£50,270 for 2021/22). Earnings in excess of the upper profits limit are liable to special Class 4 National Insurance contributions at the additional Class 4 rate (2% for 2021/22) (*SSCBA 1992, s 18(1A)*).

Recording special Class 4 National Insurance contributions

8.30 A person who is liable to pay special Class 4 National Insurance contributions must give his or her National Insurance number to the person who makes the payment of earnings. The person paying the earnings must record the earner's National Insurance number and category letter on the earner's deductions working sheet (the *Social Security (Contributions) Regulations 2001* (*SI 2001/1004*), *reg 104*).

Earnings for special Class 4 National Insurance purposes

8.31 Liability to special Class 4 National Insurance contributions arises in respect of the earner's earnings rather than his or her profits. The earnings are calculated as for Class 1 National Insurance purposes (see **3.14ff**) (the *Social Security (Contributions) Regulations 2001* (*SI 2001/1004*), *reg 105(1)*). Fractions of a pound are disregarded.

Notification and payment of special Class 4 National Insurance contributions

8.32 Unlike standard Class 4 National Insurance contributions, special Class 4 National Insurance contributions are not collected via the self-assessment system. Instead, and unless other arrangements are in place, HMRC will notify the earner of the special Class 4 National Insurance contributions payable (the *Social Security (Contributions) Regulations 2001* (*SI 2001/1004*), *reg 106*). The earner must pay any special Class 4 National Insurance contributions due within 28 days of the date of the notice, unless an appeal is lodged before the expiry of the 28-day period.

Where an appeal has been lodged and a revised notice issued, the earner must pay the special Class 4 National Insurance contributions specified on the revised notice within 28 days of the date on that notice.

Special Class 4 National Insurance contributions may also be collected under the PAYE system.

Annual maximum for special Class 4 National Insurance purposes

8.33 Where for a particular tax year an earner is liable to pay a special Class 4 National Insurance contribution and also an ordinary Class 4 National Insurance contribution, any primary Class 1 National Insurance contribution or any Class 2 National Insurance contribution, or any combination of such contributions, the maximum amount of the special Class 4 National Insurance contribution for that year cannot exceed the annual maximum for that year (the *Social Security (Contributions) Regulations 2001* (*SI 2001/1004*), *reg 108(1)*).

The maximum in the case of a special Class 4 National Insurance contribution and an ordinary Class 4 National Insurance contribution is the amount, if any, that is equal to the difference between the maximum amount of a special Class 4 National Insurance contribution (determined in accordance with *SSCBA 1992, s 18*) and the amount of the ordinary Class 4 National Insurance contributions ultimately payable for that year (the *Social Security (Contributions) Regulations 2001* (*SI 2001/1004*), *reg 108(2)(a)*).

In any other case, regardless of whether or not a Class 4 National Insurance contribution is payable, the maximum special Class 4 National Insurance contribution payable is the difference between the annual maximum computed in accordance with the rules set out at **8.21** and the amount of such Class 4, primary Class 1 and Class 2 National Insurance contributions as are ultimately payable for the year.

Reallocation of special Class 4 National Insurance contributions paid in excess or in error

8.34 In the event that special Class 4 National Insurance contributions have been paid in excess of the annual maximum for the year (see **8.33**) and in the absence of an application for the refund of such excess contributions (see **8.35**), HMRC will treat the excess contributions as being a payment made on account of other National Insurance contributions due by the earner (the *Social Security (Contributions) Regulations 2001* (*SI 2001/1004*), *reg 109*). Special Class 4 National Insurance contributions paid in error are similarly treated as payments on account of other Classes of National Insurance contributions due by the earner.

Refund of special Class 4 National Insurance contributions paid in excess or in error

8.35 Special Class 4 National Insurance contributions paid in excess of the annual maximum (see **8.33**) or in error are not refunded automatically. Instead they are treated as payments on account of other National Insurance contributions properly due (see **8.34**). However, the earner can apply to HMRC in writing for a refund (the *Social Security (Contributions) Regulations 2001* (*SI 2001/1004*), *reg 110*). The refund application must be made within a period of six years from the end of the year in which the contribution was due to be paid. Late refund applications may be accepted if HMRC are satisfied that the earner had a reasonable excuse for making the refund application late and that the application was made without unreasonable delay after the excuse had ceased.

Before making the refund, any amounts treated as payments in account of other contributions due are deducted. HMRC do not make a refund where the net amount of the refund is less than 50 pence.

COVID-19 PANDEMIC

Impact of the Covid-19 pandemic on Class 4 National Insurance contributions

8.36 Class 4 National Insurance contributions are calculated by reference to the trading profits as computed for tax purposes. Where a self-employed earner receive a grant under the Self-employment Income Support Scheme because their business was adversely affected by the Covid-19 pandemic, the grant payments should be included in the calculation of trading profits. Grant payments are taken into account in the tax year in which they are received, rather than by reference to the basis period in which they are received. The fourth and fifth grants under the SEISS are payable in 2021/22 and are taken into account in determining profits for the purpose of determining the Class 4 National Insurance liability for 2021/22.

Where a self-employed earner's profits fall below the lower profits threshold (set at £9,568 for 2021/22), no Class 4 National Insurance liability will arise for 2021/22.

PLANNING POINTS

8.37

- The Class 4 liability depends on the profits of the trade, therefore generally tax planning rules apply, including making full use of available deductions. However, some tax reliefs, such as personal reliefs and those for pension and charitable contributions, do not reduce the profits on which Class 4 NICs are calculated.
- As Class 4 National Insurance contributions are returned and collected under the self-assessment system as with tax, it is essential that returns are filed and payments made on time to avoid unnecessary interest and penalties.
- Class 4 contributions that have been made but are not due are not repaid automatically. Unless an application for repayment is made, the amounts paid are treated as payments on account of other contribution liabilities. If a refund is required, a refund application must be made.
- Class 4 National Insurance contributions do not earn pension and benefit entitlement.
- Consideration should be given as to whether it may be beneficial to incorporate the business and extract profits by way of dividends to save Class 4 contributions as National Insurance contributions are not payable on dividends. Professional advice should be sought.
- Grants received under the Self-employment Income Support Scheme to help traders affected by the Covid-19 pandemic are taxable and liable to Class 4 National Insurance and should be taken into account in the calculation of profits for the tax year in which the grants are received.

Chapter 9

International considerations

SIGNPOSTS

- There are National Insurance implications where a person goes abroad to work or comes to the UK to work from an overseas country as different countries have different social security rules (see **9.1**).
- New social security rules apply from 1 January 2021 for workers going to work in the EEA or Switzerland (see **9.2**).
- There are a number of key concepts that need to be understood when looking at National Insurance in an international context (see **9.6**).
- Residence and presence conditions determine a UK National Insurance liability (see **9.15**).
- The domestic legislation applies where there is no social security agreement in force (see **9.20**).
- The UK has reached an agreement with the EU which ensures that, from 1 January 2021, workers who move between the UK and the EU only pay into one country's social security scheme at a time (see **9.25**).
- The UK has a number of social security agreements with other countries. Where an agreement is in force, the provisions of the agreement have effect (see **9.39**).
- Special National Insurance rules apply to mariners (see **9.50**).
- Modified NIC procedures apply to certain employees (see **9.65**).

OVERVIEW OF INTERNATIONAL CONSIDERATIONS

Social security in an international context

9.1 Where a person goes abroad to work there are pension, benefit and National Insurance implications as different countries have different social security schemes. The UK scheme, in common with schemes operated by other countries, contains rules which aim to protect a person's contribution record when a person spends some time overseas. A person who is no longer required to pay UK contributions while abroad may be able to pay voluntary contributions to protect their contributions record. The rules also impose contributions liabilities on people who come from overseas to work in the UK.

When considering National Insurance liabilities for workers going abroad to work or coming from abroad to work in the UK, the rules that apply depend on whether the country is a member of the European Economic Area or Switzerland, a country with which the UK has a separate social security agreement or a country which falls outside these categories. The rules are examined further at **9.20ff**.

Impact of Brexit

9.2 In the EU referendum on 23 June 2016 the United Kingdom voted to leave the EU – the so-called 'Brexit' vote.

The *European Union (Notification of Withdrawal) Act 2017* was passed on 17 March 2017, giving the Prime Minister the power to trigger the UK's withdrawal from the EU under *Art 50* of the *Treaty on the Functioning of the European Union*. The UK invoked *Art 50* on 29 March 2017, setting an initial date for leaving the EU of 29 March 2019. However, this date was not met and in April 2019 an extension was agreed with the EU giving the UK until 31 October 2019 to leave the EU. This was extended to 31 January 2020 and the UK left the EU on that date. A transitional period applied until 31 December 2020 during which existing rules continued to apply.

The *European Union (Withdrawal) Act 2018* received Royal Assent on 26 June 2018. It repealed the *European Communities Act 1972* (which is the statute under which EU law has legislative effect in the UK) and ended the supremacy of the EU in UK law

Withdrawing from the EU meant that the UK also ceased to participate in the European Economic Area (EEA) as the UK falls outside the geographic scope and will no longer be a member of the EEA. The rules applying prior to the UK's withdrawal from the EU continued to apply until the end of the transitional period on 31 December 2020.

The UK has reached an agreement with the EU on the social security rules that apply from 1 January 2021. These rules ensure that workers who move between the UK and the EU, Norway or Switzerland will only have to pay into one country's social security scheme at a time. Separate rules apply to workers who are working only temporarily in the EU, Norway, Iceland or Switzerland, who may be able to obtain a certificate to enable them to continue to pay UK National Insurance contributions while working abroad.

Legislative framework

9.3 The legislative framework governing National Insurance contributions in an international context from a UK perspective is found in an assortment of EC Regulations, treaty provisions and UK domestic legislation. The UK domestic legislation is brief and is found mainly in the *Social Security (Contributions) Regulations 2001* (*SI 2001/1004*), *regs 145–148A*.

The Brexit transitional period came to an end on 1 January 2021. The UK has reached an agreement with the EU, the EEA and Switzerland which determines where the liability to pay National Insurance contributions falls. Prior to 1 January 2021, the treatment of workers moving within the European Economic Area (EEA) was governed by a common social security policy set out in regulations, predominantly *Regulation EC 883/2004 On the co-ordination of social security systems*. The rules applying to workers moving within the EEA and Switzerland are examined further at **9.25**. The UK has a number of social security agreements with other countries. Full reciprocal agreements (RA) cover both contribution liability and benefits. Defined contribution conventions (DCC) cover only liability for contributions. RA and DCC ensure equal treatment when employees move from one RA country to another. Although the treaty arrangements are more or less the same in each case, reference should always be made to the relevant treaty. The rules applying to RA countries are examined further at **9.39**.

HMRC guidance

9.4 Guidance on the National Insurance position of people going to and coming from abroad can be found in HMRC's National Insurance Manual at NIM 33000ff.

Guidance is available on the gov.uk website. For guidance on National Insurance implications of employees going abroad to work, see www.gov.uk/paying-employees-working-abroad and for guidance on the National Insurance position of employees coming from abroad to work in the UK, see www.gov.uk/new-employee-coming-to-work-from-abroad. Particular guidance on National Insurance for workers working in the EEA or Switzerland from 1 January 2021 can be found on the gov.uk website at www.gov.uk/guidance/national-insurance-for-workers-from-the-uk-working-in-the-eea-or-switzerland-from-1-january-2021.

Nationals of the EU, Liechtenstein, Norway or Switzerland who were living in the UK prior to 1 January 2021 had to apply for EU Settlement Scheme status by 30 June 2021 to protect their right to stay in the UK and their social security rights,

HMRC operate a helpline for queries on National Insurance status and entitlements, pension status and health care provisions for people under state pension age who live or work abroad. The National Insurance helpline for non-UK residents can be contacted on 0300 200 3506. Enquiries can also be made online by completing the form at https://online.hmrc.gov.uk/shortforms/form/CNR_NIC_SEF.

Guidance on National Insurance contributions in an international context can also be found in various HMRC booklets, including:

- NI38, *Social Security Abroad*, which is available to download from the Gov.uk website at www.gov.uk/government/publications/social-security-abroad-ni38.
- CWG2, *Employer's Further Guide to PAYE and NICs* (Ch 4), which is also available to download from the Gov.uk website (see www.gov.uk/government/publications/cwg2-further-guide-to-paye-and-national-insurance-contributions.

Planning considerations

9.5 Both contribution rates and social security provisions vary greatly from country to country. This needs to be taken into account as careful planning can save a considerable amount of money. However, it is not sufficient to consider contributions in isolation and to apply an approach of merely minimising contribution costs as the additional benefits offered by some foreign countries may well be worth the additional contribution cost.

A person can only be insured under the social security system of one country at any one time and where there is degree of choice in the matter, consideration should be given to both the contributions payable and the impact on benefit entitlement.

From 1 January 2021, the social security agreement reached between the EU and the UK ensures that workers who move between the UK and the EU only pay into one country's social security system, at a time. The agreement also applies to workers moving between the UK and Norway and Switzerland. Workers who work temporarily in the EU, Norway Iceland, Switzerland or Liechtenstein may be able to obtain a certificate or document from HMRC which allows them to continue to pay UK National Insurance contributions rather than paying contributions abroad. These rules should be considered where a worker is working in an EU, another EEA country or Switzerland. It is advisable to take expert advice prior to working abroad.

KEY CONCEPTS

Introduction to key concepts

9.6 There are a number of key concepts that need to be understood before considering National Insurance contributions in an international context. These include:

- presence: see **9.7**;
- residence: see **9.8;**

- ordinary residence: see **9.9;**
- domicile: see **9.10**;
- habitual residence: see **9.11**;
- nationality: see **9.12**;
- place of business in the UK: see **9.13**; and
- the UK: see **9.14**

It should be noted that the terms 'resident' and 'ordinarily resident' do not have the same meaning for National Insurance purposes as they do for tax. The terms, as they apply for National Insurance purposes, are explained below. Guidance can also be found in HMRC leaflet NI38, *Social Security Abroad*, which is available on the gov.uk website at www.gov.uk/government/publications/social-security-abroad-ni38.

Presence

9.7 'Presence' is an important concept in social security legislation and the requirements normally only apply if a person (including an employer) is present in a particular country.

Presence is generally a question of fact (*Colt Industries v Sarlie* [1966] 1 WLR 440). Either a person is physically present in a particular country or he or she is not.

However, the regulations may deem a person to be present in a country even if he or she is temporarily absent. Examples include presence on a British ship in territorial waters of another country.

For liability to Class 1, Class 1A or Class 2 National Insurance contributions to arise under the UK domestic legislation and for a person to be eligible to pay Class 3 National Insurance contributions, conditions as to residence and presence must be met. These are examined further at **9.15**.

Residence

9.8 The term 'residence' is used widely in the National Insurance legislation, and in *Regulation EC 883/2004* is defined in *art 1(j)* as the place where a person habitually resides. It should be noted that the definition of 'residence' applying for National Insurance purposes is not the same as that applying for tax purposes. For tax purposes, from 2013/14 onwards 'residence' is determined by reference to a statutory residence test. This test does not apply for National Insurance purposes. Further, residence for social security purposes does not automatically follow residence for tax purposes and the fact that a person is regarded as resident in the UK for tax purposes does not automatically mean that a person is resident for social security purposes.

A person may also have dual residence (*Turnball v Foster* (1904) 6 TC 206). However the concept of dual residence has little significance for UK National Insurance purposes. For National Insurance purposes HMRC interpret 'residence' to mean 'living in or at a particular place' (*Leven v IR Commrs* [1928] AC 217). It means more than simply being here. Unlike presence, a person can continue to be resident in a country throughout periods of temporary absence (*Lloyd v Sulley* (1884) 2 TC 37). However, a person must have been present in a country before residence can be established.

In an EU context, the term 'residence' has a different meaning in regard to the regulations on migrant workers and is taken to mean 'habitual residence'. This is considered further at **9.11**.

Focus

The term 'residence' has a different meaning for National Insurance purposes than for tax purposes, and the statutory residence test applying for tax is not relevant for National Insurance.

Ordinary residence

9.9 As with 'residence' the term 'ordinary residence' is used widely in the social security legislation but is not defined. It should not be confused with the concept of 'ordinary residence' which applied for tax purposes prior to the introduction of the statutory residence test from 2013/14. For National Insurance purposes, the term 'ordinary residence' is used to describe the place where someone normally lives and has a settled and regular mode of life. Occasional temporary absences are disregarded. In some circumstances, a person can be regarded as being ordinarily resident in two places at once.

When a person goes abroad, a number of factors are taken into consideration in determining whether that person is ordinarily resident in the UK. For example, returning to the UK during periods of employment abroad would indicate continued ordinary residence. The longer or more frequent the returns to the UK, the stronger the indicator of continued ordinary residence. Similarly, visits to family who have remained in the UK and holidays spent at home in the UK would indicate ordinary residence in the UK.

Maintaining a house in the UK whilst abroad would also indicate continued ordinary residence in the UK. However, this is less of an indicator of continued ordinary residence if the house is let on a long let.

Where a person has lived in the UK for a long time, this provides a strong indication of ordinary residence in the UK, despite a period of employment abroad. An intention to return to the UK at the end of the period of overseas employment again indicates ordinary residence in the UK. The earlier a person returns to the UK, the stronger the indicator that they remain ordinarily resident in the UK.

Conversely, where a person goes abroad for work, or otherwise, and is accompanied by his or her partner and/or children, this would suggest that the person does not remain ordinarily resident in the UK, particularly if a home is not retained in the UK and only occasional visits are made to the UK. Visits to the UK in connection with the overseas work do not provide a strong indicator that the person remains ordinarily resident.

The concept of ordinary residence is also relevant when someone comes to the UK to live. A person will be regarded as being ordinarily resident in the UK if he or she intends to stay here for a significant period (usually at least three years). Again, this will depend on the circumstances.

Guidance in individual cases as to whether a person is ordinarily resident in the UK can be obtained from HMRC's NIC&EO International Caseworker, contact details for which are given at **9.4**.

Domicile

9.10 Domicile is less significant than residence in a social security context. Although mainly a tax term, it is used in the National Insurance legislation in certain instances, for example in relation to aircrew and mariners. (For the special rules applying to mariners, see **9.50**.)

A person's domicile is the country in which he or she has his or her permanent home. At birth a person normally takes his or her father's domicile, regardless of the country of birth. However, the mother's domicile may be taken if at the time of the birth the parents are not married or if the father is dead (*Forbes v Forbes* (1854) Kay 341; *Udny v Udny* (1869) LR 1 Sc & D App 441). The domicile at birth is known as the domicile of origin.

After birth, a person normally takes the domicile of the person on whom he or she is dependent (*D'Etchegoyen v D'Etchegoyen* (1888) 13 PD 132). This is known as the domicile of dependency.

Once a person has reached the age of 16, he or she can replace the domicile of origin or dependency with a domicile of choice. A person can only acquire a domicile of choice where it is clearly the intention to acquire the new domicile and to give up the previous domicile. If the domicile of choice is subsequently abandoned, the person reverts back to the domicile of origin or the domicile of dependency (as relevant).

A person always has a domicile, but can only have one domicile at any time.

Habitual residence

9.11 The term 'habitual residence' is derived from the EC social security regulations. *Regulation EC 883/2004* defines residence as the place where a person habitually resides. Habitual residence is essentially the place where the person has his or her strongest personal ties. Initially, the UK regarded habitual residence as being akin to ordinary residence for tax purposes. However, a number of decisions of the European Court of Justice have challenged the view and suggest that it is more similar to domicile. The term probably lies somewhere between the two and in determining a person's habitual residence consideration is given to where the person's 'centre of interest' lies and where the worker has the strongest personal connections. (*Angenieux v Hakenberg* [1973] ECR 935; *di Paolo v Office National l'Emploi* [1977] ECR 317).

In determining where a person is habitually resident, HMRC take account of the following factors:

- where the family home is situated (and whether it is rented out or remains available to the employee if the employee is working in another Member State);
- where the worker's partner or family live and whether they have accompanied him or her abroad;
- where any children go to school;
- what connections remain with the home state, e.g. whether registered with a doctor, on the electoral role etc;
- where the worker was living before going to work in another Member State and the length and continuity of residence in the home state; and
- how long the worker intends to stay in the new Member State and whether he or she intends to return to the home country when the employment ends.

Although each case is considered on its merits, HMRC take the following general approach in determining habitual residence:

- if the worker retains accommodation in the home Member State and his family remain there whilst he is working temporarily in another state he will usually be considered as 'habitually resident' in the home state;
- if no accommodation is retained in the home state or it is rented out and the worker's family accompanies him to the other state he will not usually be considered 'habitually resident' in the home state;
- the longer the worker is abroad, for example two years or more, the more likely it is that he will be considered 'habitually resident' in the other Member State;
- if the worker has taken up stable employment in another Member State rather than short-term employment it is more likely to point to 'habitual residence' there;
- if the worker does not intend to return to the home state when the employment abroad ends this points to him no longer being considered 'habitually resident' in the home state;

- if the worker makes frequent returns to the home state whilst working abroad, for pleasure as well as for business reasons this may point to 'habitual residence' there;
- having a bank/building society account in the home state or still being registered with a doctor are not necessarily indicators pointing to habitual residence in the home state.

For details of the impact of the UK's withdrawal from the EU on 31 January 2020 and the rules apply following from 1 January 2021 following the end of the transition period on 31 December 2020, see **9.26**.

> **Focus**
>
> The concept of 'habitual residence' is important in an EU context.

Nationality

9.12 As with 'habitual residence' the concept of 'nationality' is relevant for social security purposes from an EU rather than a UK perspective. The concept of nationality also features in a number the UK's social security agreements.

For EU purposes, each Member State defines the scope of its own nationality laws. The UK definition of UK Nationals includes:

- British citizens;
- persons who are British subjects by virtue of the *British Nationality Act 1981* and who have the right to live in the UK (and are therefore exempt from UK immigration control);
- citizens of British Dependent Territories who acquire their citizenship from a connection with Gibraltar.

The definition of a UK National for these purposes excludes other British subjects and British Dependent Territories citizens. Also excluded are Commonwealth citizens other than those falling within the above bullets, British Overseas Citizens and British protected persons.

Persons from the Isle of Man or the Channel Islands are only included if they or a parent or grandparent was born, adopted, naturalised or registered in the UK (partiality) or has at any time been ordinarily resident in the UK for five years.

Individuals with a right of residence in the EU are covered by the secondment rules (see **9.30**). This reduces the importance of nationality for EU social security purposes.

Where a person has dual nationality and the National Insurance liability is determined by reference to treaty provisions, care should be taken as a double contribution liability could arise.

> **Focus**
>
> The concept of 'nationality' is relevant in an EU rather than a UK context. It is also of relevance in a number of social security agreements.

Place of business in the UK

9.13 The term 'place of business' is also a key National Insurance concept. It is relevant for Class 1, Class 1A and Class 1B National Insurance purposes as liability for employer contributions is dependent on the employer having a place of business in the UK.

HMRC guidance on determining whether an employer has a place of business in the UK can be found in Chapter 4 of booklet CWG2, *Employer's Further Guide to PAYE and NICs*.

Generally, HMRC will regard an employer as being resident, present or in the UK if the registered office of the company is in the UK, even if no actual business is carried out in the UK.

HMRC take the view that employers have a business in the UK if:

- they have a fixed address and occupy premises where they are the lawful owner or tenant or are present with the consent of the lawful owner or tenant; and
- an activity takes place which need not necessarily be remunerative in itself but is in furtherance of the purposes of the business. The business does not need to be of a trading or commercial nature.

When considering whether an employer has a place of business in the UK, HMRC will look for the following pointers:

- a name plate displayed on the door or premises;
- headed letter paper;
- a listing in a phone directory;
- a lease or rent agreement or some sort of financial transaction for the use of the premises;
- a registered office;
- registration as a company incorporated outside the UK but with a place of business in the UK for the purposes of the Companies Acts; and
- other premises in the UK.

However, an employer in another EU Member State that has employees in the UK National Insurance system is treated (from 1 May 2010 onwards) as having a place of business in the UK and as such has to pay secondary Class 1 contributions and deduct primary Class 1 contributions from UK employees (*Regulation EC 883/2004*).

For details of the impact of the UK's withdrawal from the EU on 31 January 2020 and the rules applying from 1 January 2021 following the end of the transition period on 31 December 2020, see **9.26**.

The UK

9.14 For National Insurance purposes, the UK encompasses Great Britain and Northern Ireland including the territorial waters of the UK (*SSCBA 1972, s 172*). References in the legislation to Great Britain include references to the territorial waters of the UK adjacent to Great Britain. The territorial waters are the coastal waters up to a limit of 12 miles. However, oil and gas workers on the UK continental shelf outside the 12-mile limit are within UK NIC rules as if they were in the UK.

The definition does not include Jersey, Guernsey or the Isle of Man, each of which have their own social security systems and treaties with the UK.

Also excluded from the definition of the UK for social security purposes are British embassies and consulates and territories (eg the Falkland Islands and Gibraltar).

RESIDENCE AND PRESENCE CONDITION FOR LIABILITY

Overview of residence and presence condition

9.15 A person is not liable to pay Class 1, Class 1A or Class 2 National Insurance contributions or entitled to pay Class 3 National Insurance contributions unless that person fulfils conditions as to residence or presence in Great Britain (*SSCBA 1992, s 1(6))*. The residence and presence conditions are set out in the *Social Security (Contributions) Regulations 2001* (*SI 2001/1004*), *reg 145*.

The conditions, which are set out at **9.16ff** may be overridden by EU Regulations or by provisions contained within social security agreements.

Primary Class 1 National Insurance contributions

9.16 The residence and presence condition for primary Class 1 National Insurance purposes is met if the employed earner is resident or present in Great Britain or Northern Ireland (or but for any temporary absence would be resident in Great Britain or Northern Ireland) at the time of that employment or is then ordinarily resident in Great Britain or Northern Ireland (as the case may be) (the *Social Security (Contributions) Regulations 2001* (*SI 2001/1004*), *reg 145(1)(a)*).

Secondary Class 1, Class 1A or Class 1B National Insurance contributions

9.17 For there to be a liability to secondary Class 1, Class 1A or Class 1B National Insurance contributions, the secondary contributor or person liable to pay Class 1B National Insurance contributions, as appropriate (normally the employer), must be resident or present in Great Britain or Northern Ireland when the contributions become payable or then have a place of business in Great Britain or Northern Ireland (the *Social Security (Contributions) Regulations 2001* (*SI 2001/1004*), *reg 145(1)(b)*). However, if these conditions are not met, the employer may pay the contributions if so desired.

In the event that a person who is ordinarily neither resident nor employed in the UK is employed for a time in Great Britain or Northern Ireland in relation to an employment which is mainly outside the UK and in respect of which the employer's place of business is also outside the UK, no primary or secondary Class 1 National Insurance contributions are payable in respect of the UK employment, no Class 1A National Insurance contributions are payable in respect of something provided to the employee (or his or her family) by reason of that employment and no Class 1B National Insurance contributions are payable in respect of any PAYE settlement agreement in relation to that employment after the date of the earner's last entry into Great Britain or Northern Ireland and before the earner has been resident in Great Britain or Northern Ireland for a continuous period of 52 contribution weeks from the beginning of the contribution week following that in which the date of entry into the UK falls (the *Social Security (Contributions) Regulations 2001* (*SI 2001/1004*), *reg 145(2)*).

Class 2 National Insurance contributions

9.18 Liability for Class 2 National Insurance contributions is contingent on the self-employed earner being ordinarily resident in Great Britain or Northern Ireland. If the self-employed earner is not ordinarily resident in Great Britain or Northern Ireland, liability for Class 2 National Insurance contributions only arises if that earner was resident in Great Britain or Northern Ireland for a period of at least 26 weeks in the immediately preceding 52 contributions weeks (the *Social Security (Contributions) Regulations 2001* (*SI 2001/1004*), *reg 145(1)(d)*).

A self-employed earner is entitled to pay Class 2 National Insurance contributions for a contribution week in which that earner is present in Great Britain or Northern Ireland (the *Social Security (Contributions) Regulations 2001* (*SI 2001/1004*), *reg 145(1)(c)*).

Class 3 National Insurance contributions

9.19 A person is only entitled to pay voluntary Class 3 National Insurance contributions if that person:

- is resident in Great Britain or Northern Ireland throughout the year;
- has arrived in Great Britain or Northern Ireland during the year and is liable to pay Class 1 or Class 2 National Insurance contributions in respect of an earlier period during that year;
- has arrived in Great Britain or Northern Ireland during the year and was either ordinarily resident in Great Britain or Northern Ireland throughout the whole of that year or became ordinarily resident during the course of that year;
- was not ordinarily resident in Great Britain or Northern Ireland but arrived in that year or the previous year and has been continuously present in Great Britain or Northern Ireland (as the case may be) for 26 complete contribution weeks. Such a person is only entitled to pay Class 3 contributions in the contribution year following that in which he or she arrived if the arrival was in the previous contribution year.

The residence and presence contributions for Class 3 National Insurance purposes are set out in the *Social Security (Contributions) Regulations 2001* (*SI 2001/1004*), *reg 145(1)(e)*).

GOING TO AND COMING FROM ABROAD: UK POSITION

Overview of domestic legislation

9.20 The UK treatment of persons going to or coming from abroad is set out in the *Social Security (Contributions) Regulations 2001* (*SI 2001/1004*), *regs 145–148C*. The UK legislation is overridden by the social security agreement with the EU from 1 January 2021 and prior to that by the EC Regulations where persons come from or go to another EEA country (see **9.25**) and by the relevant social security agreement where the movement is between countries which have a bilateral social security agreement in force (see **9.37**). Countries that are not covered by the social security agreement with the EU, EEA and Switzerland or by a social security agreement with the UK are referred to as 'rest of the world' (ROW) countries. Persons going to ROW countries from the UK or coming to the UK from ROW countries are subject to the UK domestic legislation (see **9.49**).

For details of the impact of the UK's withdrawal from the EU on 31 January 2020 and the rules that apply from 1 January 2021 following the end of the transition period on 31 December 2020, see **9.26**.

Payment of Class 1 contributions for periods abroad

9.21 Where a UK employer sends a person to work abroad other than in an EEA country or another country with which the UK has a social security agreement, the UK domestic rules apply under which the employee remains liable to pay UK Class 1 National Insurance contributions for the first 52 weeks of employment in the other country if the following conditions are met:

- the employer has a place of business in the UK (see **9.13**);
- the employee is ordinarily resident in the UK (see **9.9**); and
- the employee was resident in the UK immediately before starting work abroad,

(the *Social Security (Contributions) Regulations 2001* (*SI 2001/1004*), *reg 146(1)*).

Contributions are payable by the employer and the employee as if the employee were employed in the UK. The contributions are payable at normal Class 1 rates and the employer must deduct the contributions from the employee's pay and pay them over to HMRC as for UK-based employees.

The legislation sets the payment period by reference to the 'first 52 weeks of the employment' rather than by reference to the 'first 52 weeks of the employment abroad'. However, it is generally accepted that this means the first 52 weeks of the employment abroad and this is the approach that HMRC take, despite the decision in *Stevens v Ors v IR Commrs* (2004) SpC 411. This means that where an employment starts before the employee is sent abroad, the clock is effectively restarted from the date that the employee starts working abroad.

Whether the employment ceases is also a question of fact and the 52-week continuing liability may change when the employee enters into a new contract. The employment contract will indicate whether or not a new employment has been entered into. HMRC's stance is illustrated by the following example, taken from the National Insurance Manual at NIM33535.

Example 9.1—Payment of Class 1 contributions for periods abroad

- 'Ralph was posted by the UK company to work in Australia for a period of two years as a General Manager of the Sydney office
- After six months he applied for promotion as an Overseas Sales Executive with a separate department of the UK company
- He was successful and immediately took up his new position in Malaysia

The subsequent posting from Australia to Malaysia would be considered to arise in connection with the new employment with the UK company. The 52-week period would cease.

Had the UK employer simply posted him to Malaysia in connection with the original occupation/employment as a General Manager then the 52-week period would have continued in full.'

In determining whether the UK contract has ceased, HMRC will take into account a number of factors, including:

- who controls the employee's work whilst the employee is abroad;
- who has the right to suspend or dismiss the employee;
- who funds payment of the employee's earnings;
- whether the UK company has the right to recall the employee to the UK; and
- whether the employee continues to be a member of the UK pension fund.

In order to decide whether the employer has a place of business in the UK, it is important that the 'employer' is identified correctly. The relevant employer is the employer in relation to the overseas contract. This means if the employee is sent to work abroad and is under contract to an overseas company with no place of business in the UK, there is no continuing liability to UK Class 1 National Insurance contributions (other than that which may arise on any earnings paid under a UK contract).

Planning can take the employee outside the 52-week contribution rule, but the extent to whether this is beneficial will depend on the employee's contribution record and the employee's entitlement to benefits under a foreign social security scheme. If an employee does not pay Class 1 National Insurance contributions during the first 52 weeks abroad, he or she cannot pay Class 2 or Class 3 contributions instead. This will mean that there is a gap in the employee's UK contribution record, which may affect entitlement to contributory UK benefits and the UK state pension. It should be noted that to qualify for the full single-tier state pension, payable to people who reach state pension age on or after 6 April 2016, 35 qualifying years are needed, as compared to 30 qualifying years for the full basic state pension, payable to those who reached state pension age before 6 April 2016.

Liability to pay Class 1 National Insurance contributions ceases after 52 weeks. Once the 52-week period has come to an end the earner may be entitled (but not obliged) to pay voluntary Class 3 National Insurance contributions (or voluntary Class 2 contributions if also self-employed) to protect pension and benefit entitlement (the *Social Security (Contributions) Regulations 2001* (*SI 2001/1004*), *reg 146(2)*: see further **9.23**). If voluntary contributions are not paid, the employee will retain entitlement to certain benefits on his or her return to the UK.

Liability for Class 1A and Class 1B National Insurance contributions

9.22 Where an employee goes abroad to work in a country that is not covered by the UK social security agreement with the EU, EEA and Switzerland and is not one with which the UK has a separate social security agreement, the employee remains liable to pay Class 1 National Insurance contributions for the first 52 weeks of his employment aboard if certain conditions apply (see **9.21**).

The employer (or secondary contributor) remains liable for any Class 1A or Class 1B National Insurance contributions that arise in that 52-week period (the *Social Security (Contributions) Regulations 2001* (*SI 2001/1004*), *reg 146(2)(c)*). However, a Class 1A liability will only arise if there is a UK tax liability in respect of any benefits provided and this depends on the employee being UK resident for tax purposes.

Class 2 and Class 3 contributions for periods abroad

9.23 In the event that a person is self-employed in a country outside the UK (other than one governed by the UK agreement with the EU or treaty provisions) and immediately before leaving the UK, the person was either an employed or a self-employed earner, the person is entitled to pay Class 2 National Insurance contributions as a self-employed earner or voluntary Class 3 National Insurance contributions provided that certain conditions are met (the *Social Security (Contributions) Regulations 2001* (*SI 2001/1004*), *reg 147(1)*). Any periods when the person is temporarily in the UK are ignored (the *Social Security (Contributions) Regulations 2001* (*SI 2001/1004*), *reg 147(2)*).

Entitlement to pay Class 2 or Class 3 National Insurance contributions is dependent on the following conditions being met:

- the person has been resident in the UK for a continuous period of not less than three years at any time before the period for which the contributions are to be paid;
- contributions of the appropriate amount have been paid by or on behalf of that person for each of three years ending at any time before the relevant time, for each of two years ending at any time and, in addition, 52 contributions under either or both the *Social Security Act 1975* or the *National Insurance Act 1965* or, for any one year ending at any time before the relevant period and, in addition, 104 contributions under either or both the *Social Security Act 1975* or the *National Insurance Act 1965*; or
- there have been paid by or on behalf of that person, 156 contributions under either or both the *Social Security Act 1975* or the *National Insurance Act 1965*,

(the *Social Security (Contributions) Regulations 2001* (*SI 2001/1004*), *reg 147(3)*).

For these purposes, contributions of the appropriate amount are contributions, the earnings factor derived from which, is not less than 52 times the lower earnings limit for Class 1 National Insurance purposes. Contributions under either or both the *Social Security Act 1975* or the *National Insurance Act 1965* are Class 1, Class 2 or Class 3 contributions payable under *SSA 1975, ss 4, 7, 8* or *NIA 1965, s 3*, as appropriate. The relevant period is the period for which it is desired to pay the Class 2 or Class 3 National Insurance contributions (the *Social Security (Contributions) Regulations 2001* (*SI 2001/1004*), *reg 147(4)*).

A person working abroad in a self-employed capacity may choose to pay Class 2 or Class 3 National Insurance contributions to maintain entitlement to the UK state pension and to benefits on his or her return to the UK. Where a person is eligible to pay Class 2 National Insurance contributions, this will represent a cheaper option than payment of Class 3 National Insurance contributions (see also **6.15**). A person cannot pay Class 2 contributions whilst abroad for any period that they are liable to pay Class 1 contributions (see **9.21**).

Where a person wishes to pay Class 2 or Class 3 National Insurance contributions and meets the above conditions, entitlement to pay is further dependent on the payment being made within the specified time frame. The payment window applying where the contributor is abroad is the same as that where the contributor is in the UK. A person in only entitled to pay Class 2 and Class 3 National Insurance contributions for a period abroad to the same extent as the person would have been entitled to pay the contribution had he or she been present in the UK (the *Social Security (Contributions) Regulations 2001* (*SI 2001/1004*), *reg 148*).

Where a person is self-employed abroad and applies to pay Class 2 National Insurance contributions (on form CF83), HMRC may ask for proof of the self-employment abroad. Voluntary payment of Class 2 National Insurance contributions does not provide cover for health care abroad.

Coming to the UK

9.24 Liability for UK National Insurance contributions when someone comes to the UK from abroad will depend on the residence and presence conditions (*Social Security (Contributions) Regulations 2001* (*SI 2001/1004*), *reg 145*: see **9.15**) being met. Where an employee comes to the UK from an EEA or agreement country, the EU agreement or treaty provisions, as appropriate, will take precedence over the UK legislation. For details of the rules that apply from 1 January 2021 where an employee comes to work in the UK from the EU, another EEA country or Switzerland, see **9.26**.

Where an employee comes to the UK from abroad to work, from a country that is neither covered by the UK social security agreement with the EU nor an agreement country (ie from a ROW country), the basic rule is that neither the employee nor the employer is liable for Class 1 National Insurance contributions for the first 52 weeks. Liability commences from the 53rd week.

As a general rule, the employer of a person working abroad only has to pay secondary Class 1 National Insurance contributions if they have a place of business in the UK or they are resident and present in the UK. Where the employer does not have a place of business in the UK (see **9.13**), liability for secondary contributions falls on the host employer.

However, since 1 May 2010 an employer in another EU Member State that has employees in the UK National Insurance system is treated as having a place of business in the UK and as such has to pay secondary Class 1 contributions and deduct primary Class 1 contributions from UK employees.

Where there is no employer in another Member State and a person is employed by a foreign employer or by a foreign agency, the secondary contributor is specified by the *Social Security (Categorisation of Earners) Regulations 1978 (SI 1978/1689), Sch 3, para 9.* The rules, as they apply from 6 April 2014, to determine the secondary contributor are as shown in the table below.

Employment	**Secondary contributor**
by a foreign employer (other than as listed below) where the employed person, under an arrangement involving the foreign employer and the host employer provides, or is personally involved in the provision of services, to a host employer	the host employer
under or in consequence of a contract between a foreign agency and an end client where the worker provides services to that end client	the end client
by a foreign employer where the worker provides services to an end client under or in consequence of a contract between that end client and a UK agency	the UK agency who has the contractual relationship with the end client (but see notes 1 and 2 below)
by a foreign agency where the worker provides services to an end client under or in consequence of that end client and a UK agency	the UK agency who has the contractual relationship with the end client (but see notes 1 and 2 below
by a UK employer where the worker provides services to a person outside the UK under or in consequence of a contract between that person and a UK agency and the worker is liable to pay contributions in the UK in relation to that employment	the UK employer or the UK agency who has the contractual relationship with the person outside the UK
by a foreign employer where the worker provides services to a person outside the UK under or in consequence of a contract between that person and a UK agency and that worker is eligible to pay contributions in the UK in relation to that employment	the UK agency who has the contractual relationship with the person outside the UK

Notes

1. If the end client provides, at any time, to the UK agency fraudulent documents in connection with the control, direction or supervision which is to be exercised over the employed person, the secondary contributory is the end client.

2. If a person who is resident in Great Britain (and who is not the end client) who has a contractual relationship with the UK agency provides, at any time, to the UK agency fraudulent documents in connection with the

purported deduction or payment of contributions in connection with the employed person, the secondary contributor is the person who provides the fraudulent documents.

If the employer does not have a place of business in the EU, the employee will pay primary Class 1 National Insurance contributions under a modified PAYE scheme. No secondary contributions are payable.

For details of the rules applying from 1 January 2021 following the end of the Brexit transition period on 31 December 2020, see **9.2**.

EU COUNTRIES, OTHER EEA COUNTRIES AND SWITZERLAND

Rules applying prior to 1 January 2021 – overview of EC Regulations

9.25 Until the end of the Brexit transitional period on 31 December 2020, the EC Regulations continued to apply to the UK. The rules applying from 1 January 2021 following the end of the Brexit transitional period are discussed at **9.26**.

Where a worker moves between countries to work this can adversely affect his or her social security record and entitlement to state benefits. This can hinder the geographical mobility of workers.

In recognition of this and to promote free movement of workers within the EEA, the Member States of the EEA agreed a common social security policy which guarantees equality of treatment for workers and their dependants regardless of where in the EEA they live and work. This system continued to apply while the UK remained a member of the EU until the end of the Brexit transitional period on 31 December 2020. The commentary that follows reflects the position that applies until that date. The rules applying from 1 January 2021 are discussed at **9.26**.

The EEA rules are contained in *Regulation 883/2004 on the coordination of social security systems*, which replaced the rules in *Regulation 1408/71* on the application of social security schemes to employed persons, to self-employed persons and members of their family moving within the European Community from 1 May 2010 (the date of entry into force of the implementing regulation (*Regulation EC 987/2009*). The original regulations (*Regulation 1408/71*) have largely been repealed, although they remain in force for certain specified limited purposes.

The regulations ensure that a person is not, at any one time, subject to the contributions legislation of more than one Member State. They also allow contributions paid in one EEA state to count for benefit claims made in another EEA country, although the contributions are not actually transferred to the other country's social security scheme.

The EC regulations took precedence over UK law by virtue of the *European Communities Act 1972, s 2*. The regulations continued to apply until the end of the Brexit transitional period. This means that where persons came to the UK from an EEA country or went to an EEA country from the UK prior to 1 January 2021, it is the EC rules that applied, rather than the UK domestic legislation (set out at **9.20** above). The EC Regulations also overrode residence and presence tests imposed by any country's domestic legislation.

The UK left the EU on 31 January 2020. During the transitional period, which ran until 31 December 2020, the EC regulations continued to apply. From 1 January 2021, the position is governed by the social security agreement between the UK and the EU, which is discussed at **9.26**.

Rules applying from 1 January 2021

9.26 The UK left the EU on 31 January 2020. A transitional period applied until 31 December 2020 during which the EU rules in place on 31 January 2020 continued to apply. New rules apply from 1 January 2021, governed by the social security agreement reached with the EU. The rules as they apply to workers from the UK working in the EEA or Switzerland and to workers from the EEA or Switzerland working in the UK are outlined below.

Workers from the UK working in the EEA or Switzerland

From 1 January 2021, workers from the UK who work in the EU, Norway or Switzerland only have to pay into one country's social security scheme at a time. This is usually the country in which the work takes place.

However, workers who go to work temporarily in the EU, Norway, Iceland, Switzerland or Liechtenstein may be able to obtain a certificate or document from HMRC which will enable them to continue to pay National Insurance contributions in the UK, rather than in the country in which they are working. This is only possible if the worker has the relevant certificate or document from HMRC confirming their continued eligibility to pay UK contributions. An application can be made by:

- a person who is lawfully resident in the UK and who started working in the EU before 1 January 2021, and who has been working there since;
- a national of the UK or of Iceland, Liechtenstein or Norway who started working in Iceland, Lichtenstein or Norway before 1 January 2021, and who has been working there since;
- a national of the EU, Iceland, Liechtenstein, Norway or Switzerland who was resident in the UK before 1 January 2021 (including someone who has EU Settlement Scheme (EUSS) status);
- a family member of a national of the EU, Norway, Iceland, Switzerland or Liechtenstein who has status under the EUSS and who is residing in the UK;

- a person with dual nationality, one of which is the nationality of the EU, Norway, Iceland, Switzerland or Liechtenstein; or
- a multi-state worker, ie a worker who was working in two or more of the following countries – the UK, an EU country, Norway, Iceland, Switzerland or Liechtenstein – before 1 January 2021 and who continues to do so, working predominantly in the UK.

An individual may also be able to apply for a certificate or document if they are covered by any of the other conditions in the withdrawal agreement or equivalent agreements with the EU, Iceland, Liechtenstein, Norway or Switzerland.

Nationals of the EU, Iceland, Liechtenstein, Norway or Switzerland who were living in the UK prior to 1 January 2021 must apply for EUSS by 30 June 2021 to protect their right to stay in the UK and their social security rights.

A UK or Irish National or any National who is lawfully resident in the UK will only pay National Insurance in the UK if they go to work in Ireland. Multi-state workers working in the UK and one or more EU countries will also only pay UK National Insurance contributions.

Workers who go to work temporarily in one of the following countries will be able to apply to HMRC to pay UK National Insurance contributions only:

- an EU country that has decided to apply the 'detached worker' rule;
- Norway;
- Switzerland; or
- Iceland.

An EU country must decide by 1 February 2021 that they will continue to apply the 'detached worker' rules for the rules to continue to apply. Workers who go to work in an EU country before 1 February 2021 which has not opted out of the detached worker rules should apply for a certificate or document from HMRC to enable them to continue to pay National Insurance contributions only in the UK. Where the period of work starts prior to 1 February 2021 and a certificate or document has been issued by HMRC, the worker will continue to pay only UK contributions unless their circumstances change (for example, they change employers). This remains the case even if the EU country in which the worker is working no longer applies the detached worker rule. HMRC will update their guidance to reflect the decision taken by the various EU countries as to whether they will continue to apply the detached worker rule. The guidance here will be updated to reflect this once it is available.

Norway

Workers going to work temporarily in Norway for up to three years should apply for a certificate or document, ideally before going to work there. The application cannot be made later than four months from the date that the worker started work in Norway. Where the certificate or document is granted, the worker will remain in the UK scheme and will not have to pay social security contributions in Norway for the duration of the work there.

Switzerland

A worker who is going to work in Switzerland for a period of up to two years can apply for a certificate or document from HMRC to enable them to continue to pay UK National Insurance contributions. Where granted, the worker will not have to pay contributions in Switzerland while working there.

Iceland

A person who is a non-UK and non-EEA employee working in Iceland for up to one year can apply to HMRC to continue to pay UK National Insurance contributions. This can be extended by a further year if agreement is obtained from the Iceland Social Security Institution before the end of the first year.

Lichtenstein

A worker who goes to work in Liechtenstein and who is not eligible for a certificate or document entitling them to continue to pay UK National Insurance contributions will continue to pay UK contributions for the first 52 weeks under the UK domestic rules.

Paying social security contributions in the host country

A worker will need to pay social security contributions in the country in which they work if they go to work in another EU country temporarily and are not eligible for a certificate or document which enables them to continue to pay UK contributions whilst working abroad temporarily. Where contributions are paid in the host country, UK National Insurance contributions are not payable. However, the worker may be eligible to pay voluntary contributions if they wish to preserve their UK contributions record.

The forms

The form which should be used to apply for continuing eligibility to pay UK National Insurance contributions depends on the worker's circumstances. The position is summarised in the table below.

Situation	**Form**
Employer sends a worker to work temporarily in the EU, Norway, Iceland, Switzerland or Liechtenstein	CA3822
Individual is self-employed and going temporarily to carry out some activities in the EU, Norway, Iceland, Switzerland or Liechtenstein	CA3837
Individual is working in two or more of the following – EU, Norway, Iceland, Switzerland or Liechtenstein	CA8421
Flight or cabin crew with a home base in the UK	CA8421
UK-residents working on a vessel at sea with a UK flag or an EU, Norwegian, Icelandic or Swiss flag who are paid by someone in the UK	CA8421

If HMRC accept that an individual is eligible to continue to pay UK National Insurance contributions, they will issue a certificate or document as proof that contributions are not payable in the country where the worker is working temporarily.

The individual should notify HMRC if their circumstances change.

Workers from the EEA or Switzerland coming to work in the UK

From 1 January 2021, workers coming from the EU, Norway or Switzerland to work in the UK will only have to pay social security contributions in one country. This will normally be the Uk as this is the country where the work takes place.

However, workers who come to work in the UK temporarily from the EU, Norway, Iceland, Switzerland or Liechtenstein will not have to pay social security contributions in the UK if they have a certificate or document that entitles them to continue to pay social security contributions in their home country while working temporarily in the UK.

A certificate or document may be issued to:

- a person who was lawfully resident in the EU and who started working in the UK before 1 January 2021 and who has been working in the UK since;
- a national of Iceland, Liechtenstein or Norway who started working in the Uk before 1 January 2021 and who has been working in the UK since;
- a national of Switzerland who started working in the UK before 1 January 2021 and who has been working in the UK since;
- a national of the UK who was resident in the EU, Iceland, Liechtenstein, Norway or Switzerland before 1 January 2021;
- a person with dual nationality, one of which is the UK and one of which is the EU, Norway, Iceland, Switzerland or Liechtenstein;
- a multistate working, i.e. a person working in two or more countries of the EU, Norway, Iceland, Switzerland or Liechtenstein before 1 January 2021 and who continues to do so, and who works predominantly in a EU country, Norway, Iceland, Switzerland or Liechtenstein.

A person may also apply for continued liability in their home country if they are covered by any of the conditions in the withdrawal agreement or equivalent agreements with the EU, Norway, Iceland, Switzerland or Liechtenstein.

UK or Irish nationals or any national lawfully resident in Ireland who comes to work in the UK will pay EU contributions as will multi-state workers working in the UK and the EU who work predominantly in the EU.

Workers coming from an EU country that has decided to apply the detached worker rules, Norway, Switzerland or Iceland who come to the UK to work temporarily on or after 1 January 2021 are still able to apply for a certificate or document entitling them to continue to pay home country contributions rather than UK National Insurance while working in the UK. EU countries must decide by 1 February 2021 whether they are going to opt out of the detached worker rules. Workers who come to the UK to work temporarily in the UK before 1 February 2021 and who have a certificate enabling them to continue to pay home country contributions can continue to pay home contributions throughout the period of temporary work in the UK, even if their home EU country opts out of the detached worker rules, as long as their circumstances remain unchanged.

The period for which the worker is able to continue to pay home country contributions depends on their home country. Workers from Norway can apply for a certificate for a period of temporary work in the UK of up to three years. Workers from Switzerland can apply for a certificate for a period of temporary work in the UK of up to two years. Workers from Iceland can apply for a certificate for an initial period of one year, although this may be extended by a further year.

Workers who come to work in the UK from an EU or EEA country or Switzerland and who do not have a certificate or document entitling them to continue to pay home country contributions, must pay UK National Insurance while working in the UK temporarily. Workers should apply to the social security institution in their home country for a certificate. Should a worker's circumstances change while they are working temporarily in the UK, they should contact HMRC.

Guidance on the rules that apply from 1 January 2021 to workers from the UK going to work in the EEA or Switzerland and to workers from the EEA or Switzerland coming to work in the UK can be found on the gov.uk website. The guidance is updated regularly to reflect changes.

Rules applying prior to 1 January 2021 – territorial coverage of the EU Regulations

9.27 The EU Regulations (*Regulation 883/2004*) apply to EEA countries, which are the EU Member States plus the EFTA countries (Iceland, Norway and Liechtenstein). The EEA countries are as listed below. The regulation applied to EU Member States from 1 May 2010 and to EFTA countries from 1 April 2012. The regulations continued to apply to the UK following their departure from the EU on 31 January 2020 until the end of the transitional period on 31 December 2020. From 1 January 2021, new rules apply governed by the social security agreement that the UK has reached with the EU. These are discussed at **9.26**.

EEA countries

- Austria
- Belgium

- Bulgaria
- Croatia
- Cyprus
- Czech Republic
- Denmark
- Estonia
- Finland
- France
- Germany
- Gibraltar*
- Greece
- Hungary
- Iceland
- Republic of Ireland
- Italy
- Latvia
- Lithuania
- Luxembourg
- Malta
- Netherlands
- Poland
- Portugal
- Romania
- Slovakia
- Slovenia
- Spain
- Sweden
- UK

* included as a UK territory by specific agreement

The UK extended the application of *Regulation 883/2004* to Switzerland from 1 April 2012 and to Norway, Iceland and Liechtenstein from 1 June 2012.

The effect of this is that *Regulation 883/2004* applies to these countries from those dates. Prior to 1 April 2012 for Switzerland and prior to 1 June 2012 for Norway, Iceland and Liechtenstein the rules in *Regulation 1408/71* continued to apply. Where a person was subject to the old rules prior to, respectively, 1 April 2012 or 1 June 2012, and the amount that they have to pay changes as a result of the move to the new rules, transitional rules apply. Anyone potentially affected by the transitional rules is advised to contact HMRC for advice (0845 915 4811).

The Channel Islands and the Isle of Man are not members of the EU and are not constitutionally part of the UK. However, where citizens of the Isle of Man or the Channel Islands are treated as UK nationals (see **9.12**), they are within the EEA rules. Gibraltar also falls within the scope of the EC regulations because it is included as a UK territory by specific agreement.

Rules applying prior to 1 January 2021 – application of Regulation 883/2004

9.28 Prior to the end of the Brexit transitional period, the EC Regulations applied to the UK. The rules ceased to apply from 1 January 2021, for which see **9.26**. The commentary that follows covers the rules as they apply prior to 1 January 2021.

Regulation 883/2004 applies to nationals of the EU Member States (see **9.27**). The regulation also applies to stateless persons and refugees residing in a Member State, members of their families and survivors if those persons had previously been subject to the legislation of a Member State.

Regulation 883/2004 applies to Switzerland as if it were a member of the EU from 1 April 2012 and to the EFTA countries (Norway, Iceland and Liechtenstein) from 1 June 2012. Prior to these dates the previous rules as contained in *Regulation 1408/71* applied.

The UK has opted out of applying the new rules in *Regulation 883/2004* to third country nationals legally resident in Member States and continues to apply the rules in *Regulation 1408/71*. A third country national is someone who is not a national of any Member State but who resides in a Member State. HMRC regard being resident in a Member State as being legally resident in a Member State. However, a portable A1 issued to a third country national by the competent authority of another Member State should be accepted (HMRC's National Insurance Manual at NIM 33030).

The UK left the EU on 31 January 2020. The regulation will continue to apply to the UK until the end of the transitional period on 31 December 2020. At the time of writing, the position beyond 31 December 2020 was unclear.

For details of the impact of the UK's withdrawal from the EU and the continued applicability of the EU Regulations during the transitional period, see **9.2**.

Rules applying prior to 1 January 2021 – contribution liability rule

9.29 The UK left the EU on 31 January 2020. The Regulation continued to apply until the end of the transitional period on 31 December 2020. From 1 January 2021, the rules are governed by the social security agreement between the UK and the EU. The rules are outlined at **9.26**.

A key principle underpinning the EC regulations is that a person shall only be subject to pay contributions in one Member State at any given time. This remains the case from 1 January 2021 under the social security agreement between the UK and the EU (see **9.26**).

To apply this rule prior to 1 January 2021 under the Regulation, it is therefore necessary to determine the Member State in which contributions are to be paid. The rules for deciding this are found in *Regulation 1408/71, Title II, art 13(2)*.

The general rule is that an employed earner is normally subject to the rules of the Member State in which he or she works. This is known as *lex laboris* or 'pay where you work' and is given legislative effect by *Regulation 883/2004, art 11* (and previously by *Regulation 1408/71, Title II, art 13(2)*). The *lex laboris* rule applies even if the earner is habitually resident in another Member State and cross-border commutes.

This rule is subject to a number of special exceptions, including those for temporary assignments (see **9.30ff**).

Where under the EU regulations, the UK social security legislation applies, the employee and the employer (or person treated as the secondary contributor) must pay UK Class 1 National Insurance contributions and, where relevant, the employer must pay Class 1A and Class 1B contributions. All earnings are treated as arising from activity in the UK. In keeping the principle that contributions are only due in one Member State, where under the EU regulations the social security legislation of another Member State applies, no UK National Insurance contributions are due.

Special rules also apply to mariners, civil servants and members of the armed forces.

Focus

The basic premise under the EU regulations is that a worker will pay contributions where he or she works (*lex laboris);* however, there are a number of exceptions to this rule, particularly in relation to temporary assignments.

Rules applying prior to 1 January 2021 – employed posted workers – short-term assignments

9.30 Under the EC rules that apply to the UK prior to 1 January 2021, special rules apply to workers who are employed in a Member State who are posted by the employer to work in another place for a temporary period. From 1 May 2010 the rules on posted workers temporarily working in another Member State are set out in *Regulation 883/2004, art 12.* Prior to this date the rules were contained within *Regulation 1408/71, art 14(1)(a), (b).* The rules are not identical under the current and previous regulations. The most notable difference is that the former rules applied where the posting was not expected to last more than 12 months at the outset, although an extension was available for a further 12 months should the posting unexpectedly exceed 12 months, whereas the current rules apply where the posting is not expected to exceed 24 months, without the need to apply for an extension after 12 months.

The rules aim to ease the administrative burden that would otherwise arise if workers were forced to swap social security schemes each time they worked abroad by allowing them to remain in the home scheme where they undertake a short-term assignment in another Member State.

The rules as they apply under *Regulation 883/2004* from 1 May 2010 are set out at **9.31**. The UK left the EU on 31 January 2020. The regulations continued to apply to the UK until the end of the transitional period on 31 December 2020. From 1 January 2021, the rules are governed by the social security agreement between the UK and the EU, which contain provisions for workers from the UK working in the EEA or Switzerland temporarily and also for workers from the EEA or Switzerland working in the UK temporarily. The rules as they apply from 1 January 2021 are set out at **9.26**.

> **Focus**
>
> Special rules apply to short-term postings not expected to last more than 24 months, allowing workers to remain in their home social security scheme.

Rules applying prior to 1 January 2021 – EU posted workers

9.31 The rules applying to posted workers within the EU are set out in *Regulation 883/2004, art 12*, which provides that a person who pursues an activity as an employed person in a Member State on behalf of an employer who carries out its activities in that Member State and who is posted by that employer to another Member State to perform work on behalf of that employer remains subject to the legislation of first Member State provided that the anticipated duration of the work does not exceed 24 months and the worker is not sent to replace another worker.

The rules apply generally from 1 May 2020. They also apply to Switzerland from 1 April 2012 and to Norway, Iceland and Liechtenstein from 1 June 2012.

The UK left the EU on 31 January 2020. The EU posted worker rules continue to apply until the end of the transition period on 31 December 2020. The rules applying from 1 January 2021 are set out at **9.26**. To qualify for the treatment the employee and the employer have to satisfy certain conditions, most of which are set out in Administrative Commission Decision A2 on migrant workers (which replaced Administrative Commission Decision 181). For the special treatment afforded by *art 12* to apply, the conditions require:

- the existence of a direct relationship between the employee and the employer, which is maintained throughout the period of the posting; and
- the existence of ties between the employer and the Member State in which it is established.

The decision states that if the employee is made available to a third undertaking, there can no longer be any guarantee of a direct relationship between the employee and the employer. It also makes it clear that the posting rules should only be considered by undertakings that normally carry on their business in the Member State whose legislation remains applicable to the posted worker and as such only apply to undertaking that ordinarily perform substantial activities in the territory of the Member State in which they are established.

Checks may be carried out throughout the period of posting as regards the payment of contributions and the maintenance of the direct relationship and to ensure that the administrative bodies, employers and workers are suitably informed. The employer and the worker must be informed of the conditions under which the worker is allowed to remain within the legislation of the country from which he is posted.

The effect of this rule is that where a worker is sent to work abroad in another EU Member State for 24 months or less, the employee remains in the home social security scheme. Under these rules, the maximum posting period is 24 months. Where a UK employer posts a worker to another EU Member State on a short-term assignment lasting 24 months or less, the employer must apply to HMRC NIC&EO International Caseworker for Form A1 (which replaced the previous form, form E101) which shows that the employer is entitled to continue to remain within the UK scheme and remains liable to UK National Insurance contributions. Employers who are unsure as to whether the posted worker rules apply in a particular case should contact HMRC NIC&EO International Caseworker for advice.

For details of the impact of the UK's withdrawal from the EU on 31 January 2020 and on the continued applicability of the EU Regulations until the end of the transition period on 31 December 2020, see **9.2**.

> **Focus**
>
> A worker posted to another Member State for 24 months or less can remain in their home social security scheme. Workers wishing to remain in the UK scheme need to obtain Form A1.

Rules applying prior to 1 January 2021 – self-employed workers and temporary assignments

9.32 Self-employed people who go abroad to work in another country within the European Economic Area (EEA) (EU Member States plus Norway, Iceland, Liechtenstein and Switzerland) may apply to remain within the UK National Insurance scheme and for exemption from foreign contributions.

Prior to 1 January 2021, the position is governed by *Regulation 883/2004, art 12*, which provides that a person who normally pursues an activity as a self-employed person in an EEA country who goes and pursues a similar activity in another EEA country remains within subject to the legislation of the first EEA country, provided that the anticipated duration of the activity does not exceed 24 months. This is supplemented by Administrative Commission Decision A2 which sets out various conditions that must be met for the self-employed person to remain within the home country scheme. *Regulation 883/2004* and Administrative Council Decision A2 applies from 1 May 2010.

The UK left the EU on 31 January 2020. The regulation will continue to apply until the end of the transitional period on 31 December 2020. The rules that apply from 1 January 2021 are explored at **9.26**. This paragraph sets out the rules as they apply to the UK prior to 1 January 2021.Where a self-employed person goes to work temporarily in another EEA country, certain conditions must be met in order for that person to be allowed to remain within the legislation of the first EEA country. These include the requirements that the person:

- habitually carries out substantial activities in the first EEA country;
- pursues the self-employed activity in the first EEA country (usually for at least two months); and
- maintains the means to carry out the self-employment in the first EEA country on return.

A person would be regarded as maintaining the means to carry out the self-employment if, for example, they retained an office and the necessary infrastructure to continue the self-employment, such as paying taxes and social security, retaining any necessary registrations etc. However, it should be noted that what is necessary to maintain the self-employment will vary depending on the nature of the business.

Where a self-employed person in the UK goes to work on a self-employed basis in another EEA country for less than 24 months, he or she must apply for a certificate of continuing UK liability (form A1). The application is made to HMRC NIC&EC International Caseworker on form CA3837 (see **9.33**).

HMRC are likely to ask for details of contracts and work carried out in the UK and those abroad in order to ascertain whether substantial activities are habitually carried on in the UK. If less than 25% of contracts or turnover is in the UK, HMRC would not regard that as substantial.

Under the rules in *Regulation 883/2004*, a self-employed person can remain within the home country scheme if the work abroad is expected to last 24 months or less. To qualify to remain in the home country scheme for the duration of the period abroad, the self-employed worker must:

- have been self-employed in the home country before going abroad to work for and pursuing significant activities for a certain length of time (generally two years) prior to going abroad;
- be able to substantiate the work to be performed abroad (e.g. by producing details of contracts); and
- while working abroad, maintain the means to carry out self-employment in the home country on return (e.g. by maintaining office space and the infrastructure necessary to run a business etc).

Checks may be made throughout the period to ensure that the conditions for remaining in the home country scheme continue to be met. Any changes that may affect the validity of the form should be notified to HMRC NIC&EO International Caseworker.

For details of the impact of the UK's withdrawal from the EU on 31 January 2020 and on the continued applicability of the EU Regulations until the end of the transition period on 31 December 2020, see **9.2**.

Form A1

9.33 Evidence of continuing liability in the home country is provided by means of form A1 where *Regulation 883/2004* applies. This replaced form E101. Form A1 is issued for a period of 24 months at the outset.

The issue of the form confirms that person is continuing to pay contributions in the home country and exempts them from liability to contributions in the host country.

In the UK, an application for a certificate of continuing liability (form A1) is made to HMRC NIC&EO International Caseworker (formerly HMRC Residency) in Newcastle.

The relevant application form will depend on the person's circumstances. The forms are as follows:

Form	Purpose
CA3821	Employer's questionnaire when their employees are being sent to work in an European Economic Area (EEA)/reciprocal agreement country (see www.gov.uk/government/publications/national-insurance-sending-employees-to-work-abroad-ca3821).
CA3822	Application for a certificate of continuing liability to pay UK National Insurance contributions where employees are going abroad to work (see www.gov.uk/government/publications/national-insurance-employees-going-to-work-in-the-european-economic-area-ca3822).
CA3837	Self-employed temporarily working in another country in the European Union (see www.gov.uk/government/publications/national-insurance-application-for-form-e101-if-self-employed-in-european-economic-area-ca3837).
CA8421i	Normally working in two or more countries in the European Economic Area (see www.gov.uk/government/publications/national-insurance-working-in-2-or-more-countries-in-the-european-economic-area-ca8421i).

The forms are available to download from the gov.uk website. Applications can also be made online.

The forms remain the same from 1 January 2021. For their use from that date, see **9.26**.

The A1 certificate is granted in respect of a particular posting and will cease to become valid if the employer changes or the employee moves to a new country with the same employer. If the employee remains working within the same country an application should be made to the social security authorities for an amendment to the A1. However, if the employee moves to another country to work, even if the employment is with the same employer, a new application should be made.

HMRC should be notified of any changes in the posting.

Similarly, where the person in question is self-employed, HMRC should be notified if the person stops working abroad or stops working or any changes in circumstance as this may affect the validity of the certificate.

In September 2019, HMRC published a Brexit issue of *Employer Bulletin*, in which they stated that a replacement for the A1/E101 form will be issued for new applications after Brexit. The existing form can be used until the end of the transition period.

For details of the impact of the UK's withdrawal from the EU on 31 January 2020 and on the continued applicability of the EU Regulations until the end of the transition period on 31 December 2020, see **9.2**.

> **Focus**
>
> Form A1 provides evidence of continuing liability within the UK scheme.

Rules prior to 1 January 2021 – certificates lasting for a longer period

9.34 The EC regulations provide for two or more EEA countries to agree to exceptions to the rules outlined above (*Regulation 883/2004, art 16* and *Regulation 1408/71, art 17*). This makes it possible for them to agree to a person remaining under the home country legislation for a period of more than two years. In certain circumstances, it is therefore possible to seek an extension to the normal time limits or to agree to the employee remaining within the home country scheme where the posting is expected to last more than the maximum permitted period from the outset. The maximum period that can normally be agreed is five years.

Where the posting is for a longer period at the outset, an employee may be able to continue paying home country National Insurance contributions if:

- the employee has specialist knowledge or skills in that job;
- the employee has specific objectives in the other EEA country for which the employee's services are required; or
- it is in the employee's interest to remain in the home country scheme.

The rules recognise that employees may work for an extended period in another EEA country but with the intention of returning to the home country at the end of the duty. It may be important for the worker to remain in the home country scheme for when he or she returns home or retires.

The employee can only remain in the home scheme with the agreement of the host authorities. The employee must also provide a statement to the effect that he or she wishes to remain within the home country scheme.

Where an employee remains within the UK scheme HMRC NIC&EO International Caseworker will issue form A1.

In September 2019, HMRC published a Brexit issue of *Employer Bulletin*, in which they stated that a replacement for the A1/E101 form will be issued for new applications after Brexit. The existing form can be used until the end of the transition period.

The EC Regulations continued to apply to the UK until the end of the Brexit transition period on 31 December 2020. From 1 January 2021, a new social security agreement applies to the UK and the EU. This is explored at **9.26**.

Rules prior to 1 January 2021 – employment in more than one EEA country

9.35 A person may simultaneously be employed in more than one EEA country. Prior to 1 January 2021, *Regulation 883/2004* applied to the UK. Under *Regulation 883/2004, art 13* where a person works in more than one EEA country, the legislation of the country of residence applies if the person pursues a substantial part of their activity in that country. The legislation of the country of residence also applies if an employee is employed by various undertakings or by various employers whose registered office or place of business is in different EEA countries. However, if the person does not pursue a substantial part of their activity in the EEA country in which they live, they are subject to the legislation of the EEA country in which the registered office or place of business of the undertaking employing them is situated. In determining whether a person pursues substantial activities in the UK, HMRC take account of both time spent and remuneration earned pursuing those activities in the UK. HMRC regard 25% of the person's working time being spent in the UK or 25% of their remuneration being earned in the UK as substantial. Where an employee lives in the UK and pursues a substantial part of his or her activities in the UK, but also works in another EEA country, the employer should apply to HMRC NIC&EO International Caseworker for form A1 confirming continued UK liability and providing exemption from foreign contributions. However, if an employee works in the UK but resides in another EEA country, the employer should, after contacting HMRC, apply to the authorities of the country of residence who will make a decision as to which legislation applies. Where the UK legislation applies, the employer is liable for secondary Class 1 contributions and also Class 1A and Class 1B contributions where relevant.

The effect of *Regulation 883/2004, art 13* is that where a person works in more than one EEA country, in most cases that person is subject to the legislation of the country in which he or she resides.

If a worker is simultaneously employed and self-employed in different EEA countries, contribution liability arises in the country where the employment is carried out.

The UK left the EU on 31 January 2020. The regulations continue to apply until the end of the transitional period on 31 December 2020. From 1 January 2021, a new social security agreement applies. The impact of this is explored at **9.26**.

Rules applying prior to 1 January 2021 – employment in an EEA country in other circumstances

9.36 Where a person is employed in an EEA country other than in the circumstances set out at **9.32** to **9.35** above, the contribution liability will normally arise in the EEA country where the work is carried out under the general 'pay as you work' rule (see **9.31**). This would include postings of more than 24 months. Where an extension to the period of home country liability (see **9.34**) has not been granted rules apply to certain categories of workers under *Regulation 1408/71*, including mariners, transport workers, civil servants, members of staff of diplomatic or consular posts, members of staff of the European Communities, members of Her Majesty's Forces and of organisations which serve the forces. Persons falling within these categories often remain within the UK scheme. However, in the main, *Regulation 883/2004* applies to these workers as to other workers without the application of special rules.

The EC Regulations continued to apply to the UK until the end of the Brexit transition period on 31 December 2020. The rules as they apply from 1 January 2021 in accordance with the social security agreement between the UK and the EU are discussed at **9.26**.

Rules applying prior to 1 January 2021 – coming to the UK from another EEA country

9.37 Where, prior to 1 January 2021, a person comes from another EEA country to work in the UK, the general EC rules in *Regulation 883/2004* apply. If the assignment is a short-term assignment the person may be able to remain within the home social security scheme (see **9.32**). A form A1 certificate from the home country is needed for exception from liability from the UK contributions (see **9.33**). In certain circumstances, the person may be able to remain within the home scheme for longer than 24 months (see **9.34**).

In other cases, a person working in the UK will be liable for UK National Insurance contributions under the general EC 'pay where you work' rule (see **9.34**). This rule overrides the residence and presence conditions under the UK domestic legislation (see **9.15**).

The EC Regulations continued to apply to the UK until the end of the Brexit transition period on 31 December 2020. The rules as they apply from 1 January 2021 in accordance with the social security agreement between the UK and the EU are discussed at **9.26**.

Planning considerations

9.38 Contribution rates vary widely throughout the EEA as do the benefits that the contributions 'buy'. This introduces opportunities for planning. Making best use of the short-term assignment rules can reduce the contributions bill for the employer and the employee. However, it must be remembered when planning that compared to countries like France and Belgium, social security costs in the UK are low and minimising UK social security costs may not always be the best strategy if the worker is seconded to a higher contribution country. It is necessary to consider both sides of the equation – not only the cost of the contributions but also the benefits rights that those contributions buy. Depending on the individual's circumstances, it may be preferable to pay higher contributions in other Member States to benefit from the entitlement that they provide.

The short-term assignment rules also offer planning opportunities where bonuses are involved as the timing can affect whether the bonus attracts a UK or a foreign contribution liability. What represents the best course of action will depend on relative contributions rates and benefit entitlement. Contribution cost is only one side of the equation and consideration also needs to be given to the benefits provided in return for those contributions.

When undertaking any planning exercise, consideration should be given to the implications of the UK's withdrawal from the EU on 31 January 2020 and the position beyond the end of the transitional period. For details of the rules as they apply from 1 January 2021, see **9.26**.

RECIPROCAL AGREEMENT COUNTRIES

Nature of social security agreements

9.39 The UK has social security agreements with a number of other countries. Where an agreement is in force, special NIC rules apply. There are two types of social security agreement – reciprocal agreements (RAs) and double contribution conventions (DCCs). Reciprocal agreements contain provisions for both contribution liability and for benefits whereas double contribution conventions only cover contributions liability. The social security agreement with the UK applying from 1 January 2021 is discussed at **9.26**.

RAs and DCCs ensure equal treatment when an employee moves from one agreement country to another and in certain cases allows contributions to continue to be made to the home scheme. They aim to preserve benefit entitlement and prevent dual contribution liabilities from arising.

Although the agreements tend to follow a similar model, they are not identical and reference should be made to the relevant agreement in a particular case. The terms of the agreement take precedence over UK domestic legislation.

Focus

Where a social security agreement is in force, the provisions of that prevail over the UK domestic legislation.

Agreement countries

9.40 The UK has bilateral social security agreements with the following countries:

- Barbados
- Bermuda

- Bosnia-Herzegovina
- Canada
- Chile
- Croatia
- Guernsey
- Israel
- Jamaica
- Japan
- Jersey
- Mauritius
- Montenegro
- New Zealand
- North Macedonia
- Philippines
- Republic of Korea
- Serbia
- Turkey
- USA

The agreements with Japan and the Republic of Korea are DCCs and only cover social security contribution liability.

The agreement with the Isle of Man is limited and liability is general determined by place of residence.

The UK also has agreements with all EEA countries except Greece and Liechtenstein. Thus, a person who is not covered by the EC regulation may be covered by a RA when working in the EEA.

Going to an agreement country – employees

9.41 Where a person goes abroad as an employee to a country with which the UK has a bilateral social security agreement covering National Insurance contributions, the liability position will depend on the terms of that agreement.

The general rule is that a person is subject to the social security legislation of the country in which they work. However, this general rule is subject to exceptions, including those for posted workers (see **9.42**).

Special rules apply to civil servants, diplomatic posts, mariners, aircrew, and HM Forces and where a person works both in the UK and another agreement country or where a person is simultaneously employed in one country and self-employed in another.

Posted workers

9.42 The general rule that contributions are payable in the country of work is set aside in the case of posted workers. A worker sent abroad to work for a limited period may remain liable to Class 1 National Insurance contributions if the following conditions are met:

- the worker is employed in the UK:
- the worker is posted to work in another RA country; and
- the posting is for a period not exceeding the maximum period allowed by the terms of the agreement.

The permitted maximum posting period depends on the country and varies from country to country. The maximum posting periods are set out in the table below.

RA country	**Maximum posting period**
Barbados	3 years
Bermuda	12 months
Canada	5 years
Chile	5 years
Guernsey	3 years
Isle of Man	N/A – liability determined by residence. There are no time limits
Israel	2 years
Jamaica	3 years
Japan	5 years
Jersey	3 years
Korea	5 years
Mauritius	2 years
Philippines	3 years
Turkey	3 years
USA	5 years
Bosnia-Herzegovina, Montenegro, Serbia, North Macedonia	12 months – EC rules apply to Slovenia from 1 May 2004 and to Croatia from 1 July 2013

Where a worker is posted to a RA country, the employer must obtain a certificate of continuing liability from the Centre for Non-residents in Newcastle. This is similar to an A1 certificate (but is not an A1).

It is possible to secure extension to the posting periods with agreement with the foreign authority. Extensions are granted in circumstances similar to those granted under the *Regulations* (see **9.33**).

Civil servants and those treated as such posted to an overseas country where a reciprocal agreement is in place remain subject to Class 1 National Insurance contributions.

Posting from a third country

9.43 A worker may be posted to a country with which the UK has a RA whilst working outside the UK. Under the terms of the RA, the worker remains under the terms of the agreement as a posted worker and the provisions applying to a posted worker (see **9.42**) apply.

Working in both territories in the same period

9.44 Some agreements contain articles dealing with the situation where a worker works in both territories in the same period. Where this is the case, contribution liability normally falls in the country in which the employee is ordinarily resident.

Going to an agreement country – self-employed

9.45 Most of the social security agreements contain provisions which allow a person who is self-employed in the UK to continue their business in an agreement country whilst remaining within the UK social security scheme. This overrides the general rule that contributions are payable where a person works.

To remain within the UK scheme a person must apply to HMRC NIC&EO International Caseworker for a certificate of continuing UK liability. This provides exception from liability for foreign contributions.

A self-employed person who is carrying on their business in an agreement country while remaining within the UK National Insurance scheme is liable to pay Class 2 and Class 4 National Insurance contributions as if they were self-employed in the UK.

Coming to the UK from an agreement country

9.46 A person coming to the UK to work from a RA country may be able to continue paying home country contributions under the posted worker provisions. Exception from UK liability will be granted provided that the relevant certificate has been issued. Where this is not the case, the worker will pay contributions under the UK scheme under the general 'pay where you work' rule.

This rule and other treaty provisions override the residence and presence conditions under UK domestic legislation.

REST OF THE WORLD

Scope of rest of the world rules

9.47 As noted above, the world is divided into three for social security purposes. Countries that are not covered by the social security agreement with the EU with which the UK does not have a separate social security agreement are termed 'rest of the world' (ROW) countries. Most of the world falls into this category, including Australia.

Where there is an agreement in place, the treaty provisions take precedence over domestic provision; however, rest of the world (ROW) countries are subject to the UK domestic legislation (see **9.20**). This means that the UK residence and presence conditions are in point. These are discussed at **9.15**.

> **Focus**
>
> The UK domestic legislation applies to countries outside the EU with which the UK does not have a social security agreement (Rest of the World (ROW) countries).

Going to work in a ROW country

9.48 If a person is sent to work in a ROW country, he or she remains liable to UK National Insurance contributions if the following conditions are met:

- the employee remains ordinarily resident for social security purposes in the UK;
- immediately before the foreign employment began the employee was resident in the UK; and
- the employer has a place of business in the UK.

If any of these conditions is not met, liability to pay UK National Insurance contributions ceases on departure. Once mandatory UK contributions liability ends, the worker can pay UK voluntary contributions (Class 2 or Class 3 as appropriate) in order to preserve benefit and pension entitlement. Where a worker goes from the UK to work in a country which is neither covered by the EC Regulations nor by a social security agreement, the person is subject to the domestic legislation of that country from the date of arrival. This may mean that a double contribution liability may arise in the first 52 weeks if the worker also has a continuing liability to UK contributions. The UK liability can be broken by setting up a contract with an overseas employer with no place of business in the UK. However, this may not always be beneficial as it may adversely affect pension and benefit entitlement in the UK.

Coming to the UK from a ROW country

9.49 If a worker comes to the UK to work from a country which is neither an EEA country nor a country with which the UK has a social security agreement, the worker will be subject to UK domestic rules from the date of arrival in the UK. The employee is liable to primary Class 1 National Insurance contributions and the employer to secondary Class 1 National Insurance contributions. The employer is responsible for deducting the contributions and paying them over to HMRC.

However, there is an exemption from liability (by virtue of the *Social Security (Contributions) Regulations 2001* (*SI 2001/1004*), *reg 145(2)*) for the first 52 weeks if:

- the employee is not ordinarily resident in the UK;
- the employee is not ordinarily employed in the UK;
- the employee is sent to the UK in continuance of an employment that is mainly outside the UK;
- the employee is sent by an employer who has a place of business outside the UK (even if the employer also has a place of business in the UK); and
- the employee is employed in the UK for 'a time' (taken to be up to three years).

Once the employer has been resident in the UK for a continuous period of 52 weeks, a liability to UK National Insurance contributions arises.

The employer is normally responsible for deducting contributions and paying them over to HMRC. However, where the employer does not have a place of business in the UK and there is no other business that is responsible for operating UK National Insurance, the employee is responsible for paying his or her own National Insurance contributions to HMRC. This can be done using a direct payment scheme (see **9.64**).

It may be possible to benefit from a further 52 weeks exemption from UK liability if the employee returns to the overseas employment and them commences a further secondment in the UK. However, at the start of each secondment, the intention must be that the secondment will last less than three years.

MARINERS

Special National Insurance rules for mariners

9.50 Special National Insurance rules apply to mariners to ensure that they continue to be insured when working outside territorial waters. The rules are complex and depend on where the vessel is flagged. The domestic legislation governing mariners is set out in the *Social Security (Contributions) Regulations 2001* (*SI 2001/1004*), *Pt 9, Case C (regs 115–125*). These rules apply where the ship is not flagged in the EEA or country with which the UK has a social security agreement.

A mariner is defined (in the *Social Security (Contributions) Regulations 2001* (*SI 2001/1004*), *reg 115*) as a person who is or has been in employment under a contract of service either as a master or a member of a crew of any ship or vessel, or in any other capacity on board any ship or vessel where:

- the employment in that other capacity is for the purposes of that ship or vessel or the crew or any passengers or cargo or mail carried by the ship or vessel; and
- the contract is entered into in the UK with a view to its performance (in whole or in part) while the ship or vessel is on voyage,

but does not include a person in so far as his employment is as a serving member of the forces.

Due to the complex nature of the rules, HMRC have a special unit dealing with mariners, which can be contacted by telephone on 03000 582419. Guidance is also available on the Gov.uk website at www.gov.uk/national-insurance-if-you-work-on-a-ship.

Liability for UK Class 1 National Insurance contributions

9.51 Mariners are liable to pay Class 1 National Insurance contributions if they:

- work for or are paid by a UK company;
- are serving in designated inshore waters around the UK; or
- are resident and domiciled in the UK and working on a vessel flying the UK ensign.

A mariner is also liable to pay UK National Insurance contributions in respect of any work done abroad on a ship that is flying the Manx flag by virtue of a special agreement with the Isle of Man.

British ships

9.52 A mariner who is employed on a British ship and who is domiciled or resident in the UK is liable to pay Class 1 National Insurance contributions.

Secondary Class 1 National Insurance contributions are payable by the person who pays the mariner's wages, provided that person has a place of business in the UK (see **9.13**). No secondary contributions are payable if the employer does not have a place of business in the UK.

However, a secondary Class 1 National Insurance liability may fall on the host employer if the mariner works mainly in category A, B, C or D waters and is supplied by the host employer to work in UK waters.

If there is no employer, host employer or payer of wages in the UK, the mariner must pay his or her primary Class 1 National Insurance contributions direct to HMRC.

Non-British ships

9.53 The position for non-British ships depends on whether the ship is flagged in an EEA country, a reciprocal agreement country or a country that is neither an EEA country nor a reciprocal agreement country.

Vessel flagged in EEA country

9.54 Prior to 1 January 2021, the EC Regulations apply to the UK. Under the regulations, a mariner working on a vessel flagged in an EEA country is generally subject to the legislation of the state where the vessel is flagged and will pay contributions to that state (*Regulation 883/2004, art 11(4)*).

This rule does not apply if:

- the mariner has been posted to that vessel by an employer either in another EEA country or from a vessel flying the flag of another state. In this case the mariner is subject to the contribution legislation of the first state;
- the vessel is within a port of, or within territorial waters, of another EEA country and the mariner is not normally employed at sea or a crew member of the vessel, in which case the mariner is subject to the contribution legislation of the state;
- the mariner is resident in another EEA country and not paid by an employer or other person whose registered office or place of business is also in that country, in which case the mariner is subject to the contribution legislation of that state; or
- where a mariner is remunerated by an undertaking in an EEA country in which he resides, the legislation of the EEA country of residence applies. Under this rule, the person paying the remuneration is treated as the employer.

From 1 January 2021 the position is governed by the UK's social security agreement with the EU (for which see **9.26**).

Vessel flagged in agreement countries

9.55 Where a mariner who is ordinarily resident in the UK works on a vessel that is flagged in a country with which the UK has a social security agreement (either a reciprocal agreement or a defined contribution convention), the exact position will depend on the wording of the agreement, as liability can depend on:

- where the mariner, employer, payer of wages or ship owner lives;
- where the employer, payer of wages or ship owner has their place of business;
- where the ship is registered, the voyage pattern of the ship and the flag it flies.

However, in the main, the agreements provide for the mariner to pay contributions and to receive benefits in the country in which the vessel is flagged, unless the vessel is owned in the UK, the mariner is paid in the UK or the mariner works in the UK.

By virtue of the UK-Bermuda agreement, a mariner is subject to UK legislation and liable for Class 1 National Insurance contributions as if employed on a UK ship if the mariner is ordinarily resident in the UK and is employed as a mate or member of crew of a Bermudan-owned ship that calls regularly at UK ports. However, vessels that are at sea for several months at a time and which return home to UK ports several times a year are not regarded as calling 'regularly' at UK ports.

Vessel flagged in a ROW country

9.56 Mariners working on ships that are not flagged in an EEA country or a country with which the UK has a reciprocal agreement are subject to the UK domestic legislation governing mariners. This is found in the *Social Security (Contributions) Regulations 2001* (*SI 2001/1004*), *regs 115–125*.

The normal residence and presence rule are disregarded for mariners. Instead for a liability to primary Class 1 National Insurance contributions to arise, the mariner has to be domiciled or resident in the UK. A secondary Class 1 National Insurance liability arises only if the employer is resident or has a place of business in the UK.

EEA nationals on UK flagged vessels

9.57 Special rules apply to an EEA national or a person resident in an EEA country who works on a UK flagged vessel. Normally, such a person will be liable to pay UK Class 1 National insurance contributions in accordance with the general rule that contributions are payable in the state where the vessel is flagged. However, no liability to UK National Insurance contributions arises where that person has a valid A1 certificate (see **9.33**). A mariner who is subject to one of the exemptions set out at **9.53** will be required to show HMRC a valid A1 certificate from the country where contributions are payable to be excused from UK contributions.

Offshore contracts

9.58 In recent years, the UK shipping industry has transferred significant numbers of employment contracts to either non-UK members of shipping groups or to unconnected offshore employers in a bid to remain competitive by avoiding the payment of secondary National Insurance contributions by not having a place of business in the UK.

Whether there is a place of business in the UK will depend on the facts of each case.

If an entity is non-resident and does not have a place of business in the UK, HMRC will look to the following evidence to decide whether the non-resident entity is the employer (HMRC's National Insurance Manual at NIM29010):

- contracts of employment;
- agreements with shipping unions;
- disciplinary agreements;
- payroll procedures;
- liability for payment of earnings if ship owner defaults on fees due to inshore entity; and
- holder of employers' liability insurance.

EMBASSY EMPLOYEES

Special rules for people working in the UK for embassies and high commissions

9.59 Where a person is employed in the UK and has a UK employer, the general rule is that person pays Class 1 National Insurance contributions in the UK. The employer is responsible for deducting the contributions and paying them over to HMRC (see **3.127**). Where there is no UK employer, the employee is responsible for paying contributions to HMRC. This is subject to the exemptions granted to employees who come to work in the UK from EEA and agreement countries and remain within their home social security system (usually for 12 months) (see **9.36** and **9.45**).

However, certain embassies, high commissions, consulates and international organisations are exempt from operating National Insurance. Exemptions may also be in force in relation to employees who are not UK Nationals and who do not reside in the UK permanently.

Staff of embassies, high commissions and consulates of another EEA country or Switzerland

9.60 Special rules previously applied to employees of an embassy, high commission and consulates if the employee is also a national of that country. Under the special rules, the employee could choose whether to pay contributions under the UK or the home country scheme.

However, career diplomats, civil servants and people treated as civil servants by the sending country remained subject to the legislation of that country.

All other employees of EEA country or Swiss embassies, high commissions or consulates in the UK pay UK Class 1 National Insurance contributions and are covered by the UK Social Security Scheme, unless:

- the employee is a national of the Member State or consulate where they work;
- under EEA rules, each year the employee opted and was accepted by that Member State to continue to pay contributions only to that Member State; and
- that option was made prior to 1 May 2010.

The ability to opt was withdrawn from 1 May 2010 (the date on which *Regulation 883/2004* came into force). However, such employees may be able to continue to pay in their home country under transitional rules or by special agreement.

Staff of embassies, high commissions and consulates of a country that is not an EEA country or Switzerland

9.61 A person who works for an embassy, high commission or consulate of a country outside the EEA (other than Switzerland) as a member of the diplomatic, administrative, technical or domestic staff does not have to pay UK National Insurance contributions if that person is not a UK national and does not reside in the UK permanently.

However, other employees are required to pay Class 1 National Insurance contributions.

In the event that the embassy, high commission or consulate is exempt from National Insurance, an employee who is required to pay Class 1 contributions is responsible for paying the contributions to HMRC.

People working for international organisations

9.62 As a general rule, a person who works for an international organisation with a place of business in the UK is liable to pay Class 1 National Insurance contributions (subject to exemption for employees from EEA or agreement countries whilst they remain within their home country schemes).

International organisations are organisations set up under international treaties and agreements.

Some international organisations have obtained exemption for employees who are members of visiting forces, who are not UK nationals and who are not permanent residents in the UK.

DIRECT PAYMENT SCHEME

Employee operates own Class 1 National Insurance

9.63 Normally, where an employee is within liability to Class 1 National Insurance contributions, the employer deducts the contributions from the employee's pay and, together with the associated secondary contributions, pays them over to HMRC. However, where the employer is a foreign employer and there is no business in the UK with responsibility for operating National Insurance or an embassy that does not want to operate National Insurance, the employee has to work out his or her own National Insurance contributions and pay them over to HMRC. The procedures that the employee must follow will depend on whether the employee is liable to pay UK tax.

In some cases, a foreign employer may be willing to operate UK National Insurance to relieve the employee from the need to do so.

Direct payment schemes for National Insurance

9.64 There are two direct payment schemes that involve National Insurance.

DPNI schemes (also known as PAYE direct payment procedures) are appropriate where normal PAYE procedures are unsuitable. The employee is responsible for deducting his or her own income tax and employee National Insurance contributions.

DCNI schemes are used where a simplified PAYE scheme is required to enable direct payment of National Insurance contributions only.

To use a direct payment scheme for National Insurance, it is necessary to first register with HMRC, who will provide a pack containing the forms that are required. Most employees will pay standard-rate contributions. However, married women holding a valid election can pay reduced-rate contributions (see **3.118**).

The amount of National Insurance is worked out using table CA40 (employee only contributions for employees). Table A is used for standard-rate contributions and table B for reduced-rate contributions. To find the contributions payable, it is necessary to find the gross earnings figure on the table (or if the exact figure is not shown, the nearest lowest figure). The earnings figure used should be total earnings from the employment, not just UK earnings. Where payments are made in a currency other than sterling, they must be converted to sterling.

Contributions should be recorded on a deductions working sheet. Contributions are paid over to HMRC using the payslips required. At the end of the tax year, an end of year return (P14) must be sent to HMRC, as must any unpaid Class 1 National Insurance for the year.

MODIFIED NATIONAL INSURANCE CONTRIBUTION PROCEDURES

Modified NIC procedures for tax-equalised employees

9.65 Employers can elect to use modified PAYE procedures for tax-equalised employees. Employers choosing to operate these procedures can also apply to operate modified NIC procedures for such employees. These procedures, known as appendix 7a procedures, are set out in HMRC's PAYE Manual at PAYE82003.

The procedures allow employers authorised to apply the modified PAYE 'appendix 6' procedures (set out in HMRC's PAYE Manual at PAYE82002) to enter into an agreement that allows the employer more time to report and pay National Insurance contributions on overseas earnings. The employer is allowed to account for National Insurance contributions on a best estimate of earnings. Correct figures must then be submitted on a NIC settlement return by 31 March following the end of the tax year. If the procedures are followed correctly, interest and penalties are not charged.

The appendix 7a procedures can only be operated by formal agreement with HMRC. To be eligible for the arrangements, the employees must:

- be subject to an appendix 6 agreement for PAYE purposes;
- be assigned to work in the UK from abroad and have an employer or host employer in the UK who is liable for secondary contributions; and
- pay National Insurance contributions on earnings above the upper earnings limit for the year (£50,000 for 2020/21) or at or above the upper earnings limit for each earnings period in the year.

If an employee joins or leaves the employment part way through an earnings period, the agreement remains valid provided that for employees with monthly earnings periods, contributions are calculated and paid on earnings at above the upper earnings limit in all months other than the month in which the employee joined or left. If the employee has an annual earnings period, contributions are paid on earnings at or above the pro rata upper earnings limit.

Under the arrangements, the employer calculates and pays Class 1 National Insurance contributions on the best estimate of those elements of the remuneration package that attract Class 1 National Insurance contributions. The best estimate should be prepared at the start of the year or, if later, in the month in which the National Insurance liability commences. The estimate should reflect worldwide earnings, including annual salary and cash bonuses, and also non-cash benefits that attract a Class 1A National Insurance liability.

In respect of each tax month for which estimated earnings are calculated for an employee, the employer must complete and maintain a payroll record and include details about the payment, the National Insurance category letter and NIC data items on a full payment submission (FPS) which must be submitted to HMRC no later than 19th of the month following the end of the tax month.

The estimate should be reviewed in December and April to take into account any material changes, such as bonuses or National Insurance contributions on awards of securities or options. The arrangements should also be updated during the year to reflect arrivals and departures of employees. Following the review, the employer must immediately update the amount of NICs payable and when completing the next FPS, adjust the NIC data item to show the revised values to date. The employer pays 1/12th of the best estimate of the National Insurance contributions due for the year over to HMRC each month. Payments can be made quarterly if the arrangement covers five or fewer employees.

Class 1A National Insurance contributions are payable on the best estimate of the liability by 19 July following the end of the tax year. However, the employer has until 31 January following the end of the tax year to submit form P11D(b).The correct amount of Class 1A National Insurance must be paid to HMRC by 31 March following the end of the tax year.

The employer must complete a NIC settlement return no later than 31 March following the end of the tax year. Any residual National Insurance liability must be paid by the same date. The employer is given a reference number and payslip to enable the return and payment to be made.

It should be noted that to help employers affected by the Covid-19 pandemic, the 31 March 2021 deadline (the deadline for the 2019/20 settlement return) was extended to 30 June 2021.

Modified NIC procedures for certain employees working abroad

9.66 A simplified reporting procedure for National Insurance contributions can be used where the employee works overseas. The procedure, known as the appendix 7b procedure, works in a similar way to the appendix 7a procedure, but there is no requirement for the employee to be tax-equalised. The procedure is set out in HMRC's PAYE Manual at PAYE82004.

As with the appendix 7a procedures, the employer must enter into a formal agreement with HMRC before the appendix 7a procedures can be applied.

The appendix 7b procedures can be used in respect of employees who:

- are employed by a UK employer and assigned to work abroad for a period of limited duration, but for more than a complete tax year;
- have an ongoing liability to UK National Insurance contributions while abroad;
- earn above the upper earnings limit in every earnings period throughout the tax year (£967 per week for 2021/22);
- are not resident or ordinarily resident for tax purposes and not liable for tax in the UK;
- receive some earnings and benefits derived from employment other than with the UK employer.

National Insurance contributions paid during the year are paid by reference to a best estimate of earnings. The best estimate of earnings is prepared at the beginning of the tax year or, if later, at the beginning of the agreement.

For every payment of estimated earnings, the employer must complete and maintain a payroll record and include details about the payment, the National Insurance category letter and the NIC data items on a Full Payment Submission (FPS), which must be submitted to HMRC on or before the payment of regular earnings by the UK employer or no later than the 19th of the month following the end of the tax month when all earnings are paid by an overseas employer.

Class 1 National Insurance contributions based on 1/12th of the estimated liability are paid to HMRC each month, If less than five employees are covered by the agreement, payment of 3/12th of the estimated liability can be made quarterly. Details of new employees and leavers must be notified to HMRC.

An in-year review is undertaken between December and April to ensure that account is taken of bonuses and of National Insurance contributions due on shares and securities. The estimate is revised following the review and the employer must adjust the NIC data items when submitting the next FPS to show the revised values to date and adjust the next payment to HMRC if the amount paid is too little or too much.

P60s are prepared as normal. However, as these are based on estimated figures, the correct figures are supplied on a NIC settlement return by 31 March following the tax year. Any residual National Insurance liability must be settled by the same date. The issue of Class 1A National Insurance contributions does not arise as benefits provided to employees are not taxable earnings in the UK.

It should be noted that to help those affected by the Covid-19 pandemic, the deadline for the NIC settlement return for 2019/20 was extended from 31 March 2021 to 30 June 2021.

If the employee returns to the UK before he or she has completed a complete tax year abroad, the appendix 7b agreement ceases to apply to that employee and Class 1 National Insurance contributions must be computed in accordance with the normal statutory basis once the employee has returned to the UK.

OFFSHORE INTERMEDIARIES

9.67 Rules were introduced from 6 April 2014 to target avoidance of tax and National Insurance via the use of offshore intermediaries. The rules apply where workers are engaged by agencies, where workers are employed by a foreign employer and in respect of workers employed on the UK continental shelf.

Under these rules, where a worker is employed through an offshore intermediary and there is a UK agency in the contractual chain, the UK agency is responsible for operating National Insurance contributions, where there is no UK agency in the chain, the client for whom the worker works is the secondary contributor. For a summary of the application of the new rules and the hierarchy between the agency and foreign employer rules, see **9.24**.

As regards a worker on the UK continental shelf, if there is an onshore employer, it is that onshore employer who is the secondary contributory. In the absence of an onshore employer, the licensee is responsible for operating National Insurance contributions. However, if the offshore employer is meeting the National Insurance obligations, HMRC will issue a certificate exempting the licensee from such requirements. Where the certificate is in force, the licensee cannot be pursued for any National Insurance obligations.

PLANNING POINTS

9.68

- The UK left the EU on 31 January 2020. From 1 January 2021, following the end of the transitional period, new rules apply. It is important to keep abreast of changes.
- The rules relating to international social security are complex and specialist advice should be taken prior to going abroad to work or live or sending employees overseas.
- Payment of National Insurance contributions 'buys' pension and benefit entitlement. Therefore planning should consider both sides of the equation as minimising contribution cost may not always be the overriding consideration.

- Employees sent to work temporarily in the EEA or Switzerland may be able to continue to pay contributions in the UK. The rules depend on the date on which the period of temporary work commenced.
- Employees posted to countries with which the UK has a social security agreement may be able to remain in the UK scheme provided the posting does not exceed the maximum period permitted by agreement in question.
- Where a person does not pay UK contributions, this will give rise to a gap in the person's contribution record. Depending on the length of the gap, this may adversely affect UK pension and benefit entitlement. Consideration should be given to paying voluntary contributions (Class 3 or, if appropriate, Class 2) to preserve pension and benefit entitlement.
- Where a person is sent to work in a country with which there is no social security agreement, a double contributions liability may arise in the first 52 weeks as the person may be liable to UK and overseas contributions. However, UK liability can be broken by setting up an employment contract with a company that does not have a place of business in the UK, although this may not always be beneficial.
- Where a person is employed in the UK by a foreign employer with no place of business in the UK, the employee may be responsible for operating his or her own Class 1 National Insurance contributions. Where this is the case, it may be advisable to set up a direct payment scheme.
- Where an employer operates modified PAYE procedures for tax-equalised employees, employers can also take advantage of modified NIC procedures which allow more time to report and pay National Insurance contributions. Similar modified procedures can also be used for employees assigned from the UK to work overseas. The deadline for 2019/20 returns was extended from 31 March 2021 to 30 June 2021 to help employers affected by the Covid-19 pandemic.

APPENDICES

Appendix 1

Class 1 NIC rates and thresholds

	2021/22	2020/21	2019/20	2018/19	2017/18	2016/17
Lower earnings limit (LEL)	£120 per week £520 per month £6,420 per year	£120 per week £520 per month £6,420 per year	£118 per week £512 per month £6,136 per year	£116 per week £503 per month £6,032 per year	£113 per week £490 per month £5,876 per year	£112 per week £486 per month £5,824 per year
Secondary earnings threshold (ST)	£170 per week £737 per month £8,840 per year	£169 per week £732 per month £8,788 per year	£166 per week £719 per month £8,632 per year	£162 per week £702 per month £8,424 per year	£157 per week £680 per month £8,164 per year	£156 per week £676 per month £8,112 per year
Primary earnings threshold (PT)	£184 per week £797 per month; £9,567 per year	£183 per week £792 per month; £9,500 per year	£166 per week £719 per month £8,632 per year	£162 per week £702 per month £8,424 per year	£157 per week £680 per month £8,164 per year	£155 per week £672 per month £8,060 per year
Upper earnings limit (UEL)	£967 per week £4,189 per month £50,270 per year	£962 per week £4,167 per month £50,000 per year	£962 per week £4,167 per month £50,000 per year	£892 per week £3,863 per month £46,350 per year	£866 per week £3,753 per month £45,000 per year	£827 per week £3,583 per month £42,300 per year
Upper secondary threshold for U21s	£967 per week £4,189 per month £50,270 per year	£962 per week £4,167 per month £50,000 per year	£962 per week £4,167 per month £50,000 per year	£892 per week £3,863 per month £46,350 per year	£866 per week £3,753 per month £45,000 per year	£827 per week £3,583 per month £42,300 per year

Appendix 1 *Class 1 NIC rates and thresholds*

	2021/22	2020/21	2019/20	2018/19	2017/18	2016/17
Apprentice upper secondary threshold for U25s	£967 per week £4,189 per month £50,270 per year	£962 per week £4,167 per month £50,000 per year	£962 per week £4,167 per month £50,000 per year	£892 per week £3,863 per month £46,350 per year	£866 per week £3,753 per month £45,000 per year	£827 per week £3,583 per month £42,300 per year
Employment allowance	£4,000	£4,000	£3,000	£3,000	£3,000 per year, per employer	£3,000 per year, per employer
Main primary rate (on earnings between PT and UEL	12%	12%	12%	12%	12%	12%
Additional primary rate (on earnings above UEL)	2%	2%	2%	2%	2%	2%
Married women's reduced rate on earnings between PT and UEL	5.85%	5.85%	5.85%	5.85%	5.85%	5.85%
Married women's rate on earnings above UEL	2%	2%	2%	2%	2%	2%
Secondary rate on earnings above ST	13.8%	13.8%	13.8%	13.8%	13.8%	13.8%
Secondary rate on earnings above ST and below UST re U21s	0%	0%	0%	0%	0%	0%
Secondary rate on earnings above ST and below AUST re U25s	0%	0%	0%	0%	0%	0%

Appendix 2

Class 1A NIC rates

Year	Rate
2021/22	13.8%
2020/21	13.8%
2019/20	13.8%
2018/19	13.8%
2017/18	13.8%
2016/17	13.8%

Appendix 3

Class 1B NIC rates

Year	Rate
2021/22	13.8%
2020/21	13.8%
2019/20	13.8%
2018/19	13.8%
2017/18	13.8%
2016/17	13.8%

Appendix 4

Class 2 NIC rates

	2021/22	2020/21	2019/20	2018/19	2017/18	2016/17
Standard rate (per week)	£3.05	£3.05	£3.00	£2.95	£2.85	£2.80
Share fishermen (per week)	£3.70	£3.70	£3.65	£3.60	£3.50	£3.45
Volunteer development workers (per week)	£6.00	£6.00	£5.90	£5.80	£5.65	£5.60
Small profits threshold (annual)	£6,515	£6,475	£6,365	£6,205	£6,025	£5.965

Appendix 5

Class 3 NIC rates

Year	Class 3 rate (per week)
2021/22	£15.40
2020/21	£15.30
2019/20	£15.00
2018/19	£14.65
2017/18	£14.25
2016/17	£14.10

Appendix 6

Class 3A Voluntary NIC rates

TABLE SHOWING AMOUNTS OF THE CLASS 3A VOLUNTARY CONTRIBUTIONS

Age at payment date (October 2015 to April 2017)	**Rate (£) for each additional pension unit of £ 1 per week**
63 (women only)	934
64 (women only)	913
65	890
66	871
67	847
68	827
69	801
70	779
71	761
72	738
73	719
74	694
75	674
76	646
77	625
78	596
79	574
80	544
81	514
82	484
83	454
84	424
85	394
86	366
87	339
88	314
89	291

Age at payment date (October 2015 to April 2017)	Rate (£) for each additional pension unit of £ 1 per week
90	270
91	251
92	232
93	216
94	200
95	185
96	172
97	159
98	148
99	137
100	127

Appendix 7

Class 4 NIC rates

	2020/21	2020/21	2019/20	2018/19	2017/18	2016/17
Lower profits limit (annual)	£9,568	£9,500	£8,632	£8,424	£8,164	£8,060
Upper profits limit (annual)	£50,270	£50,000	£50,000	£46,350	£45,000	£43,000
Main rate	9%	9%	9%	9%	9%	9%
Additional rate	2%	2%	2%	2%	2%	2%

Index

[References are to paragraph numbers and appendices]

S